Mastering
Social welfare

Macmillan Master Series

Accounting
Accounting Skills
Advanced English Language
Advanced English Literature
Advanced Pure Mathematics
Arabic
Banking
Basic Management
Biology
British Politics
Business Administration
Business Communication
C Programming
C++ Programming
Chemistry
COBOL Programming
Communication
Computer Studies
Counselling Skills
Customer Relations
Database Design
Delphi Programming
Desktop Publishing
Economic and Social History
Economics
Electronic and Electrical Calculations
Electronics
English Grammar
English Language
English Literature
Fashion Styling
French
French 2
Geography

German
German 2
Global Information Systems
Human Resource Management
Information Technology
Internet
Italian
Italian 2
Java
Marketing
Mathematics
Microsoft Office
Microsoft Windows, Novell
   NetWare and UNIX
Modern British History
Modern European History
Modern US History
Modern World History
Networks
Organisational Behaviour
Pascal and Delphi Programming
Philosophy
Photography
Physics
Psychology
Shakespeare
Social Welfare
Sociology
Spanish
Spanish 2
Statistics
Systems Analysis and Design
Visual Basic
World Religions

Macmillan Master Series
Series Standing Order ISBN 0–333–69343–4
(*outside North America only*)

You can receive future titles in this series as they are published by placing a standing order. Please contact your bookseller or, in case of difficulty, write to us at the address below with your name and address, the title of the series and the ISBN quoted above.

Customer Services Department, Macmillan Distribution Ltd
Houndmills, Basingstoke, Hampshire RG21 6XS, England

Mastering

Social welfare

Fourth Edition

Pat Young

First edition 1985
Reprinted three times
Second edition 1989
Reprinted six times
Third edition 1995
Reprinted three times
Fourth edition 2000

Learning Resources
Centre

12234680

Published by
MACMILLAN PRESS LTD
Houndmills, Basingstoke, Hampshire RG21 6XS
and London
Companies and representatives
throughout the world

ISBN 0–333–79327–7

A catalogue record for this book is available
from the British Library.

This book is made from paper suitable for recycling and made from
fully managed and substained forest sources.

10 9 8 7 6 5 4 3 2 1
09 08 07 06 05 04 03 02 01 00

Printed in Great Britain by Creative Print & Design Ltd (Wales), Ebbw Vale

For my father

Contents

List of plates   ix
List of figures and tables   x
Acknowledgements   xi

1 People in society   **1**
   1.1 Introduction: social problems and social welfare   1
   1.2 Understanding social behaviour   10
   1.3 Social class   18
   1.4 Race and racism   24
   Further reading   40
   Useful addresses   40
   Websites   41

2 Family life   **42**
   2.1 Functions of the family   42
   2.2 Family structures   43
   2.3 Marriage   46
   2.4 Divorce   49
   2.5 Single-parent families   51
   2.6 Violence in the family   56
   2.7 The family and the welfare state   64
   Further reading   66
   Useful addresses   67
   Websites   67

3 Poverty and welfare   **68**
   3.1 Defining and measuring poverty   68
   3.2 Understanding poverty   76
   3.3 The effects of poverty   82
   3.4 The relief of poverty   82
   3.5 Issues in welfare   96
   Further reading   99
   Useful addresses   100
   Websites   100

4 Unemployment   **101**
   4.1 Types of unemployment   101
   4.2 New patterns of employment   101
   4.3 The numbers of unemployed people   102

4.4 The distribution of unemployment 104
4.5 The effects and costs of unemployment 105
4.6 Employment services 110
Further reading 117
Website 117

5 Housing and homelessness **118**
5.1 Social policy and housing 118
5.2 Types of housing tenure 121
5.3 Housing and race 132
5.4 Homelessness 133
5.5 Bad housing and rehabilitation 140
Further reading 146
Useful addresses 147
Websites 147

6 Living in cities **148**
6.1 Urban and rural societies 148
6.2 Britain's inner-cities 149
6.3 Inner-city case studies 155
6.4 Inner-city policies 158
Further reading 166
Useful addresses 167
Website 167

7 Schooling in Britain **168**
7.1 The education system 168
7.2 Provision of schooling in Britain 170
7.3 Primary and secondary education 178
7.4 Further and higher education 185
7.5 Private education 188
7.6 Special education 190
7.7 Education and welfare 193
7.8 Inequality in education 195
Further reading 203
Useful addresses 203
Website 204

8 Personal social services **205**
8.1 The origins of social service departments 205
8.2 Social work 207
8.3 Social workers 209
8.4 Organisation of social services departments 210
8.5 Race and social work 214
8.6 Home-care services 216
Further reading 218
Useful addresses 218
Website 218

9   Community care   **219**
   9.1   What is 'community care'?   219
   9.2   The history of community care development   220
   9.3   Can community care work?   225
   Further reading   233
   Useful addresses   234
   Website   234

10   Children and young people in need   **235**
   10.1   The historical background   235
   10.2   Care and protection of children   236
   10.3   Provision for children and young people   241
   10.4   Treatment or punishment for young offenders?   249
   10.5   Provision for young offenders   251
   Further reading   259
   Useful addresses   260
   Websites   260

11   Mental health issues   **261**
   11.1   Attitudes to mental health problems   261
   11.2   The causes of mental health problems   264
   11.3   The law and mental health   265
   11.4   Treatment of mental health problems   266
   Further reading   273
   Useful addresses   273
   Websites   274

12   Learning disability   **275**
   12.1   Defining 'learning disability'   275
   12.2   Provision for people with a learning disability   276
   12.3   Advocacy   281
   Further reading   282
   Useful addresses   283
   Websites   283

13   Old age   **284**
   13.1   Population trends   284
   13.2   Attitudes to old age   286
   13.3   Elderly people and poverty   287
   13.4   Housing   289
   13.5   Health   294
   13.6   Segregation   295
   Further reading   299
   Useful addresses   300
   Website   300

14   Disability   **301**
   14.1   What is a 'disability'?   301
   14.2   Acceptance   303

14.3 Taking control   304
14.4 Finance   305
14.5 Employment   309
14.6 The 1995 Disability Discrimination Act   310
14.7 Education   311
14.8 Care and support services   312
14.9 Access   315
14.10 Residential accommodation   315
Further reading   316
Useful addresses   316
Websites   317

15 **Health and the health services**   **318**
15.1 Health, society and the environment   318
15.2 The aims and organisation of the NHS   319
15.3 Policy issues   330
Further reading   342
Useful addresses   342
Websites   343

16 **The voluntary sector**   **344**
16.1 Statutory and voluntary organisations   344
16.2 Definitions of voluntary organisations   344
16.3 The work of voluntary organisations   346
16.4 The advantages and disadvantages of voluntary organisations 355
Further reading   359
Useful addresses   359
Websites   360

17 **Policy issues in welfare**   **361**
17.1 Perspectives on welfare   361
17.2 Expenditure on social services   370
17.3 Social services : a redistributor of wealth?   371
17.4 Administration of welfare   372
17.5 Privatisation   374
17.6 Universal or selective welfare   375
17.7 Positive action   376
Further reading   379

Researching and writing projects   380

Notes and references   384

Glossary of terms   399

Index   414

List of plates

1 Britain is a multi-racial society   25
2 A nuclear family consists of two parents and their dependent children   44
3 Most lone parents are women   45
4 People in relative poverty lack resources to obtain the living standards
   considered normal   69
5 There are more unemployed people than job vacancies   103
6 Some people are more vulnerable to unemployment than others   106
7 A protest outside the Ideal Home Exhibition   119
8 A roof, but is it a home for a family?   123
9 Empty houses, yet homeless families   134
10 Life in 'bed-and-breakfast' accommodation   136
11 Changes to benefit rules in 1988 caused some young people to become
    homeless and destitute   138
12 The inner-city   150
13 Isolation in the inner-city   153
14 Should nursery places be made available for all children?   170
15 Most children attend state schools   179
16 A minority of children attend private schools and even fewer go
    to public schools such as Eton   189
17 Services are available to enable people to remain in their own home   217
18 Hostels provide some support while allowing people to lead
    independent lives   231
19 Old-fashioned psychiatric hospitals are being closed down   267
20 Children with learning disabilities benefit from leisure activities   281
21 Growing old and staying fit   286
22 This cycle mechanic has no sight or hearing   308
23 New technology helps disabled people   314
24 Long waits to see the doctor at some health centres   327
25 Some people choose to pay privately for health care   334
26 Self-help in a refuge   353
27 Health care in the private sector   373

⚏ ⩔ List of figures and tables

Figures

1.1	The individual in relation to society	7
2.1	Family structures	43
3.1	Results of *Breadline Britain* survey, 1990	76
3.2	The cycle of poverty	77
5.1	Households and dwellings, 1951–86	120
5.2	Changes in housing tenure, 1914–96	121
5.3	Decline in mortgage tax relief, 1990–2000	130
5.4	Households accepted as homeless by local authorities: by main reason for loss of home, 1997–98	134
6.1	Inner-city authorities in England	161
6.2	Shifting the balance of urban group programmes, 1979/80–1988/89	162
7.1	Poverty line: the graph tracks levels of low performance linked to educational disadvantage	177
13.1	The elderly population, Great Britain, 1901–2021	285
15.1	The present structure of the NHS	325

Tables

1.1	The Registrar-General's classification of occupations	22
1.2	Racism and equality	34
3.1	Key indicators of deprivation and social exclusion	71
3.2	Proportions deeming items to be necessary, 1983 and 1990	73
3.3	Proportion of households lacking each of the items, 1983 and 1990	75
3.4	Benefit rates for income support and income-based Jobseeker's Allowance (JSA), April 1999	93
5.1	Housing legislation after 1945	144
7.1	Participation rates (percentages) in higher education, Great Britain – by social class	196
13.1	The elderly population, Great Britain, 1901–2025	285

◪ Acknowledgements

Over the years, many people have helped with this book, giving ideas, advice, support and encouragement. Heather Roberts provided invaluable assistance with the first edition, spending many Saturday afternoons reading chapters and offering constructive criticism. Arthur Rutherford, Judy Nixon, Dave Evans and Eva Garmonikow also provided useful guidance on particular chapters.

I was very grateful to Pat Newberry for her help in updating the information for the third edition of the book. She painstakingly sought out up-to-date statistics and provided invaluable information on the ever-changing scene in social welfare legislation and policy.

Thank-you also to Marilyn Billingham, Judy Nixon, Steve Leverett and Stewart Belfield who helped with the fourth edition.

The author and publishers wish to thank the following for permission to use copyright material: Guardian News Service Ltd for Figure 7.1, 'At a disadvantage', *Guardian Education*, 1/12/98 and Figure 5.3, 'The long slow death of Miras', *Guardian* 10/3/99; The Controller of Her Majesty's Stationery Office for Figures 5.2 and 5.4 from *Britain 1999* and *Social Trends 29*, Office of National Statistics, Crown copyright 2000; Routledge for Tables 3.2 and 3.3 from Joanna Mack and Stewart Lansley, *Poor Britain*, Allen and Unwin, (1991); and Sally and Richard Greenhill, Chris Schwartz, Popperfoto, Photofusion and Network Photographers for photographic material.

Every effort has been made to trace all the copyright holders, but if any have been inadvertently overlooked the publishers will be pleased to make the necessary arrangement at the first opportunity.

▼ 1 People in society

1.1 Introduction: social problems and social welfare

This book is about social problems and social policies. It is about all kinds of people, the kind of problems they encounter in their daily lives, the situations in which they live and the welfare provision which exists to help.

You may be reading this book because you are working, or intending to work, in the fields of health and social care. People whose work involves caring for others have to be able to demonstrate an almost instant understanding of a variety of human predicaments and problems. Nursery nurses will be told that a new child is expected at the nursery tomorrow, social workers will be asked to visit new clients, residential care workers will have to welcome new people into the home. In each of these situations, which are everyday events for caring workers, strangers are meeting and one will be expecting a great deal from the other. An understanding of society and social problems can provide a background of knowledge for dealing with such circumstances.

You may be reading this book because you want to understand more about social welfare provision, perhaps because of a course you are studying or perhaps simply because you are interested. You may gain a greater understanding of your own experiences in the past, or feel better prepared for issues you meet in the future. Reading the accounts of others or the ideas of researchers in these areas may reflect the way you have felt, perhaps about your education or experiences of unemployment or homelessness. You may change the way you feel. You may change your attitudes towards others.

As well as being of interest to people working in health and social care, and of general public interest, the study of social welfare is an academic subject, taught in further and higher education – nowadays usually known as Social Policy. As well as providing detailed information about social welfare and its effects, studying Social Policy gives an insight into wider social issues and helps us understand the nature of the society in which we live.

The history of Social Policy reflects the history of wider social, political and economic changes in society, illustrating changing attitudes and beliefs. Social policies concerning children, elderly people, unemployed people, disabled people, people with mental illnesses, all provide a mirrored understanding of wider social issues and make fascinating, although sometimes distressing, subjects for study. Changing attitudes can be seen in the treatment of single parents, particularly unmarried mothers, over the last hundred years or so. At one time the stigma of lone parenthood was so great that women were forced to have their babies adopted, or to marry unsuitable partners to make themselves and their babies respectable, instead of objects of shame. In numerous cases, children were brought up believing their grandmothers or other relatives to be their mothers. Any amount of deceit was thought better than the shame of illegitimacy, as it was known then. The limited provision which existed for unmarried mothers reflected these attitudes. Some women had their babies in the workhouse (see Chapter 3 for more details on how harsh life was for those in the workhouse) or they might be taken into homes run by organisations such as the Salvation Army. In either case, the girls were treated as shameful and immoral, make to work hard scrubbing and cleaning, and often forced to endure the pain and fear of labour alone – their cries of anguish believed to be just punishment for their behaviour (even though girls were kept in ignorance and many had no knowledge of the consequences of sex). Looking further behind this treatment, we can analyse wider issues about family life and the position of women in society.

Social policy also provides a more general and philosophical reflection of a society. Chapter 3 traces the historical development of the role of the state in relation to poverty and illustrates wider attitudes across a range of issues. These include the way people needing support are seen – as lazy scroungers or victims of economic or other circumstances beyond their control; the way they should be treated – as full members of society deserving dignity and respect, or as a stigmatised group, to be coerced back into work if possible. Social policy also tells us a great deal about how we think of the individual in relation to the whole society and how individual and social responsibilities are distinguished. Chapter 17 looks at these wider issues in more detail. If you are new to this study, these more complex and philosophical issues are best returned to when you get to the end of the book.

The questions which make up the first section of this chapter begin to show the way this book approaches individual and social problems.

Activity 1.1

Think about meeting a client for the first time, it could be a child starting a new school, a patient in a hospital, an older person, or an adolescent in a youth club. On a piece of paper, make a list of the sorts of things you might need to know about in order to understand and help that person. Compare what you have written with the following list.

What is the person's family background?

Most people spend some part of their lives living within a family, although family structures can vary quite considerably. Some children live in a home where there is only one adult, often the mother, but sometimes the father. Some children have step-brothers or sisters. Other families include grandparents or aunts and uncles in addition to the children and their parents. In many families the mother does a paid job, either full-time or part-time, as well as caring for the family. Some fathers participate in caring for their children, whilst in other families the father is a more distant figure. One adult may be responsible for making all the decisions or the process may be more democratic. Social services attempt to work alongside the family, helping members to cope with the demands made upon them, rather than taking over those demands. For this reason, caring workers need to understand the way the family operates.

What race is the client?

Most people in caring jobs seek to treat everyone equally, regardless of race, and this, therefore, may seem an inappropriate question to ask. However, at this time, people of different races do have different experiences and it is important to be familiar with the customs and practices of the ethnic minority communities. Many Asians, for example those who are Hindus, are vegetarian and therefore there is little point in health visitors or others telling them to give their children cod liver oil, although this has happened.[1] Practices associated with courtship and marriage vary and an adolescent girl living in an Asian community in Britain may have demands made upon her which are not shared by her white friends. Discrimination and racism are, unfortunately, social and economic realities in this country and exert particular stresses and strains on members of the ethnic minorities.

Is the person employed? Is the head of the family employed?

In this society work is very important. Not only does it bring financial reward, it also gives status; when people say 'I am a teacher', 'I am a nurse', they are using their work to define who they are as well as how they spend their day and earn their money. The worries and fears brought about by unemployment are complex and involve more than financial insecurity which itself causes stress. There is a stigma attached to unemployment. This means that the person has a feeling, reinforced by society, that he or she is somehow inadequate and a failure. Whilst it is true that not everyone experiences unemployment in exactly the same way, a general understanding of the problem throws light on a particular individual's circumstances.

How old is the person?

In this society there is a tendency to group people in terms of age, therefore it is usual to want to know the age of the client. People talk about the problems of children, adolescents, teenagers, young adults, middle-aged people, elderly people. People have different expectations at different points in the life course and may feel angry or distressed if expectations of how things should be at their stage in life are frustrated in some way. To be treated like a child is one thing if you are a child, but quite another if you are an adult, perhaps disabled and needing care, or returning to education. In neither case should people be denied adult dignity and respect. The same problem can feel different for people at earlier or later stages in life – we have a sense of events being more 'normal' at particular points in life. Many people feel they have more sympathy with people at a particular stage in their life and choose to work with a specific age group, perhaps young children or elderly people. A general understanding of the needs of children, the demands made upon adolescents and the problems faced by people as they get older will help in developing a sympathy towards a particular individual.

Is the client male or female?

Section 1.2 of this chapter looks at the different expectations society has of men and women, and the way that children learn about these differences. The differences in masculine and feminine behaviour are demonstrated in innumerable ways. A little boy and a little girl will probably react differently to stressful situations, typically, one may become aggressive or violent, while the other is withdrawn and tearful. Similarly men and women react differently to stress, and social problems like alcoholism, depression and crime are not equally prevalent amongst men and women.

What class is the person?

Different kinds of work not only provide different levels of income but also are closely associated with different life-styles and expectations. This can be summarised in the concept of social class, which is explained in detail in section 1.3 of this chapter. At this point, it is enough to say that there is research which demonstrates that class differences affect people's lives from the moment of conception through to the end of their lives.[2] Social workers need an understanding of class, as they may be required to work with people whose class background is completely different from their own. Social work itself has a class dimension, with many social workers having a middle-class background, whilst the majority of their clients are working-class. This could lead to a conflict of expectations, and misunderstandings over different ways of approaching problems.

Does the client come from a rich or a poor family?

Money cannot solve all problems but it does make many problems easier to deal with. For example, a young mother with access to a car will probably not experience the same feeling of isolation as the woman who, in order to leave the house, has to cope with public transport, with young children in tow. Strange as it may sound, lack of money can make life more expensive. The person with a car and a monthly salary can buy cheaper goods in bulk at a hypermarket while the poorer person is forced to buy small amounts at a local and more expensive store. Inadequate money is obviously the key aspect of poverty, but it results in more complex forms of deprivation and suffering. It also brings about its own problems in the form of feelings of hopelessness and degradation.

What sort of education does the person have?

Since the education system in this country combines private and state sectors and is constantly in a state of change, it is hardly surprising that people's experiences of schooling are so varied. The state sector includes some selective schools although most local areas have a comprehensive system. Education provides more than qualifications in the form of GCSEs and training for specific jobs; it also leads to a set of attitudes and expectations. The person who has attended a private school and then university may have little in common with his or her contemporary who left the local comprehensive at the earliest possible date. As a less extreme example, the child who has been able to attend a nursery school or pre-school play-group may cope better with certain situations than the child who has remained at home.

What sort of environment does the person come from?

The word 'environment' includes the home itself and the wider environment of the street and the locality. People are greatly affected by their home environment. For example, in an overcrowded home, it will be difficult for a child to find a quiet place to do homework and the child's education will therefore suffer. Similarly, lack of privacy can cause strain in a marriage and perhaps lead to the breakdown of that marriage. A child growing up in a flat at the top of a tower-block will not have the same opportunities for safe exploratory play as the child with access to a garden or a street free from traffic. Social workers and policy-makers now recognise the special problems for all the members of a family living in an overcrowded home or in high-rise housing.

The wider environment is also important. Living in a rural cottage without basic amenities, such as an inside toilet, might not result in the same feeling of deprivation as life in an identical property in a run-down inner-city area. The multiplicity of problems in run-down areas are exacerbated by the fact that living in such conditions causes people to despair of improving their situation, thus leading to further deterioration of the environment and morale. The effects of the environment on individuals can be seen by the fact that sometimes problems which appear psychological in origin, such as depression, can be solved simply by removing a person from a particular environment.

These questions are intended to show that people cannot be understood solely as individuals with individual problems but must be seen in the light of social pressures and social environments. This is why books can be of help to those planning to work with people. Reading about unemployment or poverty will increase insight into the plight of a family living on social security benefits and struggling to make ends meet.

In Britain, and indeed in most other countries, people are not allowed to do exactly as they wish, nor are they expected to cope with all difficulties in isolation. The legal system, welfare provision and voluntary organisations will intervene in people's lives, preventing them from doing certain things, enabling and assisting them to do others. There are laws, for example, to stop parents from abusing their children and there are social workers and charitable organisations who will step in if children are thought to be in danger. There are laws to prevent discrimination on the basis of sex, race or disability. In many areas of social welfare there are statutory and voluntary organisations which help people to obtain their rights. It is therefore important for people wanting to help others to know something of the relevant legislation, the welfare provision which exists to support people in need and the services provided by voluntary organisations.

It would, of course, be possible to understand all these aspects of society and still fail to understand a particular individual. However, it would be difficult to grasp an individual's needs without a general understanding of the social context, certainly without more time than most caring workers have at their disposal.

It is necessary to give two words of warning at this point. First, there is a danger in the above approach that it may appear that something called 'society' in some way causes people to do things and influences people into holding certain attitudes and beliefs. In reality, society is made up of people and it is therefore people who make society what it is. There is a two-way interaction in progress, with people changing their environment and being changed by it. For example, a child will be very influenced by the family and the home in which it grows up, but the very presence of the child will have changed the family. As adults, people influence their world through their work, political behaviour and perhaps through participation in voluntary organisations.

The second point is that, for the purpose of study, it is necessary to break up the subject area into topics which may then appear to be separate. It is clear, however, that all these areas are in fact highly interconnected. Poor housing, poverty and low achievement at school tend to go together and possibly it is the very interrelatedness of these problems that makes it so difficult for governments and social service workers to find solutions. In the same way, class is not really a separate topic, but it is significant because it is related to all the other subject-areas.

Figure 1.1 summarises this section, and illustrates the subjects covered in this book.

'Sticks and stones'

'Stick and stones will break my bones; but names cannot hurt me'. This is a saying which I often heard as a child, as adults tried to persuade me that verbal bullying could not harm me. But is it true? Is it really true that words cannot hurt?

Some people think that words can be damaging and recently the popular press have made a great joke out of so-called 'politically correct' language, poking fun out of some perhaps rather extreme attempts to avoid words with negative meanings. So-called 'politically correct' language includes avoidance of terms which might be considered sexist – suggesting that a role is limited to men or women, for example postman, dinner lady, etc. – and terms which might be considered insulting to groups such as older people, black people or people with

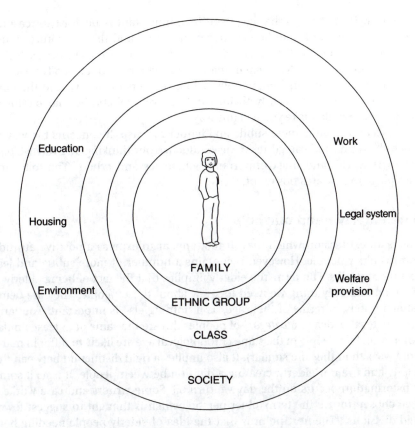

Figure 1.1   The individual in relation to society

disabilities. So does it actually matter what words we use to describe people? Has language the power to hurt or to belittle?

Activity 1.2

Are there any words which you would avoid using, perhaps to describe people with disabilities, people with mental illnesses, black people, women or older people? Are there any names you would not like to be called yourself, or which you would not like to hear used about your relatives or friends? Make a short list for yourself.

What is wrong with these words as far as you are concerned? Why do you not use them? Compare your list with those of others. Over which words do you disagree?

Although people do not agree about which words it is not okay to use, most people agree that there are some words which they do find offensive. From this it would seem that perhaps words do in fact matter.

The view taken here is that language *is* an important issue, for two reasons. The first is that words can be negative or insulting and therefore hurtful and damaging to the people they are used to describe. Words can make people feel in some way abnormal, or less than human. Words which are not actually insulting can still be belittling, making people feel like objects of charity, and thus not fully human. This point is fairly obvious and you will probably be able to think of words which would make you feel this way.

The second point is more subtle and harder to grasp. It concerns the way in which the terms and categories we use influence our thinking, the way we perceive the world, and most importantly ourselves and others. The following example demonstrates this point.

'The elderly need our help'

This is an expression which may at first appear to express a positive attitude towards older people. However, it contains a number of more subtle and less positive attitudes. The term 'the elderly' implies that the fact of being elderly is the main and only thing we need to know about these people. They are being defined purely in terms of their age, as if nothing else is important. The term also creates the idea of a *category* of people who are the same or at least similar (whereas in fact people of the same chronological age are likely to differ in many more ways than they are similar). It also implies a rigid distinction between the elderly and the not-elderly, creating a division between people. It is as if some transformation occurs on the day we turn 65. Some writers and care workers have chosen to use the term 'older person' which is thought to suggest fewer rigid divisions.[3] The next point is that the idea of elderly people needing help implies that older people are incapable of helping themselves, when in fact many are carers and work for charity. Finally, 'our help' suggests again the idea of two groups: older people who are passive and helpless and the rest of 'us' who are capable of giving help.

Activity 1.3

Look in textbooks and other sources for similar statements to that analysed above and try to work out the subtle messages contained within them.

It is not possible to lay down hard and fast rules about which words are demeaning to people and which are not. Language and meanings change constantly and words which were neutral can come to have negative connotations. An interesting example here is the term 'Borstal', which was the name given to institutions for young offenders (now no longer used). Originally this was the name of a village and was chosen for its neutral meaning. However it soon came to have powerful connotations and to conjure up an image of a harsh and rather brutal regime. The word itself began to sound unpleasant.

Sometimes it is important to change terms in order to try to shake up people's attitudes and to challenge their ways of thinking. The use of a new term can have the effect of making people think in a new way. An example of this occurred when residential homes began to talk of 'residents' instead of 'patients'. Staff were reminded that their workplace was home for the people they cared for and should be treated as such, with respect for privacy and residents' rights. A number of different terms have been used in the past to describe what we now call 'learning disability' – and it is surprising how derogatory and unacceptable some of the old terms which were once current and which can still be found in older books now sound.

The issue of language will be returned to throughout this book, for example in Chapters 11–14 looking at mental illness, learning disabilities, elderly people, and disabled people. For now, two terms which have already been used in this chapter need brief discussion.

The first such term is 'clients' which has been used to describe the people with whom care workers are involved. There is disagreement about the most appropriate word here. Other possibilities might be 'patient', in a medical setting; 'resident' in a home; or some people have advocated the term 'user' of services or 'customer'. The term 'client' has been borrowed from the private sector, and for me implies choice and rights and respect. The reasons that some prefer the word 'user' is that the word is more active, suggesting involvement, whereas 'client' perhaps implies a rather passive recipient of services.

Activity 1.4

What is implied in the following terms:
- resident
- patient
- therapist
- counsellor
- helper
- customer?

Add some terms of your own, from your own reading or experience.
In your view, which terms are most appropriate?

This may seem rather complicated and perhaps you are wondering why it matters which term is used. But think back to what was said earlier about the power of language to influence our thinking and the way we see the world. The words used in this context can influence the way the client and the worker perceive their relationship to each other. This will affect the power dynamic between the two – a point which is returned to in Chapters 8 and 9.

The other term which has been used already and which needs some explanation is 'race'. Discussion of this and other related terms can be found later in this chapter, at the beginning of section 1.4.

All areas of study have their own language, and the area of social care and social policy is no exception. To help you get to grips with the terms used, there is a Glossary at the end of the book and list of words used at the end of each chapter.

The next section of this chapter introduces the idea of *role* as a means of understanding human behaviour. This is followed by sections on class and race – both of which are referred to again in the chapters which follow.

1.2   Understanding social behaviour

There are theories which seek to explain human behaviour and which can give an insight into why people behave the way they do. Theories can also be used to anticipate situations which will cause stress. The idea described below is useful in this way and is known as *role theory*.

Role theory

A role is simply a set of ways of behaving which are expected of a person occupying a certain position. The best way to illustrate this is with an example. When a class of students meets a new teacher, even though these people are strangers, they tend not to surprise each other. This is because the individuals concerned are behaving as others expect them to act in a particular role. The teacher does not come in, stand on the table and sing a song, neither does the teacher take a seat at the back of the classroom and wait in silence. In fact the teacher will follow the detailed pattern of behaviour which makes up the role of teacher. This involves entering the classroom, sitting or standing at the appropriate place at the front, facing the other individuals and addressing them as a group. Similarly the other people in the classroom act in accordance with their role. They become students, they ask and answer questions, accepting that the teacher already knows about the subject.

This is only one example of the roles which people take up throughout their day and during their lives. The 'students' and the 'teacher' in the classroom will act in a different way on the bus going home. The bus conductor would be rather taken aback if the teacher, instead of paying the fare when asked, proceeded to give a talk to the passengers, punctuated with requests for the passengers to stop talking, sit properly and answer questions!

Activity 1.5

To show that people play a number of roles, make a list of all the roles you play. Be prepared to discuss these.

There is a danger in analysing social behaviour in terms of role theory. Stressing the way in which behaviour conforms to expected patterns can lead to a neglect of individual personality factors. There is, in reality, freedom for manoeuvre within a particular role. People interpret the role of student differently. Some students are passive, preferring only to listen, whilst others are lively and challenge the teacher. The role of teacher is also interpreted in different ways by different personalities. There are teachers who are very strict and expect complete attention from students, whilst others are more democratic and encourage students to participate in the class.

Two further ideas help to explain social behaviour within the framework of role theory. These are *role-set* and *role-conflict*. A role-set is a collection of roles which go together. Roles only make sense within a situation, and when complemented by other roles. The behaviour which makes up the role of teacher is meaningless without the presence of people acting the role of student. A teacher alone at the front of a classroom, perhaps catching up on some marking, appears somewhat lost and lonely. The way of talking associated with teaching, addressing people as a group and asking questions whilst knowing the subject, is only appropriate in conjunction with the role of student. It would be considered patronising and condescending if used in another situation, for example at a social event, even if the same individuals were present.

The other term mentioned was role-conflict. Activity 1.5 showed that people have several roles. It is possible for two or more of these roles to come into conflict and cause problems for the individual. For example, a person who is a mother or a father may also be a daughter or a son. The role of daughter is quite different from that of mother and it may be difficult for a person to play both roles simultaneously. Family visits to grandparents may produce this tension between the roles. People who are parents themselves will resent being treated as children, especially in front of their own children. From the other side, parents of grown-up children may find it difficult to adapt their behaviour and expectations to allow for the fact that their children are themselves now parents.

An understanding of role theory gives an insight into the problems people may encounter. Adjusting to a new role is not always easy. A woman with a new baby can find it difficult to adjust to the restrictions and responsibilities of motherhood, especially if she is not adequately prepared or supported in her new role. Men suffer similar problems of adjustment when they become fathers for the first time. The problems faced by young people are partly caused by their attempts to break away from the role of child and take up the role of adult. A person who has been made redundant at work will feel the loss of his or her role as worker and wage-earner, especially as that role will have carried a certain status.

Activity 1.6

List as many examples as you can where a change in role, a role-conflict or a clash of roles between individuals may cause tension.

Problems which may arise in the following situations can be analysed in terms of role theory.

Retirement

When people retire after a lifetime of work, even if they have looked forward to this event, they may experience feelings of loss of purpose and loss of identity. Their work will have given them a status and may also have been a source of power and prestige. Suddenly their identity is reduced, in the eyes of society, to that of old-age pensioners. Other members of the household may also find this a difficult time.

Mothers who work outside the home

Women who have paid jobs as well as caring for a family may experience a conflict over which role takes priority. This can be particularly acute at times when the children are ill, or have problems which seem to demand their mother's full-time attention. Whilst such demands may be unrealistic, many mothers feel guilty concerning the care of their children and women with paid employment are particularly vulnerable. Men may also feel threatened by their wives' ability to earn an income and have an independent existence and identity. Recent years have seen an increase in the numbers of families in which women are in paid employment and men are unemployed. Many of the jobs which have been lost over the last 20 or so years have been jobs traditionally done by men, whilst new jobs created in service industries have often been those seen traditionally as 'women's jobs'. Although this situation can result in a successful 'role-swap', with the men becoming 'househusbands', there are many sources of strain as people try to adjust to new roles or loss of roles, and come to terms with seeing their partners in new ways.

Unemployment

In our society, particular importance is attached to work roles. The first thing we want to know about someone is what they do: work roles are a source of status. Work takes up a large part of the day, week and year; it fills people's lives. As with retirement, unemployment can mean a loss of purpose and identity (as well as the more obvious loss of income). The effects of unemployment may be different for different people, depending on the centrality of the role of work in their lives. Although things are changing, it is still perhaps the case that loss of work has a different meaning for a man than for a woman. A woman has probably been brought up to attach importance to other roles, such as mother. Children may feel differently about unemployment affecting their father than their mother. The problems faced by young people unable to find work have aspects in common with those of older unemployed people, although there are some differences. Having the status of a job and a wage is an important aspect of adult life, and young people may find it difficult to make the transition into adulthood if they are deprived of work.

Shared households

Some young couples, newly married or living together, share a home with their parents. Lone parents may continue living with their parents, or move back in after a relationship ends. Such a situation may demand a great deal of compromise and flexibility over roles. Sometimes the difficulties cannot be overcome, and there is conflict and tension among all the people involved. Similar problems may arise when an elderly person, having difficulties in managing alone, moves in with a daughter or son. The elderly person may feel that he or she has no role at all in the new household, whilst the other adults feel there is a risk of their roles and privacy being encroached upon or taken over.

Mature students

People who return to education after years spent working or raising a family may find being a mature student more difficult than they anticipated. They may feel that teaching staff give insufficient recognition to their experience and the contribution they could make to the class. At home, women in particular may find that the family is not supportive and does not make allowances for the demands made by coursework assignments or studying for examinations. Similarly, teachers used to working with young and inexperienced people may feel that their traditional position of authority is threatened by the presence of a mature student.

Promotion

Promotion within a workplace can be a cause of conflict. The newly-promoted person may find that it takes time to become accustomed to the new position in the hierarchy. Colleagues may find it difficult to accept the authority of someone who was very recently an equal.

Step-parents

A new adult joining an existing family and taking up the role of mother or father may be resented by children who have been used to managing as a single-parent family. The situation is not made any easier by the fairy-tale tradition of the wicked stepmother, nor by the fact that the children may still feel the loss of the natural parent.

These are only a selection of the examples which exist of ways in which role theory can aid understanding of problematic situations. The fact that such situations are a source of tension is illustrated by the frequency with which they are used in fiction on television and other media. Much drama and comedy is based on circumstances such as young couples living with their parents or people marrying a second time.

Gender-roles

An important area of role differentiation in this society is that which exists between males and females. Although recent decades have seen some changes, it is still the case that differences between girls and boys, and men and women, are emphasised. In the home, certain tasks are seen as more appropriate to women and others better suited to men. In employment, women are concentrated in certain types and levels of work. In sport and leisure interests, males and females follow different activities. Males and females are thought to have different personalities and abilities.

Activity 1.7

In groups of three or four, decide which of these words describe men, women or are equally appropriate to either sex. You may need to look up some of the words in a dictionary.

aggressive	egotistic
independent	assertive
confident	helpless
sensitive	sympathetic
perceptive	passive
domesticated	caring
gossipy	gentle
emotional	self-sacrificing
catty	reliable
logical	brave
scheming	

Activity 1.8

Decide which of the words listed in Activity 1.7 describe:
(a) yourself
(b) someone of the opposite sex whom you know well.

Sexual stereotypes

Ascribing characteristics to people on the basis of factors like sex, race or age is known as *stereotyping*. Sex stereotypes are applied to males and females. It is common for women to be stereotyped as domesticated, emotional, passive and gentle, whereas men are seen as more aggressive, daring, logical and egotistic. The fact that stereotypes can be misleading is seen by the extent to which people tend not to see themselves, or people they know well, in the same way.

Stereotyping limits behaviour and development and can cause unhappiness for children and adults who cannot, or do not wish to, conform to the appropriate stereotype. Boys who do not act in an aggressive way, or who prefer quiet activities to competitive sport may be teased, bullied and called names, or in adult life may be believed to be homosexual. It is interesting that the labels applied to a 'boyish' girl are not as derogatory as those applied to a 'girlish' boy, but as a girl moves into her teens, if she does not become interested in clothes, make-up and girls' magazines, she may find herself socially isolated. These stereotypes may also limit choice of subject in school and, later on, career decisions, restricting certain types of jobs to men and others to women. This is a waste of talent and ability and also leads to the perpetuation of the existing inequality.

If it is reasonably clear that stereotypes and role divisions exist, it is less clear how this situation comes about.

Activity 1.9

In pairs or groups of three, examine each of the following statements and decide if you think each is true or false:

1 Women are naturally better at caring for babies and small children.
2 It is natural for boys to take the initiative in asking girls out.
3 Men have a stronger sex-drive than women.
4 Women are, by nature, more concerned about their appearance than men.
5 Boys are less afraid of danger than girls.
6 Women's emotional needs are stronger than those of men.
7 Boys are naturally better at scientific subjects.
8 Girls cannot do maths.
9 Males are, by nature, more aggressive than females.
10 Men are naturally more competitive than women.

Masculinity and femininity

Although many people believe that sex differences have their origins in biological factors, there is no clear evidence to prove this. For example, it may be true that women show their emotions more than men, and are less attracted to technical subjects, but it is not necessarily true that these differences exist at birth.

Studies of different societies have found that both the characteristics of men and women and notions of masculinity and femininity vary considerably across different cultures. In a tribe called the Arapesh in New Guinea:

the ideal adult has a gentle, passive, cherishing nature, and resembles the feminine type in our culture. In the relationships between the sexes, including the overtly sexual, the Arapesh recognises no temperamental differences at all. Neither is the initiator or the aggressor. The main 'work' of both adult men and women is child-bearing and child-rearing – indeed they call sexual intercourse 'work' when the object is conception ... The verb 'to bear a child' is used indiscriminately of both sexes.[4]

Within another tribe, the Tchambuli, the situation is quite different. Here, the women are practical, and men:

are skittish, wary of each other, interested in art, in the theatre, in a thousand petty bits of insult and gossip. Hurt feelings are rampant ... the pettiness of those who feel themselves weak and isolated. The men wear lovely ornaments (the women shave their heads and are unadorned), they do the shopping, they carve and paint and dance.[5]

Finally, an example from a South-west Pacific society where:

only men wear flowers in their hair and scented leaves tucked into their belts or armbands. At formal dances it is the man who dresses in the most elegant finery and ... when these young men are fully made-up and costumed for the dance they are considered so irresistible to women that they are not allowed to be alone, even for a moment, for fear some women will seduce them.[6]

It seem that sex roles are not in fact biologically determined, but are cultural in origin, and learned by the members of a particular society.

Activity 1.10

List all the ways in which you think children might learn about sex roles.

Sexual differentiation

From the moment a child is born in this society, sexual differentiation is considered very important. Babies are given different coloured clothes and toys, and people express great embarrassment if they mistake the sex of a baby. Mothers and fathers treat male and female babies in different ways and have different expectations of them. Girls are praised for being 'pretty', boys for being 'clever' and 'brave'. Parents are more protective of their daughters than of their sons. Girls are taught to stay clean and take an interest in clothes, boys to be brave and not to cry. Toys believed to be appropriate for girls and boys reflect adult sex roles, with girls being encouraged to play with dolls, and boys with building sets. Children also learn by simply observing and imitating the adults they meet, in particular their parents. Girls may be encouraged to help with housework, while boys are given other tasks around the home.

The family is not the only source of learning for children. Books, comics, magazines, computer games, videos and television shows still also portray certain activities and roles as more suitable for one sex than the other.

Activity 1.11

Collect together as many children's books and comics as you can find. Analyse the content in terms of sex roles. Look at the roles in which adults are shown. See if girls and boys are presented playing with different toys and games. Examine the books to see which children take leadership roles and show other children what to do. If you come across animal characters, are these male, female or neutral? How does this affect the personalities and behaviour of the characters?

Activity 1.12

Write a story for children which does not allocate different roles to males and females, but which encourages the interest of all children in all areas of life.

Adults outside the family also tend to treat girls and boys in different ways, encouraging them to play with particular toys and to act in certain ways. Schools continue this process and Chapter 7 on education contains a section on this subject.

Activity 1.13

If you do placements in a nursery or children's home, make an observation of any ways in which boys and girls are treated differently. Compare your findings with those of the rest of the class. What effects might such differences have on children as they grow up?

If this is not possible, carry out the same exercise, by thinking back to your own childhood.

The gender roles learned in childhood have implications which continue into adult life. One important example of this concerns the work done by men and women both inside and outside the home.

Inside the home women are more likely to be responsible for housekeeping and childcare, whilst traditionally men take on tasks such as car maintenance and home repairs. This division of labour means that women play a very significant role in informal caring: for example caring for young children, looking after people who are ill and providing support and practical help for elderly parents. This point will be referred to again in looking at the implications of the policy of developing community care.

Horizontal and vertical job segregation

In paid employment many occupations are, to a greater or lesser extent, segregated by sex. This means that the labour market is divided into jobs done predominantly by men and jobs done predominantly by women. *Horizontal segregation* refers to situations in which different jobs, perhaps of equal status, are done by men and women. An example of this is in residential care where cooks and cleaners are usually women whilst gardeners and handypersons are usually men. *Vertical segregation* refers to situations in which men and women are working in the same jobs, but one group tends to dominate the top positions and therefore receives greater rewards and has more power. This tends to be the case in social work where the majority of social workers are women but most of the directors of social services are men.[7] In private companies as well, there seems to be a 'glass ceiling' which creates a barrier preventing women from moving into top management positions.

Activity 1.14

Make a study of a local social services or educational establishment. Find out which jobs are done by men and which jobs by women. Include the jobs of the people with the power – up to the relevant Secretary of State. Analyse your findings and decide if horizontal and/or vertical segregation exists. Compare your findings to national statistics.

Activity 1.15

Discussion points:

1 Does it matter if men and women do different work?
2 Does it matter if one group tends to hold the position of power in a particular field of work?
3 What might be the causes of segregation in work?
4 What could be done to change the situation?

1.3 Social class

One of the ways of understanding British society today is by looking at it in terms of class. This involves a view of society which takes account of the fact that people do not have equal access to wealth, power and prestige. In Britain the majority of people recognise the existence of a class structure, although they may not agree on what determines class.[8] Also they may not be aware of all the implications of class. This section describes two schemes for classifying people on the basis of their social standing in the community, and looks at some of the implications of class.

Class and life-style

An understanding of the class structure is important to those who want to bring about social reforms and to help people. For example, in the field of education, policy-makers and people working in schools have aimed for a long time at achieving equality of opportunity in education. So far, changes, such as the introduction of comprehensive schools, have had little effect and educational achievement still bears a strong relationship to social class. Chapter 7 looks at this aspect of education in some detail.

The Activity that follows demonstrates some of the less serious distinctions between different classes and serves to illustrate the relationship between class and life-style.

Activity 1.16

What class are you? Without taking the questions too seriously, tick answer (a) (b) or (c) and then calculate your score.

1 At a party, which of the following drinks would you prefer?
    (a) lager
    (b) martini and lemonade
    (c) gin and tonic
2 Which of these three names would you prefer for your daughter?
    (a) Tracey

   (b) Clarissa

   (c) Hannah

3 Which of the following TV programmes would you prefer to watch?

   (a) a ballet

   (b) *Brookside*

   (c) a nature programme

4 What do you call the main meal of the evening?

   (a) tea

   (b) supper

   (c) dinner

5 Which of these three holidays would you prefer?

   (a) a week at a holiday camp

   (b) a rail trip to Birmingham to go to the 'Ideal Home' exhibition

   (c) a week in Scotland walking and fishing

6 Which newspaper do you read?

   (a) *Guardian*

   (b) *Financial Times*

   (c) *Sun*

7 To which station is your radio most often tuned?

   (a) Radio Five Live

   (b) Radio Three

   (c) Radio Four

8 How would you rather spend a Saturday evening?

   (a) betting at the greyhound races

   (b) eating out at a restaurant

   (c) at the opera

9 If you wanted a new coat which of the following would you be most likely to do?

   (a) have a look in your friend's mail order catalogue

   (b) go to the local High Street shops

   (c) wait until your next trip to London

10 After an expensive meal at a restaurant, how would you pay?

   (a) by American Express

   (b) by cheque

   (c) with cash

Award yourself marks as follows and add up the total. Question **1.** (a) 10 (b) 8 (c) 6; **2.** (a) 10 (b) 6 (c) 8; **3.** (a) 6 (b) 10 (c) 8; **4.** (a) 10 (b) 6 (c) 8; **5.** (a) 10 (b) 8 (c) 6; **6.** (a) 8 (b) 6 (c) 10; **7.** (a) 10 (b) 6 (c) 8; **8.** (a) 10 (b) 8 (c) 6; **9.** (a) 10 (b) 8 (c) 6; **10.** (a) 10 (b) 8 (c) 10.

Results of quiz

94–100   This scores indicates a person with working-class tastes and no desires to pretend to be anything else.

88–92   There are three possibilities to explain this score. One is that you ticked any answer at random. Second, you could have changed class: perhaps your parents are working class, but you have a professional occupation and associate with middle-class people. Or perhaps you pride yourself on doing whatever you feel like.

70–86   The nearer the score is to 80, the more the tastes might be described as lower-middle-class. The person who scores around 80 is definitely not working-class in his or her tastes, but cannot be described as middle-class.

60–68   This score demonstrates a middle-class life-style. A score at the lower end of the band might qualify for another term such as upper-class or upper-middle-class.

The impact of social class

There is a set of attitudes, habits and a life-style which go to make up a class stereotype. There are, also, more serious effects of class which tend to mitigate any attempts of policy-makers to move towards social equality. Educational achievement, access to wealth and top jobs, and length of life are all statistically related to social class. Statistics show that middle-class people are more likely to use contraception effectively and to have smaller families. Such people are generally healthier and less likely to suffer from serious illnesses. Working-class people are more likely to become unemployed at some time in their working life, and to have to take time off work because of illness. Smoking is more prevalent amongst the working class, as are respiratory diseases as a cause of death. Working-class people are less likely to own their own houses, and more likely to be council or housing association tenants.[9]

Activity 1.17

Using all the information in section 1.3, together with that contained in the quiz plus any additional information you have, write a brief character sketch of a real or imaginary person. Give the person a name, a job and a life-style. Read out your description and ask others to say to which class they think the person belongs.

Up to this point, words such as 'working class', 'middle class' and 'upper class' have been used loosely without much thought as to what 'class' means. Meeting Jeremy Ponsonby-Smythe who attends a public school and enjoys a game of polo, it is not difficult to apply the label 'upper-class' or 'upper-middle-class'. It is more difficult to say which particular variable indicates social class. The factors which people commonly use to define social class include the way people speak, their job, their educational background, the amount of money people have or the way they spend it, including how they dress and the car they drive.

Activity 1.18

Decide what class you think you are and write it on a piece of paper.

Occupation and class

In everyday conversation, it does not matter too much what people mean when they talk about class. However, compilation of statistical information linking class with factors such as educational achievement or death by different causes requires a strict definition of the term. The indicator most commonly used is that of occupation. There are pitfalls in grouping people on this basis but it does seem that different types of work are linked with different life-styles and attitudes. One means of demonstrating this (and becoming unpopular) is to try and convince a stranger at a party that you do a job very different from the one you really do. It is probably because class and occupation are so closely related that a conversation between strangers usually begins with the question 'What do you do?'. The man in a suit, carrying the *Financial Times* at the opera, may be a street cleaner but it is unlikely.

The Registrar-General's classification of occupations

Government reports and most other surveys which relate information to class have in the past used a form of classification known as the Registrar-General's classification of occupations. This is based on a list of some 20,000 occupational titles which are then grouped into occupational units. These groupings were intended to reflect occupational skill and qualifications. The occupations are then classified into five groups, the middle one of which is commonly split into two. Table 1.1 shows this classification. Whilst it is difficult to produce a better scheme, there are problems in the Registrar-General's classification.

Activity 1.19

Study Table 1.1 and decide which class you are. Compare this with your self-classification in Activity 1.18 and discuss any difficulties or variation.

Some of the troublesome aspects of this method of determining social class are described below. Households, children and, sometimes, married women are usually allocated to a class on the basis of the occupation of the head of the household. Where there is an adult male and an adult female, the man is taken as the head of the household. Whilst people tend to marry within a social class, it is possible, for example, for a middle-class woman to marry a working-class man. In this situation it could easily be the woman's class background which most influences the family's life-style and values.

There appears to be a group missing from the top of the scale. Whilst not numerically significant, there are titled aristocrats who live on inherited wealth. These people probably have more social standing in the community than doctors or lawyers. Also, the occupational groups are large and not clearly defined. For example, farmers vary from large-scale land-owners employing workers to tenant-farmers working a small farm alone. Their social standing and life-style cannot be assumed to be similar.

TABLE 1.1   The Registrar-General's classification of occupations

Examples of occupations		Social status	Definition
Senior executives, doctors, lawyers, accountants, bank managers, chemists, university teachers	Non-manual	I (A) — Upper middle class	Professional, higher managerial and administrative
Chiropodists, farmers, journalists, police officers, teachers, nurses	Non-manual	II (B) — Middle class	Intermediate managerial, administrative, professional
Bank clerks, technicians, sales representatives, secretaries, shop assistants, estate agents	Non-manual	III (C1) — Lower middle class	Skilled, intermediate and junior non-manual
Fitters, welders, bus drivers, miners, cooks, electricians, hairdressers, carpenters	Manual	III (C2) — Skilled working class	Skilled manual
Agricultural workers, bus conductors, machine-sewers, postmen and postwomen	Manual	IV (D) — Semi-skilled working class	Semi-skilled manual
Labourers, cleaners, window-cleaners, railway-porters, messengers	Manual	V (E) — Working class	Unskilled manual

The division between non-manual and manual work also creates some problems. It is debatable whether a secretary or a shop assistant has more status than an electrician or hairdresser. More generally, using 'present occupation' as the determining factor for class analysis does not allow for the prestige a person may have through the social standing of his or her parents.

A new way of measuring class

Towards the end of the 1990s a review of the government social classifications was carried out and a new scheme put forward. This is the National Statistics Socio-Economic Classification (NS-SEC). It was designed in time for use in the census of 2001. The new scheme has eight categories and is intended to reflect employment status but also the terms and conditions under which people work. Employers are separated from employees. Conditions of work include career prospects, the length of notice required, rights to pensions and other benefits such as health insurance. The list below shows the categories and some examples of the jobs included in each.

1 Higher managerial and professional occupations
    Company directors
    Police inspectors
    Bank managers
    Senior civil servants
    Doctors
    Lawyers
    Social workers
    Teachers

2 Lower managerial and professional occupations
    Nurses and midwives
    Journalists
    Prison officers
    Police
    Actors and musicians

3 Intermediate occupations
    Clerks
    Secretaries
    Driving instructors
    Computer operators

4 Small employers and own account workers
    Publicans
    Playgroup leaders
    Farmers
    Taxi drivers
    Window-cleaners
    Painters and decorators

5 Lower supervisory, craft and related occupations
    Printers
    Plumbers
    Butchers
    Bus inspectors
    TV engineers
    Train drivers

6 Semi-routine occupations
    Shop assistants
    Traffic wardens
    Cooks
    Bus drivers
    Hairdressers
    Postal workers

7 Routine occupations
    Waiters
    Road sweepers
    Cleaners
    Couriers
    Building labourers
    Refuse collectors
8 Never worked and long-term unemployed

David Rose, Professor of Sociology at Essex University, reviewed the old scheme and wrote the new one. He says: 'The old classification was based on occupation only and went back to the 1920s. Seventy years on, the manufacturing sector forms a declining part of the economy while the service sector forms an increasing part. Very different jobs are now dominant: coal miners are now less common than shop assistants. The old system was based on manual skills that are no longer a meaningful way of discriminating between occupations.' He also points out that women have done well out of the new scheme: 'In the uppermost class, the proportion of women has quadrupled to 11 per cent, compared with 14 per cent for men.'[10]

Class and economic production

There are other ways of looking at class. For example, there is a strong tradition of seeing class in terms of people's relationship to the means of economic production. This means that one class is defined as being the owners and controllers of the factories, machines and processes which produce goods and wealth. The other class is forced to sell its labour in order to survive. Whilst this analysis is very important, most of the references to class throughout this book will be using the term in the sense in which it is defined in the classifications of occupations.

1.4   Race and racism

This section looks at aspects of the situation of Britain's black population. It starts by looking at countries from which black people, or their parents, came to Britain and the reasons why they left their home to come here. This is followed by an examination of cultural differences between different groups. Finally the problem of racism is introduced, along with examination of some policy initiatives to combat racism. These issues are also looked at more specifically in the chapters which follow.

What is 'race'?

Section 1.1 of this chapter looked at some of the problems in finding the best words to use: these problems are especially difficult to solve in the context of talking about race. The word 'race' itself is somewhat nonsensical. It has no scientific meaning in the sense in which it was originally used to refer to genetically distinct groups. Its origins are tied up with the colonisation of other countries through the British empire and the use of the other people as slaves. The idea that some human beings were of a different 'race' – and seen at the time as inferior with less developed feelings and intellects – helped to justify slavery in white people's minds. If we actually tried to strictly divide people into racial groups – as was done under the apartheid system in South Africa – ridiculous problems of classifying particular individuals follow. However issues to do with race are significant in this society and do need to be talked about – whilst this is the case we cannot simply abandon the word race. In this book the term will be used in the same imprecise way as it is used by the general population, to refer loosely to people with different skin colours.

Source: Gina Glover, Photofusion
Britain is a multi-racial society

What is 'black'?

Another term which needs some explanation is 'black'. As used here, this includes people from India, Pakistan and Bangladesh, as well as those from Africa and the Caribbean. This convention is followed despite a recognition that the groups included may have little in common with each other in terms of culture. It is also the case that some Asians would not accept the term 'black' as applying to themselves.

UK-born ethnic groups

Another source of confusion that needs to be mentioned here concerns the convention of calling people Asian or West Indian even when they were born in the UK. A common way to avoid some of these issues is to use the term 'minority ethnic group', meaning a group with its own cultural background which does not make up the majority of the population in a given country.

Origin of Britain's black population

Activity 1.20

Make a list of countries from which Britain's black population originates.

People of Asian origin came here from two parts of the world. The first is the Indian sub-continent – India, Pakistan and Bangladesh. Second, many British Asians had been living, and perhaps had been born, in East Africa. Such people came to Britain from Tanzania, Kenya, Uganda and Malawi. There are also a small number of Africans living in Britain although more important in terms of numbers are those who come from the Caribbean, also known as the West Indies. West Indian people living in Britain have come from a number of Caribbean islands such as Jamaica, Trinidad, Barbados, Grenada or Antigua.

Activity 1.21

Have a look in an atlas to see if you know where these places are in the world.

Activity 1.22

Conduct an informal survey in the classroom to find out what people think is the proportion of black people in the population. Guess the percentage of black people in Britain and write it on a piece of paper, then collect together the information to establish an average.

Percentage of minority groups in the population

In 1991, for the first time, the government decided to include a question on ethnic origin in the census carried out on the whole population. The total population of Great Britain on the night of the census was 54,888,844. Of these people 94.5 per cent were white, and 5.5 per cent from minority ethnic groups.[11] In 1997–98, ethnic minority groups represented 6 per cent of the population of Great Britain.[12]

You can now compare these figures with your estimates in Activity 1.22. The most common result is for people to over-estimate, often hugely, the size of the minority ethnic population in relation to the white population. In my experience this is true of nearly everyone who has done this exercise, regardless of where they live. Why do people tend to do this? It is probably an aspect of racism, fuelled by the press, some politicians and general ignorance which leads people to believe that there are many more black people in Britain than is actually the case.

The historical context

Why did people come to Britain?

Racism feeds generally on lack of knowledge and one particular area of ignorance concerns the reasons why people emigrated to Britain. A full understanding of this requires an explanation which goes back some 400 years and looks at Britain's role in the slave trade and the exploitation of other countries through the British empire. It is not possible to give such an account here, and whilst it should be noted that black people have been in Britain since the sixteenth century, the explanation here focuses on the period following the Second World War, which is when many Asians and West Indians arrived.

After the Second World War Britain experienced a serious shortage of labour and many employers, especially those offering low wages or expecting people to work anti-social hours, could not find workers. It was at this time, in 1948, that the Nationality Act was passed which established two types of British subject: 'Citizens of the UK and colonies' and 'Citizens of Commonwealth Countries'. Both were free to enter and remain in the UK and, by a simple process of registration, a citizen of a commonwealth country could become a citizen of the UK and colonies. One explanation for this law was that it was a token of gratitude for the large part played by the colonies in fighting the war. However, another motive was probably to allow employers to make use of workers from the poorer countries to solve the problem of not being able to attract workers in Britain.

People were actively encouraged to come and work in Britain. For example, London Transport went to the Caribbean to recruit workers. Enoch Powell, then Conservative Minister of Health, also sought West Indians to work in the National Health Service. Employers in the textile industries looked to India and Pakistan for staff. In the words of one writer:

> The 'immigrants' came because they were invited. The Macmillan government embarked on a large-scale advertising campaign to attract them. They were extraordinary advertisments, full of hope and optimism, which made Britain out to be a land of plenty, a golden opportunity not to be missed. They worked. People travelled here in good faith, believing themselves wanted.[13]

People came for work, in order to send money back home or to achieve a better standard of living for themselves and their families.

Some Asians also came as a result of the partition of India (in 1947) into India and Pakistan, in which Britain politicians had played a major role. The partition caused disturbances at the border areas and led to a situation where people living on the Indian side of the border following the Muslim religion became a religious and cultural minority. They emigrated into Pakistan where they were refugees without work. Since they were already uprooted and living precariously some decided to come to Britain.

East African Asians were in a different situation. They had emigrated from India to Africa in the first half of this century, encouraged by the British who wanted a middle class to exist between the British rulers and the African populations. The Asians in East Africa were wealthy and owned many of the business enterprises. However, when the African countries achieved independence from Britain, the position of the Asians became insecure, and they were often forced to leave.

Restrictions on immigration

By the end of the 1950s, two things were happening. First, immigration was slowing down, as the demand for workers decreased. Second, racism in Britain was beginning to take on violent forms and become a subject of public debate. In 1962, legislation was passed, restricting immigration. It is ironic to note that racism and immigration laws sometimes had the opposite effect from that which was intended. For example, many Asian men came with the intention of earning some money, with which to return home. However, discrimination in employment forced them to set up businesses which, taking considerable time and investment to establish, they were reluctant to give up. Similarly, there was a tendency in some Indian families to send one son temporarily, to be replaced by another, on his return. The laws passed in the 1960s restricting entry made frequent trips to and from Britain impossible and resulted in the men staying on and sending for their wives and children.

By the 1970s, immigration of black people into Britain was practically non-existent and limited to dependants of those people already here. In 1981, a law was passed to come into effect on 1 January 1983, replacing the 1948 Nationality Act and incorporating aspects of immigration laws passed in the 1960s and 1970s. The 1981 Nationality Act set up three tiers of citizenship; British citizenship, British overseas citizenship and citizenship of the British dependent territories. Of these three, only the first gives an automatic right to enter and live in Britain, and being born in Britain is no longer sufficient to give British citizenship. People living abroad who are included in the category of British citizen are largely white, living in places such as Canada and Australia, whereas the people in the category of British overseas citizen are mainly black.

Cultural variation

When people move to a different country, they do not somehow forget all the things they have learned in the country from which they came. People will adapt in some ways to a new way of life, but they will probably retain their values and some aspects of their life-style.

Activity 1.23

Imagine you and your family are going to live in a very different culture, perhaps in the Middle East. How much of yourself and your life-style would you want, or be prepared to change? Think about whether you would change your religion, your way of eating, your ideas about marriage and bringing up children. Would you seek out people like yourself, or would you make friends with native inhabitants of the country?

To have a better understanding of ethnic minority groups in England, it is helpful to know something of the way of life in the countries from which they originate.

Activity 1.24

In small groups make a study of one of the countries from which Britain's black population originally came, as mentioned earlier. Cover aspects such as religion, food, education and family structure. Report your findings to the class.

Asian society

A very brief and generalised account is given here of life in the Indian sub-continent. Many people, although not all, from the Indian sub-continent, come from a rural background where the main occupation is farming. In the villages, homes commonly consist of a number of rooms built around a courtyard. People live in large family groups, which incorporate three generations. When sons marry, they bring their wives into their family home, whilst daughters join the family of their husbands. Indians have strong feelings and obligations towards their families and there are also powerful kinship relations between families.

Amrit Wilson, in her book on Asian women, argues that an important factor in Indian family life is the concept of *izzat*.[14] In one sense, *izzat* means male pride, but it also refers to the honour of the family, and it is the responsibility of everyone to maintain and enhance the *izzat* of the family. In traditional Indian families, men and women have separate roles, with the women responsible for housework and child-care. Children are given a great deal of love and attention and allowed a lot of freedom. In the large families, the women provide a great deal of support for each other. Marriage is seen, not as an individual concern, but as something which affects the whole family, and as a result, marriages are arranged by the parents of the young couple.

Religion is a very important part of Indian life, affecting clothes, food and many other aspects of life. The three main religions of India are Hinduism, Sikhism and Islam.

Caribbean society

Caribbean societies are much more similar to British society, reflecting the European influence on the islands. This influence shows in the political and legal systems, as well as in education, where schools may offer GCSE examinations from the English examining boards. The language of the West Indies is English, sometimes spoken in a dialect known as Creole. The main religion on the islands is Christianity or Rastafarianism.

West Indians see the ideal for families as being a married couple and their children. However, other forms of family group are most common. Poverty means that men need to travel to find work and as a result many families consist of a woman, her children and her mother. Common-law marriage is also as common as legal marriage. This situation means that women have considerable authority in the family. Children are brought up strictly and obedience is expected, both at home and at school.

Activity 1.25

What cultural variations exist between different ethnic groups in Britain? List any you can think of.

Ethnic minorities and British society

The following section examines some way in which ethnic minorities differ from white British society. It is important to note that what is said is very much at the level of generalisation. In reality, there are wide variations between members of minority ethnic groups, and changes occurring as the generation of black people born in Britain grows up.

Marriage and family life

Minority groups are unusual insofar as there are fewer older people than in the population as a whole. This is explained by the fact that most people who came in the 1950s and 1960s were young and are now moving into middle age. The absence of a large number of elderly people partly explains the statistical fact that minority households tend to be larger, since in the general population elderly people make up a large proportion of one- and two-person households. However, whilst most black people live in households containing one adult couple, households with more adults are more common than in the rest of society. This is in part a result of choice, but is also related to difficulties in finding housing, shortage of money and a tendency to feel the need for support, because of the difficulties of living in an alien and sometimes hostile society.

Even where people do not live in the same house, ties and obligations between relatives are stronger than tends to be the case for white people. Relatives commonly live near each other and spend leisure time in each others' company. Having said this, it is important that social workers and others do not adopt a stereotyped view of the Asian family, in particular assuming that older people will always be cared for by relatives and that services are not needed to meet their needs. One piece of research studied European, Asian and Afro-Caribbean older people in Birmingham. The study found that although 95 per cent of the Asians said that they were looked after by relatives when they came out of hospital, a quarter of the sample had no close relatives in Britain.[15]

In Asian families, there is a tendency for there to be a clear separation between male and female roles, and this is reflected in the way in which girls and boys are brought up, as well as in relationships between husbands and wives.

The Indian custom of arranged marriages continues in Britain. Whilst some young people reject the idea, others accept it as part of their culture or realise that to rebel would be to risk losing the support of their family and the Asian community. It is usual for there to be some consultation between parents and their children over arranged marriages. One Indian girl says, 'If my mum shows me a boy and I refuse, she does not mind. She asks me the reason and I tell her. If it's not my cup of tea I don't have it, and that's the case with most girls.'[16] In 1999 a working party was set up to look into the issue of forced marriages.

Young people with Asian parents live something of a double life, moving between two cultures. At home, they are expected to maintain Asian ways, whereas at school and college, they are exposed to Western culture. These two worlds are often kept strictly apart as any attempt to combine them leads to conflict. This is perhaps particularly true of Asian girls, who often have more freedom at school and college than at home. Obviously all parents want their children to be successful, but ethnic minority parents are especially ambitious for their children, wanting for them the things that they themselves could not have.

Religion and religious customs

This section focuses on people who originate from the Indian sub-continent. West Indians are mainly Christians, although Rastafarianism is becoming increasingly significant in West Indian communities.

As mentioned earlier the three main religions of India are Hinduism, Sikhism and Islam. Religious rules and customs cover many aspects of life, for example food and dress. Islamic law requires that women keep their bodies covered. Within Hinduism, a female must not show her legs, once she reaches womanhood. This at first caused problems in schools, where girls were not allowed to wear trousers or were expected to wear shorts for physical education. The clothes worn by Asian women are of several types, depending on the part of India from which they originate and the religion. Even within one kind of dress, there are many subtle variations. Examples of Asian clothes for women are saris, the *salwar-kamiz*, which is a long tunic worn with trousers, and the *dupatta*, which is a long scarf worn over the head and shoulders. Sikhism demands that men do not cut their hair, and that they should wear a turban.

Food is also governed by religion. Muslims must eat *halal meat*, which is meat slaughtered according to certain rules, and pork is forbidden. Hindus are vegetarian, as are some Sikhs. All three religions require fasting on particular days of the year.

Activity 1.26

In small groups find out more about Hinduism, Sikhism and Islam. Also find out about other religions such as Rastafarianism and the Jewish religion.

In the following extract an Asian Hindu talks about her religion and her life to Julie, who is collecting information for a project as part of her Diploma in Playgroup Practice.

On religion …

We believe in one god – Krishna. In our religion we have many gods but they are all aspects of the god Krishna. I don't find the fact that the children are taught mainly about the Christian religion a problem as we believe that all gods, the Muslim god and the Christian god, are all aspects of Krishna. I tell my children this.

Every day I have a ritual bath then I light an oil lamp to pray to Krishna. We have a special place or shrine in our house called a Mandir – the oil lamp or Dibo goes on the Mandir. When I cook I always put a little of the food on the Mandir as a 'thank you' or offering to God before we eat. If I buy fruit I always wash it and put it on the Mandir before I give it to the children to eat.

I never waste food or throw it away. I give leftovers to the birds. In India very religious people will give food to birds, cows or beggars before they eat. When I pray I say sorry to God for things that I've done wrong.

We do have a lot of festivals and sometimes we hire a hall at the college. Gorba is a kind of folk dance which carries on over nine days. The date is variable but it usually falls in October. Gorba tells the story of the Goddess Durgama or Kali who has a war with a devil. After nine days she won. We dress up in Indian clothing and dance. Diwali is another festival and there are many more.

On food …

I am a strict vegetarian and so are my husband and children. Some Hindus will eat fish and other meats but no beef as the cow is sacred. In Gujerat where I come from people are mostly vegetarian but they will eat chicken if they live on a farm.

My best friend is a Hindu but she eats meat. She thinks that it is important to do as the English do in this country. I don't think one should give up one's beliefs and we have many arguments about it.

The children are very strict about it too. When Srina was two we went to visit a relative and she was offered curry with chicken in it. I didn't tell her not to eat it, and the relative encouraged her to try it but she refused.

Although school will provide vegetarian meals they will assume that the children will eat fish. I have to be careful to specify no meat or fish. The children take a packed lunch. Even things like biscuits have animal fats in them so I have to be careful. When the children were at playgroup I asked the staff to check the ingredients on the packet to make sure there were no animal products in the food.

On marriage and family life …

We usually have marriages arranged for us but we do have a choice. If we have a meeting with our potential husband or wife and don't like them we can refuse. My brother saw fifteen girls before he said okay.

I was born in Uganda then lived in India from age three to fourteen. My parents then came to England. My husband's family came from Kenya. I agreed to marry my husband although he was the first man I was introduced to as a prospective husband. I liked him and he was quite religious and also a vegetarian. If he was not a vegetarian I would have refused him as I could not cook meat.

We were very happy at first then we moved in with his parents and lived with them for eight years. We had three small children and slept in one room. I don't get on with my in-laws. They are very critical, particularly my mother-in-law, and I could do nothing right. When we got our own house, it was much better.

The family in Hindu life is very important but like anyone there may be personal clashes. My parents live in London but I don't get on with my mother because our temperaments are too similar. We fight quite a lot but if they needed me to look after them I would.

Caste is more important in India when choosing a husband or wife. If a man or woman really wants to marry someone of a different caste the family will usually object but come round to it eventually in this country.

I have a friend from Rajastan. Her parents objected to her marrying a Patel as they wanted her to marry from her own community. The pair insisted and now they all get on very well.

I have a cousin who married an English woman. My uncle was furious although my aunt was not so angry. In the end they gave in and the couple married. Funnily enough they ended up getting divorced and my cousin married another English woman. Now they are very happy and are accepted by the family.

Most Hindus will eventually accept marriage to an English woman but would object if a Hindu married an African or West Indian. This is crazy as a lot of Indians lived in Africa. How can we condemn racism if we are prejudiced ourselves? I am very against this.

Weddings are huge affairs. In India if a girl is born the family start saving for the wedding straight away as they are so expensive.

I have read about people aborting female foetuses in India. It is terrible. My husband was really pleased when Sita was born and the nurses said 'I'm surprised you're happy to have a girl, most Indian people want boys.'

Valuing minority cultures

Activity 1.27

What steps can be taken by a nursery school or children's home in a multiracial area to reflect the different cultures of the children?

It is not difficult for a nursery or other organisation, having recognised the need, to provide an atmosphere in which all children can feel at home. There is a need for teachers and other staff from ethnic minorities, and for white teachers to know something of the different cultures. Perhaps staff who speak only English could learn something of the languages spoken by people in the area, and they certainly should make sure they are able to pronounce the children's names correctly.

The nursery or other children's home should generally reflect the fact that the children are from different backgrounds. This can be done with posters, toys, dressing-up clothes, musical instruments, stories and books. It is particularly important that books and posters show black people in everyday situations in Britain. Where food is provided, different diets must be recognised and respected and all religious festivals should be celebrated, not just Christmas and Easter.

Activity 1.28

Why is it important for a nursery, or any other provision, to reflect the different cultures its children come from?

There are several points to be made here, all of which are very important. People settle much more quickly in a familiar environment, especially young children who may have little experience outside the home. Where a child's or adult's culture is ignored a feeling of conflict may result, or a feeling that a particular type of background is not valued by society. Also, if white and black children are educated to understand and accept different cultures, they may grow up to be more tolerant adults.

Racial disadvantage

So far, this section has looked at the reasons why black people came to Britain, the backgrounds from which they came and variations in life-style and beliefs. Little has been said about the experience and treatment of ethnic groups in this country.

TABLE 1.2   Racism and equality

	Racism	*Equality and justice*
Power, participation and influence	White people control all or most positions of management, government, influence and power; black people are disproportionately involved in menial work, or are unemployed or under-employed	Black people are proportionately represented in management and government at all levels, and are not over-represented in lowest-paid and lowest-status occupations or in unemployment or under-employment
Practices, procedures and customs	Practices, procedures and customs affecting life-chances and the allocation of scarce resources benefit white people rather than black, and work to the disadvantage therefore of black	Practice, procedures and customs do not discriminate to the advantage of white people and to the disadvantage of black. On the contrary, they are fair to all
Beliefs and attitudes	White people believe in white superiority, have negative views and expectations of black people, and are ignorant or indifferent with regard to the nature of racism. Black people in consequence develop negative views of white people	There is mutual respect and appreciation: black people and white are ready to learn and benefit from each others' history, culture, insights and experiences, and to work together co-operatively on the solution of common problems

Source: Berkshire County Council, *Education for Racial Equality* (1983).

Activity 1.29

Make a list of areas of life where you think black people might have suffered from discrimination.

The theme of this section is racism and ways in which society operates in such a way as to disadvantage black people. Racism and disadvantage take many forms and the aspects covered here give an indication rather than a total picture of the problem. The term racism, as used here, has several aspects. First, it refers to attitudes and behaviour of individuals who discriminate between black and white people, or who believe, consciously or unconsciously, that white people are superior. Second, racism describes procedures and practices of individuals or institutions, which, intentionally or unintentionally, work to the disadvantage of ethnic minorities.

Table 1.2 is a chart produced by an advisory committee of Berkshire County Council, showing the various aspects of racism, compared with a situation of equality.[17]

Black people suffer from racism in a variety of ways, they are abused and ridiculed, their culture is ignored or denigrated and they live in a society which, in terms of advertising and other media, treats them either as non-existent or in terms of stereotypes. The following extracts show how black children can feel, on realising that they are not white. This experience is particularly painful for black children who have grown up in a white world. The two women referred to in the first extract were both brought up by white foster parents.

> When Susie Crawford first went to school, she was called a wog and a golliwog. Later in the bath she scrubbed her skin until it was red. Mary Titchmarsh recalls going riding with a (white) friend on her horse. When it refused at a jump she called it a silly wog – without knowing what the word meant. Her friend said, 'My horse is not a silly wog. You're a wog'. 'That really hurt', says Mary. 'She was my best friend'.[18]

A black man who was educated at an English boarding school tells how:

> The social brainwashing has its desired effect. If I wanted to be better, to be like them, I had to be white. So I tried. At Easter 1960, when I was fourteen – Easter, because that was when Jesus was in the mood to forgive *all* sins and by now black had become a sin – I went down on my knees and prayed, real hard. Every time I was alone I prayed, sometimes for hours. I prayed with tears in my eyes, imploring God to listen to my plea. I prayed to God to make me white. The myth of black inferiority, having been preached at me for so long, convinced me that the way out was to become a white man.[19]

Activity 1.30

Susie and Mary in the first extract above were fostered by white parents. There has been a lot of debate about mixed race fostering and adoption. The Commission for Racial Equality have a booklet on this called *Adopting a Better Policy* which contains useful evidence, recommendations and further readings.

For the address of the CRE, see the Further reading section at the end of this chapter. Do some library research on the arguments surrounding adoption and fostering of ethnic minority children and decide your own view on this issue.

Activity 1.31

As a class, carry out a survey of media to discover the way in which ethnic groups are presented or ignored by the media. Include books, comics, magazines, newspapers, television and videos in your study.

Racism does not only consist of verbal attacks and lack of respect for black people and their culture, it can also erupt in violence. It is difficult to find figures to illustrate the level of racist attacks on people in Britain. This is partly because of the way in which records have been kept. Also there has been a reluctance on the part of members of ethnic minorities to report incidents to the police, perhaps because they feel the police cannot, or will not help them. Local newspapers in areas like Southall in London and Handsworth in Birmingham regularly report attacks on Asians.

Amrit Wilson, in the introduction to her book on Asian women, tells of a woman who will not open the door until she hears a greeting in Bengali and another whose child was badly beaten up on the way to school. These women feel that Asians must live near each other for protection from violence. In Amrit Wilson's book, one woman describes an incident as follows:

> It was just an ordinary evening. I had done all the cooking and was waiting for my husband to come home. Suddenly I heard a loud scream and rushed to the front door. Half a dozen white teenagers were beating someone up. There was blood on the pavement. I couldn't see who it was at first, then I realised it was my husband. He was unconscious on the ground. They were kicking and beating him. I screamed for help. the neighbours rushed out and we beat off the thugs with sticks and broom-handles. We called the police and ambulance but it was a long time before the police arrived. They went to see my husband in hospital and asked him to see them when he came out. But when he did, they showed no interest at all, they just said the officer concerned was not there. They made no attempt to catch the thugs.[20]

The Macpherson report, published in 1999, investigated the handling by the police of the murder of a black teenager, Stephen Lawrence. Six years earlier, Stephen Lawrence had been killed while he waited at a bus stop in south east London. No-one was convicted for this crime. The Macpherson report was severely critical of the way the Metropolitan Police Force carried out the investigation. It concluded that the investigation was marred by 'a combination of professional incompetence, institutional racism and a failure of leadership by senior officers.'[21] Amongst many examples of incompetence and racism the report was critical of the way the police immediately assumed that Stephen Lawrence had been in a fight, refusing to believe that a racist attack could have occurred. The investigating officers ignored leads which could have led to an early arrest of the white boys suspected of the attack. They were also racist in their stereotyping of Stephen's friend Duwayne Brooks who was in shock after witnessing the attack. He says, 'at the scene the police treated me like a liar, like a suspect instead of a victim, because I was black and they could not believe that white boys would attack us for nothing. They tried on the night (of the murder) at the police station to get me to say that the attackers didn't call us nigger. They described me as violent, unco-operative and intimidating. They were stereotyping me as a young black male. They didn't care about what I told them. They weren't bothered that Stephen was lying there dying.'[22] The report also heard how the police had treated Stephen's parents, Neville and Doreen in a patronising and unsympathetic manner. The persistence of Neville and Doreen Lawrence's need for justice resulted finally in the Macpherson investigation, six long years after Stephen's death. As well as focusing on the prejudice which exists within the police force, the report took a much wider view, arguing that racism exists in all organisations and institutions.

Benjamin Zephaniah is a black poet. His poem *What Stephen Lawrence has taught us* includes the following verse:

The death of Stephen Lawrence
has taught us
That we cannot let the illusion of freedom
Endow us with a false sense of security as we walk the streets,
The whole world can now watch
The academics and the super cops
Struggling to find a definition of institutionalised racism
As we continue to die in custody
As we continue emptying our pockets on the pavements,
And we continue to ask ourselves
Why is it so official
That black people are so often killed
Without killers?[22]

The Macpherson report's many recommendations recognised the need to eliminate racism across the whole of society with policy changes needed in education, housing and the rest of the public sector as well as within the police service and the criminal justice system as a whole. The report received a great deal of publicity at the time of its publication and led to considerable debate about the extent of racism throughout the various institutions of society. Only time will tell if any real changes came as a result of the horrific death of Stephen Lawrence.

Other aspects of racial disadvantage, such as in employment, education and housing, are examined in Chapters 4, 5 and 7 of this book.

Policy on racism

1976 Race Relations Act

The discrimination and disadvantage suffered by black people persist despite the existence of legislation which makes discrimination illegal. The Act of Parliament which covers this is the 1976 Race Relations Act. The law makes discrimination illegal in a variety of circumstances including employment, housing, education and the provision of goods and services. The Race Relations Act is concerned with discrimination on racial grounds, which is defined in terms of colour, race, nationality or ethnic origins. Discrimination is defined in three ways. First, it is against the law to treat a person less favourably, on the grounds of race. Second, indirect discrimination consists of applying criteria which work to the disadvantage of one person over another, for no justifiable reason. An example of this might be an employer requiring a high standard of English for a job which does not need this qualification. Third, it is illegal to victimise someone for being involved in making a complaint about discrimination.

People who believe that they have been illegally discriminated against must prove in a court (or industrial tribunal in the case of employment) that they have been treated less favourably because of their race. If people are successful in proving that discrimination occurred they can be awarded compensation and sometimes have the situation put right. The Commission for Racial Equality, which was set up by the government to work towards the elimination of discrimination, can help in the preparation of Race Relations Act cases and in representation at tribunals.

Activity 1.32

Why might the Race Relations Act have limitations as a means of stopping discrimination?

The first and most obvious problem of the existing anti-discrimination legislation is that people have to prove that the law was broken. This is extremely difficult, since few employers are going to admit that they are acting illegally. If, for example, someone is not given a job, it is difficult to prove that discrimination on the grounds of race was the reason. Also, people may feel that they will lose more than they will gain by bringing a case to court or to a tribunal. However, the 1976 legislation is important and its existence may serve to prevent some discrimination from occurring and perhaps act to change attitudes towards race.

Equal opportunities policies

Many organisations in the public and the private sectors have adopted policies to promote equal opportunities. These can cover various aspects of the organisation and the services it provides. In terms of employment practices, an equal opportunities policy could involve the following aspects. The first step might be to examine current practices in case any are discriminatory in the sense of preventing black people from competing for jobs on an equal basis with whites.

Secondly, positive action can be taken in terms of advertising posts in such a way as to attract black people to areas of work where they are needed. Finally, in areas of work where a particular racial group is under-represented, training can be provided or people can be encouraged to go for training.

The following is an example of how the positive action already outlined could be used in a social services department. A social services division in an area of the country with a large population has no black social workers. When vacancies arise, the employing authority could use positive action in the following ways:

- The advertisement for posts could include a statement that applications from members of ethnic minorities are welcomed.
- The authority could encourage black people to train as social workers (although cannot guarantee a job afterwards, since this would count as unlawful discrimination).
- If there is a job which involves providing people from a particular racial group with personal services to promote their welfare, the law allows the employer to appoint someone of the same racial group. An example of this might be a post of warden in a hostel for Asian girls.

This chapter has attempted to demonstrate the importance of recognising that Britain is a culturally and racially diverse society. Alongside this, is the necessity of understanding the causes and effects of disadvantage. This understanding is perhaps particularly important for those who work in the caring professions, whether in nurseries, children's homes or in the community. It may be that such an understanding will be the first step towards moving away from the situation, described by Salman Rushdie, where, 'Britain is now two entirely different worlds, and the one you inherit is determined by the colour of your skin.'[23]

Activity 1.33

Make sure that you understand the following expressions used in this chapter. Check in the Glossary at the end of the book if you need to.

census	psychological
class structure	racism
comprehensive school	role
cultural differences	role-conflict
depression	role-set
deprivation	selective schooling
discrimination	social services
equality of opportunity	state sector
ethnic minority	status
'glass ceiling'	statutory organisation
learning disability	stereotype
legal system	stigma
positive action	voluntary organisation
private sector	welfare provision

Further reading

There are a number of introductory textbooks on social welfare, covering the subject from a range of different angles. Some are more difficult than others, covering material in more depth or writing in a more challenging style. *Developments in British Social Policy*, edited by Nick Ellison and Chris Pierson (Macmillan, 1998) is a comprehensive book which covers most relevant areas of social policy with some more general chapters. A book which is perhaps more accessible at an introductory level is Stephen Moore's *Social Welfare Alive*, 2nd edn (Cheltenham: Stanley Thornes, 1998).

Any book in this area quickly becomes out of date as the rate of change in social policy is so rapid. Newspapers and journals are a source of more up-to-date information. *The Guardian* is a newspaper with an excellent reputation for coverage of welfare issues. Journals published for the caring professions, such as *Community Care*, contain useful and relevant articles. Other more specialist and academic journals will be available in college libraries. *Social Trends* is an annual summary of statistical data published by HMSO. It is available in reference sections of libraries. Also see below for the government's website on statistics.

Each year The Family Welfare Association publish a new and up-to-date edition of their *Guide to the Social Services* which lists and describes services and organisations.

Thinking more specifically about the areas covered in this chapter, *Social Issues for Carers*, 2nd edn by Richard Webb and David Tossell (Edward Arnold, 1999) focuses on social inequality within British society. Topics of race, gender and class are covered from the point of view of carers. The book also covers discrimination against other groups such as homeless people and travellers.

On gender issues, the Equal Opportunities Commission is a useful source of information (the address is given below). For information on race issues, try the Commission for Racial Equality (see below for address and website).

Useful addresses

EOC
Overseas House
Quay Street
Manchester M3 3HN
tel. 0161 833 9244

CRE
Elliot House
10–12 Allington Street
London SW1E 5EH
tel. 0207 828 7022

Institute of Race Relations
2–6 Leeke Street
King's Cross Road
London WC1X 9HS
tel. 0207 837 0041

Joint Council for the Welfare of Immigrants
115 Old Street
London EC1V 9JR
tel. 0207 251 8706

Websites

Equal Opportunities Commission **www.eoc.org.uk**

Commission for Racial Equality **www.cre.gov.uk**

UK in Figures **www.statistics.gov.uk**

▼ **2** Family life

The family is the most important social group in our society. The vast majority of people spend at least part of their lives living as a member of a family. Families exert a huge influence on children and varying degrees of influence on us all. Although there is a tendency to regard family life as a very private area, it is a subject of concern, both to academic writers and to policy-makers. The reason for this interest is that the family plays a key role in society.

Activity 2.1

Think about the family as a social group. List all the ways in which the family meets the needs of individuals, and of society at large.

2.1 Functions of the family

Social scientists talk about the *functions* of the family. This is simply a way of looking at the role the family plays in the context of the whole society. An important set of functions concerns children. The family, in whatever form, is the unit which provides a home and care for dependent children. In addition to physical care, children also receive a great deal of informal education within the family. They learn to walk, to talk, and the correct way to behave in society. A teacher in a nursery school will be aware how much a child knows, on arrival. For example, most children know that chairs are for sitting on, that they should obey grown-ups, and countless other details of social behaviour. This learning process is known as *socialisation*. It is not done exclusively by the family, although the family is the key agent. The way children are brought up is of obvious concern to society, since children grow up to be future citizens. In a very real way, the future of society depends upon the family.

Adults also expect to have certain needs met within the family. The family is expected to provide for emotional and sexual needs. Family groups form economic units in the sense that income is pooled and goods consumed are shared. Physical needs – for food, and care in times of ill-health – are primarily met within the family. Finally, the family exercises control over social behaviour which extends far beyond childhood, for example, someone might hesitate before leaving a partner, because of anticipated disapproval from relatives.

Activity 2.2

In some societies – for example in the kibbutz in Israel – the family, in the sense that we understand it, does not exist. Imagine what life would be like without the family. Write an account of a day in the life of a person in such a society.

It is probably becoming clear that discussion of the family takes in many different areas. Relationships within the family include marriage, parenthood and links with other relatives such as grandparents. The relationship between the family and the state is also an area of interest. This chapter will look at different types of family, marriage and divorce, violence in marriage and the relationship between welfare provision and the family.

2.2 Family structures

Over time, between societies, and even within one society, there is variation in the way in which the family is structured. Different terms are used to describe different kinds of families. Activity 2.3 is an introduction to looking at different family structures.

Activity 2.3

Take a particular family you know well. Obviously, this could be a family of which you are a member or in which you grew up. Construct a family tree, using Figure 2.1 as an example. (The symbol ○ means a female, △ means a male, and a line through the symbol ⧄ shows that the person is deceased. I have also indicated divorce by ⌊⫽_⫽⌋ and you may need to add a way of showing people who are living together without being married.)

Using the family tree, consider how much contact there is between family members. Note down how near people live to one another, and how regularly they visit. Do family members support each other, for example by

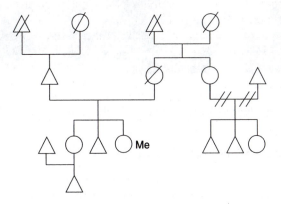

Figure 2.1   Family structures

lending money or offering to help someone to move house? Do families rally round in the event of a death or divorce? Do people feel obliged to attend weddings and to visit on festival occasions?

Nuclear, extended and modified extended families

Families vary, both in terms of the number of people living under one roof, and the amount of contact and support given. Two common types of family are *nuclear families* and *extended families*. The nuclear family consists of one man, one woman and their dependent children. The extended family is a wider grouping, including grandparents when vertically extended, and aunts and uncles when horizontally extended. A recently-invented third term is the *modified extended family*. This consists of separate nuclear families, related to each other, who do not have a great deal of actual physical contact, but who exchange significant services. An example of this would be families who live in different parts of the country, but who help each other out, for instance, in raising money for one member to start a business.

Source: Crispin Hughes, Photofusion
A nuclear family consists of two parents and their dependent children

Lone-parent and reconstituted families

Lone- or *single-parent families* have become increasingly common in recent years and are looked at in section 2.5 later in this chapter. The increase in divorce and re-marriage has given rise to another new term, *reconstituted families*. These are families including step-parents, half- or step-children.

Source: Bob Watkins, Photofusion
Most lone parents are women

Activity 2.4

Decide the most appropriate term for the family for which you drew the family tree in Activity 2.3. Find out which type of family is the most common in the area where you live.

Changes in family life

Whilst there is disagreement among social historians, it seems that in the past, extended families were more common than they are today. Family structures have altered as a result of changes in the wider society, for example, the economy demands that people should be prepared to move away from their relatives to find work. This trend has implications for social policy, for instance in terms of the needs of the elderly and of mothers of young children. However, extended families still exist, particularly in traditional working-class communities and among the Asian population. The ideal family, as portrayed in advertising images, consists of one man, one woman and children. In reality, only 23 per cent of households are made up of a married couple and their dependent children.[1]

Activity 2.5

What do you think are the advantages and disadvantages of living in a nuclear or extended family, from the point of view of:
  (i) a child
 (ii) a teenager
(iii) a mother with young children?

Other changes in family life include the fact that most families have a smaller number of children. In Victorian times, the average family would have included about six children. The statistical average now is just under two. There are several reasons for this trend, including improved and more freely available contraception, and the fact that whereas children were once a financial asset, working on family farms, they are now a financial liability, costing their parents thousands of pounds. The trend towards smaller families, together with the tendency for elderly people to live longer, has implications for the care and support of elderly people (see Chapter 13). At a time when there is an increasing expectation that relatives will care for elderly people, there are proportionately fewer people available to provide care.

2.3   Marriage

Types of marriage

The kind of marriage practised in our society, and enforced by law, is the marriage of one woman and one man. This type of marriage is known as *monogamy*. Other types of marriage which exist in other countries are *polygyny*, which involves one man and several women, and *polyandry*, where a woman has several husbands. The term *polygamy* is sometimes used to cover polygyny and polyandry. These kinds of marriage are often found where the population has an unequal number of men and women.

Trends concerning marriage

In the UK, statistics demonstrate changing trends concerning marriage. Marriage rates peaked in the early 1970s and have fluctuated since, with current trends showing a decrease in the number of marriages. Trends also indicate that people were marrying younger, although recent figures show a move back to later marriage.[2]

Why do people marry?

Activity 2.6

Why do people want to get married? List as many reasons as you can think of, indicating if you think that some reasons apply more to women than to men, or vice versa.

People marry for many different reasons. For many people, marriage gives a sense of emotional security and sometimes is a source of financial security. It is probably still the case that married women have higher status than single women. Whether married men have more status than single men is less clear; certainly the term 'bachelor' conjures up an attractive image whereas the term spinster, hardly used now, implied something quite different. Traditional values and most religions encourage marriage as a form of recognition of a relationship. Marriage also integrates partners into wider families and gives a social seal of approval to a relationship.

It is obviously possible to have children without being married – and attitudes towards women who do so have changed a great deal in recent years (see below) – but there is still some element of social disapproval in some social groups. For men, marriage provides someone to care for them. It has been shown that married men suffer far less than single men from psychiatric problems.[3] Whilst this could be interpreted in more than one way, it is likely that men benefit from having the support of a wife.

Changing attitudes towards marriage

Attitudes towards marriage seem to be changing quite significantly with trends showing an increase in the number of people who live together. A survey found that three-quarters of people under 30 did not think it is wrong for people to live together without being married. The figure is lower for older age groups.[4] It used to be that people lived together before getting married and this still is the case for a lot of people, although there is a significant increase in the number of people who live together instead of getting married. A significant proportion of the people living together are people who have been married to someone else previously and are either divorced or in the process of getting divorced.

The basis for choice of a partner in marriage varies from society to society, and has changed over time. At one time, marriage was more concerned with benefits to the wider family group, such as bringing together adjoining land, than with romantic love. Amongst the Asian population in Britain, as discussed in Chapter 1, it is more common for marriages to be arranged by the parents, and love is seen to come after marriage, not before. In 1999, the government set up a working party, led by Asians, to look into the issue of forced marriages, believed to involve around a thousand people a year. This followed the case of a Bradford couple, in hiding for six years after death-threats from the wife's family, after her refusal to marry a cousin in Pakistan. However, when romance and sexual attraction are seen as the basis for selecting a partner, other factors intervene. For example there is a tendency for marriage partners to be of the same age, the same religion, the same race and the same class background. People do not fall in love in a completely random way.

Working parents

There has been an increase in the number of married women who work outside the home. The image of the male breadwinner and dependent housewife no longer reflects the reality of the family. In 1961, 29.7 per cent of married women were in paid employment, compared with a figure of 70 per cent in 1997.[5] Many women leave paid employment while their children are below school-age, although a significant minority are remaining in the labour force. In 1997, 64 per cent of women with children aged 0–4 were employed on a part-time basis, while 480,000 women were employed in full-time jobs.[6]

There are several explanations for the increased numbers of married women working outside the home. The two world wars brought women into areas of work previously considered suitable only for men. Although women were encouraged to give up their jobs when the wars ended, attitudes about the role of women had been challenged. The 1960s was a period of full employment with expansion in the areas of work traditionally seen as women's work, for example, in the service, commercial and administrative sectors of the economy. Even with high unemployment rates in later decades, these jobs have not been lost at the same rate as jobs traditionally done by men in areas of the economy such as manufacturing. It is becoming increasingly common for women to have work whilst their husbands are unemployed. Other explanations for the number of women in paid employment include the facts that families are smaller and that people live longer. It is no longer the case that child-bearing and child-care take up the whole of a woman's life. On an individual level, women may work outside the home for various reasons. The need for money is obviously a significant factor. Other reasons might include the desire for social contact, the need to have an identity other than housewife, a wish to escape from the routines of housework and, for some women, the desire to use their skills in a job which they enjoy.

Women with children sometimes feel guilty about having a job. There is, however, no conclusive evidence proving that relationships or children suffer in a family where both parents are in paid employment.

New rights for working parents were introduced in 1999. Fathers have the legal right to time off when a child is born or adopted. Parents are entitled to up to 13 weeks unpaid leave during the first five years of their child's life. Entitlement to short periods of time off means that employees cannot be sacked if they are called to school to pick up a sick child or deal with some other problem.

Activity 2.7

Do you think women with young children should continue to work? Give reasons for your answer and be prepared to discuss your ideas.

Segregated and joint roles

The sort of relationship a man and a woman have in marriage can, and does, vary. One way of looking at this is to talk of *segregated* and *joint* roles. In a segregated-role relationship, housework and child-care are seen as the concern of the wife only. Leisure and social activities are also separate, in that the man will have his own friends and hobbies, and the woman her own. In a marriage with joint roles, divisions are less distinct, and housework, interest and friends are shared.

There have been changes in men's and women's roles in marriage over the last 50 or so years, but there is also a tendency to exaggerate the extent of these changes.

One obvious change which has already been looked at is the increased likelihood for women to be working outside the home. This has not however been accompanied by an equivalent change in the amount of work done by men inside the home.

A market research company carried out a survey on gender roles, interviewing 1500 men and women.[7] They tried to interview couples who shared equally the shopping, cooking and laundry but were forced to give up when they could only find one man in a 100 who did his fair share of housework; 85 per cent of working women said they almost always did all of the laundry and ironing and a similar number said they were entirely responsible for cooking the main meal. The consumer research manager of the company commented:

> Men seem to set out with good intentions to share the domestic chores but the catalyst appears to be the arrival of children. At this stage, the man appears to abdicate responsibility for his share, regardless of whether his partner is working.

Other surveys have found similar results: people tend to think that men and women should share housework, but in reality it is the women who carry the main burden, even where they have paid work.

Things have changed a little more with regard to children. Men are taking a bigger role in the care of their children than was previously the case. A study called *Looking after Baby* carried out in Bristol found that 80 per cent of fathers were involved in tasks such as bathing, walking, feeding and putting children to sleep. The study suggested that men nowadays feel able to be soft, tender and caring with their children without being seen as a 'wimp'.[8]

Activity 2.8

Carry out a survey to investigate roles in marriage. Design a questionnaire to put to married couples, including questions on housework, child-care, decision-making, money management and social activities. Write up the results and conclusions in a report.

Activity 2.9

Imagine a situation where a couple are about to marry and have decided that they want an equal marriage. Draw up a contract which they could both sign. Bear in mind the areas of married life mentioned in Activity 2.8.

2.4 Divorce

Statistics show that the divorce rate has increased dramatically over the last thirty years, although there has been a more recent decrease. In 1961, 27,000 decrees absolute were granted to end marriages in the UK. The peak figure was in 1993, when there were 180,000 divorces. In 1996 the figure dropped slightly to 171,000.[9] The likelihood of divorce increases where people marry in their teens.

When can people get divorced?

Under the 1969 Divorce Reform Act, divorce is allowed when a marriage has irretrievably broken down. There are several ways in which this can be said to have happened. People can get divorced if they have lived apart for two years and both agree to the divorce. Where one partner does not agree, a divorce can be granted after they have lived separately for five years. Other grounds for divorce are unreasonable behaviour or adultery which the other partner finds intolerable. Since the 1984 Matrimonial and Family Proceedings Act, couples can petition for divorce after one year of marriage.

A new Family Law Act is expected to come into force in 2000. This will do away with the idea that one of the partners has done something wrong or that there has been a period of separation. The only reason for a divorce will be the irretrievable breakdown of the marriage. In this sense the law seems to make divorce easier. However, couples will have to go through a lengthy process of waiting and mediation meetings. First the couple must attend an information meeting to learn what services are available – from counselling to mediation to legal advice. Then they must wait three months before they can file a statement of marital breakdown. During this period the couple should consider whether the marriage is really over. Then they must wait a further six months, which is extended to nine months if there are children under 16. This can be lengthened further if one partner requests a longer time. Couples are expected to use the time to work out their new financial and childcare arrangements through a series of meetings with a mediator who will help them work out their own solutions.

Explanations for increased divorce rates

The rise in the divorce rate does not necessarily indicate an increasing disillusionment with marriage, since many divorced people remarry. Neither does the trend in divorce mean that marriages are less happy than they used to be. The reverse may be true, in that it may be that people have a higher expectation of marriage and are less prepared to remain unhappily married. Those marriages which do continue may be of a better quality. One explanation of the increase in divorce lies in the fact that people now marry younger and live longer. This means that marriages are expected to last longer. It is possible that a new phenomenon now exists which can be termed *serial monogamy*. This means that it is normal for people to have more than one monogamous marriage in the course of their life. Another possible reason for increase in divorce is the greater independence enjoyed by women, which makes it possible for unhappily married women to consider leaving their husbands. As has been described, the changes in the divorce laws have made this much easier. Attitudes to marriage and divorce have changed and the stigma of divorce is very much reduced.

Children and divorce

One reason why people express concern over divorce is that it may have a bad effect on children. This is a difficult area in which it is dangerous to generalise.

There are situations in which children are suffering as a result of very unhappy marriages and experience relief when their parents split up. In other situations, children show symptoms of emotional distress and anxiety, perhaps in the form of bed-wetting or tantrums in a younger child. The long-term effects of divorce on children have not been sufficiently researched for any positive conclusions to be drawn.

The 1989 Children Act introduced new provisions for children in cases of divorce. These are known as Section 8 orders and can apply to others such as grandparents as well as the child's parents. The orders are made by a court after all the evidence has been heard and the aim of the court will be to provide the best for the child. Section 8 orders are only used when necessary and the court can decide not to go ahead with an order at all.

There are four types of orders which the court can make:

- A *residence order* decides where the child will live. This can be in more than one place. The order also gives parental responsibility for the child and this too can go to more than one person.
- A *contact order* replaces the old idea of 'access'. This gives a person with whom the child does not live the right to contact with the child. The court can say exactly how much contact there will be and what conditions there might be. This might mean, for example, that the contact has to be supervised.
- A *specific issue order* takes away the parents' responsibility over particular issues and means decisions must be made by the court. An example of this could be decisions on education.
- A *prohibited steps order* stops something from being done, for example stating that the child must not be taken abroad.

Activity 2.10

Questions for discussion:
1 Should divorce be made easier, remain as it is, or be made more difficult to obtain?
2 Should divorce be allowed in the first year of marriage?
3 Should people wait until their children grow up before seeking a divorce?
4 In view of the increased likelihood of those who marry young getting divorced, should the age for marriage be increased to 21, or perhaps 25?
5 What provision would offer the best support for family members experiencing divorce?

2.5 Single-parent families

At present, there are about 1.7 million single-parent families in Britain. They consist of people who are divorced, separated, widowed or unmarried. Families where one parent is in prison can also be considered as single-parent families, since they will experience the same sorts of difficulties.

There is a tendency to see single parenthood as something abnormal, in spite of the fact that in some areas, the majority of children in a school live with one parent only. Similarly, single-parent families are sometimes assumed to be problem families, a view which overlooks the unhappiness in many two-parent families. Both these attitudes arise from the fact that society has in the past been geared to couples and nuclear families. However, whilst single-parent families should not be characterised as problem families, they do encounter special difficulties, many of which could be alleviated by legislation and better welfare provision.

Activity 2.11

What sort of problems do you think a single parent might encounter? Make a list of them.

Problems for single-parent families

The problems experienced by widows and widowers, divorcees and unmarried parents vary to some extent, although there are common factors. The stigma attached to single parenthood has reduced very significantly but it is still there to some extent, especially for unmarried mothers. Loneliness is a potential problem for all single parents and people who are widowed have special burdens in coping with bereavement at the same time as adjusting to life as a single parent. The problems of stigma and loneliness are both the concerns of *Gingerbread*, which is a national organisation of single parents. Gingerbread campaigns for a better deal for lone parents, as well as providing local groups offering advice and support.

Other emotional problems for single parents include their feeling of guilt towards their children. Children may feel deprived and express resentment towards the parent with whom they live. This may be caused partly by treatment received from other children at school, or even by tactless comments by teachers. Concern for children can also make it difficult for single parents to form new relationships, since children may feel threatened by the entry of a new adult into their lives. These problems are too complex to be more than indicated here. More information on this, and other aspects of single parenthood, can be obtained from Gingerbread.

Single-parent families tend, as a group, to be less well-off than other families. The costs of running a home are not substantially reduced because there is only one adult. Rents, mortgages and heating bills, for example, remain the same. In addition, many two-parent families benefit from having two incomes. Single parents face extra costs for child-care, if they want to work or have a social life.

Even where a lone parent has employment, the family is likely to be less well-off than other families. There are several reasons for this. First, the majority of single parents are women and women tend to earn less than men, despite the existence of equal pay legislation. Second, working often involves paying for child-care. Work is not organised in such a way as to make running a family at the same time an easy task. Even in the best situations – for example, teaching – school holidays do not always coincide, evening meetings are held and all plans are thrown into chaos if a child is ill.

The problems of working and the limited availability of suitable child-care result in many single parents being forced to rely on income support. These benefits are means-tested and barely provide for existence.

Teenage mothers

Particular concerns have been voiced in recent years about young single women who become pregnant and keep their babies. England and Wales have the highest rates of teenage pregnancies in the European Union. A report published in 1998 tried to dispel some of the myths about teenage mothers as well as suggesting some solutions:[10]

- Teenage mothers should not be seen in universal terms. They come from a variety of social and educational backgrounds.
- Teenagers do not become pregnant deliberately in order to get council housing or social security benefits

However, 81 per cent of the girls interviewed for the report ended up claiming income support. The report says there is a need for improved education of young people about sex, personal relations and the harsh realities of life as a teenage mother. It also calls for measures to help lone parents to improve their qualifications so they can find decent jobs and become more independent. The fathers are not forgotten. The report says: 'There must be a change in the culture that accepts that young men can abandon all responsibility for their babies ... .'

Activity 2.12

Imagine you are a member of a committee set up to investigate the issue of teenage mothers and make proposals for policies:

- What would you need to find out?
- What would your policy objectives be?
- How would you try to achieve your objectives?
- Are there any problems with any of your ideas?

Child support and maintenance

Financial and emotional hardship for single parents has also resulted from problems concerning maintenance payments. Until April 1993, all maintenance payments to lone parents were dealt with by the courts. In many cases this system did not work, with the result that 70 per cent of lone parents received no maintenance at all and many others received very small sums of money. The effect was that many lone parent families lived in poverty.[11]

Creation of the CSA

In 1991 the Child Support Act was passed. In April of 1993 the *Child Support Agency* (CSA) was set up by the government to gradually take over the task of dealing with maintenance of children by 'absent parents'. The agency uses the term 'absent parent' to describe the parent not living with the children; this is usually, but not always, the father. Fathers – who may in fact be seeing their children for several days a week – have objected to the implications of this term (see below).

The job of the agency is to assess the financial situations of both parents and to set an amount of maintenance to be paid. It is also responsible for making sure that the maintenance is actually paid. Where a lone parent is claiming income support, the maintenance is deducted from the income support paid. In most cases, lone mothers refusing to give information about the father of a child lose benefit. The law, however, states that people are exempt from assessment where there are reasonable grounds for believing that harm or undue distress will be caused by a maintenance assessment. An example of such a situation would be a case of a violent partner.

Reaction from 'absent fathers'

There was a strong reaction from fathers to the Child Support Agency and their campaign was well publicised in the media. It appears that the CSA targeted particular types of situations for the first wave of their assessments. These tended to be middle-class men in regular employment who were already paying maintenance. Many of these men had agreed to what were known as 'clean break' arrangements under the old system. These arrangements were favoured by the courts and encouraged in government legislation. The thinking behind a 'clean break' was that it was important for the children to have a home. Solicitors representing the husband and the wife (separately) would agree that the house – or a large part of the capital invested in the house – would be given to the woman in order that she and the children should have a home. In return, maintenance payments were set very low. These arrangements were believed to be permanent and legally binding. The CSA overturned this approach. In situations where men had already given over the house, they are now finding that they had higher maintenance costs to pay as well. In an average case, a man previously paying £80 a month for two children might now be expected to pay £300. It is argued that this has forced some fathers to give up work and go on to benefits; others say they are no longer able to afford to visit their children.

It has been stated that the views of absent fathers have been well publicised and indeed responded to by the government, with a series of amendments. Not long after the setting up of the CSA, the government announced radical changes to the formulas used to assess the amount fathers should pay for their children. This is a good example of how more powerful voices are heard. Much less well publicised has been the views of lone parents themselves – a less powerful group. As a result of pressure from fathers, the rules were changed to make sure that non-resident parents (usually the father) keep more money than they would get if they were on means-tested benefits such as income-based Jobseeker's

Allowance and are not required to pay more than 30 per cent of their income after tax.

NCOPF and NACAB criticisms

The National Council for One Parent Families (NCOPF) supported the principles behind the Child Support Act, believing there is a need for more equality between lone parents and their ex-partner. They argued that for too long lone parents have lived in poverty with their children whilst absent fathers have enjoyed a higher standard of living on their own or with second families. However NCOPF are still critical of the CSA, arguing it has failed those people it was set up to help. NCOPF monitored the working of the agency and in a report published in 1994 criticised it for delays and inefficiencies. They also felt the agency was weak in enforcing payments of maintenance.[12]

The CSA has been criticised from all sides for being more concerned with saving the government's money than with helping lone parents or children. The National Association of Citizens' Advice Bureaux (NACAB) carried out a major survey of the Agency's first year. They wrote:

> It is the conclusion of the CAB service that the Government's concern to maximise public expenditure savings has serious consequences for the success of the child support scheme.

Although the CSA was originally intended to deal with all lone parents, its task was adjusted to mean that only lone parents on social security benefits are required to apply for a child maintenance assessment. Parents who are not on benefits may apply.

On the basis of their survey NACAB made a number of recommendations, including that lone parents should be able to keep the first £15 of maintenance before it is deducted from social security payments. This has been implemented for lone parents who are working and receiving a top-up payment through Family Credit, but not for people on income support or Jobseeker's Allowance. A further step came in 1999 when the government proposed to take lone parents receiving Family Credit away from the control of the CSA, allowing them to keep all the maintenance paid. The Citizens' Advice Bureaus also argued that the government should take account of previous 'clean break' settlements in creating a fairer system for absent parents.[13]

CSA successes and failures

From the mother's point of view:

> Kate Lister is an example of how the CSA was intended to work. Divorced six years ago, she says she received intermittent maintenance under a court order for her 10-year-old son Oliver and 7-year-old daughter Amy.
>
> The agency last year ordered her former husband to pay £78 a week which has left her £30 a week better off and enabled her to take a part-time job and come off income support. She says: 'For the first time in six years I have had some independence.'

Carol Pallister is typical of many women who feel the CSA is failing them. Although her former husband has his own company, he has been told he need pay no money towards their son, 13-year-old James.

Ms Pallister says her former husband left her six weeks before James was born. For the first eight weeks she had no idea of his whereabouts. She lives on income support after being made redundant last year.

Having received a 'nil' maintenance assessment, Ms Pallister is bitter at what she sees as the CSA's inability to deal with self-employed fathers. She says: 'The agency should not be targeting men who are honourably fulfilling their promises.'[14]

From the father's point of view:

Tony Walentowicz is an angry man. His marriage broke down. It was his wife's idea to split, but it was termed an amicable divorce.

They agreed the financial arrangements. Jenny McLean, his wife of seven years, kept their £60,000 home. He was to pay £120 a month towards the upkeep of their daughter, Amy, now six.

It has been a struggle for Mr Walentowicz, aged 41. He earns £19,000 a year as keeper of natural science with the council museums in Chelmsford, Essex. Mortgage payments on his new home are proving tough to meet.

The settlement ... runs until 2004, when Amy will be 17. But last month the letter from the Child Support Agency arrived.

The agency says it will be reassessing what he pays each year. It will charge him £44 annually to do so ...

He says: 'What I really object to is that they wrote to me as an absent father. That is really unfair. I've never ducked my responsibilities. I've always paid up. It's insulting to say that about me.

'There are thousands of others in my position ... We fully recognise our responsibilities. But it seems we are the ones who will be hit hardest, whilst those who have done a runner are quietly ignored.'[15]

Activity 2.13

In groups of three or four, decide on policies which central government could implement to improve the position of single-parent families. Agree on a priority order for these issues.

2.6 Violence in the family

Violence between partners

Newspaper and television reports are full of stories concerning violence on the streets. Yet many violent incidents take place within the home, between people who are close to each other: we have much more cause to fear people we live with than assault by a stranger.

It is difficult to know the full extent of violence between partners, since it is probable that many incidents go unrecorded. This may occur because people feel shame or guilt about admitting that their relationship has gone wrong. Alternatively, they may fear that telling someone will lead to further attacks or that nothing can be done to help them. The following statistics provide no more than an indication of the extent of the problem. One study found that 25 per cent of all reported crime was domestic violence.[16] Other studies have estimated that there is severe and repeated violence in more than 1 in 100 marriages[17] and that in one in seven relationships there is violence at some point.[18] A survey of 1000 married women conducted by *World in Action* found that 28 per cent had been hit by their husbands and a further 5 per cent threatened with physical violence. Amongst women who had been separated or divorced the overall proportion of those either hit or threatened rose to 63 per cent.[19]

Violence in the family is most commonly directed against women. One survey found 75.8 per cent of assaults involving family members were assaults on the wife; in only 1.1 per cent of cases were husbands the victims of marital violence.[20] Other studies have suggested a higher proportion of men experiencing violence. The British Crime Survey found that there were 6.6 million assaults in the home each year, evenly spilt between men and women.[21] However the research also showed that women are twice as likely to be injured and to suffer repeated attacks. They are also less likely to be in a financial position to leave a violent relationship.

The particular form of violence inflicted on women by their partners obviously varies, but is often of a very serious nature and results in severe injuries, and sometimes death. Here, one woman describes the results of an attack, which continued after she lost consciousness:

> He grabbed me from the chair, dragged me back into the sitting-room, to the hall, pulled me halfway up the stairs, then pulled me back down and started to kick and stand on me. And that was in front of his own mum. I was knocked out with the first couple of blows he gave me. He was hammering into something that was just like a cushion on the floor. I had a broken rib, broken leg on the right side, two front teeth knocked out, burst chin – I've still got the scar – I had five stitches, and a broken arm on the right side.[22]

Another woman describes her husband's threats to her life:

> He threatened to kill me no end of times. He used to put ropes round my neck and try to strangle me – he even once tried with wire – that's when I left. The worst time he locked me and the children in a bedroom, put a gaspipe underneath and turned the gas on – nailed the door up with 6 in. nails.[23]

The effects of violence are not only physical. Imagine not knowing when you are going to be assaulted and living in constant fear of violence. Such fear takes away self-respect and self-esteem. It is exhausting and draining. It leaves women powerless.

Why does violence occur in marriage?

Activity 2.14

Why do you think violence occurs in marriages? Make a list of possible causes.

Different ways of looking at this question will produce different sorts of answers. A survey which looked into immediate causes of violent episodes found several common themes. Sexual jealousy was frequently referred to, often flaring up simply as a result of a wife speaking to a neighbour who happened to be male, or where the husband imagined that something had happened. Another common source of conflict was housework. Some men considered it their right to set the standards for housework and for these standards to be met by their wives. Other explanations for violent episodes included disputes over money, the husband's drinking behaviour and the man's assumption that it was his right to have sex when he wanted.[24] At the time of the survey, this last point was backed by law, since there was no legal concept of rape within marriage. More recently, a legal precedent has been set whereby a man who forces his wife to have sex can be found guilty of rape.

Violence tends to begin with marriage rather than earlier and men who assault their wives are not necessarily violent towards friends or other relatives. Bearing this in mind, explanations can be sought in marriage itself. Within marriage, the wife is vulnerable because she is dependent on her husband, and leaving means risking losing a home, breaking up a family and admitting to failure. The cause of wife-assault can be related to the way in which society has seen a woman as the property of her husband, and subject to his control. The home is regarded as a private area in which people are allowed to behave as they wish. Linked to these points, there is a tendency for domestic violence to be seen as acceptable, trivialised, or treated as a joke, as in 'Punch and Judy' shows. The following quotation illustrates the acceptance of violence against women in marriage:

There are times when a man is justified in using violence, hitting a woman. Yes. A man is justified when he has sufficient provocation. And there are many, many, many circumstances in which a man should react in this way.[25]

Help for victims of domestic violence

The discussion of the helping agencies which follows also demonstrates this acceptance of violence as a normal part of marriage.

Activity 2.15

Imagine that you discover that a neighbour is regularly beaten by her husband. She asks you for advice. Which agencies might be able to help her?

Many women feel trapped in a violent relationship because they do not know where to seek help, or because the people they have approached have proved unhelpful. There are several sources of help, although some are of limited use, primarily because of the sort of attitudes people have towards battered women. Friends and relatives may be the first people to whom a woman turns, although some feel too ashamed to tell of their suffering and attempt to explain away visible injuries. Also, most people do not have big enough houses to take in a woman and her children, and therefore may be unable to offer more than advice and support. Women may be reluctant to put their friends or relatives at risk of repercussions from an angry husband. Neighbours are often aware of violence, but ideas about privacy, together with fear, result in their being reluctant to intervene in a violent situation.

The police

Battered women often contact the police in fear and desperation, but in the past have rarely been satisfied with the response they have received. The police called violence to wives a 'domestic dispute' and were often unwilling to get involved. One woman reports her attempt to seek help from the police in the following account.

> When we lived in Newark he hit me all over – I was black. I was very fright-ened. I ran out of the house to the phone box – I was really petrified. The police came and just sat me in the car outside and said 'Look, you've got a nice house, you're a young couple, kiss and make up. Be friends.'[26]

The police sometimes refused to believe the woman's story. Even if they turned up, it was rare for the man to be charged. There are several explanations for police conduct in cases of marital violence. They tend to see the home as a private area and distinguish between assaults in the home and the same behav-iour in a street or public house. The police argue that women are unwilling to pursue a charge against their husbands. However, this may well be as a result of fear, since the woman will be expected to live with her attacker while awaiting a court hearing.

There is however some evidence that police attitudes are changing. A survey of 100 Women's Aid refuges in September 1992 found that in a number of areas, police officers are giving a higher priority to domestic violence, are giving out more information to women and are following up cases and generally showing more sympathy and understanding.[27] The survey also found that in some areas little had changed.

Where there have been changes in police behaviour, this is a result of chang-ing policy guidelines. In 1987, the Metropolitan Police issued an order stating that domestic violence was a crime and should be treated as such. This was fol-lowed in 1990 by a circular from the Home Office to all police forces in England and Wales. This emphasised that violence which occurs within the home is 'no less serious than a violent assault by a stranger' and recommended that the widespread practice of 'no-criming' domestic assaults should cease. In response to this circular, many forces, particularly in London, set up domestic violence

ecialise in this area of work. Women's Aid Federation England (WAFE)
hese units but expressed some concerns also:

give a cautious welcome to the setting up of specialist domestic
ence units, we also have some concerns about this approach. It appears
that many police forces have seen domestic violence units as 'the answer' to
domestic violence, whilst at the same time failing to put sufficient resources
into them. Most domestic violence units are staffed by one or two officers
only. This means that any women calling the unit will invariably receive an
answerphone message requesting her to leave her name and number so that
an officer can get back to her. This is useless to women who have no phone or
who are staying in Bed and Breakfast or other temporary accommodation,
who feel unable to give out a refuge number or who are fearful that their
abuser may intercept a call intended for them.[28]

Even in cases where the police press charges, the courts are unwilling to take
effective action to protect the wife. The following account from a battered
woman shows this:

He was charged with Actual Bodily Harm, common assault and unlawful
assault. He got fined, bound over and was given a suspended sentence. It was
useless because he wouldn't pay the fine and I had to. They threatened to take
the furniture if I didn't. And it didn't stop him beating me.[29]

The courts

In theory the courts are a potential source of protection for women. Under the
1978 Domestic Proceedings and Magistrates' Court Act, married women can be
granted a protection order by the magistrates' court. This will state that the
husband is not to use or threaten violence and can order him to leave the home.
In some circumstances, powers of arrest can be attached to the protection order
meaning that the police will arrest the man if he breaks the order. Under the
1976 Domestic Violence and Matrimonial Proceedings Act, the county court can
offer protection to people living together as well as those who are married. The
judge can order the man not to molest his wife – this includes violence, but also
harassment such as verbal abuse or persistent telephoning. As in the magistrates' court, powers of arrest can be attached to the order and in some circumstances the man can be ordered to stay away from the house. In practice the
usefulness of these orders is limited as they tend not be fully enforced.

1999 saw the opening of the first magistrates' court to deal solely with domestic violence. The court can call on staff from the National Society for the
Prevention of Cruelty to Children and a national pilot project known as Stop
(Stop Terrorising and Oppressing Partners) for background on both the victim
and the perpetrator and referral to support programmes.

The social services and doctors

The social services are another agency upon which battered women might call
for help. The problem here is that social workers have a commitment to the

family as a unit and attempt to dissuade the woman from leaving her husband. Like the police, social workers are reluctant to intervene in a marriage; also, they may be as afraid of a violent man as is his wife. Social services have limited ability to offer practical help and are felt by women to be more concerned about the risk to the children than with the plight of the woman.

General practitioners come into contact with victims of domestic violence. They tend to concentrate on treating the medical aspects of the problem and to solve any other difficulties by prescribing tranquilisers or anti-depressants. These drugs may inhibit the woman's ability to think through her situation and to take positive decisions. Doctors tend to be unaware of resources available to battered women, and are therefore not in a position to offer constructive advice.

Alternative housing

Women attempting to escape a violent marriage may approach the local authority housing department for help in finding alternative housing. Under the 1985 Housing (Homeless Persons) Act, women who cannot occupy their home because of violence should be treated as homeless. However, many local authorities have been slow to accept their responsibilities under the Act. Women have reported unhelpful attitudes on the part of housing officers, for example:

> They had no right to treat me as they did. I came out in tears many times. The housing officer says he hits his wife and vice versa – and that's the way of happy marriage.[30]

Even where local authorities accept battered women as homeless, the provision offered is often highly unsatisfactory, for example, in bed and breakfast accommodation.

Voluntary organisations

There are voluntary organisations which will offer assistance to battered women. Gingerbread, as we have seen, is one, although the group specifically concerned with marital violence is Women's Aid. Women's Aid has a national office and nearly 200 local groups offering safe, temporary accommodation in refuges, advice, support and help in finding permanent accommodation, if this is what the woman wants. Refuges are run by residents, support groups of volunteers and paid workers. Most refuges have little financial support and are often in poor physical condition. The pressure of demand means that many are overcrowded. An important aspect of refuges is that women regain confidence through meeting others who share their experiences and the women are able to help one another.

Activity 2.16

Find out if there is a refuge in your local town. It may not be in the telephone book, since it is important that violent men are not able to find their wives and children. The refuge can be contacted through the Samaritans, the Citizens' Advice Bureau or the police. You may be able to arrange for people from the refuge to give a talk to the class.

The effects of violence

Men who are violent towards their wives are not necessarily child-abusers. Battered women are often reluctant to leave their husbands because they do not want to deprive their children of a father. On the other hand, others leave because they fear their children will be subjected to violence. Children can get involved through trying to protect their mothers. Even where children are not in physical danger themselves, they suffer the anxiety of seeing or hearing their mothers beaten up.

There is no real evidence to support the idea that children of violent fathers will be violent in their own adult relationships. Even where researchers have found that the father of a violent man was himself violent, this does not explain wife-battering, since not all the boys in the family have been shown to have been violent in their marriages. Being exposed to a violent marriage can have the effect of making boys determined not to behave in this way. Little is really known about the effects on children of violence between parents and it may be that individuals react in different ways.

This lack of understanding extends to other areas of the problem of marital violence and one of the tasks of Women's Aid is to help the public, the government, the police, doctors and social workers to gain a better understanding of the needs of victims of domestic violence.

Child abuse

The problem of cruelty to children in the family was first recognised in the 1960s. At that time the term used was 'child battering', although this later changed to 'non-accidental injury' and, more recently, to 'child abuse'. The changes in name have reflected the way the issue has become broader in definition, now including physical injury, emotional damage, neglect and sexual abuse of children. Sexual abuse was rarely mentioned until the late 1970s, but recently has become an issue of major public and professional concern.

Since the 1960s, and especially in recent years, there has been a rapid increase in cases of child abuse. However, it seems likely that this does not mean there has been a real increase in cruelty, but rather an increase in public and professional awareness which means that more and more cases come to light.

The following case-studies from the National Society for the Prevention of Cruelty to Children (NSPCC) illustrate the nature of the problem:

When the NSPCC was called to Mark's home – after a serious row between his parents – [the] Inspector found a little boy, tiny for his two and a half years and very pale. He was suffering from what the experts call 'non-organic failure to thrive'. In other words, Mark's failure to grow and develop healthily was not due to a disease or medical condition but due to lack of loving care and nourishment.

Sarah was 15 and her young sister, Jo, 13 when the girls told their older brother, Michael, that their father had been sexually interfering with them ... the girls had been sexually abused since they were very young. Their father fondled them, used sexually explicit language and, as they got older, had full sexual intercourse with them.

Six-year-old Kate was beaten by her mother. Thankfully she was not badly injured. But her mother felt terribly guilty. She contacted her family doctor and explained how she just couldn't cope with Kate and her four-year-old sister, Mandy.[31]

Agencies involved

Many different professionals are involved in cases of child abuse. These include doctors, both in general practice and in various hospital departments; other health workers such as health visitors and midwives; social workers and child guidance therapists; teachers and other school staff, educational welfare officers and educational psychologists; the police; workers in voluntary organisations such as the NSPCC; and perhaps the church. Others who may be involved work in housing departments, the probation service and social security offices. A key issue in dealing with child abuse, often referred to in official reports, is effective liaison between so many people. The geography and the bureaucracy of the different departments often divide people and make communication difficult. There are also different ways of seeing the issues and these can prevent people working together effectively. For example, the police may see the achieving of justice for the offending adult as their priority, the medical profession may prioritise clinical diagnosis and medical treatment, whilst social workers may be more concerned with a therapeutic approach to the whole family.

In 1988 the Butler–Sloss report was published following an inquiry into procedures for dealing with child sexual abuse in the county of Cleveland. The report said that there were three main reasons why things had gone wrong in Cleveland. First, the agencies involved failed to understand each others' function in relation to child abuse; secondly, they did not communicate sufficiently with each other; and thirdly, there were differences of view at middle-management level which were not recognised by senior staff. Many local authorities have begun to develop multi-disciplinary teams for child abuse cases and joint training sessions for the different professions.

Protection of children at risk

Area Review Committees were set up in 1974 to co-ordinate multi-agency work on child abuse. These committees are responsible for keeping *At Risk Registers* in their local area. These registers record names of children thought to be at risk of child abuse. They are sometimes managed by the NSPCC. In 1980 a government circular from the then DHSS, now Department of Health, tried to standardise the criteria for the registers across the country. The circular recommended that the criteria be broadened to include physical injuries where there is a suspicion of abuse, physical neglect, failure to thrive, emotional abuse and situations where a child is in a house with, or visited by, a person who has abused another child.

When a case of child abuse is discovered, the child can be admitted to hospital or removed to a safe place under an *emergency protection order*. Both of these actions can be taken very quickly. Then a case conference will be called, bringing together various professionals to decide on a course of action. The possibilities include returning the child to its home, with social work support for the parents or with supervision under a care order, or taking the child into the care of the local authority, either voluntarily or through care proceedings in the juvenile court. (These procedures are explained in Chapter 10 on children in trouble.)

Cases of child abuse can be particularly difficult for social workers as they can feel torn between their duty to protect children and their commitment to keeping families together and avoiding compulsory care orders where possible. There is a feeling that social workers will be condemned by the media and the public both for taking children into care and for not taking children into care. The public attention given to child abuse has tended to make this seem the most important aspect of social work and to lead to a draining of funds from other areas such as work with elderly people or people with disabilities.

Activity 2.17

There have been a number of official inquiries into deaths of children, from the Maria Colwell case in 1974 to that of Stephanie Fox in London in 1990. Find out about one of these cases. What went wrong – in the family and in the social service department? What could have prevented the death of the child? Could it happen again?

2.7   The family and the welfare state

In 1977, Patrick Jenkins, then Secretary of State for Social Services, warned of the dangers of the state taking over the responsibilities of the family. The extent to which this fear is based on reality is the subject of this section.

This chapter began by establishing the important role which the family plays in society. To summarise the aspects of this role, the family provides care and socialisation for children and meets many physical and emotional needs of both adults and children. However, we have seen that both the structure and the functions of the family have changed. For example, at one time, all education and training in skills for work was provided by the family. Similarly the family had sole responsibility for the care of the elderly, the sick and the disabled family members. Changes in the economy and the wider society have resulted in modifications in the family. Legislation and increased welfare provision mean that the family is no longer the sole provider of all education and care.

However, welfare provision has not taken over the responsibilities of the family in the sense of making the family redundant. The example of education demonstrates this point. It is compulsory for children to go to school from the age of five to sixteen. This does not mean that the state completely takes over all aspects of education. It was pointed out at the beginning of the chapter that children have learned a great deal by the time they go to school and they continue to learn at home, as well as at school. Schools do not completely take over the care of children and tend to expect mothers to be at home on call during school hours. Staying on in post-compulsory education is difficult for young people without parental support. In many ways, the state and the family have a joint role in educating children and young people.

Similarly, in the area of health care, the family plays a key role, but is supported by doctors and hospitals. It is women in the family who provide most basic health care. Social services see their main aim as being to support the family. It is only in unusual circumstances that social workers take over the care of children or elderly relatives. Relatives are, for most people, a major source of support in times of need. The current policy of care in the community means that the family is being increasingly relied upon to meet the needs of those who might previously have been cared for in residential institutions.

Taxation and social security policies have been geared to a traditional view of the family, viewing married women as dependants and carers. In writing the report (in 1942) which created the basis of the present social security system, Beveridge tended to think of the needs and life-patterns of working men and to regard married women not as earners or claimants in their own right, but as dependants of their husbands. He wrote, 'The attitude of the housewife to gainful employment outside the home is not and should not be the same as the single woman – she has other duties.'[32] This attitude continued long after the post-war years as the following quotation from the then DHSS shows:

> It is normal for a married woman in this country to be primarily supported by her husband, and she looks to him for support when not actually working, rather than to a social security benefit. Indeed, it continues to be a widespread view that a husband who is capable of work has a duty to society, as well as to his wife, to provide the primary support for his family.[33]

There have been a number of ways in which these ideas have affected rules concerning benefits and taxes. For example, it was not until 1986, as a result of a case won in the European Court, that married women could claim the Invalid Care Allowance when caring for a sick or disabled relative. Previously only men and single women could claim, since it was thought that caring for relatives was part of a married woman's role. Another example, unchanged until 1989, was that of the married man's tax allowance, based on the idea of a married man as head of a dependent household.

Although a number of reforms have been made to the social security and taxation systems it can be argued still that these reflect traditional ideas about the family and the role of women in the family.[34]

It would seem that there is little need to fear that welfare provision is making the family redundant. The family continues to be the primary source of care for most people and state provision exists to support, rather than threaten, the family. In spite of changes in family life, the family is a key part of society today.

Activity 2.18

Throughout this chapter, there have been many references to changes in the family. List and explain the changes you think most important.

Activity 2.19

Make sure that you understand the following expressions used in this chapter. Check in the Glossary at the end of the book if you need to.

anti-depressant
At Risk Register
case conference
Child Support Agency
contact order
contempt of court
division of labour
divorce rate
extended family
higher education
income support
injunction
invalid care allowance
joint roles
maintenance payments
married man's tax allowance
matrifocal family
means-tested

modified extended family
monogamy
norm
nuclear family
polyandry
polygamy
polygyny
prohibited steps order
reconstituted family
residence order
segregated roles
social security
socialisation
specific issue order
stigma
tax relief
tranquiliser
voluntary organisation
welfare provision

Further reading

The Family Policy Studies Centre publishes up-to-date research on family life in Britain.

Detailed information on legal aspects relating to the family can be found in Hugh Brayne and Gerry Martin, *Law for Social Workers* (London: Blackstone Press), updated regularly.

Women's Aid Federation England (WAFE) are a useful source of information relating to domestic violence (for address, see below).

The NSPCC have information on child abuse (see below).

Useful addresses

WAFE
PO Box 391
Bristol BS99 7WS
tel. 0117 9444411

The National Council for One Parent Families
255 Kentish Town Road
London NW5 2LX
tel. 0207 267 1361

NSPCC
42 Curtain Road
London EC2A 3NH
tel. 0207 825 2500

Family Policy Studies Centre
9 Tavistock Place
London WC1H 9SN
tel. 0207 388 5600

Websites

The Joseph Rowntree Foundation publish research online at **www.jrf.org.uk**

Information on the child support agency can be found through **www.dss.gov.uk**

⍌ **3** Poverty and welfare

In comparison to many places in the world, Britain is a wealthy country with a high standard of living. Yet this chapter will show that, for a significant number of people, poverty is a harsh reality, impacting on many aspects of daily life. The chapter begins by looking at the difficulties in defining poverty and measuring the extent of the problem, followed by an examination of explanations for the continuation of poverty (section 3.2). Sections 3.3–3.5 examine social policies designed to tackle poverty and look in some detail at the social security system in Britain.

3.1 Defining and measuring poverty

The first stumbling block in any discussion of poverty is the definition of the term. It is meaningless to say that so many people live in poverty, without first establishing the criteria for deciding who is 'poor'. The usual procedure involves calculating a weekly income which is required to meet the needs of an individual or family. This, in turn, means that needs have to be established. Activity 3.1 illustrates the difficulty of this task.

Activity 3.1

Make a list of the things you consider necessary for a family living in Britain. This means that you would consider a family who could not afford such items to be poor. Be precise, giving details, rather than simply writing 'food' or 'clothes'. Compare your list with those of your fellow-students and attempt to reach agreement on items for inclusion in the list.

Poverty and society

People have quite different ideas about the standard of living below which people should be considered poor. This is a major element in the problem of defining poverty. For example, some people might consider a computer or a car a necessity, whilst others may see these as signs of wealth. Alcohol can be considered a necessary part of social life or as a luxury item. In spite of these differences, few people would limit the list to the necessities for physical survival. It could be argued that anyone with the barest shelter, a few rags for clothing and a sack of potatoes or rice, could survive. However, a person living this way in Britain would certainly be considered to be living in poverty.

Source: Crispin Hughes, Photofusion
People in relative poverty lack the resources to obtain the living standards considered normal in the society in which they live

It will become clear that poverty is defined and experienced in the context of a particular society. A family which did not have a washing machine would not feel deprived in a society in which everyone washed by hand. Tea and coffee are not necessary to physical survival, but for many people, they are a key part of social life, such that a person who could afford neither tea nor coffee would experience hardship.

The idea that poverty is defined in relation to the society in which a person lives is expressed in the distinction made between *relative* and *absolute* poverty. Absolute poverty refers to the lack of basic necessities for life. Throughout the world, absolute poverty is a problem on an immense scale and there are many people who cannot survive because of lack of resources. In Britain, absolute poverty, although it does exist, is less common. This is primarily due to the existence of the welfare state. Discussion of poverty in this country is concerned with the second concept, that of relative poverty. This is poverty relative to the standard of living which is considered by most people to be normal. Such a standard varies from society to society, and changes over time. In any society with wide inequalities of wealth, there will be those who exist at a level below the accepted standards. These people are described as living in relative poverty. The following quotations illustrate the idea of relative poverty:

> to have one bowl of rice in a society where all other people have half a bowl may well be a sign of achievement and intelligence … to have five bowls of rice in a society where the majority have a decent, balanced diet is a tragedy.[1]

Peter Townsend, in his classic study of poverty published in 1979, defined poverty in the following way:

Individuals, families and groups can be said to be in poverty when they lack the resources to obtain the types of diet, participate in the activities and have the living conditions and amenities which are customary, or at least widely encouraged or approved, in the societies to which they belong.[2]

Activity 3.2

In your own words, write a definition of 'relative poverty'.

Social exclusion

This is term which is intended to be wider in its focus than poverty and which includes a variety of ways in which people are denied participation in society and full and effective rights of citizenship.[3] The Social Exclusion Unit which was set up by the Labour Government says:

Social exclusion is a shorthand label for what can happen when individuals or areas suffer from a combination of linked problems such as unemployment, poor skills, low incomes, poor housing, high crime environments, bad health and family breakdown.[4]

The New Policy Institute constructed a set of indicators to present a wide view of social exclusion in Britain.[5] Forty-six indicators show the numbers of people facing difficulties at different points in their lives, covering childhood, the transition to adulthood, adulthood and old age. The indicators cover areas of life such as education, employment, crime, housing and health and can be updated and used by the government to monitor change.

Table 3.1 shows the indicators which relate to children and young people with statistics to show the extent of the disadvantage and the trend over recent years.[6]

Activity 3.3

Which of the indicators would you feel were the most and least important influences in demonstrating degrees of social exclusion? Rank the indicators in significance. Give reasons for the choices at the top and bottom of your scale.

Choose three of the indicators and find out some more statistics on these areas of young people's lives.

Choose four of the indicators and explain why you think the trend is rising, falling or steady. Can you find out if the trend is still the same as when the statistics were produced?

Choose one of the indicators and design a set of policies which you think would be effective in tackling the issue. Would there be any obstacles in the way of improvements?

TABLE 3.1   Key indicators of deprivation and social exclusion

Indicator	Extent		Trend
Living in workless household	2.5 million	25% children in poorest 20% of income distribution	Falling
Children in families below half average income	3.3 million	Children are 25% more likely than average to be in low-income families	Falling
Low birthweight babies (%)	7.1 per cent	25% higher rate among mothers in lowest social classes	Rising
Accidental deaths	620 per year	Double the rate among children in social classes IV and V than social classes I, II and III (see Chapter 1)	Falling
Pupils gaining no GCSE Grade C or above	222,000 per year	Numbers fell by 40,000 between 1992 and 1996	Falling
Permanently excluded from school	12,500 per year	Three times the rate among black children compared with white children	Steady
Children whose parents divorce	166,000 per year	Double the rate for unskilled husbands compared with the average	Steady
Births to girls conceiving under age 16	4250 per year	Girls aged 13 to 15 account for 4.3 in every 1000 births	Rising
Children in young offenders institutions	11,000 per year	Numbers have risen by 38% since 1993	Rising
Unemployed	600,000	The unemployment rate among young adults is double the overall rate	Falling
On low rates of pay	1.2 million	One in three young adults earns less than half the wage of an average male	Steady
16/17-year-olds with severe hardship payments	100,000 per year	Two thirds claimed hardship payments in 1997	Falling
Starting drug treatment episodes	23,000 per year	Number of 15 to 24-year-olds treated for addiction has risen by 50% since 1993	Rising
Suicides	600 per year	60% higher rate for 20 to 24-year-olds in lowest social groups	Steady
19-year-olds without a basic qualification	200,000	30% of age group are without an NVQ level 2, a GNVQ or higher grade GCSEs	Falling
23-year-olds with a criminal record	90,000	Numbers have fallen by more than a third in the past decade	Falling

Studies of poverty

The first studies of poverty in Britain were carried out a century ago. These studies are important, both in their own right, and because of the continued influence of the ideas behind the research.

Joseph Rowntree

Probably the most famous poverty study was conducted in 1899 by Seebohm Rowntree.[7] The research was done in York where Rowntree's chocolate and cocoa factory was a major employer. Rowntree established the idea of a 'poverty line'. This concept, still in use, sets a level of income below which people are considered to be living in poverty.

Rowntree considered that people were poor if their income was so low that the resulting deprivation affected their health. For example, to calculate the amount of money required for food, Rowntree worked out the number of calories necessary for physical efficiency. He then found an inexpensive diet which provided the calorie requirement and established the cost. Rowntree admitted that the poverty line was based on an extremely austere scale and explained that he had designed it in this way to offset possible accusations of exaggeration. For example, no allowance was made for bus- or rail-fares, for newspapers or for stamps to write to children living away from home. The poverty line excluded money for toys and sweets, tobacco and alcohol.

In considering poverty, Rowntree distinguished between 'primary' and 'secondary' poverty. Families were in primary poverty if their income was not sufficient to maintain their physical existence. Secondary poverty meant that the income would have been sufficient, were it not that some was spent on items not in the scale, whether useful or wasteful. Even on the basis of a far from generous definition of poverty, Rowntree found that 10 per cent of the population of York were living in primary poverty and a further 18 per cent in secondary poverty.

Rowntree conducted two later surveys, one in 1936 and one in 1950.[8] He changed his definition of poverty to some extent, recognising that poverty could not be defined simply as the lack of necessities for physical survival. This led to an acceptance of the social dimension of poverty, in terms of the inability to participate in the life of the community. As a result, the 1936 study included allowance for a radio, books, newspapers, beer, tobacco, presents and a holiday.

As mentioned earlier, Rowntree's work set a precedent for more recent research into poverty. It also influenced Beveridge in the design, in 1942, of the social security system. Rowntree himself was a member of a committee appointed to calculate the rates for Social Security benefits.

Breadline Britain

In 1983 a major survey on poverty in Britain was carried out for a London Weekend Television series called *Breadline Britain*. The results were written up in a book by Joanna Mack and Stewart Lansley called *Poor Britain*. In 1990 the survey was repeated to update it for the new decade.[9]

This survey defines poverty as 'an enforced lack of socially perceived necessities'.[10] In order to find out what were 'socially perceived necessities', the public were questioned using a set of cards with different items written on them. People were asked to place in one box the cards showing items felt to be necessary for all adults in Britain, and in another those which they did not feel were

TABLE 3.2   Proportions deeming items to be necessary, 1983 and 1990

	1990 (%)	1983 (%)	Change (%, +/−)
A damp-free home	98	96	+2
An inside toilet (not shared with another household)	97	96	+1
Heating to warm living areas of home if it's cold	97	97	0
Beds for everyone in the household	95	94	+1
Bath, not shared with another household	95	94	+1
A decent state of decoration in the home[2]	92	–	–
Fridge	92	77	+15
Warm waterproof coat	91	87	+4
Three meals a day for children[1]	90	82	+8
Two meals a day (for adults)[4]	90	64	+26
Insurance[2]	88	–	–
Fresh fruit[2]	88	–	–
Toys for children, e.g. dolls or models[1]	84	71	+13
Separate bedrooms for every child over 10 of different sexes[1]	82	77	+5
Carpets in living rooms and bedrooms in the home	78	70	+8
Meat or fish or vegetarian equivalent every other day[3]	77	63	+14
Celebrations on special occasions such as Christmas	74	69	+5
Two pairs of all-weather shoes	74	78	−4
Washing machine	73	67	+6
Presents for friends or family once a year	69	63	+6
Out of school activities, e.g. sports, orchestra, Scouts[1,2]	69	–	–
Regular savings of £10 a month for 'rainy days' or retirement[2]	68	–	–
Hobby or leisure activity	67	64	+3
New, not secondhand, clothes	65	64	+1
A roast joint or its vegetarian equivalent once a week[3]	64	67	−3
Leisure equipment for children, e.g. sports equipment or bicycle[1]	61	57	+4
A television	58	51	+7
Telephone	56	43	+13
An annual week's holiday away, not with relatives	54	63	−9
A 'best outfit' for special occasions	54	48	+6
An outing for children once a week[1]	53	40	+13
Children's friends round for tea/snack fortnightly[1]	52	37	+15
A dressing gown	42	38	+4
A night out fortnightly	42	36	+6
Fares to visit friends in other parts of the country 4 times a year[2]	39	–	–
Special lessons such as music, dance or sport[1,2]	39	–	–
Friends/family for a meal monthly	37	32	+5
A car	26	22	+4
Pack of cigarettes every other day	18	14	+4
Restaurant meal monthly[2]	17	–	–
Holidays abroad annually[2]	17	–	–
A video[2]	13	–	–
A home computer[2]	5	–	–
A dishwasher	4	–	–

The descriptions of items have been abbreviated.
[1]For families with children.
[2]Not included in the 1983 survey.
[3]Vegetarian option added in 1990.
[4]Two hot meals in the 1983 survey.
Source: Joanna Mack and Stewart Lansley, *Poor Britain* (London: Allen & Unwin, 1985, 1991).

necessary. Table 3.2 shows the results of this first part of the survey, in 1983 and 1990.

Activity 3.4

Use the items in Table 3.2 to carry out your own small-scale survey. Compare your findings with those of the study.

In the earlier study in 1983, 26 out of a list of 35 items were considered to be necessities by a majority of the population. in 1991 there were 44 items on the list and 32 were classed as necessities by a majority of the people questioned.

The next step was to find out how many people lacked these necessities. In the second stage of the survey, respondents were asked which of the items they had. If they did not have an item, they were asked if this was by choice or not. Table 3.3 shows the proportions of people lacking each of the 44 items and the changes since the earlier study.[11]

One of the points that makes this survey better than previous attempts to measure poverty is that the survey took account of personal choice by asking people who lacked a particular item whether or not this was by choice. It is certainly true that there are quite well-off people who choose not to have carpets (scrubbed and varnished wooden floors are fashionable) or who prefer not to own a television. However, the question of choice is not as simple as it may appear. There are people who say they go without through choice, but for whom this does not really seem to be the case. The following example illustrates this point. Ernie is a 79-year-old pensioner living alone. He is unable to cook for himself and relies on meals-on-wheels. Instead of getting a lunch every day, he takes one every other day and eats half the main course at lunch time and half the sweet in the evening. He saves the rest for the next day. He tells the interviewer:

> I can't eat them. To be fair to myself, I know I haven't got the appetite I used to have. Therefore I just have enough to eat and then I have the rest the next day. It's an economic idea to have as much as you can afford. You can't go beyond your means. I mean, the point is I get the meals Mondays, Wednesdays and Fridays and that costs over a pound, £1.40 for that. I would have to pay twice that if I had it Tuesdays and Thursdays. See what I mean.[12]

The designers of the survey decided to take those who could not afford three or more of the items as an indication of the numbers of people in poverty. With this definition, the 1990 survey found 11 million people in Britain living in poverty (see Figure 3.1). This is one in five of the population.[13]

Official statistics

There is no official poverty line in Britain. However it is possible to use government statistics on income to create an unofficial measure of poverty. This is done by calculating the average income for the country, excluding housing costs, and halving the figure. Those people whose income falls below this point are

TABLE 3.3 Proportion of households lacking each of the items, 1983 and 1990

	1990 (%)	1983 (%)	Change (%, +/−)
A damp-free home	2	7	−5
An inside toilet (not shared with another household)	*	2	−2
Heating to warm living areas of home if it's cold	3	5	−2
Beds for everyone in the household	1	1	0
Bath, not shared with another household	*	2	−2
A decent state of decoration in the home[2]	15	−	−
Fridge	1	2	−1
Warm waterproof coat	4	7	−3
Three meals a day for children[1]	*	2	−2
Two meals a day (for adults)[4]	1	3	−2
Insurance[2]	10	−	−
Fresh fruit[2]	6	−	−
Toys for children, e.g. dolls or models[1]	2	2	0
Separate bedrooms for every child over 10 of different sexes[1]	7	3	+4
Carpets in living rooms and bedrooms in the home	2	2	0
Meat or fish or vegetarian equivalent every other day[3]	4	8	−4
Celebrations on special occasions such as Christmas	4	4	0
Two pairs of all-weather shoes	5	9	−4
Washing machine	4	6	−2
Presents for friends or family once a year	5	5	0
Out of school activities, e.g. sports, orchestra, Scouts[1,2]	10	−	−
Regular savings of £10 a month for 'rainy days' or retirement[2]	30	−	−
Hobby or leisure activity	7	7	0
New, not secondhand, clothes	4	6	−2
A roast joint or its vegetarian equivalent once a week[3]	6	7	−1
Leisure equipment for children, e.g. sports equipment or bicycle[1]	6	6	0
A television	1	*	+1
Telephone	7	11	−4
An annual week's holiday away, not with relatives	20	21	−1
A 'best outfit' for special occasions	8	10	−2
An outing for children once a week[1]	14	9	+5
Children's friends round for tea/snack fortnightly[1]	8	5	+3
A dressing gown	2	3	−1
A night out fortnightly	14	17	−3
Fares to visit friends in other parts of the country 4 times a year[2]	19	−	−
Special lessons such as music, dance or sport[1,2]	20	−	−
Friends/family for a meal monthly	10	11	−1
A car	18	22	−4
Pack of cigarettes every other day	5	6	−1
Restaurant meal monthly[2]	22	−	−
Holidays abroad annually[2]	32	−	−
A video[2]	10	−	−
A home computer[2]	16	−	−
A dishwasher	18	−	−

Items are listed in the order of Table 3.2, with necessities above the break.
The descriptions of items have been abbreviated to fit the page.
*Less than 0.5 per cent.
[1]For families with children.
[2]Not included in the 1983 survey.
[3]Vegetarian option added in 1990.
[4]Two hot meals in the 1983 survey.
Source: Joanna Mack and Stewart Lapsley, *Poor Britain* (London: Allen & Unwin, 1985, 1991)

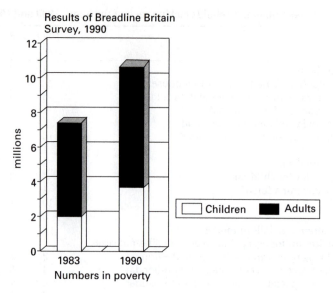

Figure 3.1   Results of *Breadline Britain* survey, 1990

considered to be living in poverty. Figures released by the government in 1998 showed that 24 per cent of households had incomes which were below half of average incomes, after housing costs.[14] These figures show a big increase in poverty over the last 25 years.

3.2   Understanding poverty

The poverty cycle

Measures of poverty such as that used in the *Breadline Britain* survey give a snapshot view of society, showing how many people are poor at a particular moment in time. These figures do not show the number of people who will experience poverty at some point during their lives. Rowntree was the first person to describe the poverty cycle, a process whereby people move in and out of poverty at different times in their lives.

Activity 3.5

Describe a typical life-cycle, indicating whether you would expect a person to be richer or poorer at each point.

The poverty cycle, as outlined by Rowntree, included five alternating periods of poverty and comparative prosperity. The first stage of early childhood would be spent in poverty, until the time when elder brothers and sisters began to earn money for the family. This more prosperous period would continue into young adulthood and the early years of marriage, until the arrival of children. Rowntree

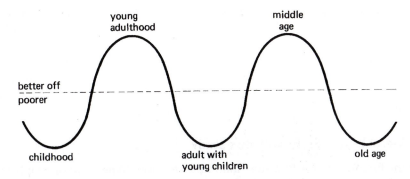

Figure 3.2 The cycle of poverty

saw the following period of poverty as lasting about ten years until the children began to supplement the family income through employment. The fourth stage, when the children are older, would be one of relative prosperity. The final period when the person was too old to work, would again be a period of poverty. Figure 3.2 is a diagrammatic representation of the idea of the cycle of poverty.

Activity 3.6

Consider the advantages of the concept of the poverty cycle as a means of understanding poverty.

Rowntree acknowledged that the poverty cycle was not relevant to everyone. There are many people who are never poor, having sufficient wealth and income for the presence of dependent children, for example, to have no effect on their life-style. On the other hand, there are those who never escape poverty, perhaps because a disability prevents them from working or because they are low-paid workers. The poverty cycle does not *explain* why poverty exists – it is rather a *description* of the life-cycle of certain sections of the population.

The relative poverty or prosperity of families is affected by wider economic conditions as well as by individual circumstances. Unemployment is an example of such an economic factor. Partly as a result of high rates of youth unemployment, the majority of young people continue in education or join training schemes. Few young people are able to help their families financially when they reach the end of compulsory schooling.

The poverty cycle is useful in understanding poverty in two respects. It indicates points to which state help might be best directed, for instance, to the old and to families with young children. It also gives an extra dimension to poverty statistics by showing that many people experience poverty at some stage in their lives.

The immediate causes of poverty

The causes of poverty in Britain can be stated quite simply. Either the wages people earn are insufficient to meet their needs or they are unable to work and the benefits they receive are inadequate. This does of course leave unanswered questions such as *why* people are paid low wages and *why* benefit rates are low. These political and economic questions are beyond the scope of this book. This section focuses on poverty at a more individual level, examining immediate causes of poverty. These immediate causes do not explain why people are poor, but show which groups are particularly vulnerable and illustrate changes over time.

Vulnerable groups: Rowntree's study

In the first York study, Rowntree found that for over 30 per cent of people who were living in poverty, the explanation was low wages. Other reasons he discovered were unemployment, old age, sickness, the death of the chief wage-earner in a family, and large numbers of children in a family. In the 1936 study, unemployment had increased in significance as a cause of poverty, although inadequate wages were still a crucial factor.

Vulnerable groups: modern Britain

In Britain today, the groups most vulnerable are lone-parent families, unemployed people, people with badly-paid jobs, people who are sick or disabled, and older people.

- Government figures show that the majority of lone parents have below average incomes.[15] Lack of child-care provision makes it difficult for many lone parents to work. Also most lone parents are women and, as we saw in Chapter 2, women's wages are lower than men's.
- A growing number of people are living in poverty owing to unemployment. With long-term unemployment the effects of poverty deepen, as people have fewer and fewer resources to fall back on.
- The figures also show an increase in the numbers of people who are working but living in poverty. Low pay tends to be concentrated in particular types of work and industries. These include catering, hairdressing, shop work, farm work, the textiles industry, and parts of the public sector such as nursing and care work. In 1999, for the first time, a minimum wage was introduced in Britain. This was set at £3.60 per hour for all adults aged 22 and over. There is a lower rate of £3 for 18–21-year-olds. The minimum wage increased the pay of more than two million workers.
- About a third of disabled people are living in poverty. Where disabled people are employed their incomes tend to be lower than those of able-bodied people. Many disabled people are unable to work or unable to save and therefore reliant on state benefits. Often disability creates extra costs.
- Older people make up a significant proportion of those living in poverty, although clearly not all elderly people are poor. Some continue to work beyond the state retirement age and are better off; others have more generous occupational or other pensions. Elderly women are more likely to be living in poverty than elderly men – mainly because of men's better pensions. Some of these issues are dealt with in more detail in Chapters 2, 13 and 14.

The culture of poverty

This concept is part of an attempt to explain the persistence of poverty, and the complexities of deprivation from a wider viewpoint than one which focuses entirely on financial aspects. An American writer, Oscar Lewis, is most closely associated with the idea of a culture of poverty.[16] He suggests that poor people form a separate group within wider societies. Poverty is associated with a distinctive way of life which is passed from generation to generation. The features of the culture of poverty, as described by Lewis, cover most aspects of life from family relationships to attitudes towards money. For example, Lewis says that in many different countries, the family life of poor people is characterised by freer sexual relationships and more frequent resort to violence than is found in families of the rest of society. Lewis argues that the culture of poverty instils a lack of interest in saving and a short-term, day-to-day attitude to money. On a more general level, the poor are unwilling to plan for the future and have a resigned and fatalistic attitude to life.

Lewis sees the culture of poverty as a positive attempt by poor people to cope with their situation and to defend themselves against the effects of deprivation. It also means that people are not psychologically equipped to take advantage of any improvements in opportunity. Further, the way in which aspects of deprivation are related to each other means that government attempts to solve problems one at a time are doomed to failure.

The cycle of deprivation

A similar theme is expressed in the idea of the cycle of deprivation, a concept popular in Britain in the late 1960s and early 1970s. Publicity was given to this notion by Sir Keith Joseph, when Secretary of State for Social Services, in a speech made in 1972. Joseph was looking at the problem of the persistence of deprivation. He suggested that there may be little-understood processes by which poverty continues in spite of relative prosperity and state intervention. These processes lead to the reproduction of the problems of one generation in the following one. The cycle of deprivation was seen as having four types of cause. These were economic factors such as unemployment; environmental factors such as poor housing; circumstances seen as personal such as illness and hereditary make-up; and, finally, child-rearing practices. Having outlined these four areas of concern, Sir Keith Joseph then ignored most of the issues and emphasised the need for government policies on family planning and preparation for parenthood.

Both the cycle of deprivation and the culture of poverty focus on the idea that people who are disadvantaged in childhood will be unable to break out of their situation and will become the parents of deprived families. Coates and Silburn considered the usefulness of these concepts in their study of a poor area of Nottingham in the 1960s.[17] They found that poverty did tend to lead to feelings of helplessness and despair over the possibility of any improvement. However, they did not find any evidence that poor people shared a separate culture, and concluded that poor people in Britain are not essentially different from anyone else.

Activity 3.7

List the advantages of using the concept of the culture of poverty as a means of explaining poverty.

Criticisms of culture and cycle theories

The idea of the culture of poverty has been criticised on several grounds. As already mentioned, there is little evidence that those living in poverty do not go along with the standard values in society. For example, in Britain, poor and non-poor alike believe in the Royal Family and share many other values. Lewis has also been criticised for confusing working-class culture with something associated with poverty. It is sometimes said that putting off pleasures for the future, for example by saving money, is a middle-class habit, and that working-class people live in a more day-to-day fashion. Many of the characteristics described by Lewis can also be seen simply as effects of lack of resources. Financial insecurity could lead to less permanent sexual relationships, if, for instance, people are unable to afford to set up house together, or have to move around in search of work.

Both the cycle of deprivation and the culture of poverty focus on the characteristics of the poor. This carries the implication that poverty is the *fault* of poor people. Such an approach can be used by governments as an excuse for their inability or unwillingness to tackle problems of poverty.

However, the ideas are useful to the extent that they illustrate the complexity of the issues. The concepts show that poverty is not simply one problem, but a multiplicity of interrelated problems. This understanding means that governments are less likely to propose simple solutions, expecting to end the problem. For example, the elimination of poverty will not mean the end of the culture of poverty. The style of life based on apathy and despair starts from a situation of economic deprivation but becomes in itself, a much more complex problem. Lewis's approach is also important in that it sees positive aspects of poverty and explains ways in which the poor cope with their situation.

A dependency culture

This is an idea which dates back to the nineteenth century (see section 3.4) but which has more recently attracted attention, especially from right-wing politicians. The idea of the dependency culture is that people on benefits become reliant on the state and as a result have no interest in trying to find work or in living as economically as possible.

A survey of low-income families in five inner-city areas found no evidence of the dependency culture among the people interviewed.[18] One of the authors of the study said:

There is no culture of dependency that people prefer to stay on benefits rather than work. What they wanted above all else was work. Men wanted to earn their living and women wanted part-time jobs which they could combine with looking after children. They did not want increased benefits, even if that was politically feasible.[19]

The growth of an 'underclass'

Some writers have argued a new phenomenon now exists in Britain: an underclass. There are two main ways in which the term has been used. Firstly it refers to people who are seen as being outside the class system based on work (discussed in Chapter 1) and living on the margins of society, without access to full citizenship. In this sense it is similar to the idea of social exclusion. From this point of view, the focus is on economic and social structures which create a division between the underclass and the rest of the population. This is the left-wing use of the term. People are seen as trapped in a situation which is not of their own making. An underclass is created by changes in the economy, for example the wholesale loss of jobs in particular areas, such as the towns in South Wales which were previously dependent on coal mines for work.

However the term has also been used by writers taking a right-wing perspective who tend to blame the individuals concerned for their marginal position in society. An American writer called Charles Murray wrote an influential article in which he argued that problems he had observed in America had spread to Britain. Murray takes a strongly judgemental view, particularly of single parents and people who are experiencing long-term unemployment. They are, according to Murray, lacking in morals and the desire to do anything about their situation.

The distribution of wealth and income

A different way of looking at the problem of poverty is to see it as a problem of wealth. Perhaps it would be more useful for people concerned about poverty to focus their attention on rich, rather than poor, people.

In this country, there is considerable inequality in the distribution of wealth, as shown in government figures. These statistics reveal that, in 1995, 19 per cent of the country's wealth was owned by 1 per cent of the population. The most wealthy 10 per cent owned 50 per cent of the wealth. Looking at the situation from the other end of the scale, the least wealthy 50 per cent of the population owned only 8 per cent of the wealth.[20] This distribution has remained relatively unchanged, over time, in spite of different taxation policies. The only change which has occurred is between the wealthiest groups, where there has been a redistribution of wealth from the very rich to the rich. The proportion of wealth owned by the majority of people has changed very little.

The situation is similar, if less dramatic, in the case of the distribution of income. Figures published in 1994 revealed that the top 10 per cent of people in the country received 25 per cent of the total income. The bottom 10 per cent received only 3 per cent. The last 30 years have seen a widening of the gap between those with the very highest and those with the very lowest incomes.[22]

3.3 The effects of poverty

Poverty has effects for individuals, communities and the whole of society. It is hard to describe the full effects of poverty on an individual family or person. CPAG reports this comment from someone living on state benefits.

> Sometimes I don't have enough money for food for my kids. Sometimes I go without. It makes me feel like a pauper ... It makes me feel cross, I feel hurt because I cannot give my children proper nourishing meals.[23]

Poverty means going without and constantly thinking about money. It leads to humiliation, shame and feelings of failure. People trying to live on low incomes suffer from mental and physical health problems. The frustration and anxiety experienced as a result of poverty can lead to family violence or cause people to resort to alcohol or drugs (prescribed or illegal). Poverty leads to feelings of powerlessness and a real inability to participate fully in society.

Poor communities become run-down physically and are characterised by general feelings of despair. Crime and juvenile delinquency are related to poverty and lack of employment. This, in turn, causes problems for poor communities and society in general.

Activity 3.8

Write a letter, maybe the kind which could be sent to a local newspaper, imagining you are a child or an adult living in poverty, saying how you cope with poverty and describing the obstacles you have to overcome.

Activity 3.9

Examine each of the following statements. Write about a paragraph arguing for or against the view expressed in the statement:

1 Few people in Britain will experience poverty through much of their lives.
2 More people could get off benefits if they weren't so choosy about the jobs they were willing to take or the level of pay.
3 With Child Benefit people can afford to have more children.
4 Unemployed people can live comfortably on the money they receive from the state.
5 With state pensions, there is no need for anyone to fear poverty in old age.

3.4 The relief of poverty

The Poor Law

By looking back in history it is possible to see different attitudes to poverty and to trace the development of the present system. The first law about poverty was the Elizabethan Poor Law in 1601 which allowed officials in each village or parish to collect money, known as the poor rate, from each household and distribute help to those in need. The help given would take various forms, depending on the individual needs of the family. Sick or elderly people might be taken into places known as almshouses; others would be given work to do in return for money; widows might be given a small pension or have bills paid. The following account, based on records kept at the time, shows how varied the help could be:

> In 1775 the Collins family was subsidised during the illness of Mrs Collins to the amount of £18 11s 1d. The children were boarded at the blacksmith's; they were shod and the boy breeched. Fuel, soap and meat were provided. Mrs Collins had a nurse ... wine and brandy [eighteenth-century invalid foods] and oatmeal. Evidently she died, for her funeral cost £1 – after which Mr Collins was removed to another parish.[24]

This system was run on a local basis and people could not be helped if they were not settled in the parish. Help was classified as *outdoor relief* or *indoor relief*. With outdoor relief the family received help in their own home; indoor relief meant moving into an institution of some sort.

Activity 3.10

Find out from history books what sort of society Britain was in the eighteenth century. Where did people live? What did they do? What changes occurred in society between 1700 and 1900?

Speenhamland and other local systems

As time went on, this system of poor relief became increasingly impractical. Parishes were very small and whilst this did not matter in country areas with small populations, it was a problem when towns began to develop. The laws of settlement whereby newcomers would not be helped, but returned to their original parish, also created problems. The rules were complicated and could be very harsh. The laws were also thought to deter people from seeking jobs in other areas.

Towards the end of the eighteenth century conditions in Britain began to change very dramatically, bringing new needs, new ideas and demands for change in the Poor Law. There were wars, especially with France, which meant that food could not be imported to compensate for a bad harvest. This resulted in very high food prices so that people could not afford to buy bread, even when they had work. Several parishes began to develop schemes such as that tried in Speenhamland in Berkshire. The Speenhamland system gave allowances from the parish based on the price of bread and the number of children in the family. This meant that people would be working and receiving poor relief. It was criticised for a number of reasons: it allowed employers to pay low wages, knowing their workers would be subsidised; it demoralised workers, making them rely on the parish even when in work; and it was said to encourage large families and deter people from seeking better-paid work, perhaps in the towns. Another change was enclosure, which meant that poor people could no longer keep animals or grow food. Finally and probably most importantly, the population was increasing very fast. From 1781 it rose from nearly nine million people to twenty million people in 1851.

As a result of all these factors the poor rate began to rise rapidly and people became reluctant to pay it. Attitudes towards the poor began to change. People became less sympathetic and began to blame poor people for their situation.

1832 Royal Commission

In 1832 a Royal Commission was set up to investigate the workings of the poor law. Twenty-six commissioners travelled the country, visiting 3000 parishes. It seems however that the Commissioners had decided what to say in the report before they completed the research. The report was critical of a number of aspects of the Poor Law and made strong recommendations for change. Firstly, they suggested that a central board be set up to make sure that the same system existed throughout the country. Secondly, parishes would join together to provide workhouses for the poor. It should be illegal for anyone who was physically able to work to be helped other than in the workhouse. The Commissioners believed that conditions in the workhouse must be worse than the living conditions of the poorest person in work. This was known as the *principle of less eligibility*. It was thought that this would deter people from coming to the parishes for relief and make them find work. The following extract explains this idea in the Commissioners' own words:

> Every penny bestowed, that tends to render the condition of the pauper more eligible than that of the independent labourer, is a bounty on indolence and vice. But once the condition of the pauper is made more uncomfortable than that of the independent labourer then new life, new energy, is infused into the constitution of the pauper; he is aroused like one from sleep, his relation with his neighbours high and low is changed; he surveys his former employers with new eyes. He begs a job – he will not take a denial, he discovers that everyone wants something done.[25]

Unions and workhouses

There were many things wrong with the ideas of the Royal Commission of 1832, but since it was likely to cut the poor rate it was popular with better-off people and its ideas became law in the Poor Law Amendment Act of 1834. This act set up a central commission of three Commissioners and nine assistants. It called for parishes to group into Unions and to elect Boards of Guardians to oversee a workhouse. Outdoor relief would only be available for those who were sick or disabled and all others would be offered relief only in the workhouse. The Commissioners would set the standards for the workhouses.

Within a few years of the law being passed, most parishes had formed Unions and set up workhouses.

Activity 3.11

Find out if there were workhouses locally. Quite often these are still standing, converted into hospitals or flats. It may be possible to visit one. Ask older members of the community if they remember the workhouse. Ask them what it was like and how people felt about it.

The new commissioners supervised the task of building new workhouses and adapting already existing ones to their way of thinking – in the words of one commissioner, to make them 'wholesomely repulsive'.[26] The furniture in the workhouse was basic with people sharing beds, packed into rooms, with coarse and uncomfortable bedding. Inmates had to wear uniforms which were uncomfortable and marked them out as being in the workhouse. The food was dull and tasteless, consisting mostly of gruel and bread and cheese. The routine of the day was boring and the work which inmates had to do was deliberately made very hard and uninteresting.

The following poem was written by John Withers Reynolds who spent some time in Newmarket workhouse in 1846.[27]

Since I cannot, dear sister, with you hold communion,
I'll give you a sketch of our life in the union.
But how to begin I don't know, I declare;
Let me see: well, the first is our grand bill of fare.
We've skilly for breakfast; at night bread and cheese,
And we eat it and then go to bed if you please.
Two days in the week we have puddings for dinner.
And two, we have broth, so like water but thinner;
Two, meat and potatoes, of this none to spare;
One day, bread and cheese – and this is our fare.

And now then my clothes I will try to portray;
They're made of coarse cloth and the colour is grey,
My jacket and waistcoat don't fit me at all;
My shirt is too short, or I am too tall;
My shoes are not pairs, although of course I have two,
They are down at the heel and my stockings are blue …
A sort of Scotch bonnet we wear on our heads,
And I sleep in a room where there are just fourteen beds.
Some are sleeping, some are snoring, some talking, some playing,
Some fighting, some swearing, but very few praying.

Here are nine at a time who work on the mill;
We take it in turns so it never stands still;
A half hour each gang, so 'tis not very hard,
And when we are off we can walk in the yard …

I sometimes look up to a bit of blue sky
High over my head, with a tear in my eye.

Surrounded by walls that are too high to climb,
Confined like a felon without any crime;
Not a field nor a house nor a hedge can I see –
Not a plant, not a flower, nor a bush nor a tree …
But I'm getting I find, too pathetic by half,
And my object was only to cause you to laugh;
So my love to yourself, your husband and daughter,
I'll drink to your health in a tin of cold water:

Of course, we've no wine nor porter nor beer,
So you see that we all are teetotallers here.

Break-up of the Poor Law

The 1834 Poor Law Amendment Act was in some ways a success. People's fear and hatred of the workhouse was so great that they would do everything in their power to avoid it. Therefore in some parts of the country at least the poor rate was reduced as people starved rather than enter the dreaded workhouse. However things began to go wrong very quickly and the so-called *break-up of the poor law* began almost as soon as the act was passed (although the system was not completely abolished until after the Second World War, and some people would say that remnants of it still exist today). Many scandals occurred and attracted bad publicity, such as that at Andover where men working on crushing bones were found to be eating bits of rotten meat and gristle left on the bones. Different groups of people were mixed together in some workhouses, so that children shared rooms with adults who were mentally or physically ill. There was confusion over the application of the principle of less eligibility: were elderly people to be included on the basis that they should have saved for their old age? Most importantly, the system was based on the false idea that poverty is the fault of the poor.

There was a great deal of opposition to the workhouses. Riots occurred in some areas; petitions were sent to parliament. Some areas refused to elect guardians, others broke the rules and continued to give outdoor relief. The poor law was gradually eroded over the hundred years that followed its passing. Several administrative changes were made until finally in 1948 the relief of poverty was taken over entirely by central government (see below). Social inquiries, such as that done by Rowntree, showed poverty not to be the fault of the poor. Several Royal Commissions, especially that of 1905, gave support to those opposed to the poor law. Economic depressions in the 1880s and 1930s showed that poverty and unemployment were not caused by the laziness of the poor, but by economic factors.

Changing government attitudes

Attitudes to the role of government in helping people began to change. Previously, the attitude had been one of *laissez-faire*, that the government should not interfere in the workings of the economy. Increasingly, in the first half of the twentieth century, it was believed that the government should take a more active role. Finally, the Poor Law was eroded as other forms of help developed and fewer and fewer people depended on it for help. These other forms included self-help groups, such as friendly societies, charities and employment-based insurance schemes. Also, alternatives were introduced by the government at the beginning of the twentieth century.

Significant reforms were brought in by a *Liberal government* which came to power in 1905. In terms of the relief of poverty, the acts were the ones that brought in old age pensions and sickness and unemployment insurance. In 1909 a pension of 5 shillings (25p) was given to people over 70 whose income was not more than 10 shillings (50p) a week. A couple received seven shillings and six-pence ($37\frac{1}{2}$). The 1911 National Insurance Act covered health and unemployment benefits. Workers earning less than £160 a year were provided with free medical attention, free medicine and sick pay of seven shillings (35 pence) a week. They and their employers had to pay contributions towards these benefits. The treatment was available for the worker only and did not include his wife or children. Contributions were also made to receive unemployment benefit of seven shillings (35p) to cover fifteen weeks in any year. At first this did not apply to all workers but only those in industries likely to experience intermittent unemployment.

Activity 3.12

Interview a person who can remember times before the introduction of the welfare state after the Second World War. This means they will have been born around 1920. Find out what life was like, for example what happened when someone was ill, when someone was unemployed, if a child was orphaned, or an elderly person unable to look after themselves.

The following account comes from an interview carried out and written up by Val Derrett, a student on the In-Service Course in Social Care at Colchester Institute in 1987–88.

Alf is a tall, active, grey-haired man aged 81 years. He is slightly hard-of-hearing but has a keen brain and a good memory.

Alf's Dad worked on the railway, he and his wife had six children. He died young leaving his wife to bring up the children, all under ten, on a widow's pension. She was unable to cope financially and applied to the Board of Guardians to get assistance and had to undergo a means test to get 'parish money'. The two eldest children were sent to the Railway Servants orphanage in Derby, a crippled sister was sent to a home for the physically handicapped in Winchmore Hill, London.

'They only came home once a year at Christmas,' said Alf, 'so we didn't get to know each other very well.'

Alf and his two brothers attended a Charity School in Currier's Lane, Ipswich. Each child had a well-to-do sponsor who bought a suit of clothes and a pair of shoes per year for their child. The uniform was very distinctive and they stood out as 'charity boys' and they felt looked down upon. The children had to attend church every day and three times on Sundays and had to doff their caps to the Vicar and to the teacher. Once a year, at Easter, they had to pay a visit to their sponsor dressed up in their school uniform. There was also Ipswich Ragged School for children too poor or deprived to be suitable for the ordinary charity schools.

Alf started work at 14 with the railway in Ipswich and received a boy's pay until he was 21. He belonged to the NUR (National Union of Railwaymen) and came out on strike in 1926 in sympathy with the NUM (National Union of Mineworkers). He received only strike pay for over a year and 'times were hard'.

At the age of 21 he met his wife Mary, aged 23. They were courting for six years before they married as they had to save up from Alf's small wage of £2.4s.0d [£2.20p] and Mary's £1.5s.0d [£1.25p] as a machinist at a clothing factory. They rented a six-roomed house (no bathroom or central heating) for nine shillings [45p] a week which was a big part of their income, especially when Mary left work because she was expecting their first baby.

Alf changed his job to work at a tent-maker's in town. It was better hours and not such dirty work as at the railway. He was never unemployed as such but knew plenty who were. If a job was offered, a man had to take it or lose the dole. Many families suffered terribly, he remembered an account in the newspaper of a man who cut his throat because he could not bear to see his children starve. Unemployed men were sent to the 'spike' (workhouse) to do menial work such as chopping wood and stone picking.

Alf said there was a system of insurance whereby a small deduction was made from his pay towards sickness benefit, but there were no paid holidays. They also paid two pence [just less than 1p] a week to a doctor's club and a friendly society, because at that time if you called out or attended a doctor, you had to pay him. Old folk had a small old age pension and managed as best they could. Some went to live with their children, others ended up in a hospital or workhouse. Orphans and other children from destitute homes were cared for by charitable bodies such as Dr Barnardo's or the Church of England Children's Society. Children from the same family were often split up when they were adopted and many ended up in different countries such as Canada and Australia. Mentally and physically handicapped people were largely cared for by their parents and relatives, if not they ended up in an asylum or workhouse.

Activity 3.13

Look back over the history of welfare before the Second World War. Note things which have changed and things which remain the same. Look especially for evidence of ideas which continue, although perhaps in a different form.

The welfare state

The Beveridge report

In 1942, William Beveridge wrote the report which formed the basis of the present welfare system.[28] Beveridge said that there were five 'giants' which had to be slain by government in the post-war period. These were Want (poverty),

Disease (ill-health), Squalor (poor housing), Idleness (unemployment) and Ignorance (lack of education). His report was concerned with the abolition of want. He saw poverty as having two causes: loss of income due to old age, unemployment, sickness, etc., and the costs of children.

To help families with the costs of children, Beveridge proposed that children's allowances be paid to meet the full subsistence costs of all children except the first in each family. To replace lost earnings, Beveridge proposed a system of social insurance. The idea was that people would qualify, on the basis of contributions made, for payments when they could not work. All people in work would pay a set sum per week and receive, as of right, a set payment in times of need. These benefits would be contributory, non-means-tested benefits since people received them on the basis of having contributed and without being questioned about their means. Beveridge believed that most cases of need could be met by the insurance benefits but he recognised that there would be some people not covered. This is because benefits would be payable only to those who have contributed, and there will always be people, for reasons of disability for example, who cannot contribute. Therefore a safety net was added, termed national assistance. This would be subject to a means-test.

The social security system

Beveridge's report was very well received by the public and several acts were passed to implement his ideas. The 1945 Family Allowance Act brought in allowances for all children, except the first in each family, of five shillings (25p) a week. This was not, as Beveridge had suggested, the full basic cost of keeping a child. The 1946 National Insurance and 1946 National Insurance (Industrial Injuries) Acts provided a system of flat-rate contributions and benefits to provide for unemployment, retirement, sickness, disability, widowhood, maternity and funeral costs. The levels of the benefits were lower than Beveridge had intended and unemployment benefit was to be payable for 180 days only. The 1948 National Assistance Act brought in a non-contributory, means-tested benefit for those not covered by national insurance.

Many piecemeal changes have been made to the social security system set up after the Second World War, but the basic structure remains. National Insurance still exists, but its importance has been eroded and the significance of means-tested and other benefits increased. Contributions are no longer flat-rate but are earnings-related. Beveridge believed that for most cases of loss of income, the working population could earn its own cover through insurance. Theoretically, the social security system could therefore pay for itself. This has not worked for two main reasons. First, it is only recently that there have started to be people who have paid into the system for the whole of their working lives. Until about 1990, people were receiving benefits which, in a sense, had not been paid for. Second, Beveridge allowed for 8 per cent unemployment, which proved to be too low a figure. Because of these factors, national insurance benefits are financed partly out of weekly contributions from employees and employers and partly from general taxation. The contributions paid include a token payment towards the health service and a payment towards the Redundancy Fund.

National Assistance came to be highly stigmatised and its name was changed in 1965 to supplementary benefit. Further changes came as a result of the 1986 Social Security Act and supplementary benefit was replaced by income support. In 1996 people required to look for work moved to a new benefit: Jobseeker's Allowance. In 1976, the family allowance system was changed, and the new 'child benefit' is payable in respect of all children. Child benefit is non-contributory and non-means-tested. Changes in taxation accompanied the increased payments. The fourth sector of the post-war social security system was tax relief for dependent children. This was abolished in 1976 and the only people who received tax relief for children were single parents. From 2001 children's tax credits replace the married person's allowance, reintroducing the idea of tax relief for people with children.

Social security benefits

The main social security benefits are described below. It is important to note that the rules concerning benefits are extremely complicated and this book does not provide a comprehensive guide to welfare rights.[29] The benefit rates given are correct from April 1999 and are revised each April by the government. The benefits are arranged, as far as possible, on the basis of entitlement. Anyone wondering if they are entitled to a benefit should first think about whether the benefit is only available to those who have paid national insurance contributions – these are the contributory benefits. Then consider if the benefit is only paid to people with a low income – these are the means-tested benefits. As the list below shows, there are also some non-contributory, non-means-tested benefits, available to anyone in a particular group, for example child benefit for people with dependent children. To confuse matters further, some benefits cross over these boundaries. Jobseeker's Allowance includes a contributions-based element and a means-tested element. Some parts of the Social Fund are means-tested and other parts are not.

Non-contributory, non-means-tested benefits

The first set of benefits described here are those which are available to people because of some aspect of their situation – people who are disabled, caring for someone with a disability, or parents of dependent children. Entitlement to these benefits does not rely on a record of national insurance contributions, so someone who has not been working is as entitled to the benefits as someone who has been in work. Neither are the benefits means-tested. So even if people have a high income, from whatever source, and savings in a bank, building society or elsewhere, they are still entitled to receive the benefit.

- Industrial injuries benefits are paid to people who have been disabled at work or who suffer from a disease caused by their job. *Disablement benefit* is paid at a weekly rate which varies depending on the extent of the disability. Another benefit exclusively for people disabled due to an industrial accident or illness is constant attendance allowance (see below).

- The *disability living allowance* (DLA) is for people who are disabled and need help with extra costs for personal care or getting about. (This benefit replaced the mobility allowance and the attendance allowance in 1992.) For the *mobility component* the claimant must be over 5 and under 66 when first claiming. There are two rates of payment depending on the extent of the disability: a higher rate of £37.00 a week and a lower rate of £14.05 a week. The *care component* of DLA has three rates of payment, depending on the amount of help needed. These are £14.05, £35.40 and £52.95. The *attendance allowance* is still paid to those who began to need care after the age of 65. There is also a *constant attendance allowance* for people severely injured at work. The highest rate for this benefit is £86.60 although the amount depends on the extent of the disability and the need for care.
- *Invalid care allowance* is for people of working age who spend at least 35 hours a week caring for a person who is receiving a benefit for people with disabilities needing care. The weekly rate is £39.95, plus £23.90 for an adult dependant and £11.35 for a child.
- A £10 Christmas bonus is payable to people receiving certain contributory and non-contributory benefits. The benefits which entitle people to the bonus include the retirement pension, the invalid care allowance, the widowed mother's allowance and the attendance allowance.
- *Child benefit* is payable to all those responsible for a child under 16 or aged 16–19 and in full-time education. The rate is £14.40 for an only child or the eldest child and £9.60 for other children in the family. The higher rate for lone parents was abolished in 1998 but is still paid to lone parents who received the extra amount before that date.

Contributory, non-means-tested benefits

The benefits which are described under this heading are contributory which means that people must have paid national insurance contributions of the right sort and amount. Most employed people have national insurance contributions taken directly from their wages and there are means by which self-employed people and others can make contributions. The rules about contribution records are too complex to explain here: more details can be found, if needed, in the CPAG books described in the Further reading section at the end of the chapter. These benefits are not means-tested, so that people are entitled to claim on the basis of their national insurance contributions and it does not make any difference if they have income from other sources or savings.

- National insurance *retirement pensions* are currently paid to men over 65 and women over 60 who have paid sufficient contributions. The retirement age for women is to be increased to 65 between 2010 and 2020. The change will affect women born after 5 April 1950. The standard rate is £66.75 for the claimant, £39.95 for an adult dependant and £11.35 for a child. In 1978, a new system of earnings-related pensions was introduced. This is described in Chapter 13 along with other developments in pensions' provision.
- *Statutory sickness benefit* is paid by employers for 28 weeks. It is not paid for the first three days and then it is paid at a rate of £59.55 a week. Statutory sick

pay is not paid to people whose normal weekly earnings are below the lower earnings limit for national insurance contributions, which is £66.00 a week. The rate for statutory sick pay is a legal minimum: many employers pay a higher amount. After 28 weeks, *incapacity benefit* replaces statutory sick pay for people assessed as incapable of work. The weekly rates vary according to the length of time the person has been receiving the benefit and the age of the claimant.

- *Statutory maternity pay* is paid by employers for a maximum of 18 weeks. For the first six weeks the payment is 90 per cent of weekly earnings, for the rest of the time the amount is £59.55. Like statutory sick pay, this is the legal minimum and many employers pay more.

- A woman whose husband dies will receive certain benefits if he paid sufficient contributions before his death. Widows under 60 whose husbands have paid contributions receive a *widow's payment* of £1000. This is a one-off lump sum. Widows with children receive a *widowed mother's allowance* of £66.75 until the children have grown up. For middle-aged women there is a *widow's pension* also of £66.75 a week for those aged 55 and over, and lower amounts for women between 45 and 54 years of age. In 2001 widows' benefits are to be replaced with a set of benefits which do not discriminate between men and women in the way that the old system did. A £2000 lump sum bereavement payment replaces the widow's payment. A widowed parent's allowance is paid to men and women with dependent children. For those widows or widowers aged over 45 without dependent children a transitional bereavement allowance is paid for 6 months.

Jobseeker's Allowance (JSA)

Jobseeker's Allowance is given a heading of its own here because it includes both a contributory and a non-contributory, means-tested benefit. It therefore falls inside two categories of benefit. In 1996 the government announced that unemployment benefit (and income support for those out of work) would be abolished and replaced by a benefit to be called *Jobseeker's Allowance (JSA)*. JSA is for people who are unemployed or working less than 16 hours a week. *Contributions-based JSA* is paid to people who have sufficient national insurance contributions. This is paid for six months only. Others receive *income-based JSA*, which involves a means-test. To receive JSA people must be available for employment and actively seeking employment. Claimants are required to sign an agreement that they will take certain steps to look for work.

The rates for contribution-based JSA are £30.95 for someone under 18, £40.70 for someone between 18 and 24, and £51.40 for people 25 and over. There are no increases for partners or children. Income-based JSA tops up incomes to a set level. To calculate the amount received it is necessary to work out the person's or family's needs and to subtract their income from this; the amount remaining is the amount of JSA paid. Table 3.4 shows the personal allowances for different people and the premiums. These, plus some housing costs, equal needs.

There is not enough space here for all the details of how people qualify for premiums. A family in which the child was disabled would be eligible for two

TABLE 3.4   Benefit rates for income support and income-based Jobseeker's Allowance (JSA), April 1999

Personal allowances	£
Single	
– aged 16–17	30.95
– aged 18–24	40.70
– aged 25 or over	51.40
Lone parent	
– under 18 (usual rate)	30.95
– under 18 (in certain circumstances)	40.70
– aged 18 or over	51.40
Couple	
– both under 18	maximum 61.35
– both 18 or over	80.65
Dependent children	
– under 11	24.90
– aged 11–15	25.90
– aged 16–17	27.50
– aged 18	30.95
Premiums	
Family – ordinary rate	13.90
Family – lone parent rate	15.75
Pensioner	
– single	23.60
– couple	35.95
Enhanced pensioner	
– single	25.90
– couple	39.20
Higher pensioner	
– single	30.85
– couple	44.65
Disability	
– single	21.90
– couple	31.25
Severe disability, per qualifying person	39.75
Disabled child	21.90
Carer	13.95

premiums: the family premium and the disabled child premium, in addition to their personal allowances. From the figure for needs must be subtracted any income such as child benefit, maintenance payments and earnings, although a small part of earnings is not counted. The rates for income-based JSA are shown in the table which also applies to income support (see below).

Income-based JSA and income support (see below) are sometimes described as '*passport' benefits*. This means that they automatically entitle recipients to certain other benefits. These include free prescriptions, dental treatment, milk and vitamins for expectant mothers and children under five, eyesight tests and school meals.

Several benefits are now subject to tax. Jobseeker's Allowance is taxable. The effect of this change is that a refund of tax is not made when a person becomes unemployed, but when unemployment benefit stops, or at the end of the tax year, whichever comes first. The calculation of the refund includes the benefit paid. Other taxable benefits are pensions, the invalid care allowance and the widowed mother's allowance.

Some people who have received JSA and people under 60 receiving income support are entitled to a *Back to Work Bonus*. This is for people who have worked part-time whilst on benefit and then stop claiming because they have started working full-time or because their level of pay no longer entitles them to JSA. The bonus depends on the amount earned in part-time work and goes up to £1000.

Means-tested benefits

The benefits in this section do not require people to have paid national insurance contributions, so it does not matter if people have not worked for some time, or indeed ever worked. The benefits are however means-tested. This requires an assessment of an individual's or couple's income, from all sources such as part-time work, child support, pensions, and rent from a lodger. Savings and investments are also assessed and people are disqualified from benefits if they have savings over a particular amount. Again the details of the rules are complicated and more information can be found from the sources listed at the end of the chapter.

- *Income support* is a benefit for people on a low income who are not in full-time work and are not required to be available for work. This includes people over 60 and lone parents. The amount of income support is calculated in the same way as has already been described for income-based JSA (see above and Table 3.4). People are not eligible for income support if they have savings worth more than £8000.
- *Housing benefit* is paid by local councils and helps low-income families and individuals with rent. People on income support and income-based JSA are eligible for the maximum amount which is all of the rent. Others receive an amount which is calculated using the same needs' allowances as for income support and income-based JSA. However, since 1996 there are rules limiting the amount of rent which can be paid. The local authority may decide that the rent is too high or the accommodation is too large and therefore not pay all the rent. For single people under 25 the rent is likely to be restricted to the cost of a single room with shared facilities.
- *Council tax benefit* is calculated in a similar way to housing benefit and can be claimed by anyone liable for council tax. The maximum benefit is all the tax due.
- Tax credits were introduced in 1999, replacing family credit and disability working allowance. The main difference is that claims are dealt with by the Inland Revenue instead of the Benefits Agency. After March 2000 payments will be made by employers and claimed back from the Inland Revenue. *Working families tax credit* is for people with children, in full-time work (at least 16 hours a week) on a low income. The amount paid is calculated by looking at the number of children in the family, the hours worked, income,

savings and child-care costs. The amount people receive is the difference between their income and the maximum amount of tax credit for their family. If the income is below the threshold level of £90, they receive the full tax credit for their family. If the income is higher than the threshold, the tax credit is reduced by 55 per cent of the difference. As an example, a family with three children aged 8, 10 and 13 in which one of the parents works over 30 hours a week and earns £200 after deductions for tax and national insurance would receive £63.55.

- *Disabled Person's Tax Credit* is paid to low-paid workers with a disability. The amount payable is calculated in a similar way to family credit. The threshold is £70 for single claimants and £90 for couples or lone parents. For people whose income exceeds the threshold, the amount they are entitled to is reduced by 55 per cent of the difference between their income and the threshold amount.

The social fund

The 1986 Social Security Act set up the social fund. The fund has two parts, which is why it is given its own heading here. The first provides grants for funerals, maternity needs and cold weather fuel allowances. People are entitled to these grants when they meet the conditions agreed by Parliament. The maternity expenses payment is paid to people receiving income support or family credit and is £100. People on income support, disability working allowance and family credit are entitled to the grant, although the amount is reduced if people have savings over £500. *Funeral payments* from the social fund are designed to meet reasonable funeral costs for people on low incomes who are responsible for a funeral. These are payable to people on income support, family credit, housing benefit and the disability working allowance.

The second part of the social fund is made up of payments made at the discretion of the social fund officers and must come out of a set budget available to each social fund office. There are three categories of discretionary payments. The first category consists of non-repayable *community care grants*. These are for vulnerable people such as those with learning difficulties moving into the community from an institution, but also can be paid to help with exceptional pressures on families or with certain essential travelling expenses. *Budgeting loans* are interest-free loans for people on income support who need help with exceptional expenses. An example might be the purchase of a bed or a cooker. These loans are paid back through deductions from benefit. Finally, *crisis loans* are payable to anyone who has no other means of avoiding damage to their health or safety.

The social fund has been criticised on a number of points. The fact that it is discretionary may mean that different people are treated differently by local officers. There is no procedure for appeal against a decision which seems unfair. The fund is cash-limited which may mean that people in desperate need at the end of the financial year cannot be helped if the money has run out. Also it will be very difficult for people on income support to pay back loans. Attempting to do so will push them below the poverty line.

Activity 3.14

Select a social fund benefit and find out the details of entitlement and the current rates. The local benefits office will provide leaflets which contain this information. Report your findings to the class.

Activity 3.15

The social security system is very complicated and not even officials or advice workers are expected to know all the details off by heart. The following questions will help you check your understanding of the main benefits.

1 Jane Nixon is a single parent with two children of school age. She lives in a council house and works 30 hours a week. Are there any benefits she can claim?

2 Mike, who is 18, has just finished a training scheme and is unable to find a job. To which benefit is he entitled?

3 Mr Ruprah has been made redundant after working for 10 years. In addition to redundancy pay, what can he claim?

4 Ms Andrews stays at home to look after her severely disabled mother who receives a disability living allowance. To which benefit could Ms Andrews be entitled?

5 Ben has a disability and is receiving benefits. He has just been offered a job. Although the pay is low he will gain valuable experience. Is there a benefit to help him manage?

6 Janice is a single parent. She has been receiving income support for some time. She is about to be re-housed from a furnished flat into a council house. She has no money for furniture. What help might be available?

7 Mrs Bal's husband has died. Before his death he was employed and she stayed at home to care for their three young children. She is worried that she will now have to go out to work. Which benefit can she claim?

8 Richard is 7 and severely handicapped. He requires assistance with feeding, going to the toilet and cannot be left alone. Which benefits can be claimed for him?

9 A home care worker is worried about an elderly client who does not have enough money to buy food for the week. Which benefits might help her client?

10 Mr Jones is about to be discharged from a psychiatric hospital to live in the community. What help will he be entitled to?

3.5　Issues in welfare

Take-up of benefits

Despite all the fuss made about 'welfare scroungers' in the popular press, many people do not claim benefits for which they are eligible. 'Take-up' is defined as the percentage of people eligible for a benefit who successfully claim it. The benefits with the lowest take-up rates are the means-tested benefits. The total amount of unclaimed benefits is estimated to be as much as £3.5 billion. Pensioners are the group with the lowest take-up rates.

Activity 3.16

List all the reasons you can think of why people might not receive benefits to which they are entitled. What could be done to improve their situation?

There are many possible explanations for low take-up rates. Social security benefits are very complicated and not widely understood. Many people will not have heard of benefits such as family credit, let alone realise that they are eligible to claim. There is a feeling, especially common among the elderly, that benefits are a form of charity. Pride can therefore prevent people who are aware of benefits from claiming.

Explanations for the problem of low take-up rates can be found by comparing the rates for different benefits. The means-tested benefits have the worst records probably because a means-test carries a stigma. People may feel that to claim family credit (now working families tax credit), for example, labels them as 'poor' or 'inadequate', setting them apart from other people. Many people find it humiliating to be questioned about their income and resources. These points can be illustrated by considering the difference between child benefit and other benefits. Child benefit is paid in respect of all children and therefore has no means-test and no associated stigma.

Although the funding for child benefit comes from the Department of Social Security, people have never had to go to benefits offices to apply for child benefit or to collect their money. Instead, this has been done through post offices. Explanations for low take-up rates must consider the treatment which claimants receive at the local benefits office. People can be put off claiming benefits by their experience or by rumours they have heard.

There are families in need who do not claim free school meals because of the stigma attached and the treatment by schools of children receiving this benefit. CPAG produced a report on the subject, quoting from letters they had received. One parent wrote:

I know Matthew is entitled to free school dinners but I have never accepted this for him as some children can be so cruel about these things and I do not want Matthew to have to face that so my earnings pay for his dinner.[30]

It would be possible to improve take-up rates, if the government was committed to this. However, it is possible that the expense concerned is too great. The benefit system could be simplified, although the trend has been for it to become more complex. Benefits could be better publicised, in ways which ensured that the information reached people. More advice workers could be provided to inform individuals of their rights and to initiate publicity campaigns. Efforts have been made in these respects and the benefits leaflets, for example, clearly explain people's entitlements. When Family Credit was first introduced the government was keen for it to succeed in encouraging people into work and it was well publicised, on buses and other public places and even on television. Child benefit books continue to be used as a means of telling parents how much they could earn and still qualify for the benefit. Education could not only inform but attempt to change attitudes, so that people understand that social security benefits are a right, not a form of charity.

Stigma could be reduced by a move away from means-tested benefits, towards benefits for categories of people. For example, instead of single parents relying on income support, they could receive a non-means-tested benefit. Procedures could be simplified and improved, and officials could be encouraged to see claimants as people claiming their rights. In the specific case of free school meals, it is possible for the procedures to be organised in such a way that no-one knows which children receive free dinners. This is already done in some schools.

These measures are all possible but they do require a level of commitment from the government not at present found. Also, any campaigns to change attitudes are working against the powerful influence of the popular press, with their stories of 'scroungers' falsely claiming massive amounts of social security money.

The poverty trap

The term 'poverty trap' is used to describe situations in which people attempt to improve their position but end up no better off. The poverty trap discourages some people from seeking work and leads to increased feelings of hopelessness and despair. The poverty trap occurs as a result of the system of taxation, contributions and benefits. A person may begin work or receive an increase in wages but lose entitlement to benefits, while paying more in tax and national insurance.

Efforts have been made by governments to improve the situation for people in low-paid work. Entitlement to family credit was intended to mean that a family with a low-paid job should not be worse off than on income support. The disability working allowance protected people with disabilities in a similar way. People in work can continue to claim housing benefit if their income is low. However the poverty trap can still affect childless people who are only entitled to claim housing benefit and who may find themselves no longer entitled to free prescriptions or dental care. Single parents have long complained that the high costs of child-care mean they cannot afford to work. The introduction of tax credits for working parents, which include child-care costs, and for people with disabilities, as well as the minimum wage, are further attempts to tackle this issue and encourage people to find and keep employment.

'Deserving' and 'undeserving' poor

The idea that people can be categorised as 'deserving' and 'undeserving' poor dates back to the Victorian era. Yet this way of seeing poverty continues and is built into the welfare system. Certain groups living in poverty attract more public sympathy than others. This tends to be reflected in benefit levels. For example, the child of an unmarried mother is forced to live at a lower level of poverty than a child whose mother is a widow. The payment of the Christmas bonus highlights this situation, with beneficiaries of certain benefits included and others excluded.

The idea of deserving and undeserving poor is also behind the different sorts of treatment different categories of claimants receive. People entitled to contributory benefits are treated more as people claiming their rights than are those applying for income support, for example.

The expectation of the social security system was that it would bring an end to poverty. It fails in this aim in two basic ways. First, there continue to be large numbers of people living below the poverty line. Second, those who live on means-tested benefits experience hardship which is tantamount to poverty in the context of today's society. Fundamental problems exist in the over-worked social security system which is attempting to do a job far larger than that for which it was designed. To some extent, the system has been weakened, rather than strengthened, by the piecemeal reforms which have been made.

This chapter emphasised the complexity of the problem of poverty. It is not a problem which can be solved easily. Solutions require a commitment from the government and the public which has not always been in evidence. A full understanding of the complexities and the interrelationships of the problem is also necessary as a basis for real change. In the meantime, people continue to suffer.

Activity 3.17

Make sure that you understand the following expressions used in this chapter. Check in the Glossary at the end of the book if you need to.

absolute poverty	poverty trap
dependency culture	primary poverty
deprivation	redistribution of wealth
disabled person's tax credit	relative poverty
earnings-related	secondary poverty
eligibility	social exclusion
less eligibility	social security
means-tested	stigma
National Insurance contributions	take-up
passport benefit	welfare state
poverty cycle	workhouse
poverty line	working families tax credit

Further reading

A useful review of issues around poverty can be found in the second edition of a book called *Understanding Poverty* by Pete Alcock (London: Macmillan, 1997).

The best source of information on poverty and welfare benefits is the *Child Poverty Action Group* (CPAG) which publishes results of surveys, statistical information and a regular journal. The organisation also produces comprehensive guides to benefits which are updated each year.

Useful addresses

CPAG
94 White Lion Street
London N1 9PF
tel. 0207 837 7979

Department of Social Security
Room 114
Adelphi
1–11 John Adam Street
London WC2N 6HT
tel: 0207 712 2171

Websites

You can find information on benefits through the Citizens' Advice Bureaus website **www.adviceguide.org.uk**

The Department of Social Security provide information through **www.dss.gov.uk**

The Joseph Rowntree Foundation publish findings on research – some of which relates to poverty and social exclusion at **www.jrf.org.uk**

▼ **4** Unemployment

Unemployment causes suffering to people who are made redundant or who cannot find a job on leaving school or college. The families of these people also experience financial difficulties, anxiety and stress. In areas where a high proportion of people are out of work, communities become demoralised and depressed. High unemployment means that even people in work suffer, through reduced opportunities to change jobs, and the feeling of vulnerability which spreads throughout society. The costs of unemployment are borne by the society as a whole, both in terms of financial and social factors. Increased demands are made on social workers, doctors and other caring workers as they are called upon to deal with the effects of unemployment on the physical and mental health of individuals, families and communities. Unemployment is thus an issue of individual and national concern.

4.1 Types of unemployment

Economists have distinguished several types of unemployment, related to particular causes. First, *structural unemployment* is caused by changes in the industrial structure, for example, the decline in manufacturing industry or the introduction of new technologies which reduce the need for labour. The second type is *cyclical unemployment*, which is caused by a tendency for the economy to go through periods of boom and recession in demand and production. Third, *frictional unemployment* results from people being unemployed between jobs or before they start work. Finally, there is *voluntary unemployment*, where people choose not to work, perhaps because wages are too low to provide an incentive.

Activity 4.1

―――――

Which of these definitions of unemployment seems most appropriate to describe Britain's situation at the present time?

4.2 New patterns of employment

The 1950s and 1960s were a period of full employment. The post-war boom lasted for thirty years and in most parts of the country jobs were plentiful. The majority of the workforce were men and most expected to stay with the same firm all of their working lives. Things changed in the 1980s when a series of recessions led to much higher levels of unemployment, initially concentrated in the North of the country and spreading to the relatively affluent South-East in the 1990s.

Continuing high rates of unemployment have led commentators to talk of a new kind of society: one in which full-time, permanent jobs will be rare, and people will instead be employed in several part-time jobs on a more casual basis. This pattern of employment has of course always been common for women. The 1980s and 1990s saw a decrease in the types of jobs traditionally done by men; where new jobs were created, many were of the type traditionally done by women. These trends suggest changes ahead for men as they increasingly find themselves either unemployed whilst their partners are in work or working in situations previously associated with women.

4.3   The numbers of unemployed people

In February 1999 government figures showed there to be 1,305,300 people unemployed and claiming benefits. Although still high in comparison to earlier decades, this was the lowest level since June 1980.[1] There is however considerable disagreement as to whether or not these figures give true indications of the numbers unemployed.

Activity 4.2

Why might the official statistics not be a real measure of the extent of unemployment?

Calculating the number of unemployed people requires a definition of unemployment and an accurate method of counting. Recent years have seen around 20 changes in the way the government calculates the figure. In 1982 a major change was introduced when the figure stopped being those registered as 'unemployed' and became those 'claiming benefits'. The Unemployment Unit has estimated that use of the old criteria would increase the figure by some 400,000.[2] The claimant count excludes many people with working partners who have been unemployed too long to qualify for contributions-based Jobseeker's Allowance (more than six months). Also not counted are men aged 60–64. Similarly, the figure does not include people on training schemes. Some argue that people in part-time work who want full-time work should be included in the figures, especially since some two-thirds of the jobs created in recent years are part-time jobs. From a different point of view the International Labour Organisation (ILO) use a narrower definition of unemployment. This requires that a person must be without a paid job, be available to start work within a fortnight, and have looked for work in the last four weeks or be waiting to start work. This definition reduces the figures by 200,000. ILO figures are now commonly used in government sources in addition to the claimant count. Taking the whole

Source: Crispin Hughes, Photofusion
There are more unemployed people than job vacancies

range of definitions of unemployment, estimates have ranged between 1 and 5 million people without work.[3]

The acceptance of mass unemployment is hard to understand but perhaps is partly explained in terms of the prevalence of myths about unemployment. These myths include the idea that the existence of the system of benefits for people out of work means that unemployment does not cause suffering. There are also people who believe that no-one is unemployed for very long and that it is quite nice to have a period off work, living on welfare benefits. Finally, despite the high level of unemployment, there are those who argue that there is no genuine unemployment and that people could get a job if they wanted to.

Activity 4.3

Discuss with your fellow students the following statements, which represent some people's view on unemployment. Draw on your experience or that of friends or relatives, and information you might have from reading newspapers or books.

1 There are jobs available if people really want to work.
2 Benefits are high enough that people don't feel the need to look seriously for work.
3 Some people are better off on benefits than in work.
4 People who are made redundant will find another job in a few weeks.
5 Many people manage to cheat the system by working on the side whilst claiming unemployment benefits.

4.4 The distribution of unemployment

In a period of high unemployment, work becomes a scarce resource, and like most scarce resources, is not shared out equally. If unemployment was divided equally among the whole working population, each person would be unemployed every six years or so – about eight times in their working life.[4] This is not the case, many people are never unemployed, while other more vulnerable groups are unemployed for long periods and at frequent intervals.

Activity 4.4

Which groups of people might be more vulnerable to unemployment? Why?

Regional inequalities

Throughout the 1980s there were large variations in the unemployment rates of the different regions in the UK. In 1989 the highest rate of unemployment, in Northern Ireland, was five times that of the lowest region, East Anglia. Other areas of particularly high unemployment were the North, the North-West and Scotland. The South of England generally had low rates of unemployment. The 1990s saw striking changes in patterns of unemployment with massive job losses occurring in areas previously experiencing little unemployment. The rate for Northern Ireland, although still amongst the highest, fell; whereas figures for the South and East Anglia rose almost to a par with those for the North. The ordering of the regions has remained pretty much the same, but the differences are much smaller than they were. Within regions unemployment is often concentrated in particular areas, leading to particularly high rates in particular towns or parts of the regions. For example, the rate for the coastal town of Harwich is almost twice as high as that of the rest of the county of Essex.[5]

The reasons for regional inequalities are complex, but one explanation lies in the concentration of particular industries in particular areas. The large variations in the 1970s and 1980s were partly caused by the decline of older industries such as ship-building, engineering and metal-manufacturing. These industries were concentrated in the North and in Scotland. Unemployment in the South in the 1990s has resulted from cutting back of staff in many different areas of work such as banking, the public sector and telecommunications, as well as closures of firms in newer industries.

Vulnerable groups

Young people are vulnerable in times of high unemployment. Statistics show that youth unemployment rises faster than overall unemployment, although it also falls more quickly as unemployment decreases.[6] This is because, in a recession, employers do not take on new workers. The unemployment rate for people aged 18–24 is double the overall rate.[7]

Older people who are made redundant find it difficult to find a new job, as employers tend to think that people over 50 or so are unable to adapt to a new situation.

Women are also vulnerable to unemployment, although the fact that married or cohabiting women may not be eligible for benefit makes it difficult to estimate the extent of female unemployment and the figures from the government show relatively low levels. Many women work part-time and a firm wishing to reduce its workforce may dismiss the part-time workers first, since their conditions of service offer less protection and more limited rights to redundancy pay.

Research shows that ethnic minorities are more likely to be unemployed than white people. Black and Asian workers are more than twice as likely to be unemployed as white workers. Discrimination by employers is illegal under the 1976 Race Relations Act (as we saw in Chapter 1), but continues on a very significant scale. This has been shown in research using black and white actors matched for qualifications and experience. In these tests, Asian and West Indian applicants were discriminated against in 46 per cent of cases.[8] In the same research project, written applications for jobs were sent, making it clear that some applicants were not white. The letters received from employers clearly demonstrate the existence of racial discrimination. In one case, the white applicant is invited to arrange an interview, while the other is told the vacancy no longer exists as a result of the fuel crisis of the time. In another case, a married woman is invited to telephone for an appointment, while another is told that 'we have a policy in the office not to employ married women.'[9]

People without skills or qualifications find it more difficult to secure employment, since many of the vacancies which exist are for skilled workers. Related to this, manual workers are more likely to be unemployed than non-manual workers. Finally, people who are discriminated against by employers are less likely to find work when there is a high level of unemployment. These people have included those with a learning disability or physical disability and people who have suffered from mental illnesses. The 1995 Disability Discrimination Act has made it illegal for employers to treat disabled people less favourably than others and employers are required to make reasonable adjustments to working conditions and environments to overcome the effects of a disability. (There are more details on the DDA in Chapter 14.) Ex-prisoners are another group of people who are likely to find it difficult to get work in times of high unemployment.

4.5 The effects and costs of unemployment

Activity 4.5

What might be the effects of unemployment on an individual or a family? Do you think that the experience of unemployment is different for some people than for others, for example, for a school-leaver as opposed to a parent?

Source: Janis Austin, Photofusion
Some people are more vulnerable to unemployment than others

Effects of unemployment

We live in a society in which work plays a major part in people's lives. People
who are in work may complain about it and say they only work for money, but

the experience of unemployment highlights the fact that work provides more than just an income. Employment is a source of status and gives people a role in society, as well as structuring the day, week and year. People who are without work dread being asked what they do, and there is no pleasure in Friday evening, the weekend or bank holidays when all the days are the same.

Personal

The following section includes several quotations from people who are unemployed, to show how they feel about their situation. These illustrations of people's experiences are taken from research carried out by Jeremy Seabrook in various parts of the country.

When people are first unemployed, they may experience a certain elation, especially those who receive redundancy money. A man from Sunderland tells how, at first, he:

> felt like a millionaire. At first, great, you don't have to get up in the morning. That goes on for a few weeks. Then you have a twinge of anxiety. You think 'Next week I'll look for a job.' You put it off for a week or two. Then you have a casual look round, and the thing that strikes you is the shortage of work. You get more anxious; you see your money dwindle.[10]

With or without redundancy money, being unemployed gets worse as time goes on. Many people tell how at first they enjoy the change and the opportunity to catch up on decorating and other jobs around the home. Gradually, feelings change as jobs are completed or the motivation goes. Long-term and recurrent unemployment are both becoming more and more significant. Nearly one in two unemployed men has been unemployed for more than a year.[11]

People's feelings about unemployment vary, and for some people the experience is one of shock that redundancy could happen to them. This initial feeling changes as lethargy and boredom set in. The same man quoted above goes on to say:

> You don't realise just how much your life was parcelled out to fit the needs of the company you worked for. You're not used to constructing it for yourself; and when you get to a certain age it becomes harder.[12]

This problem of structuring the day without work leads many people to stay in bed late and to spend hours watching television. It is easy to put things off when endless days stretch ahead.

Common themes in people's accounts of unemployment are feelings of shame and uselessness. People start to feel that they are on the scrap-heap of society and that they have nothing to offer, or that society has no need of their talents and abilities. The woman speaking in this quotation has just heard that a neighbour, out of work for fifteen months, has committed suicide:

> Of course, I've no evidence that it was anything to do with his being out of work, but I could understand if it was. If you're able-bodied you've got to have a reason for living; and for most people, their job is the main reason for living. If you can't do that, you feel you're on the scrap-heap; you feel a burden to society.[13]

Unemployment is a source of stigma and leads to feelings of shame and failure. People with children are ashamed that they cannot provide them with everything they need and want. Many people feel that they are a failure in the eyes of their children. People who are out of work also feel isolated, missing the social life at work and avoiding people out of embarrassment. It is difficult for someone to go out for a drink knowing they cannot afford to buy a round if they meet their friends. People fear the charity and pity of those still working, or, perhaps worse still, criticisms of the way they spend their money or the fact that they are unable to find work.

Unemployment can also have a brutalising effect and, in Seabrook's book there are accounts of young people who turn to violence, racism and brutalised sexual fantasy to escape the boredom and meaninglessness of their days.

Unemployment can also affect health. A government-sponsored report found that unemployed people had much poorer health than those in work.[14] Another study, based on official statistics, found that unemployed men were more than twice as likely to commit suicide as the rest of the population. The author of the study argues that stress is probably the cause of the increased rate of illness amongst unemployed men.[15]

Financial

Little has been said so far about the financial aspects of unemployment. Unemployment is a major factor in explaining poverty and leads to considerable anxiety over money. Only people on very low wages with large families do not experience a significant drop in income on becoming unemployed. Benefit rates, as set out in Chapter 3 on poverty and welfare, are well below the national average income. For a single person, benefits provide about a quarter of the average net wage; for a family with four children, it is about half. Many people who are unemployed have problems with debts and difficulty in paying for basic needs like heating and housing. A survey carried out by the National Association of Citizens' Advice Bureaus found that nearly 50 per cent of CAB clients in debt were not in full-time employment.[16]

A further factor in understanding the stigma and humiliation felt by people without work is the treatment people receive when claiming benefits. Many people feel that they are subjected to unnecessary rudeness and tactless questioning when claiming benefits to which they have a right.

Family problems

The effects of unemployment reach further than just those individuals without work. Whole families suffer from poverty and the anxiety of having a member out of work. Problems occur in a variety of different situations and anxiety is expressed in different ways. In this society, it is considered to be normal for a man to go out to work and be the main source of financial support for the family. Families who exchange roles with the woman working and the man looking after the home often find this situation stressful, especially if it is not voluntarily chosen, but a result of external factors, such as unemployment. However, there can also be problems when both partners are at home. Women who are used to being alone to get on with the housework may resent the continual presence of their husbands. Men may feel that there is nothing for them to do in the home and that they are in the way.

There is a tendency for people to take out feelings of frustration on people close to them. Stress can cause family quarrels and ultimately marital breakdown. There is also the risk of violence when frustration and resentment build up. In the account given below, a man living in Newcastle-upon-Tyne tells how he came to leave his family in Scotland, after a long period of unemployment:

> I couldn't stand the pressure. I hated being at home. I felt useless. I was no good to them. They're better off without me. I've four kids, the eldest is nine now. But when I was there, I was shouting at them all the time. I never spoke to them in a normal tone of voice. One night I got that mad, the baby wouldn't stop crying, I went to pick her up, but I knew if I did, that would be it. I'd've broken her like a doll. That was it. I had to get out. It makes me feel bad, what I did. But I don't know what I would have done if I'd stayed there. It's best for all of us.[17]

Up to this point, the emphasis has been on negative aspects of unemployment. This is representative of most people's experiences, although there are those who manage to cope with their situation without being demoralised. As the man quoted next explains, feelings about unemployment are related to the importance which society attaches to work. This man was a joiner and his wife does not work because she suffers from angina.

> I don't feel I've been destroyed by not having a job. I've had a set-back, yes; time hangs heavy sometimes. But my purpose now is the same as it's ever been – to look after the kids and now I've got the added job of looking after my wife as well. That isn't unworthy of a man. Quite the opposite. Being out of work is an attack on dignity and self-respect, but maybe that's because we set too much store on things that don't matter – dignity and self-respect should come through your relationship.[18]

There are also people who make use of their time and gain satisfaction and self-esteem through involvement in community work or political activity.

Community and social problems

Unemployment causes problems for communities and for society as a whole as well as for individuals and families.

Activity 4.6

Consider ways in which unemployment has implications for a local community, and for the whole of society.

Communities become demoralised when a high proportion of people are out of work and no employment is available. Poverty also leads to physical deterioration of properties and empty factories or warehouses give a feeling of decay to an area. High unemployment leads to a deterioration in services as health visitors, doctors and social workers attempt to cope with the increased pressure.

Commercial and shopping facilities are also affected and big supermarkets are reluctant to open branches in areas where people have no money to spend.

The level of crime and vandalism in poor districts may be caused by unemployment, although this relationship is difficult to prove conclusively. Jeremy Seabrook's book contains several accounts of young people who take to crime, either as a source of money or to relieve boredom and create excitement. In this account, a woman who was trained as a nursery teacher, tells how her feelings of frustration gave her an understanding of vandalism:

> one day when I came out of the JobCentre, I was so pent-up, I felt a sudden overwhelming desire to smash every window in the street. It was quite overpowering. I just stood there and said 'Calm yourself down, this isn't going to get you anywhere.' But I felt I suddenly got a great insight into vandalism and violence because there it was in myself.[19]

Unemployment can lead to an increase in crime in that people feel that they have nothing to lose. Someone who is unemployed already need not fear losing their job. Unemployed people cannot pay large fines, although obviously they can still be fined. For some young people, there is even a feeling that being sent to prison would not make much difference to their lives. Communities already suffering the effects of unemployment are also victims of high crime rates and a high level of vandalism.

Trade unions also suffer in periods of high unemployment and are the main pressure group campaigning for a policy of full employment. Trade unions lose members and funds as a result of unemployment and are placed in a weak position for bargaining when jobs are few and far between. The Trade Union Congress has been involved in establishing centres for the unemployed to help people without work. The loss of strength of trade unions in a period of high unemployment extends to the whole of the working class who become demoralised and less able to make demands for improved pay and working conditions.

Increased pressure on health and social services and on the police means increased costs for society as a whole. The riots which took place in the summer of 1981 are considered by most people to have been related to unemployment. The cost to society of such events is immeasurable although more direct costs of unemployment can be calculated. The most obvious cost of unemployment is in terms of benefits and special employment measures, paid for by the state, through taxation and national insurance contributions. The price of these is measured in billions of pounds. The social security bill for unemployed people is £5420 million.[20] The figure is much higher if the loss in taxes caused by people not working is added.

4.6   Employment services

Activity 4.7

List any government schemes for advice and training for the unemployed of which you have heard or have experienced.

Unemployment is an issue of national concern and over the years a number of initiatives and programmes have been devised by successive governments. There have been many changes to these programmes and this is quite a complicated area with a lot of different acronyms (words made up of the initial letters of words) being used.

Organisation of services

The government department with the overall responsibility for the various employment services is the Department for Education and Employment (DfEE). Services are administered through the Employment Service, which is part of the DfEE. The financial aspects of the main benefit for unemployed people, Jobseeker's Allowance, are dealt with by the Benefits Agency, which is part of the Department for Social Security. This benefit has been described in Chapter 3.

In 1990 the running of many of the training schemes for unemployed people was transferred to local organisations. In England and Wales, there are 78 *Training and Enterprise Councils* (TECs), led by employers, with a budget and performance targets set by the government. In Scotland 22 *Local Enterprise Council* (LECs) fulfilled a similar role but with wider-ranging responsibilities. The abolition of the TECs is proposed for 2001 under a plan to create a national council for training and 50 local councils. In 1997 a network of National Training Organisations was set up. These have played a key role in developing Modern Apprenticeships and National Traineeships which provide work-based training for young people.

Advice

Advice and information services are run by the government through the Employment Service, which is part of the Department for Education and Employment. Services are provided through a national network of over a thousand JobCentres. These provide information on job vacancies and training opportunities. There is a Jobseeker's Charter which sets standards for the service. In 1998 a major programme was started to upgrade the physical environment of the JobCentres and to make more use of information technology, for example through touch screen information kiosks. A year later the Employment Service and the Benefits Agency started pilots for a 'single gateway' to bring together in a one-stop shop all the benefits, including housing benefit, and the employment services. The old set-up often involves people traipsing across town to access different services administered by the Employment Service, the Benefits Agency and the local authority.

Employment Service advisors see everyone who claims Jobseeker's Allowance to decide if they are eligible for the benefit and to advise on work and training opportunities. Claimants complete a Jobseeker's Agreement which includes steps to be taken in looking for work. People are then expected to 'sign on' every fortnight and a short job-search review takes place to make sure people are keeping to their Jobseeker's Agreement. After about

13 weeks people are called in for a more in-depth interview to discuss their attempts to find work. Unemployed people are then called in every six months for the compulsory Restart interview and the Agreement is revised. At various points in this process, people who are still without work will be directed to the programmes described below. Additional compulsory interviews can be required if the staff are not happy with the answers given at the fortnightly review.

The Employment Service also helps people with disabilities to find work. All the programmes available for unemployed people are open to people with disabilities. *Disability Service Teams* provide specialist advisory services for people with disabilities. They also offer the Access to Work programme which helps people with disabilities to overcome barriers to employment and the Supported Employment Programme which provides supported employment schemes for over 22,000 more severely disabled people. There is more detail of these schemes in Chapter 14.

Programmes available

The Labour government elected in 1997 brought in New Deal schemes under the banner of Welfare to Work (see below). Many of the previously existing programmes are being restructured under the New Deal. Those still running in 1999 included the following:

- *Travel to Interview Scheme* – For people who have been unemployed for three months, this scheme pays the cost of travelling to interviews further away from home.
- *Job Interview Guarantee* – This provides an interview with an employer for people who have been unemployed for six months or more. The skills and experience of the unemployed person are matched to the needs of the employer.
- *Work Trials* – Another scheme for people who have been unemployed for six months. Work Trials are with employers who have vacancies and last up to three weeks. People continue to receive Jobseeker's Allowance with an extra £10 a week and help with travel and meals' expenses.
- *Jobclubs* – Here people who have been unemployed for over six months meet together and receive training and advice on skills in looking for work. Jobclubs provide free access to facilities such as telephones, newspapers, stamps and stationery.
- *Jobfinder Plus* – People over 25 who have been unemployed for over 18 months may be asked to attend a series of interviews with an advisor. The aim of Jobfinder Plus is to work out achievable goals and actions and to provide support and guidance.
- *Jobplan Workshop* – People who haven't found a job after one year are required to attend workshops lasting four and a half days with a further half day a couple of weeks later. These are intended to improve confidence and job-seeking skills.
- *Jobfinder's Grant* – People who have been unemployed for two years or more are encouraged to take a job they would not otherwise have taken, perhaps

because costs of special clothing etc. are involved, by being offered a one-off payment of £200.

The Labour government elected in 1997 introduced the Welfare to Work programme. This is a series of measures attempting to tackle youth and long-term unemployment and move people from welfare to work. The programme includes the 'New Deals'. The programme is funded through the windfall taxes imposed on excess profits of the privatised utilities and involved an initial investment of some £5200 million.

The New Deal for young people

This was introduced in 1988 for young people aged 18–24 who have been unemployed for more than six months. The programme begins with a 'Gateway' period lasting up to four months. Here young people are given careers' advice and help with looking for work and training in the skills needed in work. After this time there are four options:

- working with an employer and receiving at least one day a week to study for a qualification – a wage subsidy of £60 a week is paid to the employer for a period of up to six months;
- a work placement with a voluntary organisation for six months, with day release to study;
- a six-month work placement with an Environmental Task Force, including day release;
- for people without basic qualifications, a place on a full-time education and training course for up to one year.

The New Deal for long-term unemployed people

Also introduced in 1998, this scheme is for adults who have been unemployed for two years or longer. Pilot programmes are being run in several areas of the country for people unemployed for shorter periods. The programme begins with an advisory interview, followed by support in seeking work (see above). Someone who still has not found work may be offered one of the following:

- work with an employer who receives a subsidy of £75 for up to six months;
- access to an employment-related course which can last for up to one year.

The New Deal for lone parents

This programme attempts to help lone parents on income support begin work. It consists of a series of interviews with a New Deal Personal Advisor to provide advice on job-seeking, benefits for working families and child-care.

Career development loans

These are operated by the Department of Employment in partnership with four banks. The loans are for people to pay for their own training. Loans of between £300 and £8000 are available to pay for 80 per cent of the costs of course fees and other expenses such as books. The loan can be for a course lasting up to two years or for the first two years of a longer course. No repayments need to be made during the course or for a month after the course ends. During this time the interest is paid by the Department for Education and Employment. Afterwards the repayments must be made with interest. People who are still unemployed after the course ends can apply to defer payments for a further five months.

Youth Training

Most 16- and 17-year-olds are not entitled to income support or Jobseeker's Allowance. Instead, young people who are not in education or work at this age are guaranteed a training place through Work-Based Training for Young People (WBTYP).

Training for all young people began in the 1970s with the Youth Opportunities Programme (YOP). In 1981, the government announced a massive Youth Training Scheme (YTS) which was to provide training and work experience for all 16-year-olds not in full-time education or work. The scheme was initially for one year but was extended to two years in 1985. YTS was originally run by the Manpower Services Commission but in 1988 this organisation was replaced by a Training Agency within the Department of Employment.

YTS was replaced in 1990 with Youth Training (YT). This was run by the local Training and Enterprise Councils (TECs). All young people aged 16 and 17 are eligible for YT and the government have guaranteed that a place is available for all who want one. The training is not limited to one or two years but gives the opportunity to train to National Vocational Qualification (NVQ) Level 2. Trainees receive a weekly allowance of £29.50 which increases to £35 on their seventeenth birthday. This can be topped up by the employer.

The various youth training schemes have been criticised for a number of reasons. In the beginning it was said that the schemes would not be made compulsory but in 1988 income support was withdrawn from 16- and 17-year-olds. In effect this meant the training scheme became compulsory. There is no guarantee of employment at the end of a training scheme and many young people have resented the idea of working for such low pay. Also schemes have varied in quality a great deal. Some are very good, offering high-quality training and valuable work experience; others do not meet this standard and offer routine and boring work with little training. Indeed, not all jobs require training or experience. In these cases, trainees feel they are being used as a source of cheap labour. Some schemes have provoked accusations of substitution, whereby employers have used trainees instead of workers on full pay. To the extent that this is the case, the schemes serve to increase, rather than decrease, unemployment. Figures from 1987 showed that just over half of young people on YTS found a job after training. The details were as follows:[21]

- 28 per cent found a full-time job with the employer with whom they had trained;

- 25 per cent found a full-time job with another employer;
- 4 per cent found a part-time job;
- 3 per cent went on to a full-time course;
- 6 per cent went on to another training scheme;
- 6 per cent did something else;
- 28 per cent were unemployed.

In 1997 a new strategy planned the replacement of Youth Training with Modern Apprenticeships and National Traineeships. Modern Apprenticeships train young people for jobs at craft, technician and trainee management level. They will eventually cover all sectors of the economy; early schemes included ones in banking, insurance and engineering. They offer NVQ/SVQ Level 3 qualifications. Modern apprenticeships are popular with young people intending to enter jobs in these areas. National traineeships offer broader learning programmes, focusing on key skills of communication, numeracy and information technology.

In 1997/98 there were 320,300 young people on the main government training programmes: Youth Training, Modern Apprenticeships and National Traineeships.[22] These three schemes are known together as 'Work-Based Training for Young People'. The programmes are run locally by TECs in England and Wales and LECs in Scotland. The minimum training allowance is £30 although some TECs and LECs set higher minimums.

Problems with government schemes

Although it is undoubtedly true that people have been helped by the programmes provided by the government there are problems with the various schemes.

One of the most obvious criticisms lies in the confusion caused by constant changes of names and rules and the bewildering numbers of acronyms used. Even the staff working in this area are said to have difficulty in keeping up to date with the changes and certainly this is the case for unemployed people, employers and the general public. There is also confusion over who is responsible for what scheme and sometimes a lack of co-ordination between trainers, colleges, TECs, the Employment Service and careers advisors.

It has been argued that schemes have been more concerned with reducing numbers of people on unemployment benefit than with helping long-term unemployed people. Many unemployed people found the letters they received worrying and felt anxious that the purpose of the interview was to somehow catch them out and withdraw their benefit. Certainly it is the case that along with these measures the government has introduced a number of methods to check on people's 'availability for work' and therefore entitlement to benefits.

Schemes such as the Jobclubs imply that people could get jobs if they were better at looking for work. With redundancies being announced each month, this seems a rather unfair blaming of unemployed people for a situation which is beyond their control. At best many unemployed people feel these courses are a pointless waste of time. The training provided on schemes is often too short and insufficiently funded to give people the kind of skills which are needed. A report on the New Deal found employers failing to provide any training at all.[23]

Many people have been concerned by the element of compulsion included when there is the threat of loss of benefits if people do not accept places on schemes.

The early years of the New Deal suggested it was more successful than other schemes, both in the response of unemployed people and employers and in its achievements in getting people into work. The New Deal is a more comprehensive and better-funded scheme than any which have gone before. It is however hard to evaluate the success of the New Deal since it has coincided with a growth in jobs which would in any case have reduced the number of people unemployed. A report from the National Centre for Social Research suggested however that many young people left the New Deal for short-term jobs and were unemployed again after a few months.[24]

Positive experiences on the New Deal for young people

Penny Pritchard, Plumber
Penny, 22 says: 'I was initially sceptical of the scheme, because they'd been other ones before which didn't work, but this one was different. The advisor was very helpful and didn't try to fob me off. I'd been on benefits for two years. I now install central heating systems. I'm taking driving lessons after Christmas so I can get to more customers. I'm also doing an NVQ Level 2 in plumbing. Some women customers like having a female plumber. I earn £72 a week take home pay.'

Barry Perkins, Warehouseman
Barry, 22 says: 'I had been unemployed for three years and was getting very depressed before I started on the New Deal. As soon as people heard I'd been unemployed for so long, they didn't want to know. But it only took two weeks for my New Deal adviser to get me this position. Some parts of the job were new to me, like health and safety and dealing with customers, but as numbers was my best subject at school, I've found I can do the stock-taking job quite well. As far as the New Deal being compulsory, people who can't be bothered to work shouldn't expect to get money for doing nothing.'[25]

Activity 4.8

Find out more about these and other schemes concerned with unemployment. The local JobCentre will have information and literature. Or go to the end of the chapter for websites and other sources of information.

Activity 4.9

In groups of three or four, think of policies which the government could implement in an attempt to solve the problem of unemployment. Note down arguments for and against each idea.

Work-sharing and job creation

The initiatives which have been described do little to solve the problem of there being more people wanting work than there is work available. There are proposals for more radical policies which would have a greater impact on unemployment. One such suggestion is for work-sharing. Work-sharing is not the same as job-sharing. Job-sharing refers to a situation where more than one person does a job. Work-sharing would mean adjusting working patterns of the whole society to fit the amount of work which is available. This has happened before in the sense that working hours have been reduced from the time when people worked an 80-hour, six-day week. Work-sharing could be achieved by reducing the working week to 35 hours with a statutory limit on overtime. This would be a way of allowing everyone to work for a shorter period, rather than having some people not working at all, whilst others work 40 hours and often more with overtime.

Another way of tackling unemployment was put forward by the Labour Party, whilst in opposition. Labour argued that government money should be used to create jobs in the public sector as a means of reducing unemployment. It is certainly true that although there is a shortage of jobs, many needs are not being met. Old people's homes and hospitals are two examples of areas of provision with a desperate need for more staff. Obviously, both the proposals outlined here cost money, but then so does unemployment.

Activity 4.10

Make sure that you understand the following expressions used in this chapter. Check in the Glossary at the end of the book if you need to.

acronym	status
cyclical unemployment	stigma
Disability Service Teams	structural unemployment
ethnic minority	Training and Enterprise
frictional unemployment	Councils (TECs)
National Vocational Qualification (NVQ)	voluntary organisation
pressure group	work-sharing
Restart	

Further reading

The Independent Unemployment Unit and Youthaid publish booklets providing information on training schemes and programmes for unemployed people. Their *Unemployment and Training Rights Handbook*, updated each year, provides full details of all the benefits and schemes for unemployed people.

Website

The Employment Service website can be found at **www.employmentservice.gov.uk**

⬛ ☑ **5** Housing and homelessness

People need shelter from the environment in the same way as they need food, as a condition for survival. Housing is also a necessary base for many other aspects of life, such as raising children. Housing is a political issue in that it reflects ideas about the way society should be organised. For example, housing can be seen as a social service, provided by the state, or as an area of life to be left to private individuals and free enterprise. Houses can be owned communally, by individuals or by various social groups. The size of buildings reflects ideas about ideal social groupings. For instance, in this society at this time most housing is designed for occupation by small groups of around four people, living as one household.

Activity 5.1

> Whilst there is a certain level of agreement on housing ideals, individual preferences do vary. Imagine you are looking for a home and think about the factors which are most important to you. Would you prefer to share with others or live alone? Would you rather rent or buy? Is your ideal location in a city, the country or a suburb? Would you like to live at the top of a high-rise block of flats or in a cottage with a garden? Compare your ideas with those of the rest of the group.

5.1 Social policy and housing

Since housing is so important and has political dimensions, it is not surprising that there is considerable state intervention. This began in the nineteenth century and takes many forms, including central and local government subsidies, control of planning, building of council houses and regulation of relations between landlords and tenants.

Housing is an extremely complex area of social policy. Housing shortages can only be prevented by anticipation of future housing needs. This is difficult to achieve since needs alter as society changes. It is not sufficient to predict changes in the population, since the number of households can also vary independently. For example, an increase in the number of single-parent families creates a demand for more housing, as does a tendency for young people to live apart from their parents. The prevention of problems associated with housing

Source: Martin Mayer, Network Photographers
A protest outside the Ideal Home Exhibition

also requires co-ordination of planning, building and the availability of money for housing. A number of agencies are involved in housing. Central government, through the Department of the Environment, Transport and the Regions (DETR) is responsible for establishing housing policies. Local authorities are involved in the implementation of these policies. Building societies and banks largely control the availability of mortgages, which affect house prices. Architects and

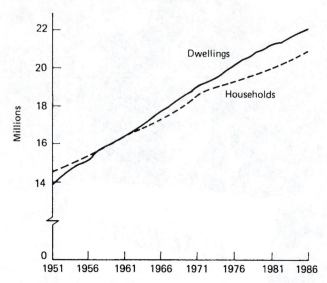

Source: Department of the Environment, Transport and the Regions
Figure 5.1   Households and dwellings, 1951–86

builders are also involved, as, of course, are ordinary people as 'consumers' of housing.

In Britain, at present, there is what is called a 'crude surplus' of housing. This means that there are more dwellings than households, by which is meant individuals or groups of people, living as separate units. Figure 5.1 shows the trend from 1951 to 1986.[1] Updating these figures with recent government statistics does not change the situation. The total number of dwellings in 1997 was 24.8 million. The number of households for 1998 was 23.6 million.[2] This is still a surplus of just over 1 million.

The fact that there is a crude surplus of housing does not however mean that there are no housing problems.

Activity 5.2

Make a list of reasons why it is possible for there to be both a crude surplus of housing and a housing shortage, at the same time.

There are several explanations for this seemingly contradictory situation. Housing is of little use if it is in the wrong place, for example where there is no employment. The properties may be unsuitable, too big or too small, unfit, or too expensive for people to be able to afford. A number of people own more than one house, and a number of properties are used for holiday lets. Also, the number of households may be misleading, in that some people live with others because they cannot find separate accommodation, for example, people who have to live with their parents.

5.2 Types of housing tenure

Housing can be seen as being made up of different sectors or types of *tenure.* Tenure describes the way in which houses are occupied. There are three main types of tenure: owner-occupation, where people are buying or already own their home; social housing, which includes renting from the local housing authority (council housing), a housing association or other landlord registered with the Housing Corporation (registered social landlords); and privately rented housing. These three types of tenure will be examined separately, although it should be remembered that they are not entirely distinct, in the sense that changes in one sector will have implications for the other two. Figure 5.2 shows the changes in tenure since 1914. [3]

Activity 5.3

Carry out a local survey of availability and costs of housing in each of the three sectors. In order to make a comparison, it is best to decide on a particular sort of property, for example a three-bedroomed estate house. Consult newspapers, the council, estate agents and letting agencies for information.

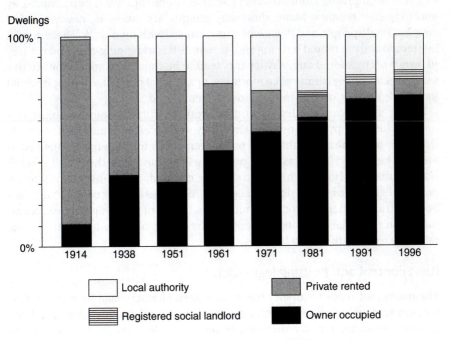

Source: Office for National Statistics, *Britain 1999.*
Figures 5.2   Changes in housing tenure, 1914–96

Privately-rented accommodation

Declining housing sector

At the time of the Second World War, the majority of homes were privately rented. The trend has been for this sector of housing to decline. This has happened as a result of several factors. At one time, buying or building property to rent was a good investment. Changes in taxation policies, and in interest rates for other forms of investment, now mean that rented property brings a comparatively low level of return on money invested. Inflation has also resulted in increased maintenance and repair costs. A number of rented properties were lost in the 1950s and 1960s as a result of slum-clearance programmes. The availability of improvement grants encouraged landlords to improve property and there was a tendency for such property then to be sold for owner-occupation. Tax relief on mortgages (abolished in 1999) increased the possibility and desirability of home-ownership. An important factor was also the introduction of legislation giving tenants security of tenure and controlling rents. For all these reasons, the decline in private renting has been such that, while in 1951, 52 per cent of homes were rented, only 10 per cent were privately rented in 1999.[4]

Least-favoured tenants

In Britain today, the worst-quality housing is concentrated in the privately-rented sector. There is a high proportion of accommodation which is old, lacking in basic amenities such as baths and inside toilets, and in a poor state of repair. The people who rent from private landlords can be seen as falling into two groups, short-stay and long-stay tenants. Many short-stay tenants are students, newly-married couples, single people and those who move around with their work. These groups live temporarily in rented housing and, for some, it is a stepping-stone on the way to owner-occupation. Long-stay tenants tend to be those who are trapped in this sector, because they cannot get a mortgage, or a council house. Such people would include those on a low income or who are unemployed.

Private tenants are the least-favoured group in current housing policy. Not only do they occupy the worst housing, they also receive no automatic subsidy from the state. The only subsidy to private tenants is through the means-tested housing benefits. Unlike tax relief on mortgages (now abolished) and council house subsidies, housing benefit has to be claimed, and consequently many people eligible for benefit do not receive it. Since 1994 the housing benefit has been restricted where the local authorities feel the rent is too high or the accommodation too large, and single people under 25 are likely to be limited to the rent for a room with shared facilities.

Rent control and housing legislation

The market for rented property has always been characterised by scarcity. This leads to unequal relations between landlords and tenants. Attempts have been made by governments to redress the balance and since the Second World War, rents have been controlled and de-controlled in a zig-zag fashion. The first period after the war was a period of rent control. In legislation passed in 1954

A roof, but is it a home for a family?

and 1957, the Conservative government removed rent controls. Some properties were to be decontrolled as tenants left and this led to cases of harassment and eviction of tenants by landlords. This phase ended in 1965, when tenants of unfurnished accommodation were given security of tenure, which meant they could not be evicted at the whim of the landlord. At the same time, the concept of a '*fair rent*' was introduced. This is a rent assessed on the basis of all aspects of the property, except scarcity value. The 1974 Housing Act extended security of tenure to furnished properties.

In 1980 a measure of decontrol was introduced by the Conservative government with the introduction of *shorthold* and *assured tenancies*. Shorthold tenancies are for a fixed period of between one and five years. Initially they had to be assessed for a fair rent by the rent officer, but this requirement was dropped. Assured tenancies replaced 'fair rent' tenancies and can be used by all private landlords and registered social landlords on new lettings. There is no limit to the rent that is agreed by the landlord and tenant at the beginning of a term, which can be for any period of time (in practice often six months). The tenancy automatically continues at the end of the term, unless either party gives notice for the tenancy to be ended or renewed on a new basis.

In 1988 controls were reduced further. Under this legislation, effective from 1989, all new tenancies are to be either shorthold or assured tenancies. This did not affect existing tenants. At the same time the laws against harassment were strengthened.

Activity 5.4

Do you think that relations between landlords and tenants should be regulated by law? Give reasons for your answer.

Landlords are in a more powerful position than tenants and the laws exist to correct the balance. Whilst the landlord is the owner of the property, it is important to remember that it is the tenant's home. People cannot enjoy their home if they can be evicted at any moment, or if the rent can suddenly increase to a level which means that they have to leave. Existing legislation does, however, have disadvantages. Many landlords exploit loopholes in the law, leaving tenants with no rights whatsoever. It is also the case that requests for a rent assessment often result in rents being increased. Legislation designed to help tenants can also work to their disadvantage, in that landlords are deterred from renting out property. It is also interesting to note that the decrease in controls on landlords has contributed to the huge rise in the cost to the government of *housing benefit*, since many tenants of private landlords are claiming benefits. This forced the government to introduce restrictions on housing benefit in 1994 (see above). Further proposals to reduce the cost of housing benefit by using tax credits were announced in 1999.

Social housing

Housing societies and housing associations

A proportion of rented property is available from organisations within the voluntary housing movement, which operate on a non-profit-making basis. Voluntary housing has a long history in terms of small-scale provision of rented accommodation for the homeless, the elderly and the disabled. However, in the 1950s, the decline in private rented property caused Conservative politicians to be concerned about the dominant role being assumed by local authority housing, a concern based on a belief that council tenants voted Labour. The Conservatives saw housing societies as an alternative form of housing in this situation.

Housing societies and housing associations had been similar sorts of organisations up to this point. Following the 1961 Housing Act, housing societies were defined as organisations which built new houses and let them at cost-rents. The Act gave the societies access to low-interest government loans for this purpose. Since cost rents would be relatively high, this form of housing was only available to those with a higher than average income. In 1964 the loan provision was extended and the Housing Corporation set up to act as a clearing-house for government funds. However, by the 1970s, high interest rates meant that it was no longer feasible to charge cost-rents on new houses. This prevented any further expansion in the role of housing societies.

The 1974 Housing Act allowed housing associations, as well as housing societies, to receive money through the Housing Corporation. Housing association priorities were outlined as being to improve housing, increase the amount of property available for rent and help people in special need such as those with disabilities. Following this legislation, housing societies increased in importance. They have been particularly active in buying up older, inner-city property, improving it and letting it to existing tenants and people in need.

The role of housing associations changed again and expanded as a result of legislation in 1988. This encouraged housing associations to set up housing schemes with half the funds coming from the Housing Corporation and half raised from the private sector. The rents charged have to be high enough to pay back the loan from the private sector.

The Conservative government made it clear that from 1988 onwards housing associations would be the major providers of new social housing – the role previously of the local authorities. The Labour government elected in 1997 has continued the commitment to the housing associations' role in social housing. As a result, the housing association sector is expanding rapidly. From owning just over 500,000 homes in 1988 they grew to own over a million.[5] In the late 1990s housing associations were building 50 houses for every one built by a local council. *Registered Social Landlords*, which include housing associations and other non-profit-making organisations providing housing to rent or buy, receive grants from the Housing Corporation. In 1998–99 the Housing Corporation had provision for about £900 million in grants.[6] Housing associations also continue to supplement the money raised from grants with private-sector loans.

The recent expansion of the role of housing associations has led to some concern that they will inherit the problems traditionally associated with council housing: the bad image which attached to some council estates may now be transferred to housing association developments.

Council housing

In Britain, the state has in the past played an active part in providing housing for rent. However, since the Second World War, there have been changes, both in terms of the priority given to public housing and the role allocated to such provision. In the period immediately after the war, providing council-housing was an important part of housing policy. The aim was to build good-quality houses available at rents which people could afford. The houses were to be for any citizen and not restricted to the poor or those living in slums. Later, council housing came to be seen as a second-class alternative for disadvantaged people.

Eligibility

The fact that generally the demand for council housing is greater than the supply has resulted in provision being limited to certain categories of people. People eligible for housing are those needing to be rehoused as a result of redevelopment, those in need and homeless people. Need is usually decided on the basis of a points system, taking into account factors such as length of residence in the area, existing housing, the size of the household and health problems. Most councils have long waiting-lists, on which applicants are placed according to the urgency of their need for housing. In 1977 the Homeless Persons Act gave local authorities the duty to house homeless people. This tended to give homeless people priority over others on the waiting-list for local authority housing. The 1996 Housing Act took away homeless people's right to permanent housing and set up the National Housing Register as a single route into permanent social housing. When the Labour Party were elected a year later, they reintroduced a 'reasonable preference' which allows councils to use their discretion in giving homeless people priority. People on the register have the right to see their entry and to be given information about how long they are likely to have to wait.

Activity 5.5

Find out from your local council the policy for selection of tenants, and the number of people on the waiting-list. Do you think some people, such as those who are homeless, should have priority over others, who have been on the waiting-list for a longer time?

Responsibilities and allocation

Council housing is administered by local authority housing departments. Since these are controlled by councillors, there is considerable regional variation, according to the political composition of the council. For example, Labour-controlled councils have tended to be more committed to providing public housing and keeping rents as low as possible. Housing departments have a variety of responsibilities. These include the designing and building of houses and flats. The housing department also decides the rents to be charged. However, local authorities are restricted by central government regulations and limits imposed on expenditure.

Tenant's Charter

In 1992, the Conservative government introduced a Tenant's Charter for council tenants, setting out their rights. This covers areas such as allocation of housing, security of tenure and repairs.

Sale of council houses

The most important issue in public housing has been the sale of council houses. Legislation was passed in 1957 which allowed councils to sell off property. As a result, some councils, mainly those with a Conservative majority, did pursue this policy. The 1980 Housing Act established the 'right to buy'. Under this clause of the Act, tenants can buy their homes with discounts of 33 per cent for those who have been tenants for three years, rising to 50 per cent for tenants of thirty years' occupancy. In 1983, the qualifying period was reduced from three to two years. People who wish to take up this option are also entitled to a mortgage which covers 100 per cent of the cost of the property and the legal fees involved.

In 1986 a new scale of discounts was introduced for flats. The discount starts at 44 per cent for a tenant of two years' standing and goes up to 70 per cent for a tenant who has been with the council for 15 years or more. It was Conservative policy to encourage tenants to buy in two ways: first, through the discount scheme, and second, by increasing rents. In the period 1979–80, council rents rose by 117 per cent.[7] Some Labour-controlled authorities attempted to resist the right-to-buy policy, but in 1982, it was ruled in court that one such council must speed up its sales process or have its housing department taken over by central government. Between April 1979 and the end of 1991 some 1.8 million council, housing association and new town homes were sold in Great Britain.[8] Although dropping below the 1982 peak of 200,000 sales, in 1997 57,000 dwellings were sold.[9] In 1993 new legislation introduced a Rent-to-Mortgage Scheme whereby local authority tenants can buy their homes by initially paying only the amount they would have been paying in rent. Also some local authorities operate a Cash Incentive Scheme which gives tenants cash towards buying a house in the private sector.

Activity 5.6

What are the advantages, and the disadvantages, of giving council tenants the right to buy their home at a discount price?

The question of council house sales can be looked at in two ways, from the point of view of the tenant wishing to buy and from an approach taking into account the interests of others. Home-ownership is seen as desirable and therefore individual tenants benefit from being able to realise this ideal, with the help of generous discounts and mortgage provision. People who buy have greater freedom to carry out repairs and to 'personalise' their homes. However, home-ownership can become a burden and a liability. There is the fear of not being able to keep up with mortgage repayments and consequent court orders, with ultimate repossession of the property by the lender. There is also the responsibility of repairs which can be an unforeseen cost. Balancing these factors, the majority of council tenants who buy their home probably do benefit from the transaction.

The disadvantages become clearer when the issue is looked at from a more general point of view. Council housing was introduced in order to provide decent homes at rents which people could afford. Once houses are sold, they are no longer available for future tenants. This will lead to problems where little council housing is available and local authorities are required to house victims of redevelopment schemes and other homeless people. In financial terms, it has been calculated that the sale of council houses means a long-term net loss to the state.[10]

The properties which are being sold are the better council houses. Few people would consider buying a high-rise flat, or a low-quality house on a disreputable estate. Also, the allocation policies described above mean that the better-off tenants, those most likely to be in a position to buy, have the best housing. This situation has several consequences. It means that government discounts are available to those least in need, many of whom could afford to buy on the open market if they so wished. Councils are left with older, less desirable properties in which to house needy families. This increases the already-present stigma attached to local authority housing. Finally, council tenants in low-quality accommodation have less chance of moving into better housing. However, it is possible that a revised policy could avoid these disadvantages of selling rented properties.

Changing government policy

Government policy in the 1980s and 1990s has been to reduce the role of local authorities as providers of housing. It is argued that local authorities should rather work with housing associations and the private sector, allowing them to take over the role of providing rented property. The 'right to buy' is an aspect of this policy.

In the 1980s other schemes were introduced to transfer housing from local authorities. Tenants Choice and Housing Action Trusts were intended to allow tenants to opt to transfer to a new landlord. Neither of the schemes were popular with tenants; Tenants Choice has been scrapped and Housing Action Trusts proved very expensive and are being wound up. Large-Scale Voluntary Transfers have been much more significant in reducing the number of properties owned by local councils. Around 60 local authorities have transferred all or part of their housing to Registered Social Landlords, usually housing associations, involving the transfer of 250,000 properties by the end of 1997.[11] In most cases the local authority has transferred all property and therefore is no longer required to manage a waiting-list for housing. The local authority can use the money gained for other services or to pay off debts. Most of the transfers in the 1990s have been in the South of England.

Owner-occupation

Since the Second World War, there has been a considerable increase in the proportion of people who own their homes. In 1951, for example, only 30 per cent were owner-occupiers, while in 1997 the figure was 67 per cent.[12]

Activity 5.7

Why might people want to own a home of their own?

Incentives to buy

Government papers in the 1970s suggested that the desire to own property is natural.[13] Yet it is a recent phenomenon and can be seen as resulting from several political and economic factors. Government policies resulted in strong financial incentives to buy. Tax relief has been given on mortgage-interest payments (this was abolished in 2000 – see below) and housing made free from capital gains tax. Also, inflation in the 1980s meant that home-ownership was a wise investment, since repayments remained the same, while wages and the value of the property increased (but see the discussion of 'negative equity' below). Many schemes such as the Right to Buy, shared ownership and cash incentive schemes have more recently encouraged people on lower incomes to move into home ownership.

Some people buy a house because there is no other alternative. Privately-rented property is scarce, expensive and does not provide security of tenure. In most areas of the country, council accommodation is not available to those without children. Other advantages of owner-occupation are the degree of choice and freedom from restrictions, both of which are greater than in the other two housing sectors. There is also considerable social status attached to home-ownership.

The ideal of owner-occupation has been an integral part of Conservative party policy. Labour governments in the past were less committed to the philosophy of home-ownership, but always conscious of the numbers of people who own, or want to own, a house, and mindful of the potential vote-loss involved in withdrawing the privileges attached to owning property. The 1990s saw a coming together of Conservative and Labour approaches to housing as Labour withdrew their commitment to public housing. There are still differences between the two parties, but these are much less clear-cut than in earlier times.

Government funds have been channelled into building societies and the tax relief on private housing has constituted a major housing subsidy. In 1990–91 the cost to the government of mortgage interest tax relief (known as MIRAS) was £8.3 billion.[14] Through the 1990s the figure dropped as interest rates fell and the government reduced the amount of relief allowed. Mortgage tax relief has been abolished altogether from 2000 (see Figure 5.3).[15] Decreasing interest rates and therefore housing costs made it easier for the government to make what had been previously a politically difficult and unpopular decision. These changes, although perhaps not liked by home-owners, have been welcomed by housing policy experts who had long criticised the unfair subsidy to home-owners. In the past this was especially unfair, as those in owner-occupation were generally much better off than people in rented accommodation. Also the larger the house, and therefore mortgage, people had, the larger the subsidy they received. (As house prices overtook the limit of the tax relief, this second point no longer

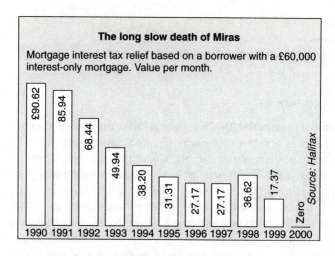

Source: *Guardian*, 10 March 1999, p. 17

Figure 5.3   Decline in mortgage tax relief, 1990–2000

applied.) Mortgage tax relief was therefore an example of a *regressive subsidy* – one which benefited the better-off and least in need of state support – and this is why it was criticised.

Mortgages and loans for housing

Few people can afford to buy a house outright, and therefore most have to obtain a loan. There are several ways of raising a mortgage, which is simply a type of loan, whereby the lender owns the property until the money owed is paid off. The four most common sources of funds are building societies, banks and insurance companies. Building societies have a long history and still play the largest part in providing mortgages. They were originally literally building societies, in which skilled workers clubbed together to build houses. The role of building societies has changed to the extent that today they do not build properties, but provide investment and lending facilities.

Initially building societies were reluctant to take risks with the money available to them. This meant that they would only lend to people who meet certain conditions, and who wanted to buy particular sorts of properties. The ideal borrower was probably a young professional married man with a high and secure salary. In terms of property, the societies were conscious that, in the event of non-repayment of the loan, they would have to be able to sell the house or flat. The ideal property was seen as being a family-sized, modern house in a residential suburb and better terms were available for such properties.

In the 1970s, it was discovered that building societies were operating a policy which came to be known as 'red-lining'. The term originates from the idea of lines marked on a map of a town and the implication is that societies will not provide money for properties in certain areas. The way in which this policy works is demonstrated in the following quotation from Short's research on housing:

> During an interview with a branch manager of a major building society the term red-lining came up. The manager stated categorically, 'we do not red-line'. Later in the discussion he pointed to the St Paul's district of Bristol on the map and said that 'there are certain areas in the city, however, where we won't lend.'[16]

The significance of red-lining was that the building societies, despite their benevolent image, were contributing to the circular process of inner-city decay.

Although there are still people who find it difficult to get a mortgage from a building society, changes in building society policies and competition from banks have made it much easier for a more diverse group of people to get mortgages on a wider range of housing. Owner-occupation is no longer limited to well-off people with secure incomes. As well as providing benefits, this has created some problems of its own, as the next section shows.

Repossession, mortgage arrears and 'negative equity'

The extension of owner-occupation to people who are not so well off as previously has begun to create problems for some. The 1980s and 1990s saw a rapid rise in the numbers of repossessions of houses by building societies for non-payment of mortgages. In 1997, 32,770 home-owners had their houses repossessed and 236,900 people were more than three months behind with their mortgage payments and therefore in danger of repossession.[17]

In 1991, the government announced measures to prevent repossessions in cases of arrears. These include provisions for benefits to be paid direct to lenders and encouragements to banks and building societies to develop schemes to allow people to remain in their homes. The increase in repossessions since 1984 slowed in 1992.

A new problem for home-owners in the 1990s was been that of 'negative equity'. For a long time it was believed that house prices could only go up and that housing was always a good investment. Massive price rises in the early 1980s created a rush to buy and many people, particularly in the South, bought at hugely inflated prices. This period was however followed by one in which house prices, again particularly in the South, fell rapidly. People who bought at the peak of the rise were left with properties worth less than the price they paid and therefore loans higher than the value of the property. Figures from the Bank of England revealed that, in 1993, 1.3 million owners were in this situation, known as 'negative equity'.[18] This creates anxiety for people wanting to move or needing to sell for other reasons. It also means that people who have houses repossessed will still owe money on their mortgage after the house has been sold.

Lenders have introduced schemes to alleviate this situation but these are not well publicised. Negative Equity Mortgage Schemes allow people to move, transferring the negative equity to their new house.

5.3 Housing and race

When black people came to Britain in the 1950s, work was available, but not housing. As a result of discrimination and existing housing problems, ethnic minorities became concentrated in areas of poor housing and general deprivation. Ironically, some sections of the white population then argued that black people created poor housing conditions, and for some reason liked to live in slums. However, in the words of the Community Relations Council:

> All the evidence shows that there are no differences between black and white households in the quality of housing they aspire to. Inadequate space standards and poor conditions are largely the result of the weak position of minority households in the housing market.[19]

Statistics show there to be a number of differences between black and white people in terms of housing. Indian people are the group most likely to own their own home with four out of five (80 per cent) doing so. Black Caribbeans are less likely than the general population to own their own homes.[20] The unusually high incidence of owner-occupation amongst Asians is explained by the existence of direct and indirect discrimination in other sectors of housing. Private landlords have discriminated against black people, although this is of course against the law. A black actor tested accommodation agencies for a survey carried out by the Commission for Racial Equality. He was shocked when the white tester who went in after him came out with more addresses in the same area and the same price range. 'I'd never have known', said the black tester, 'She was so friendly and helpful.'[21]

In the public sector there has been evidence of some direct discrimination together with indirect discrimination in the form of clauses stating that applicants must have been resident in the area for a certain period of time. The Commission for Racial Equality found that in Liverpool ethnic minority families had to wait longer for a council home, and had far less chance than white people of getting a house with central heating and a garden.[22] It is also the case that the type of local authority housing available does not meet the needs of some Asian families.

In all racial groups, the majority of people borrowed money from building societies for purchase of a house, but other forms of finance are more common for Asian and West Indians than for whites.[23] A relatively large proportion of Asians have loans from a bank. This reflects the difficulties they have experienced when seeking property they can afford which is large enough for their households. Such properties are often in inner-city areas not popular with building societies or in need of too much repair.

Estate agents have been found to be illegally discriminating against ethnic minorities. An estate agent told white people in a survey carried out by the Commission for Racial Equality they would not want to live in certain areas 'because of the Asians'. They did not tell this to Asian people.[24] This discrimination has the effect of segregating people by race and also makes it harder for Asians to sell houses as fewer people are sent to view and forces prices down for Asian owners.

The overall trend in housing is that the best-quality housing is that which is owner-occupied. In spite of this and the fact that a high proportion of black people own their own homes, a higher percentage of black than white households live in poor-quality homes. Black home-owners are more likely than whites to be sharing, to be overcrowded and to live in houses which lack basic amenities such as inside toilets. Members of ethnic minorities are concentrated in older housing in inner-city areas. Similarly those members of ethnic groups who are in council housing are allocated to less desirable properties, and are again more likely to be sharing, to be overcrowded and to lack basic facilities.[25]

5.4   Homelessness

Who is 'homeless'?

Despite the surplus of housing referred to at the beginning of this chapter, there are people in Britain without a home. Understanding of this problem is hindered by the lack of statistics showing the full extent of the situation. The official statistics on homelessness are restricted to the number of people accepted by local authorities as homeless. These statistics have several limitations. Homelessness is defined in the narrow sense of 'being without accommodation'. People who are homeless may not approach the council or may be turned away. The voluntary organisation most concerned with homelessness, Shelter, argues that the definition should be broadened to include those who do not have a home, rather than simply counting the number of people without a roof over their heads.

Activity 5.8

Think about what is implied by the term 'home'. Write a full definition of what it means to have a home. Discuss your ideas with the rest of the class.

In its definition of homelessness, Shelter includes people who have accommodation which is insecure, overcrowded, dangerous, damp or lacking in basic amenities. People who are 'squatting' are considered homeless, as are those living with relatives, for example, married couples living with their parents.

In 1997, 165,790 households were accepted as homeless by local authorities in Great Britain.[26] The number of people homeless in terms of a wider definition is unknown.

Causes of homelessness

The causes of homelessness can be looked at in several ways. At one level, homelessness is caused by a national shortage of adequate and suitable housing in the right places and available at the right price. It is also possible to examine immediate reasons for particular cases of homelessness. Figure 5.4 shows the reasons given by people accepted as homeless by local authorities in 1997–98.[27] It should be borne in mind however that statistics do not necessarily tell the

Percentages

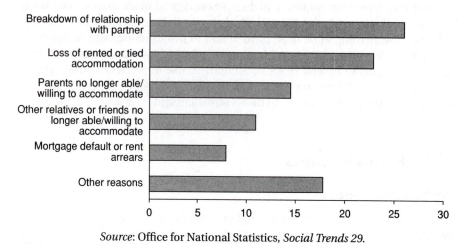

Source: Office for National Statistics, *Social Trends 29.*

Figure 5.4   Households accepted as homeless by local authorities: by main reason for loss of last settled home, 1997–98

Empty houses, yet homeless families

whole story, since a breakdown in a relationship for example could be caused by poverty or over-crowding.

A third way to think about the causes of homelessness involves considering groups of people who are excluded from access to particular types of housing. People who are low-paid or unemployed find it more difficult to get mortgages – this would include many single-parent families. Black people have, as we have seen, suffered from discrimination by building societies, estate agents and private landlords. Local authority housing policies have also indirectly discriminated against immigrants through residence clauses. Landlords are sometimes reluctant to let to people with children and usually demand references which can be a problem for people who have been in prison and other institutions. Local authority policies operate to the disadvantage of single and childless people.

Activity 5.9

People leaving community homes and psychiatric hospitals often experience particular housing difficulties. Find out from your local social services department if any special help is given to such people in your area.

The consequences of homelessness

Homelessness has severe consequences for the individuals concerned and for society. It can lead to unemployment and to the break-up of families and can result in children being taken into care. The physical effects on health and the psychological effects are also serious. It is likely that homelessness will increase in future years. This is mainly because there has been a decrease in the building of new houses. In 1980, a start was made on 152,000 houses – the lowest figure in peace-time since the 1920s.[28] The number has risen a little since this time, but is still much lower than in previous decades.

Temporary housing for homeless people

Local authorities have had duties towards homeless people for some time. Between 1948 and 1977, the legal requirements were set out in Part III of the 1948 National Assistance Act. This stated that local authorities had to provide temporary accommodation for people in urgent need. The provision came to be known as Part III accommodation. Local authority temporary housing was often in a poor state of repair and characterised by restrictive rules, for example, banning husbands (housing women and their children only and not allowing men to stay with their families, even overnight). The demand for Part III accommodation increased in the 1950s as a result of the decline in privately-rented property.

The pressure on temporary housing continued to increase in the 1960s and 1970s. In response, local authorities in London began to use bed-and-breakfast accommodation as a solution to the problem. This policy has since spread to other areas of the country, reaching a peak in 1991 with 12,200 families in bed and breakfast.[29]

The unsatisfactory nature of bed-and-breakfast provision for homeless families is illustrated in the following description:

Life in such places was awful. Often a whole family would live in one room, with nowhere to cook – meals had to be bought in a local cafe. Facilities for washing clothes would often be non-existent. In many places families were required to leave the guest-house after breakfast and walk the streets all day, until they were allowed back in the evening. Families with babies would often have to smuggle in electric kettles or small stoves in order to be able to heat up bottles. As one family told me, 'We do our ironing on a tiny coffee table or on the floor. The only meal you can get here is breakfast and you can't cook so we either live on sandwiches or fish and chips. The kids have to sit on the beds and eat their chips. We haven't had a Sunday dinner for nearly a year.' In short, bed-and-breakfast is no 'holiday on the rates' – rather it makes normal family life impossible.[30]

Despite the inadequacy of guest-house accommodation for a homeless family, it costs local authorities considerable sums of money. The cost in 1986 to the London boroughs alone was £63 million.[31] More recent figures calculated by Shelter show that the annual cost of building a new home would be less than councils pay to keep people in bed and breakfast.[32]

Some hotels were set up specifically to exploit the situation and the high profits to be made. A report in a newspaper in 1987 told of a group of three London hotels who were found to be charging more than twice their usual rate to the council to provide fewer facilities. Tourists paid £8 to £15 a night whilst council tenants paid £17.50 to £34. Up to six people shared one room.[33]

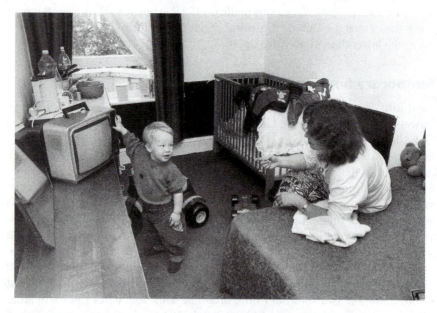

Source: Crispin Hughes, Photofusion
Life in 'bed-and-breakfast' accommodation

At the end of March 1998 local councils were housing 47,080 households in temporary accommodation. Of these 4770 households were in bed-and-breakfast hostels. The rest were in hostels, social housing or private-sector rented accommodation. The cost of providing temporary accommodation between 1996 and 1997 was over £185 million.[34] Shelter argues that living in temporary accommodation seriously affects the quality of people's lives and is never a substitute for a permanent home.

Activity 5.10

Find out from your local housing department what provision is made for homeless people in your area. What kind of accommodation is used for temporary housing of homeless people? Maybe you can visit a hostel and see what life there is like.

Homelessness legislation

The 1977 Housing (Homeless Persons) Act gave new responsibilities to local authorities and a right to a permanent home for homeless people. The same rights were included in the updating of the legislation in the 1985 Housing Act. As mentioned earlier, the Act defines people as homeless if they have no accommodation which they are entitled to occupy. People can also be considered homeless if they cannot occupy their home because of violence or the threat of violence. While the Housing Act was passed as a result of pressure put on the government by groups concerned with homelessness and is an improvement on the previous situation, problems remained. The Act contained a clause freeing local authorities from responsibility for those who are considered to have 'intentionally' made themselves homeless. The interpretation of this clause can cause problems for homeless people. For example, people who accept advice from bank managers to sell their homes to pay off debts can be argued to be intentionally homeless. Similarly, eviction following rent arrears can be looked at in this way. The clause on intentional homelessness can also be used against people who, not understanding their rights, leave rented property when told to do so by the landlord.

The following extract from a Shelter report shows how the intentional homelessness clause has been used:

Mr and Mrs H and their two children rented a flat from a landlord who later fell into arrears with the mortgage on it. Repossession was on the cards, which would mean the tenants would be evicted at the same time. The H family decided to move out before the inevitable happened, and accepted an offer from Mr H's employer to put them up in a caravan. But as there was no planning permission for the site the Council forced the employer to put the family out. The Council then declared them 'intentionally' homeless because they had given up their initial accommodation, which the Council regarded as 'secure'. The Council discharged its responsibility to the family by finding them accommodation in a hotel at their own expense.[35]

Priority need

Another problem with the legislation on homelessness was that the Act only required local authorities to house homeless people who are defined as being in 'priority need'. Priority-need groups include households with dependent children or pregnant women, the elderly and people with health problems.

1996 Housing Act

The 1996 Housing Act made the situation more difficult still for homeless families. Since the Act was passed, local authorities are only required to provide temporary accommodation for households in priority need.

Single homeless people: living on the streets

The system of priority need ignores the problems faced by single homeless people. As a result of this and other policies such as the withdrawal of benefit for 16- and 17-year-olds, increased numbers of people began sleeping rough. Considerable publicity was given to people living on the streets in towns like London. The 1991 Census recorded 2674 people sleeping rough in England.

Source: J. Southworth, Photofusion
Changes to benefit rules in 1988 caused some young people to become homeless and destitute

Shelter however argue that the figure is much higher, estimating there are 8600 people sleeping rough.[36] There are a number of shelters and hostels run by voluntary organisations such as Centrepoint in London. In 1990–91 the government introduced the *Rough Sleepers' Initiative* to provide additional beds in hostels and other temporary accommodation. Some £96 million was spent in three years and surveys have shown a drop in the number of people living on the streets.

In 1991 the *Big Issue* was set up in London. The newspaper is produced and sold by homeless people and the profits ploughed back into helping homeless people. From an original circulation of 30,000, the *Big Issue* is now sold nationally with sales over 271,000.[37]

Foyers

Foyers began in the United Kingdom in 1992, inspired by a movement of the same name in France.[38] Foyers involve a partnership between government, the private sector and voluntary organisations, including housing associations and the YMCA, to provide accommodation, training and support for young people in need aged between 16 and 25. 'Drop-in' resource areas provide support for residents and non-residents in looking for work and in dealing with other personal and social problems. By 1999 around 60 Foyers had been set up in Britain and another 40 were planned. Research on Foyers has found that most people find the services provided useful although in other reports young people complained they had too little freedom and not enough support:[39]

> Sarah [not her real name] left school at 16 and was thrown out of her home soon afterwards. For five years she went from job to job until she was taken on to a New Deal programme. There she decided she wanted more education and started a GNVQ in Health and Social Care at Brighton College of Technology. About the same time she split up with her boyfriend and found herself without a home. She went to live at Brighton Foyer so she could continue with her course.[40]

Squatting

Homelessness, combined with the existence of a large number of empty properties, led to an increase in squatting in the late 1960s and early 1970s. Squatters occupy empty houses illegally. This attracted considerable attention from the media, focusing mainly on mythical cases of squatters moving into houses while the owners were on holiday. An important consequence of the actions of squatters was that, in 1969, the government issued a circular urging local authorities to use their empty property as short-life housing. Such housing was let, on a temporary basis, to licensed tenants or turned over for management by housing associations. Surveys have suggested that in 1990 there were some 30,000 squatters in London and about 50,000 in the UK as a whole.[35]

In 1977, squatting was made into a criminal offence instead of a civil offence, as previously. As a result, squatters can be arrested by the police and, if convicted, fined £1000 or given a six-month prison sentence. In 1994 the Criminal Justice and Public Order Act brought in new measures to speed up removal of squatters. Under an 'interim possession order' a judge will require squatters to leave within 24 hours. Anyone not leaving is then committing a criminal offence and can be evicted by the police.

5.5   Bad housing and rehabilitation

Housing standards have risen this century and Britain is one of the best-housed countries in the world. However, there remains a significant proportion of housing which is unfit or without basic amenities. In 1996, 7.2 per cent of dwellings were judged unfit for human habitation because of inadequate facilitities for cooking or disrepair and dampness. The highest proportion of unfit housing was in the private rented sector where 15.1 per cent of properties were unfit for human habitation.[41] In the same year there were 207,000 dwellings in which people lacked basic amenities, such as a bath or shower with hot and cold water and an inside toilet.[42]

Social effects

The effects of poor housing on those who live in such conditions are considerable. Damp or dangerous houses are a risk to health. When houses are in a poor state of repair, attempts at improving or maintaining living conditions often produce little result. For example, decorating quickly becomes a pointless exercise if damp means that wallpaper will not stay on the wall. Old, poorly-maintained houses are difficult to keep clean. These factors have a morale-reducing effect on people trying to maintain a home in such conditions. The risk of marital breakdown or domestic violence is present if partners blame each other for their situation or express their frustration through violence. Poor housing can result in children being taken into the care of the local authority. Young people living in inadequate housing may spend more time on the streets and risk getting into trouble with the police. These problems are of concern to society as well as to the individuals concerned.

Possible solutions: rehouse or rehabilitate?

There are several possible solutions to the problem of bad housing. In the period following the Second World War, local authorities were encouraged to demolish older properties and build new estates, often in the form of tower blocks. Some twenty years later, disillusionment with such policies led to increased interest in the rehabilitation of housing.

Changing government thinking

The following extract demonstrates the shift in government thinking:

> The Government believes that, in the majority of cases, it is no longer preferable to attempt to solve the problems arising from bad housing by schemes of

widespread, comprehensive redevelopment. Such an approach often involves massive and unacceptable disruption of communities and leaves vast areas of our cities standing derelict and devastated for far too long. Regardless of the financial compensation they receive, many people suffer distress when their homes are compulsorily acquired. Increasing local opposition to redevelopment proposals is largely attributable to people's understandable preference for the familiar and, in many ways, more convenient environment in which they have lived for years. Large-scale redevelopment frequently diminishes rather than widens the choice available to people in terms of style of houses, their form of tenure, and their price.[43]

Activity 5.11

List as many advantages as you can think of for rehabilitation rather than demolition of older properties.

It has been increasingly recognised that redevelopment has costs and disadvantages. In purely financial terms it is cheaper to improve existing properties than to build new ones. In 1969, it was estimated that it would cost £600 million per annum to construct 200,000 council houses, while the same number of properties could be rehabilitated for £115 million.[44] While costs of building fluctuate, it is probably still cheaper to renovate old houses than to pull them down and build new ones.

The social costs of breaking up established communities are now acknowledged. This can be seen in the following quotation from Peter Walker, when Secretary of State for the Environment:

New homes are not enough. We need many more new houses, but it should be remembered that whilst new homes take a matter of months to build, it takes much longer to build a new community ... We have established communities with their local churches, their local schools, their local pubs and their local football teams, where the inhabitants are friends and neighbours of each other. It is important that where possible, instead of using the bulldozer we retain the community and improve the quality of the housing and the environment.[45]

Dangers of community break-up

Whilst there is a danger of becoming too romantic about the virtues of areas of older housing, research such as that carried out by Young and Willmott demonstrated the existence of extended families and community network.[46] Breaking up such communities can have far-reaching and unforeseen effects. It can mean the loss of support for people such as young mothers and the elderly, resulting in increased pressure on social services departments. In long-established communities, the inhabitants know one another and this can constitute a form of self-policing. For example, a stranger entering a property will be noticed or young people getting into trouble reported to their parents. Many of the newer estates are characterised by a high level of crime and vandalism.

Demolition often meant that people were moved out of city areas to estates on the edge of the town. This could lead to isolation and increased costs for travel to work or to visit friends and relatives. The policy of moving people into high-rise flats is now acknowledged as having created many new problems. It is difficult for inhabitants of such housing to feel a sense of territory, either as individuals or as a community. There is a feeling of being cut off from social contact, especially for people remaining at home during the day. Practical problems also arise – for example, parents cannot allow children to play out alone. Many of the tower blocks were shoddily constructed and not maintained adequately. Commonly, lifts break down, and there is a high level of vandalism to the buildings. High-rise flats are not necessarily always unsuitable as places to live, but they cause problems for families with young children and elderly people.

Finally, re-housing people who already have homes adversely affects those on council waiting-lists, delaying the possibility of their being offered housing.

Improvement policy

There has been legislation allowing local authorities to improve housing for some fifty years. However, little was done as a result of early legislation, as the impetus was towards redevelopment, rather than rehabilitation. From 1959, local authorities were required to make grants available to owners installing basic amenities such as baths. In 1964, local authorities were given the power to compel owners to renovate properties in designated improvement areas. This provision was extended in 1969 through legislation which followed the publication of the government paper 'Old Houses into New Homes'. The following extract from the paper describes local authorities' new powers to create General Improvement Areas:

> Local authorities should have power to declare General Improvement Areas. The aim in these areas would be to help and persuade owners to improve their houses and to help them also by improving the environment. Authorities would be able to buy land and buildings and carry out work for this purpose. They would also have power to buy houses for improvement and conversion and to buy any houses which were unfit and which stood in the way of improvement of the whole area.[47]

The General Improvement Areas were introduced in the 1969 Housing Act as small areas of approximately 300 houses. As a result of this legislation, the number of grants allocated increased considerably. In 1974, Housing Action Areas (HAAs) were introduced. These were also small areas and were to be characterised by social factors such as overcrowding, the proportion of large families and elderly people. In these areas, local authorities could work directly on improvement, and housing associations were encouraged to acquire and manage property.

As is often the case in social policy, even with well-intentioned proposals, the laws did not always work to the advantage of those it intended to benefit. Problems arose as landlords improved properties with the assistance of grants, only to sell the property or evict poor tenants and bring in better-off people who could afford higher rents. People were thus pushed out of the improved areas, and forced to move into other run-down properties. Restrictions were introduced in an attempt to prevent this process, but they were inadequate and came too late to be fully effective.

In the 1990s, the government's emphasis has been on improving existing housing stock, rather than demolition. The *Estate Action Programme* began in 1985, providing local authorities with extra resources to regenerate run-down estates. Run-down estates are now improved through the Single Regeneration Budget Challenge Fund which supports housing improvements undertaken by local partnerships. Over 200 local Housing Improvement Agencies operate schemes known as 'Care and Repair' or 'Staying Put' which provide independent advice and help for older people, disabled people and those on low incomes carrying out repairs and improvements to their properties.

The 1988 Housing Act provided for housing estates to be taken out of the control of the local authorities and run by *Housing Action Trusts* (HATs). The HATs would improve the estate with money from central government and then sell them to a new landlord within 5 years. The first batch of estates, 18 in six inner-city areas, was announced for a programme starting in 1988 with a budget of £125 million. As a result of protests by tenants, a House of Lords' amendment allowed tenants to vote on their change of landlord. HATs proved unpopular with tenants and only six HATs were established in Hull, Liverpool, Birmingham and the London boroughs of Waltham Forest, Tower Hamlets and Brent. The programme has now been wound down.

Grants to enable owner-occupiers to improve their houses have been cut. The 1989 Local Government and Housing Act allows grants to be given only to the poorest people living in the worst houses. There are mandatory grants to pay for work to make property fit for human habitation; discretionary grants can be given by the local authority for improvements beyond this standard. There are also grants available for special facilities for people with disabilities. All grants are, however, means-tested.

Houses in Multiple Occupation (HMOs) are properties divided up into bedsits or lived in as a shared house. Local authorities have special powers to deal with unsatisfactory conditions in these properties. Owners can be required to carry out repairs or have the council carry out the work instead. Local authorities can also limit the number of tenants in an HMO. Councils in some areas operate a registration scheme for HMOs. Registration of unsuitable properties can be refused or withdrawn.

The role of housing in society

The politics of grants for owner-occupiers raises wider issues about the role of housing in society and who should take responsibility for housing. For some housing is a social issue – the effects of bad housing spread wider than the individual and the nation should take responsibility for maintaining the housing stock of the country. In a report looking at the results of the 1991 Housing Condition Survey, the National Housing Forum argued that poor housing had a

TABLE 5.1   Housing legislation after 1945

Government	Date	Name of Act	Summary
Labour	1946	Housing Act	Encouraged council house building by increasing subsidies and allowing local authorities to borrow money at low interest rates
	1949	Housing Act	Local authorities allowed to provide housing for all, not just working-class people
Conservative	1952	Housing Act	Stimulated all house building, increased subsidies to local authorities
	1954	Housing Repairs and Rent Act	Rent increases allowed in private rented sector after improvements
	1956	Housing Subsidies Act	Reduction in subsidies to local authorities, larger subsidies given for high-rise building
	1957	Rent Act	Partial decontrol of rents in private sector
	1957	Housing Act	Allowed sales of council houses
	1961	Housing Act	Subsidies reintroduced for housing; low-interest loans available for housing societies
	1964	Housing Act	Extended housing society support; set up Housing Corporation
			Local authorities could compel landlords to improve property
Labour	1965	Rent Act	Security of tenure for unfurnished accommodation tenants. Introduction of fair rents
	1967	Housing Subsidies Act	Subsidy to local authorities to help with increased interest rates. Introduction of option mortgages
	1969	Housing Act	Increased improvement grants. Introduction of General Improvement Areas
Conservative	1972	Housing Finance Act	Reduced subsidies to local authorities; increased council rents
Labour	1974	Housing Act	Increased improvement grants; expanded role of housing associations
			Introduction of Housing Action Areas; removed 1972 Housing Finance Act
			Security of tenure to tenants of furnished rented property
	1975	Housing Rent and Subsidies Act	Increased subsidies to local authorities
	1977	Housing (Homeless Persons) Act	Gave local authorities a duty to house homeless persons
Conservative	1980	Housing Act	Increased control of local authority spending, introduction of shorthold tenancies in private renting, increased rents in private and public sector, introduction of right to buy for council tenants
	1984	Housing and Building Control Act	Gave more rights to council tenants

TABLE 5.1   Continued

Government	Date	Name of Act	Summary
	1988	Housing Act	Reduced control on rents in private rented properties; allowed housing associations to use private loans; allowed council tenants to choose a new landlord; introduced Housing Action Trusts to renovate council estates
	1989	Local Government and Housing Act	New finance arrangements for local authorities; new system of grants for improvements; allowed for renewal areas
	1993	Leasehold Reform, Development Act	Introduced Rent-to-Housing and Urban Mortgage Scheme
	1996	Housing Act	Enabled the Housing Corporation to register a wider range of social landlords; revised homelessness legislation to create one waiting-ist and place homeless people in temporary rather than permanent housing; allowed more action to be taken against anti-social tenants; strengthened local authority powers over Houses in Multiple Occupation

bad effect on the whole nation's well-being. The chairperson of the Forum added that:

> Neglecting housing makes no sense in economic terms because the public purse has to bear the costs of the increased health and social care which results from poor quality housing. There is also the cost of ultimately demolishing homes which are in the most serious disrepair.

The government take a different line, with a spokesperson for the Department of Environment saying that:

> The primary responsibility for repairing a home is the owner's. Public resources to help private owners are necessarily limited and are therefore targeted on the needy.[48]

Activity 5.12

Most parts of the country have areas of housing problems, whether they be old council estates, newer high-rise blocks or inner-city slums. As a class, decide where such areas are located locally. What policies could the local council implement to improve these areas?

This chapter has attempted to demonstrate the complexity of housing issues. It can be seen that many of the current problems have their origins in history. Housing policies have failed to take an overall view of the issues, but rather have tended to deal with single aspects of problems as they become apparent. Partly because of this, policies have rarely provided solutions, and in some cases, have then created new problems. Inequalities in housing persist, and some policies, such as the sale of council houses, increase the polarisation of different people into different types of tenure and into good and bad housing.

Table 5.1 gives a summary of the main aspects of post-war legislation on housing.

Activity 5.13

In small groups, discuss the following statements:

1 Housing is a basic right and should be provided for all.
2 People should not be allowed to live in houses which are larger than they need.
3 Houses should not be individually-owned, but allocated to people and re-allocated in the event of death.
4 There should be no state involvement in housing and no subsidies. People should simply buy or rent privately homes they can afford.

Activity 5.14

Make sure that you understand the following expressions used in this chapter. Check in the Glossary at the end of the book if you need to.

bureaucratic	Part III accommodation
fair rent	paternalistic
General Improvement Area	'red-lining'
Houses in Multiple Occupation (HMOs)	redevelopment
Housing Action Area	registered social landlord
Housing Action Trust (HAT)	regressive subsidy
housing association	rehabilitation
Housing Corporation	rent arrears
interest rate	security of tenure
	shorthold tenancy
large-scale voluntary transfer	short-life property
mortgage	social housing
mortgage default	squatting
negative equity	tenure

Further reading

There are relatively few books on housing policy and those available are quickly out-of-date. *Housing Policy* by Jean Conway (Gildredge Press, 1999) provides a very readable and comprehensive overview of housing issues. Another to try is *Homelessness and Social Policy* by Roger Burrows, Nicholas Pleace and Deborah Quilgars (London: Routledge, 1997).

Shelter is the best source of up-to-date information on homelessness, housing needs and housing policy. See below for the address and website.

Useful addresses

Shelter
88 Old Street
London ECIV 9HU
tel. 0207 505 2000

The National Federation of Housing Associations (NFHA)
175 Gray's Inn Road
London WC1X 8UP
tel. 0207 278 6571

The Department of the Environment, Transport and the Regions, which is responsible for government policies on housing, provide free publications from:

Department of the Environment, Transport and the Regions
DETR Free Literature
PO Box No 236
Wetherby LS23 7NB
tel. 0870 1226 236

Priced publications are available from:

Publications Sales Centre
Department of the Environment, Transport and the Regions
Unit 21, Goldthorpe Industrial Estate
Goldthorpe, Rotherham S63 9BL
tel. 01709 891 318

Websites

The government department responsible for housing has an informative site at **www.detr.gov.uk**

Find The Big Issue at **www.bigissue.com**

Summaries of past research and useful links can be found at the University of York Centre for Housing Policy website **www.york.ac.uk/inst/chp**

Shelter provide a mass of accessible information on homelessness at **www.shelter.org.uk**

Some of the research published on the web by the Joseph Rowntree Foundation concerns housing. Find them at **www.jrf.org.uk**

The Department of the Environment, Transport and the Regions (responsible for housing) can be found at **www.detr.gov.uk**

6 Living in cities

Most of Britain's population lives in urban areas. This chapter looks briefly at the implications of urban life for social services and then focuses on problems of the inner-city areas. This is followed by a discussion of policies relating to improvement of the inner-city environment.

6.1 Urban and rural societies

Within sociology, attempts have been made to draw distinctions between urban and rural societies.[1] Typically, urban societies are said to consist of larger communities, in contrast to the small communities found in rural areas. This is believed to result in different types of relationships between people. In a small community, it is possible for everyone to know everyone else and for people to have a strong sense of belonging to a group. Both these factors lead to informal social control by the community. For example, in a close-knit community, people will be controlled by local gossip. Similarly, a person doing something wrong, perhaps committing an act of vandalism, will be recognised and may have his or her act reported to parents or dealt with on the spot. In contrast, in urban areas, day-to-day life is seen as consisting of many social encounters with strangers. Relationships between people are superficial and urban dwellers have little sense of belonging to a community with shared values.

Activity 6.1

> To what extent, in your experience, is this view of urban and rural life accurate? If this is a true picture of urban life, what implications might this have for social services?

In areas where people are strangers to each other, or have only superficial relationship, more demands will be made upon local social services. There will be a lack of support for people such as parents of young children, the elderly or people with disabilities living at home. Such people will feel isolated and lonely. The lack of informal social control can lead to increased levels of crime and vandalism as well as other forms of anti-social behaviour. Sociologists have argued that people who have no sense of belonging to a group are more vulnerable to mental illness and more likely to contemplate suicide. The current trend towards a policy of care in the community is unlikely to be successful in areas where no community exists to give support to those in need. The implications of this are discussed further in Chapter 9.

However, it has been argued that the features described above are not necessarily part of urban life, although they may exist in areas with a large number of new arrivals or where people live temporarily before moving on. Young and Willmott's study of Bethnal Green, in London's East End, conducted in the 1950s (see Chapter 5), found a strong sense of community in this urban area. Within a small locality, people were surrounded by relatives and close friends, providing mutual support for one another.

It may be that both these conflicting views of urban life are true and that it is not possible to generalise any further. Within large cities, there are small local communities, such as that found in Bethnal Green, and areas where people are strangers and which provide no sense of belonging and no community support. These features are of course attractive to many people and experienced as a freedom from interference and social convention. People whose life-style might result in condemnation from a rural community find the anonymity of city life allows them the freedom to live in the way they wish.

6.2 Britain's inner-cities

The inner-city problem has attracted considerable publicity over the years, culminating in the riots of the summer of 1981 in many inner-city areas. There have been a series of government policies aimed at improving the environment and quality of life in these areas. The relative lack of success of these policies is in part related to the difficulty in pin-pointing the nature and origin of deprivation. The best way of conceptualising the inner-city problem is through the term 'multiple deprivation'. This emphasises the fact that the urban problem is not a single problem but one of the concentration of a number of problems in one area, which added together lead to a situation of deprivation.

Activity 6.2

Make a list of the sort of problems which add up to multiple deprivation.

The Urban Task Force was set up by the Labour government in 1998 to identify causes of urban decline and make recommendations for the regeneration of cities. They produced the following Urban Factfile:[2]

- Urban areas in England account for 90 per cent of population, 91 per cent of economic output and 89 per cent of jobs.
- The public sector spends over £200 billion a year on English towns and cities and the people who live there – almost 60 per cent of total UK public expenditure.
- Government projections estimate that 3.8 million extra households will form between 1996 and 2021 – a 19 per cent increase.

The inner-city

- One in four people living in urban neighbourhoods think their area has got worse in recent years, compared with only one in ten who think it has got better.
- More than 90 per cent of the urban buildings and infrastructure that will exist in 30 years' time, has already been built.
- Traffic is predicted to grow by a third in the next 20 years. Average commuting time is 40 per cent higher than 20 years ago.
- Unemployment in inner-cities runs at more than double the rate elsewhere.
- 40 per cent of inner-urban housing stock is subsidised 'social' housing.
- Around 1.3 million residential and commercial buildings are currently empty.

Loss of population

As has been said, most of Britain's population live in urban areas, yet the inner-cities have suffered a loss of population. The introduction of cheap transport and the desire for gardens and clean air first led people to move from the urban centres to the suburbs of towns and cities. This emigration was initially supported by government policies. These included the funding priority given to the new towns developed under the 1947 New Towns Act, grants for 'over-spill' estates on the edges of towns, and money for housing and industrial development in 'expanded towns' such as King's Lynn in Norfolk. There was also pressure on people to move as commercial development in the cities led to rapidly rising land values. Some commercial developers, anxious to make a quick profit, used harassment to shift tenants from these areas. The city centres experienced a sharp drop in population, beginning in the 1950s and accelerating in the 1960s. However, not everyone was in a position to move, and those who did so tended to be young and to be skilled or professional workers. As a result, the populations of the inner-cities became unbalanced with a high proportion of elderly people and people living on a low income. This trend, whereby people have moved out of large urban areas into more rural areas has continued: in the period 1971–81, populations in all metropolitan areas fell as people moved from cities such as London to more rural areas like East Anglia. New reasons for leaving the cities include the fear of crime and poor schools.

Loss of industry and employment

There has also been a loss of industry from the urban areas, caused by a general decline in manufacturing and relocation of industry, encouraged initially by generous government grants. To the extent that industry has been replaced, it has been replaced by commercial enterprises and warehousing, which do not tend to provide employment opportunities for unskilled manual workers. There has been an overall loss of employment in the urban centres – for example, in Liverpool, the number of jobs for men fell by 18 per cent between 1966 and 1971.[3] The jobs lost were mainly unskilled manual work, such as in building, engineering and on the docks.

Loss of services

Recent years have seen a reduction of services in urban and especially inner-city areas. The development of out-of-town shopping centres with large car-parks, often only accessible for those with cars, has affected shopping facilities in the town centres. Of particular concern is the threat from out-of-town supermarkets like Sainsbury's and Tesco's to local grocery shops, butchers, bakers and fishmongers. Closure of small local shops has led to 'food deserts' – areas where fresh food cannot be bought by those without access to cars. Similarly, financial exclusion is a growing issue as banks rationalise provision and close branches.

Environment and housing

Environmentally, inner-cities have suffered in a variety of ways. Commercial development often occurred as a result of a slow process whereby developers gradually bought up areas, boarding up empty properties and spreading a general sense of decay. High-rise office buildings dwarf many urban centres, creating impersonal environments in which few people can feel at home. Local authorities have also played a part in the deterioration of inner-cities through 'planning blight'. There was a tendency for councils to plan over-ambitious renewal schemes. They would purchase properties compulsorily, only to delay or reverse their plans. This contributed to the decay of the physical environment and led to uncertainty and a run-down of local facilities.

Inner-city areas are characterised by housing stress, with long council waiting-lists and a high incidence of overcrowding. Environmental and economic problems of unemployment and poverty lead in turn to social problems. Many inner-city areas have high numbers of people suffering from physical and mental illnesses and handicaps and an unusually large number of children in the care of the local authority. All these factors mean that there is a great deal of demand on already over-stretched local authority budgets. The urban problem is not a simple one, but rather the sum of a variety of problems with complex causes. Multiple deprivation refers to the interaction of all these environmental, social and economic problems.

'Gentrification'

This section has so far focused on negative aspects of life in Britain's inner-cities. Although a government-sponsored survey of Lambeth in South London found that 42 per cent of people surveyed wanted to move out, there are people who live in urban centres by choice.[4] Such people are attracted by the proximity to facilities such as theatres and the excitement and pace of city life. Recent years have seen a process which has been termed 'gentrification', describing the fashion amongst professional people for renovating old properties in inner-city areas. This process has been aided by the systems of generous improvement grants described in Chapter 5. Other schemes encouraged the revitalisation of quayside areas, and city dock areas in towns like London, Hull,

Source: Gina Glover, Photofusion
Isolation in the inner-city

Manchester and Liverpool have been restored and become fashionable and highly desirable places to live. Gentrification tended to mean that poorer people were pushed out of areas as more middle-class buyers moved in, pushing up house prices. The two-sided nature of this trend is illustrated in the following quotation:

Many inner residential areas in the major cities now became in fashionable demand, and very nice they looked with bright new paint, shining brass and cheerful plants in tubs and window-boxes. The only snag to this happy burst of environment improvement was the question of the previous tenants, who had been moved out of their rented homes so that lawyers, architects, advertising executives, teachers, university and polytechnic lecturers and such like could move in.[5]

Many urban centres have fashionable streets inhabited by comparatively wealthy people neighbouring on areas of poverty and deprivation. The huge price rises in all areas of London in the 1980s accelerated this trend to the extent that it is common for so-called 'yuppies' to live next door to longer-standing working-class residents.

Activity 6.3

Make a list of areas of the country where you might expect to find multiple deprivation.

Measuring and comparing deprivation

It is important to establish the location of areas of deprivation for the allocation of funds available from central government. It is, however, very difficult to establish criteria for the evaluation of need.

Multiple deprivation means that areas are seen as falling into decline as a result of a combination of factors such as unemployment, overcrowding and unbalanced populations, for example, consisting of a high proportion of elderly and poorer people. To measure and compare deprivation, indicators have to be established. These are factors which are not necessarily problems in themselves, but which indicate deprivation. A range of indicators has been used over the last thirty years to produce ways of measuring deprivation and ranking local areas. The Department of the Environment, Transport and the Regions 1998 Index of Local deprivation has twelve indicators, designed to measure seven aspects of deprivation across 354 local authority districts. [6] These are shown below:

Economic	Total unemployment
	Male long-term unemployment
Low income	Number of people receiving income support
	Number of people who do not get income support but who receive council tax benefit
	Dependent children of people receiving income support
Health	Death rates of people under 75 measured through Standardised Mortality Rates (under 75s)
Education	Low educational attainment – percentage of 15-year-olds with no GCSE passes or gaining GCSE passes at grades D–G only
	Low educational participation – percentage of 17-year-olds no longer in full-time education
Environment	Derelict land
Crime	Weightings for home insurance
Housing	Households lacking basic amenities plus all households in temporary accommodation
	Overcrowded households (more than 1 person per room)

Since there can be small pockets of deprivation within districts, there are also sets of indicators for smaller areas within districts. To distinguish wards within a local authority district, the index measures:

- unemployment;
- children in low-earning households;
- households with no car;
- households lacking basic amenities;

- overcrowded households;
- 17-year-olds no longer in full-time education.

Activity 6.4

Consider the indicators of deprivation used by the Department of the Environment, Transport and the Regions. Could any other factors be more relevant in comparing different areas? Bear in mind that social indicators are not intended to be problems in themselves, but rather a way of measuring a problem.

6.3   Inner-city case studies

This section illustrates the problems of inner-city areas by looking at a particular area.

Brixton

The information used here is taken from the Scarman report, written in response to the 1981 riots.[7] Brixton is part of the London Borough of Lambeth in South London. It is an inner-city environment with a mixture of residential, industrial and commercial premises. In the late nineteenth century and early twentieth century, Brixton was a prosperous area. It was inhabited by professional people who enjoyed the easy access into the centre of London, and others for whom there were good local employment opportunities.

The economic decline of Brixton began after the First World War, continuing to the present day. The physical appearance and standard of amenities in Brixton are typical of inner-cities areas. There has been a decline in shopping facilities and the physical environment has been affected by indecision in planning. For example, the Railton and Mayall Roads area was to be redeveloped until the plans were overruled by central government, leaving boarded-up sites at the junction of Railton and Mayall Roads.

Brixton is an area of housing stress. In 1977 a Housing Action Area was declared and some areas have been improved as a result. There is a housing shortage, although there are also empty properties, into which squatters have moved. Some households are overcrowded and some of the housing is below standard. The newer council estates of high-rise flats also have problems. The housing problems combined with the deterioration in the physical environment give a sense of decay to the area. Brixton has few leisure and recreational facilities, especially for young people in the area. This is in spite of the availability of funding under the schemes described in section 6.4 of this chapter.

The population of Brixton is falling as people, in particular those aged between 25 and 60, move away. There is a high rate of population movement, with a net loss of professional and unskilled workers. Brixton has a high proportion of children in care and a high level of mental illness and disability. There is also a large proportion of families with only one parent. All these factors, together with high unemployment and a large number of low-income families, lead to high expenditure on social services.

Brixton, in common with some, but not all, inner-city areas, has a relatively large black population, although white people make up the majority. Many Asian and West Indian people came to Britain in the 1950s around the same time as people were moving from the inner-cities to the suburbs. As has been noted in Chapter 5, the immigrants found work easily but housing was more of a problem. As newcomers, they had to accept any available housing and many were pushed into the privately-rented sector in the cities. Since then, many have become owner-occupiers although they have continued to be restricted to less desirable properties. Although black people have been blamed for the problems of the inner-city areas, it is important to note that these problems already existed before they arrived.

Hackney

The information in this section is taken from Paul Harrison's 1983 book on Hackney.[8] Harrison suggests, probably rightly, that the London borough of Hackney, with low-paid employment, unemployment, poverty, poor housing, dereliction, educational failure and a high crime rate, is 'one of two or three contenders for the title of the Most Awful Place in Britain'.[9] Like many inner-city areas Hackney was once a pleasant residential area housing the rich. The turning-point came towards the end of the nineteenth century when a development boom led to rapid building of poor-quality housing. The local economy, based on clothes manufacture, was notorious for its poor working conditions and low pay. These two factors created a vicious circle of deteriorating conditions. The bad housing could be rented cheaply by unskilled workers on low incomes. The resulting lack of skills in the population affected the type of employment attracted to the area. The circle continues as poverty leads to further decline when people are too poor to maintain and repair properties.

The industries of Hackney have been those particularly vulnerable to recession and the move of manufacture from Britain to Third World countries. This has obviously led to redundancies and cuts in wages as the remaining firms try to compete and stay in business. Even people who have work struggle to survive on low wages with frequent periods of lay-off. The inner-city problem results from the combined effect of several problems and Hackney has all the typical inner-city problems. In the following extract a woman who is relatively well-off insofar as her husband has work and they do not live on the worst estate, describes the problems of life in a high-rise flat:

> I didn't want to move in ... but they said we had only one choice, and we had nowhere else to go. I don't like heights, I feel closed in, I get very depressed. I hate this area. I know everywhere is rough these days, but Hackney is *really* rough. I hate the thought of my kids going to school here. I got attacked in the lift once ... I have a terrible fear of getting stuck in the lift. If our lift (serving 'odd' floors) is broken, we have to use the other (serving 'even' floors) and walk

down from the twelfth floor. Andrew carries the kids and I carry the double-buggy. You shouldn't have to do that sort of thing just to get in at your own front door. My gran who's 77, she came one day when both lifts were broke, she had to walk up twenty-six flights of stairs. There's glue-sniffers using the top of the staircases and there's people who dirty in the lifts, they go to the toilet in there.[10]

Poor areas like Hackney have the greatest need for health and social services provision yet have the worst facilities for providing care. Such areas lack populations of middle-class people involved in voluntary organisations and campaigning for improvements in services. Poor housing and schools and unattractive environments mean that doctors and teachers do not want to live and work in such areas. Those who do are over-stretched and risk disillusionment as problems overwhelm them.

Inner London's educational record is poor and Hackney has a high level of educational failure. Schools are unable to compensate for the poverty of the children's home-life. Children come from overcrowded homes where tension and conflict are part of the normal environment. Few houses have decent gardens, yet play areas are lacking or in states of disrepair because of the pressure on land, the high density population, vandalism and the local authority's lack of money for facilities. Children are forced to play on roads and other unsafe areas, risking injury. The following list was taken from a survey of playgrounds in Hackney:

Somerford Gardens   A dismal little playground that local parents find too dangerous for children to use.
Clissold Park   Umbrella immobilised since April; see-saw chained up since July, playground unchanged since Victorian days. If dangerous equipment is removed little remains.
Springfield Park   Paddling-pool empty for a year; sandpit fouled by cats and dogs; swing chained up; never seems to be open.
Millfields   Roundabout has exposed nails and rotten board seats; sand has broken glass in it.
Hackney Downs   Rocking-horse removed; slide irreparable, must be removed immediately; dogs a problem.[11]

Parents face the choice of cooping up their children, depriving them of the opportunity to explore, have adventures and mix with other children, or allowing them to risk accidents and the possibility of getting into trouble with the police.

The high crime rate in Hackney includes crimes committed for money or to fund a drug habit and acts which provide no benefit to anyone, except perhaps a release of frustration. The effects of crime are felt by people who live in fear or lose their few possessions, as well as by the community as a whole. Shops and businesses suffer as insurance premiums are increased or as areas become uninsurable. These effects are passed on to the community in price-rises or when firms move out of the area. No types of facility are immune from crime and vandalism, even when they are provided by residents for the benefit of the local community. For example, a tenants' association attempt to improve the quality of life on a particularly bleak estate was victim to the following set-backs:

> in July 1981, an old people's party had to be cancelled because the food and drink had been stolen. In August the social club had to close for a time after two burglaries had cleaned them out of bar stock worth £300. And in January 1982 the disco equipment was stolen from the community centre – for the second time.[12]

The list of problems in Hackney is long and the combination of poverty, crime and the inner-city environment lead to low morale and feelings of hopelessness which cause further deterioration in a circle difficult to break.

Activity 6.5

> Find out about a local inner-city area. The local authority or the Department of the Environment, Transport and the Regions and libraries are all possible sources of information. Or try the Internet.

6.4 Inner-city policies

The policies described here are those dating from the 1960s to the present. There have been government schemes for specific areas for longer than this but the programmes discussed are distinctive in that they are concerned with the problems characterised in terms of social and economic factors.

1960s

The first measure to use this approach was included in Section 11 of the 1966 Local Government Act. This allowed special aid for areas with a concentration of commonwealth immigrants. Local authorities could claim a 75 per cent grant from central government for approved expenditure in areas such as education, child care or maternity services. In practice, however, most of the money was spent on education. This source of funding is still available.

The second programme to combat deprivation followed the Plowden Report in 1967. This established Educational Priority Areas (EPAs). The thinking behind EPAs was based on the theory of the culture of poverty and the cycle of deprivation, discussed in Chapter 3. EPAs were to be given extra resources and to be designated on the basis of social indicators, although the factors to be used were never clearly established. The criteria suggested by Plowden were: the occupation of the head of household; size of families; the extent of overcrowding and sharing of basic facilities; the number of people relying on welfare benefits; poor attendance at school; the proportion of children with disabilities; the number of 'incomplete' families; and the number of pupils unable to speak English.

In 1968, the Urban Programme was set up. This resulted from a speech by Enoch Powell which caused great alarm at the time, predicting social unrest caused by urban deprivation and concentration of immigrants in cities. The

Urban Programme was based on the idea that there existed small localised pockets of deprivation, defined in terms of social factors such as overcrowding, large families, unemployment, poor environments, immigrant populations, and large proportions of children in the care of the local authority. As was the case with the EPAs, these factors were never quantified. Under the Urban Programme, central government would provide 75 per cent of funds for projects expected to produce quick results. Initially, these projects were mainly concerned with the provision of nursery facilities. Later the scheme diversified and expanded. It is now linked to the Partnership and Programme Area schemes and described as the Traditional Urban Programme. It takes up a small part of the larger budget and consists of a variety of community projects.

In 1969, the Home Office set up the Community Development Project (CDP). The emphasis was on raising local people from a position of 'fatalistic dependence' on local authorities to self-sufficiency and independence. Twelve local teams were employed to work with local communities in deprived areas, with a research team to monitor the results. The assumptions in the CDP plan were that it was the 'deprived' who were the cause of deprivation and that the problem could be overcome by tackling apathy in communities. The CDP teams soon ran into trouble with local authorities and central government as they began to criticise policies and the approach they were expected to take to their work. In the words of a CDP report:

> A few months' field-work in areas suffering long-term economic decline and high unemployment was enough to provoke the first teams of CDP workers to question the Home Office's original assumptions. There might certainly be in these areas a high proportion of the sick and the elderly for whom a better co-ordination of services would undoubtedly be helpful, but the vast majority were ordinary working-class men and women who, through forces outside their control, happened to be living in areas where bad housing conditions, redundancies, lay-offs, and low wages were commonplace.[13]

This criticism of a small-scale localised approach to the problem of deprivation led to the development of a different analysis, focusing on structual problems in society. The following quotation from the Newcastle CDP team demonstrates the approach taken:

> The team had moved away from the original assumptions of the CDP programme that the causes of deprivation are to be found in the local community, and in the shortcomings of local policies and services. Our experience in Benwell convinces us that much of the disadvantage to be observed arises from structural causes. In other words, we would argue that the workings of the general economic and associated political system are inherently liable to create wide inequalities between groups in society.[14]

1970s

As a result of this switch in approach, the CDP programme was abruptly ended in 1976. In 1974, Comprehensive Community Programmes (CCPs) were set up as a more acceptable substitute for the CDPs. The new project analysed problems and put forward recommendations, although they had little overall impact. The Community Development Project was successful in challenging the assumptions behind inner-city policies and a change in approach was to come in later schemes.

The Housing Action Areas, set up in 1974, and discussed in Chapter 5, were another attempt to deal with small areas of deprivation. Briefly the idea was to provide special levels of grants for owner-occupiers and landlords in small areas of older housing. The scheme intended that improvement of housing would lead to an upgrading of whole areas. The programme achieved little success for several reasons. Cuts in expenditure were introduced shortly after the introduction of the scheme which seriously curtailed the efforts at improvement. Some local authorities were not enthusiastic about the programme since funds were inadequate, the improvements did not have to conform to traditional standards and there was a fear that the establishment of Housing Action Areas would divert attention from other areas of need. These factors contributed to the failure of the programme to make any great impact on the urban problem. However, it has been argued that even if these problems had not existed, the limited scope of the policy would have meant that it had little effect where problems were caused by poverty and lack of investment in inner-city areas.

The change in emphasis in urban policy began with the Inner Area Studies. These were studies carried out by consultant architects for the Department of the Environment, Transport and the Regions between 1972 and 1977. The brief was to look at the problems of a small area, taking a wide approach to the task. The Inner Area Studies suggested the need for economic regeneration, the need for sensitivity towards local people, the need for improved housing and – perhaps most importantly – the need for an overall approach to inner-city problems, taking account of social and economic factors.

The Inner Area Studies resulted in a government White Paper, 'Policies for the Inner City', published in 1977. In line with the new approach, the White Paper placed the emphasis on economic rather than social problems, and economic solutions to deprivation.

The Act which followed – the Inner Urban Areas Act 1978 – continued the policy of area-based positive discrimination with a social-services orientation, but with a new focus on economic revival. The new policy for the inner-cities included a specific commitment to urban centres which was a reversal of earlier policies for economic and demographic dispersal. The aim was to work on three fronts outlined as economic, environmental and social aspects of deprivation. Inner-cities were to be given a priority second only to the assisted areas in the provision of grants for industry. Local authorities were empowered to make loans for up to 90 per cent for land purchase, and could declare Industrial Improvement Areas, providing help with the cost of site preparation. The act retained the traditional Urban Programme and expanded this provision. Finally, Partnerships were set up between local and central government in seven areas: Liverpool, Birmingham, Glasgow, Manchester/Salford, the London boroughs of Lambeth and Islington/Hackney, and the London docklands. Each partnership had a team to analyse the needs of the area and to draw up a programme for regeneration. The map in Figure 6.1 shows the areas coverd by these policies.[15]

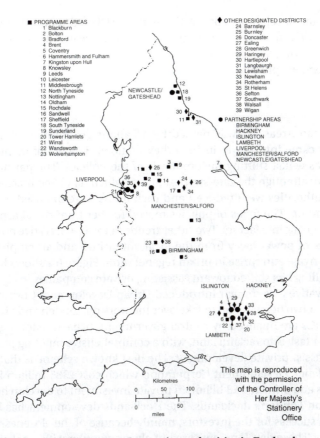

PROGRAMME AREAS
1 Blackburn
2 Bolton
3 Bradford
4 Brent
5 Coventry
6 Hammersmith and Fulham
7 Kingston upon Hull
8 Knowsley
9 Leeds
10 Leicester
11 Middlesbrough
12 North Tyneside
13 Nottingham
14 Oldham
15 Rochdale
16 Sandwell
17 Sheffield
18 South Tyneside
19 Sunderland
20 Tower Hamlets
21 Wirral
22 Wandsworth
23 Wolverhampton

OTHER DESIGNATED DISTRICTS
24 Barnsley
25 Burnley
26 Doncaster
27 Ealing
28 Greenwich
29 Haringey
30 Hartlepool
31 Langbaurgh
32 Lewisham
33 Newham
34 Rotherham
35 St Helens
36 Sefton
37 Southwark
38 Walsall
39 Wigan

PARTNERSHIP AREAS
BIRMINGHAM
HACKNEY
ISLINGTON
LAMBETH
LIVERPOOL
MANCHESTER/SALFORD
NEWCASTLE/GATESHEAD

NEWCASTLE/GATESHEAD

LIVERPOOL

MANCHESTER/SALFORD

BIRMINGHAM

ISLINGTON   HACKNEY

LAMBETH

This map is reproduced with the permission of the Controller of Her Majesty's Stationery Office

Kilometres
0   50   100

0   50
miles

Figure 6.1   Inner-city authorities in England

The following sections give an idea of the scope of the Urban Programme by describing four examples from over 5000 projects. The projects are selected from a Department of the Environment, Transport and the Regions document.[16]

In *Lambeth*, a craft workshop for people with learning disabilities received funding under the Urban Programme. It is a branch of *L'Arche* which is a national association of communities for people with a learning disability. People are referred from the local social services department and are involved in working on contracts for industry or making craft items for sale. The second example comes from *Manchester*, where a group received £15,000 for an anti-vandalism campaign. The scheme involves local residents and the activities include publicity, making repairs following acts of vandalism, and organising activities like football in the hope of preventing vandalism.

A very different project on *Merseyside* received £110,000 for a maritime museum on a derelict site in the city. The museum is in the Canning Dock area and includes restored quaysides with horse-drawn wagons and steam lorries on display. The final example was of an industrial project in the Derwenthaugh Industrial Improvement Area in *Gateshead* in the North East of England. This was a five-year project with an annual grant of £300,000. The task was the improvement and development of run-down industrial land, aiming to revitalise existing industry and to attract new industry to the areas. The borough was involved in improving the site in the hope that firms would take up the initiative to improve their own premises.

1980s

The Inner Urban Areas Act was passed by a Labour government. When the Conservatives came into power in 1979 they retained the commitment to the inner-city areas whilst shifting the emphasis of the policies. The partnerships were to remain, although the rate-support grants which had been increased for urban local authorities were reduced and cash limits were imposed on local-authority spending. The focus of policies moved further from social aspects of deprivation to economic factors. Two other trends in the Conservative approach were a transfer of power away from the local authorities and an emphasis on encouraging private enterprise in urban regeneration. Figure 6.2 shows how the balance of funding has shifted towards assisting private companies.[17]

The Conservative government introduced Urban Development Corporations (UDCs), the first two being set up to take over the work on London and Liverpool docklands. UDCs are financed by central government, bypassing local government, and their task is to reclaim land, with a comprehensive building plan, and to financially assist private development. The best known scheme is that of the London Docklands Development Corporation which cost £385 million in government funds and attracted £3 billion in private investment to develop housing and industry on London's docklands. The Docklands development has been a huge financial success for the investors, mainly because of the closeness of the area to the City. These developments are not always popular with local authorities since they mean a loss of control and can be criticised for being undemocratic. John Banham, director-general of the CBI, has also criticised the way that UDCs cut across the work of local councils and can spoil good relationships between industry and local government. He said:

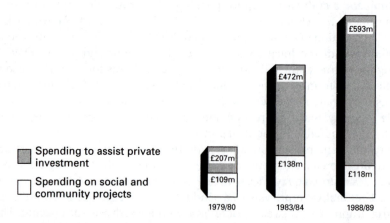

Figure 6.2   Shifting the balance of urban group programmes, 1979/80–1988/89

Local authorities cannot be by-passed – they are there and in many respects they are efficient and effective ... We're not going to get there by depriving them of resources ... penalising them by spending money they ought to be spending ... or worse still, holding them up to public ridicule.[18]

In 1987, several further UDCs were set up, including those in the Black Country (West Midlands), Tyne and Wear, and Teesside.

The Conservative government also introduced Enterprise Zones (in 1981) which are areas free from planning and other controls and where industries pay no rates. Enterprise Zones have been subjected to criticism on the basis that they do little to create employment since it is often existing firms who benefit from reduced costs or those who make short-distance relocations to cut cost. A report by an independent urban research centre, the Centre for Environmental Studies, concludes:

EZs have not resulted in a net job gain to either the local or the national economy. Although they have strongly influenced the choice of location within an area, almost all establishments and jobs would have been created anyway.[19]

It is argued that the greatest benefit from the zones is to industrial and commercial development companies, especially in the context of the recent extension of the scheme to areas like North Kent and Wellingborough, which cannot be described as deprived inner-city areas.

In 1985, five City Action Teams (CATs) were set up to encourage co-ordination in their areas. They aim to bring together civil servants from the three departments concerned with inner-city policies. These are the Department of the Environment, Transport and the Regions, the Department of Employment and the Department of Trade and Industry. There are also 16 Task Forces which operate more at a local level to bring together people from industry and government. Urban Development Grants and Urban Regeneration Grants are schemes whereby government money is available in some areas of the country for private companies to use in plans to develop run-down and derelict sites.

These policies achieved only limited success, for when Mrs Thatcher took office for her third term she announced that a central priority for the government that term would be the improvement of the inner-cities. A year later, in 1988, a glossy document called Action for Cities was published by the government setting out the various policies for the inner-cities. These include the following:

- An increased number of Urban Development Corporations;
- Additional City Action Teams;
- Replacing the Urban Development Grant and Urban Regeneration Grant with a simplified City Grant;
- Continuation of Inner Area Partnerships and other earlier schemes;
- A series of breakfast meetings around the country, costing £450,000, where business people can discuss plans over breakfast with government officials.

1990s

The early 1990s saw a continuation of the trend for involving the private sector in initiatives to improve inner-city areas.[20]

By 1994 the number of CATs had increased to eight. These work on co-ordinating government activities in their areas and encouraging participation from the private sector and other organisations. Each has a small budget for this work and can give grants to local authorities, businesses, local community groups and voluntary organisations working in or moving to an inner-city area.

Task forces were first set up in 1986 and are small teams of civil servants and others which work in the most deprived urban areas. They concentrate on improving employment prospects for local people by supporting training and education and other projects aimed at removing barriers to employment. They also promote local enterprises in business and community initiatives to solve local problems. The idea is that a Task Force will exist only as long as necessary and once local organisations are strengthened the Task Force will be closed down. In 1994 there were 16 Task Forces.

The Urban Programme was one of the longest established initiatives, although it moved through a number of changes as political ideas have changed. In 1994 the Urban Programme was concentrated on 57 target areas with the greatest problems and the most severe deprivation. As was stated on page 159, the Urban Programme provides grants for projects with 75 per cent of the funding coming from central government and the remainder from the local authority. From 1993–94 there were no new projects supported through the Urban Programme, although previously approved projects continued to be funded.

A new scheme announced in 1991 was the City Challenge. Under this scheme local authorities, in partnership with private and voluntary organisations, local communities and government agencies were invited to offer imaginative and comprehensive plans for improving local deprived areas. The best of the proposals received government funding over a period of five years.

Urban Development Corporations (UDCs) have been mentioned already. By 1994 there were 13 UDCs. The initial ones were in London's Docklands and Merseyside. Additional UDCs have now been established in Birmingham Heartlands, Bristol, Leeds, Central Manchester, Plymouth, Sheffield, Trafford Park (Greater Manchester) and Cardiff.

Action for Cities (1988) included the establishment of City Grants. These exist to encourage private development in inner-cities. By May 1993, 330 schemes had been approved.

The Enterprise Zones established in 1981, as already described, ran for 10 years. In 1994 there were 10 Enterprise Zones, although five ended in that year. Three new zones were designated in 1994 in areas affected by job losses in the mining industry. A related idea was that of Simplified Planning Zones (SPZs) which also last for 10 years. These allowed planning permission for certain types of development. In 1993 there were six SPZs.

New Labour policies

The new Labour government, elected in 1997, has continued the approach to urban regeneration which looks to a partnership between government, private and voluntary organisations. Local priorities are set by the Regional Development Agencies, established from April 1999, and it is hoped that local involvement will avoid some of the mistakes of the past. The focus links wide-ranging aspects of social and economic deprivation including the physical environment, poverty, employment, training and education, crime and health issues. As over the previous thirty years, some initiatives have ended and new ones have been started.

In 1998 the City Challenge initiative and the twelve Urban Development Corporations (both described above) came to an end. Other programmes which have been described above and are now closed include the Urban Programme, City Grants, Task Forces and City Action Teams. English Partnerships, set up as part of the package created under the previous Conservative government, were initially retained, taking over some of the unfinished projects started by the Urban Development Corporations. This government agency was responsible for improving housing and the environment and creating jobs through the reclamation of vacant and derelict land. By 2000 these duties passed to the newly established Regional Development Agencies and the Commission for New Towns.

Two significant new developments in England are the Single Regeneration Budget (SRB) and the New Deal for Communties (NDC).

The Single Regeneration Budget funds local regeneration schemes administered by Regional Development Agencies set up in April 1999. The schemes focus on social exclusion, employment, training, education, housing, community safety, drug misuse prevention, healthcare and child-care. They are funded through a combination of government money, private sector support and European Union funding.

The New Deal for Communities was launched in 1998 with the aim of tackling multiple deprivation in the poorest areas. It involves targeting small areas with special resources through partnerships from private, community and voluntary organisations. The scheme begins with 17 'pathfinder' neighbourhoods, of which all but two are in big cities with large clusters of poverty. The partnerships are to adopt a long-term approach to neighbourhood regeneration and last up to 10 years, hoping to improve on the limited successes of previous shorter-term schemes. Although including upgrading of the physical environment, the scheme is intended to be people-based with a focus on skills, jobs and education. The re-introduction of caretakers and wardens is hoped to tackle some of the complaints of people living on poorly maintained and supervised estates.

EC funding

Money is available from the European Community (EC, now known as European Union, EU) for inner-cities. This can come from the European Regional Development Fund and the European Social Fund. These, together with other sources of finance, are know as the European Structural Fund. The funding is focused on the following objectives:

(1) to promote the development of regions lagging behind the rest of the European Union;

(2) to redevelop regions that are seriously affected by industrial decline;

(3) to promote the development of rural areas.

It is difficult to evaluate the success or failure of the various urban policies outlined in this chapter. Certainly, the earlier programmes tackling specific aspects such as housing or education in small areas had a limited impact on the overall problem of multiple deprivation. The newer policies have still had little effect on the unemployment in poorer areas which is a major factor in deprivation. As this chapter shows, very many short-term initiatives have been started by whichever government is in power, and then wound down, perhaps by a new government, only to be replaced by another initiative with similar sounding aims. There has been little sense of long-term vision, sufficient investment or of genuine community involvement. It is hard to be any more optimistic about the latest batch of schemes.

Activity 6.6

Make sure that you understand the following expressions used in this chapter. Check in the Glossary at the end of the book if you need to.

community care	multiple deprivation
culture of poverty	planning blight
cycle of deprivation	positive discrimination
economic regeneration	Single Regeneration Budget
gentrification	social exclusion
informal social control	social indicator

Further reading

Up-to-date information on inner-city initiatives can be obtained from the Department of the Environment, Transport and the Regions or from a very useful reference book called (in 1999) *Britain 1999*. This book is produced each year by the government and covers all aspects of life in Britain.

Useful addresses

The Department of the Environment, Transport and the Regions is responsible for government policies on inner-cities. Free publications are available from:

Department of the Environment, Transport and the Regions
DETR Free Literature
PO Box No 236
Wetherby LS23 7NB
tel. 0870 1226 236

Priced publications are available from:

Publications Sales Centre
Department of the Environment, Transport and the Regions
Unit 21, Goldthorpe Industrial Estate
Goldthorpe, Rotherham S63 9BL
tel. 01709 891 318

Website

The Department of the Environment, Transport and the Regions (responsible for urban regeneration) **www.detr.gov.uk**

▧ **7** Schooling in Britain

Education is important for society as a whole as well as for each individual. Education plays a role in giving people the skills and abilities needed for work and other aspects of social life. Education also contributes to wider attitudes, beliefs and ways of behaving. Future life chances are, in part, determined by educational achievements and experiences. Access to jobs is often based on qualifications achieved at school or college. Most people have strong and powerful memories of their school days, long after these are over. As well as requiring individual investment of time and money, education is a major consumer of public expenditure. In the year 1996–97 total government expenditure on education was £32,640 million.[1]

This chapter examines some of the important issues in education. It begins by describing provision within state and private schools and across pre-school, primary, secondary, further and higher education sectors. The role of special educational provision for children with learning disabilities is considered in another section. The chapter also looks at educational welfare benefits and the work of careers guidance. Education, perhaps more than any other aspect of the welfare state, has been subject to a great deal of research, controversy and public, political and academic debate. The final part of the chapter examines some issues of continuing concern in education.

In spite of the importance now attached to education, compulsory education is a relatively recent phenomenon. It was only in 1870 that education was made compulsory, and then only for children up to the age of 10. Over the following 30 years the school-leaving age was gradually raised to 13. In 1918, legislation made it compulsory for children to remain in school until they were 14. The 1944 Education Act, of which more is said later, raised the school-leaving age to 15. Today, as a result of legislation passed in 1972, young people are required to be in school until they are 16. Increasing numbers of people remain in post-compulsory education well beyond the minimum school-leaving age.

7.1 The education system

This section is given the title 'The education system', yet it will quickly become apparent that education in this country is hard to think of as one single system, but is better described as including several different systems, varying considerably from area to area. There are several reasons for this diversity of provision, the main one being the complex and changing relationship between central government and the local education authorities. The Department for Education and Employment (DfEE) is the government department in charge of education, responsible for overall policies and legislation. Some aspects of education are governed by legislation passed through Parliament and are therefore the same throughout the whole country. For example, the school-leaving age is 16 for all children, whether they live in Devon, Sheffield or Newcastle.

Local education authorities (LEAs) have traditionally been responsible for the actual provision of state education: building schools and colleges, employing teachers and other staff, and exercising considerable control of the organisation of education in their areas. This changed in the late 1980s and 1990s: first, because of the introduction of the national curriculum which, as mentioned above, set national standards and reduced local decision-making; and secondly as a result of schools being allowed to opt out of LEA control. Both of these changes were introduced by the 1988 Education Reform Act.

The 1988 Education Reform Act allowed schools to become independent of the local education authority and by 1999 six per cent of all schools and 23 per cent of secondary schools[2] had done so. Parents could vote for a school to become 'grant maintained'. Grant-maintained schools were funded from central government with a governing body responsible for all aspects of the management of the school. Reducing the powers of the local authorities in this kind of way was part of Conservative party philosophy. The Labour government, elected in 1997, inherited a system with three types of mainstream state school: county schools owned and funded by the local education authority; voluntary schools, established by churches and other organisations and funded by the local authority; and grant-maintained schools. In 1999 grant-maintained schools were abolished as a result of the School Standards and Framework Act, passed in July 1998. This establishes three types of schools: *community schools* which include the old county schools; *foundation schools*, which include previously grant-maintained schools; and *voluntary schools*. All state schools will receive funding through the local authorities (as before the 1988 Education Act) but schools will continue to have governing bodies which will manage the school's budget.

Colleges of further education are now self-governing with funds allocated through further education funding councils. Similarly there is another funding council to allocate central government money to universities.

Activity 7.1

What was your experience of the education system? Begin with any pre-school education, including the kind of secondary school you attended, and whether or not you had to take an examination before you went there. Compare your experience with that of the rest of the class.

7.2 Provision of schooling in Britain

Several variations can be expected in the educational experiences of a group of people. Some will have attended a private nursery school, others a nursery class attached to a primary school, whilst others will have had no pre-school education. From the age of 5, members of the group may have gone to an ordinary state school, a school run by a Church or an independent school. In terms of secondary schooling, many areas have comprehensive schools, while others retain some grammar schools. Some people will have had to sit an examination before transferring to a secondary school. Some members of the group may have changed schools at the age of 11 whilst others may have attended middle schools and moved into secondary education at 12 years of age.

Pre-school education

In Britain, there has been little systematic nursery provision, although the 1944 Education Act stated that local education authorities should provide nursery education. This was clarified in the 1980 Education Act, where provision for the under-5s is stated to be at the discretion of the local authorities. During the war, when women were required to work, nursery provision expanded, but the trend was reversed in the period after the war and government money was withdrawn. By the 1960s, only 5 per cent of children could be given nursery education.

During the 1960s, there was increasing concern over the lack of child care and nursery facilities. In 1967, the report of the Plowden Committee, 'Children and

Source: Gina Glover, Photofusion
Should nursery places be made available for all children?

their Primary Schools', was published, recommending the expansion of nursery provision. In 1969, as we saw in Chapter 6, the government established the Urban Aid Programme which provided financial resources for areas of the country thought to be in particular need. In the initial years of the Urban Programme, much of the money was spent on day-care for children. The Conservative government, in 1972, promised to expand nursery provision, but this plan fell victim to public expenditure cuts after 1973. In the extract below, Helen Penn – an expert on education – made strong criticisms of Britain's treatment of under-5s in the early 1990s:

> We have a crazy system which offers 25 per cent of children nursery education in shifts, shoves four-year-olds into school before they can cope with it, segregates depressed and forlorn children into a different and temporary system in social services, family centres and day nurseries, and considers children of working parents best catered for in the private pay-as-(or if)-you-earn sector. We refuse to listen to the evidence about parents' views, and if we have no idea how much we spend or what on, nor will we contemplate any more expenditure. We have a Children Act and an Education Reform Act, and national and local economic and employment initiatives concerning young children; but each of them ignores the other, and none of them takes early years' education into account.
>
> Children beginning formal school at five have already experienced very different levels of intervention. Should we continue to believe, as the Government does, that we have a system which offers 'choice' or would it be more apt to call our system unjust, wasteful and very nearly pointless?[3]

Successive governments have acknowledged the need for expansion in pre-school education to provide sufficient places for all children whose parents want their child to attend. This has often, however, been made dependent on availability of resources and as a result the promised expansion has not materialised. In 1993 the then Prime Minister, John Major, stated that nursery education was the government's top spending priority in education and that he wanted to see universal nursery education. He refused, however, to set a date for this expansion and said that the government did not have the resources for it. Three months later he said: 'as and when resources are available we shall move towards further nursery education, towards universal nursery education.'[4]

The Labour government which began office in 1997 was committed to increasing the availability of pre-school education and child-care and the number of child-care places doubled by 1999. Free nursery education is now available to all 4-year-olds whose parents want their children to attend. This is to be expanded to cater for 3-year-olds as well. Local education authorities have been required to draw up 'early years development plans' for meeting these targets through co-operation between private nurseries, playgroups and schools. The introduction of child-care tax credit in 1999 is likely to increase the demand for child-care places as parents are entitled to a government subsidy for child-care costs. These changes have had the effect of creating a shortage of child-care workers to provide education and child-care, and there are plans to train people for this fast-growing area of employment.

Activity 7.2

What facilities for children under 5 exist in your area? Carry out a survey of local provision, looking at the various types of facilities in nurseries, play-groups and with child-minders. Find out where the funding comes from and the kind of activities the children are involved in.

Provision of pre-school education has been limited and varied across the country. Patchy state provision has resulted in the development of private and voluntary nurseries and playgroups and a range of different types of provision.

Since 1999, regulation of child-care services, including child-minders, nurseries and playgroups, has been the responsibility of the education watchdog, OFSTED.

Nursery schools and classes

Nursery schools and classes are provided free by local education authorities, opening for school hours in term-time. These have been available for some time but demand for places has always outstripped supply. From 1998, places have been guaranteed for all parents who want their 4-year-old children to attend. The majority of children attend nursery classes on a part-time basis. Since nurseries take children for short hours during term-time only, they are of little help to working parents needing child-care. As a result, it may be that the children who would most benefit from pre-school education are most likely to be those deprived of it. Local education authority nurseries are staffed by nursery teachers and emphasise the development of the child by means of stimulating play. In 1999 the debate over pre-school education intensified after 'learning goals' for children in nursery education were proposed.

Targets for Toddlers[5]

- Naming and sounding all the letters of the alphabet.
- Reading a range of common words and simple sentences independently.
- Showing comprehension of stories.
- Holding a pencil effectively and forming recognisable letters.
- Using phonetic knowledge to make plausible attempts at complex words.
- Writing their own names and forming sentences, sometimes using punctuation.
- Counting reliably up to 10 everyday objects.
- Recognising numerals 1 to 9.
- Understanding the vocabulary or adding and subtracting.
- Asking about why things happen and how things work.

Activity 7.3

Whilst some people agree that children's time should be used in a structured way which prepares them for school, others feel children under five
are not mature enough for structured learning and should spend their time
at play. What are the arguments for and against each of these points of
view? What do you think is most appropriate for children under five?

Playgroups

Playgroups are usually run by voluntary organisations, the most successful being
the Pre-School Learning Alliance. This organisation was started in 1961, in
response to the lack of pre-school provision at the time. The movement
expanded rapidly and in 1999 there were 850,000 children in playgroups.[6]
Playgroups emphasise the importance of play and education activities for young
children. They usually take children over 3 years of age, and involve parents in
the running of groups. Pre-school playgroups are not evenly spread throughout
the country and can be criticised for being predominantly middle-class in
appeal. A survey carried out in the 1980s by the Pre-School Learning Alliance
found that only 10 per cent of groups were in inner-city urban areas, whilst 38
per cent were in villages. The Pre-School Learning Alliance receives a grant from
the government and, whilst the Alliance is successful and popular, possibly it is
encouraged by the government because they provide a cheap means of meeting
a need.

Playgroups came under threat in the late 1990s with a number of groups
around the country closing – first as a result of the vouchers scheme set up by
the Conservative government, and now abolished, and then from the guaranteed places in nursery schools offered from 1998.

Local-authority day nurseries

In 1997, 20,000 children had places in day nurseries provided by local authorities.[7] Within this overall figure there is considerable local variation. London
boroughs, for example, tend to have a higher ratio of places than rural areas.

Local-authority day nurseries are provided by social-service departments and
take children from a few months old to the age of 5. They are open up to 10
hours a day, including school holidays. Places are mainly reserved for children
thought to be in special need, such as children at risk of non-accidental injury or
those living in areas with no play facilities. Nurseries are staffed by trained
nursery nurses. The demand for places far exceeds the availability and long
waiting-lists are common. Fees are charged, on a sliding scale, depending on the
income of the parents.

Private nurseries

Private nurseries are overseen by OFSTED (Office for Standards in Education)
and must comply with regulations concerning staffing and facilities. It is difficult

for a private nursery to run successfully without charging fees which most parents would be unable to afford. As a result, there are few private nurseries.

Education and work-place nurseries

There are a small number of nurseries attached to places of work and colleges of further and higher education. This type of provision is most useful to parents who want to work or study, happy in the knowledge that their children are safe and close-by.

Child-minders

The lack of availability of places in nursery schools and day centres means that many parents leave their young children with private child-minders. In 1999 the role of ensuring that standards are met was transferred from the local-authority social-services department to OFSTED. It is probable that there are unregistered child-minders operating illegally. In 1972, 383,000 children (under 8) were cared for in the UK by registered child-minders.[8] Child-minders work long hours and receive little money.

Activity 7.4

What are the advantages of making state provision of nursery education available to all 3–5-year-olds?

There are several advantages for children, parents and the wider society in state provision of pre-school day-care. Nurseries prepare children for school, helping them to adjust not only to leaving their parents but also to school routines. This preparation means that children will settle in quickly at school and that schools can get on with the task of teaching. Nursery classes in schools and nursery schools attached to infant schools are especially useful in this respect, introducing the child gradually to school. Children aged 3–5 are at a stage in their development when they are eager and willing to learn. The trained teacher or nursery nurse can make use of this, and provide an environment to stimulate learning. Play facilities provided by nurseries are of a better standard and less restrictive than those available in most homes. For children from poor or over-crowded homes, or those living in high-rise flats, the nursery may provide the only opportunity for creative play.

Pre-school education teaches children to socialise and to mix with other children, which is particularly important for children from families where there are no other small children. Nursery schools can be involved in preventative work, in that the staff watch for signs of health or development difficulties in children. Early recognition of problems, whilst of benefit to the child, could also save money for the health or educational services. Also, children who are at risk of abuse can be recognised at an early point.

Providing facilities for disadvantaged children only (as do many local authorities at present) groups together and isolates such children. Full-scale provision would avoid the problems inherent in putting all these children together, separate from others. Looking at the present situation from another point of view, much of the provision is more readily available to middle-class families. Comprehensive state provision would lead to greater equality in access to pre-school education.

Nursery schools give greater freedom to parents of children aged 3–5, allowing them to work, develop their own interests or devote time to younger children in the family.

Finally, state provision might ensure that day-care for under-5s was of an adequate and uniform standard. The present lack of facilities means that parents have to use private child-minders, where the care provided may not be satisfactory.

Compulsory schooling

Primary and secondary education is provided for all children between the ages of 5 to 16. Children are legally required to attend school between these ages. There are several different types of schools (these are described in more detail at secondary level in the section on secondary education):

- *Community* and *foundation schools* are owned and maintained by the LEA.
- *Voluntary schools*, usually set up by religious organisations, are also maintained by the LEA, but some of the costs for the buildings might be paid for by a Church.
- *Independent schools* are privately run and parents pay fees for their children to attend. They benefit from tax exemptions – as a result of their status as charities.

The national curriculum

In 1988, the government introduced the *national curriculum* for all maintained primary and secondary schools in the country. This sets out what must be taught to children and standards they should reach. Compulsory education is divided into four key stages:

- Key Stage 1 – Pupils aged 5 to 7.
- Key Stage 2 – Pupils aged 7 to 11.
- Key Stage 3 – Pupils aged 11 to 14.
- Key Stage 4 – Pupils aged 14 to 16.

Pupils at Key Stages 1 and 2 study English, mathematics, science, design and technology, history, geography, art, music and physical education. At Key Stage 3 a foreign language is added. At Key Stage 4 pupils have more choice and time to add vocational courses if they wish: they study English, mathematics, science, physical education, technology and a modern foreign language.

In each subject there are *statutory attainment targets* setting what children should know and be able to do at each *key stage. Standardised assessment tasks* (SATs) are taken by all children towards the end of Key Stages 1, 2 and 3 in English, mathematics and science. There are also formal teacher assessments in the other subjects. GCSEs provide the assessment at the end of Key Stage 4. Results are made available to parents. The government agency in charge of the national curriculum and all assessment and examinations in schools and vocational training is the Qualifications and Curriculum Authority (QCA).

The national curriculum, when first introduced, proved very controversial, particularly with teachers. The conflict which arose between teachers and the government reached a head in 1993 with a successful boycott of tests by teachers. Teachers basically objected to the amount of extra work involved in teaching to the national curriculum, the amount of material to be covered, the time taken up with the testing procedures, and the lack of freedom for teachers to plan their own teaching – for example, English teachers objected to the mandatory lists of authors to be covered. In 1993 Sir Ron Dearing was asked to review the national curriculum and make recommendations for change. The Dearing Report introduced a slimming down of the national curriculum to make it more manageable and to allow time for schools to offer other options. Dearing also recommended that the tests and gradings be simplified and no further changes to the curriculum be introduced in the short-term future. In the summer of 1994 the government also announced that teachers would not be expected to mark tests as part of their ordinary workload and outside examiners would be paid to do so.

'League tables' of school achievements

Schools are required by law to publish their results and all schools have to be included in the annual 'league tables' which are published in newspapers and on the DfEE website. League tables were introduced in 1992 for secondary schools and then in 1996 for primary schools. The league tables for primary schools show the annual results of tests in English, mathematics and science together with teacher assessments of work done in class throughout the year. The tables for secondary schools provide information about achievements in GCSEs and entries for 'A' levels. In 1998 a 'school progress measure' was added – to indicate secondary schools which, on the basis of the results of the children at Key Stage 3, had achieved better than expected GCSE results. This is an attempt to show the 'value added' factor in education.

School league tables are controversial. In their favour, it is argued that the lists allow parents to make comparisons between different schools. Whereas schools provide information to sell the school to parents, and try to show themselves at their best on open evenings, league tables cannot lie. Research has suggested that league tables have created greater equality in the information to which parents from different backgrounds have access:

> Middle-class parents have always tended to make sure they were informed about the schools in their area. The attention given to the league tables – particularly in the local press – has encouraged many working-class parents to take a more active role in school selection. … Many middle-class parents know teachers and other academics and are able to get an inside track on which schools are currently doing well. Working-class parents don't have this cultural capital and a lot of their information is out of date.[9]

However, there are many people who believe league tables are dangerously misleading. The main argument against the publication of the tables is based on the

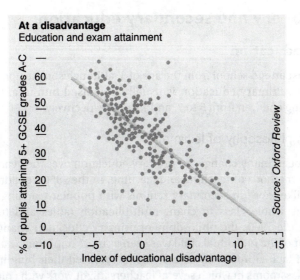

At a disadvantage
Education and exam attainment

Source: Oxford Review

Source: *Guardian Education* (1 December 1998)/*Oxford Review*.

Figure 7.1   Poverty line: the graph tracks levels of low performance linked to educational disadvantage

very close relationship between exam results achieved by a school and the poverty or prosperity of the pupils. Figure 7.1[10] shows a graph which plots the percentage of children gaining five A* to C grades at GCSE against an index of educational disadvantage. Each dot is a school – the more disadvantaged the area, the more likely the school is to be at the bottom right of the graph, with comparatively low performance. The league tables do not make enough allowance for these social and economic differences in the backgrounds of the children, or of cultural differences between schools. They create the impression that a school is not as good a provider of education, which lowers morale amongst the staff, the pupils and their parents, and creates or adds to prejudice against schools in poor areas. A vicious circle then means that schools which are doing well can attract higher-ability pupils, at the expense of schools further down the tables, which do not appear to be doing so well. This would have the effect of widening the gap between schools and creating greater educational disadvantage.

Standards in schools

Standards in schools are monitored by the Office for Standards in Education (OFSTED). Inspectors contracted by OFSTED visit schools at least every six years and produce a report – a summary of this is sent to all parents.

Schools which are judged to be 'failing' can be taken over from the local authority and run by a private or other type of organisation. The first private sector takeover was of King's Manor School in Guildford which had been branded by OFSTED as one of the worst schools in the country.

7.3 Primary and secondary education

Primary education

Children must attend school from the age of 5, although some begin before their fifth birthday. Primary education is usually organised into infant and junior schools, taking children from 5 to 7, and 7 to 11 respectively.

Changes in philosophy of learning

There have been many changes in primary education over the years, mainly in terms of the methods of teaching and learning. In the 1950s, children learnt in classrooms like those in secondary schools with popular teaching techniques requiring the whole class to chant multiplication tables and to memorise spellings. In the 1960s the philosophy of primary education changed and the development of the individual child was seen as more important than learning a great deal of factual information. Schools reorganised their buildings to allow open-plan classrooms in which several teachers might work with children sitting in small groups. Much primary teaching was based on projects covering many skills rather than separate subjects, as in secondary school. Classes were mixed ability without any attempt to grade children into ability groups and children were encouraged to work at their own pace on individualised learning schemes. Also at this time there were a number of experiments with new ways of learning reading and mathematics.

The trend is currently back to more formal and conventional styles of teaching and learning. In 1987 the national curriculum (described above) was introduced, encouraging a return to a more structured approach to assessment of learning in primary school. Poor results in SATs – only 64 per cent of pupils reached their target in English and 57.9 in mathematics – have increased the pressure to put more emphasis on teaching of basic skills. Daily mathematics and literacy lessons have been introduced in a drive to improve numeracy and literacy standards.

Reduction in primary school class sizes was an election promise in 1997 when the Labour government was elected. Local authorities are working towards a goal of classes of 30 children or fewer by the year 2001.

The Plowden Report

In 1967, as mentioned in the previous section, a major government report on primary education – the Plowden Report – was published, containing many recommendations. These included the idea that parents should be more involved with their children's education. Plowden was also in favour of middle schools, for children from 8 to 12 years of age. The most important recommendation, however, of the Plowden report, was that Educational Priority Areas (EPAs) be established. This idea was based on a conclusion of the report that poorer areas tended to have poor schools, and that positive discrimination was necessary to bring these schools up to the standards of the best in the country. The policy of positive discrimination meant that schools in deprived areas would qualify for additional resources. The money would be spent on more buildings and materi-

Source: Gina Glover, Photofusion
Most children attend state schools

als, extra pay for teachers, the provision of teachers' assistants and better ratios of teachers to pupils.

The government has never actually designated EPAs, but in 1967, local authorities were invited to submit claims for government money. The money was available for areas of multiple deprivation (see Chapter 6), characterised by factors such as overcrowding, a high incidence of families needing financial support from the state and a rapid turnover of teachers. The money available was a comparatively small sum, insufficient to meet the need. In 1968, it was agreed that teachers in schools in deprived areas should receive an extra £75 per year. Again the criteria suggested for designating deprived areas were vague. The factors to be considered were: the social class of parents in the area, the incidence of homes without basic amenities and the numbers of children receiving free school meals. By the end of 1968, approximately 2.5 per cent of maintained primary schools received some form of special help.

Considerable hope was raised by the Plowden Report and the subsequent government proposals. However, the implementation of the policies has achieved little, for a variety of reasons. The means of deciding the areas in need of extra resources have never been satisfactorily settled. The amount of help provided has been inadequate to deal with the massive problems of poor areas. Also, there is less acceptance now of the idea that improvements in educational provision can affect wider problems in society, such as poverty and deprivation.

Secondary education

Secondary education was made compulsory by the 1944 Education Act, sometimes known as the Butler Act. The Act was based on a report produced in 1943, by the Norwood Committee. The Norwood Committee believed that there are three types of children; first those who enjoy learning for its own sake, can grasp ideas and are interested in finding out why things happen; second, those whose abilities lie in applied sciences and arts; and finally those who are not interested in ideas, but in practical work.

The 1944 Educational Act introduced universal secondary education which most local authorities provided in the form of a tripartite system, under which there would be grammar schools for academic pupils, technical schools for vocationally-oriented pupils, and secondary modern schools to provide a general education for the remainder of children. It was believed that the 11-plus examination could determine which type of education was most suitable for each child. In practice, few technical schools were established and so there were mainly two types of schools, grammar schools for about 20 per cent of children, and secondary modern schools for the rest. The grammar schools prepared children for examinations which led into higher education. Secondary modern schools did not usually offer any examinations until 1965, when the Certificate of Secondary Education was introduced. In theory, the different types of schools were equal, although providing different sorts of education. They were to have 'parity of esteem' which means equal status. In practice, however, there was a hierarchy, with grammar schools having more status than secondary modern schools.

The Crowther Report

Two important reports concerned with secondary education were published following the 1944 Act. The first was the Crowther Report, in 1959, which focused on young people aged 15–18. The report looked for reasons why many children failed to progress in school, and why working-class children tended to leave school at the earliest possible date. The Crowther Report found a relationship between home background and success at school, and indicated that educational attainment was more closely linked with social class than with ability.

The Crowther Report contained many recommendations, including the suggestions that the school-leaving age be raised to 16, an examination provided for secondary modern pupils and that education in schools should be more orientated to technology. The report recommended an expansion in all forms of further education, and the establishment of county colleges for sixth-form students. Little was done by the government in immediate response to the report, although many of the recommendations were taken up in later years.

The Newsom Report

The Crowther Report was followed in 1963 by the Newsom Report, entitled 'Half Our Future', meaning that the less privileged 50 per cent of children with whom the report was concerned would, in time, be half the country's citizens, workers and parents. The report found that many secondary modern schools were deficient and argued that the less privileged 50 per cent of children did not receive their fair share of resources. The Newsom Report found wide differences in educational attainment between one school and another, and in different parts of the country. The Report supported the idea that it was social factors which held children back and argued that this led to a waste of talent and ability, which was not in the interest of the economic development of the nation.

The Newsom Report recommended that the school-leaving age be raised to 16 and that the school day be lengthened. Newsom sought to establish a government working party to look at the social and educational problems of slum areas. The Report further suggested that schools should provide learning more closely related to the everyday lives of the pupils. In common with the Crowther Report, little was done by the government at the time of the publication of the report, although some of the recommendations were implemented at a later date.

Comprehensive education

Both the Crowther Report and the Newsom Report supported the tripartite system of education, but in 1965 a major change was initiated. All local authorities were sent a central government circular, known as Circular 10/65, asking them to submit plans to abolish selective secondary education and introduce a comprehensive system. The circular described various ways in which local authorities might effect this change. Circular 10/65 came as a result of many years of debate by politicians, educationalists and others over the merits and problems of selective schools.

Activity 7.5

What are the advantages, and the disadvantages, of comprehensive schools? Discuss the points you have listed with the rest of the class.

Many different points have been put forward in the long debate over selective and non-selective schooling. Sometimes the same argument is used by both sides, each believing that it proves their case. For example, those in favour of comprehensive schools argue that such schools improve educational standards while those against comprehensive schools claim that they mean a reduction in standards.

In favour Several of the criticisms of the tripartite system concerned the process of selecting children for different schools. The 11-plus examination has been attacked on several grounds. A child, for reasons of sickness or nervousness, could produce results on the day of the examination which would not be an accurate reflection of his or her ability. It has been increasingly recognised that some children are 'late developers' and that assessment at the age of 11 does not provide an indication of their future ability. It was possible for children to change schools after the age of 11, but in practice, this rarely happened.

It was argued that 'failing' the 11-plus examination had an adverse effect on children, although strictly it is not possible to fail an IQ test, since it simply measures and compares certain sorts of ability. The IQ test was criticised for being biased in favour of middle-class children, enabling a greater proportion of them to gain access to grammar schools. Both Crowther and Newsom found children wrongly placed as a result of errors in the test.

Other arguments for comprehensive schools included the fact that such a system would eliminate regional variation, which meant that some children had a better chance of going to a grammar school because they lived in an area where there were more grammar-school places. In addition, the fact that comprehensive schools would be bigger than selective schools would mean they could provide better facilities with a wider range of subject options. Finally, those in favour of comprehensive schools argue that selective schools increase social divisions in society and that comprehensive schools promote greater equality.

Against On the other side of the debate, there are those who argue that large schools are impersonal institutions. It is said that comprehensive schools hold back brighter pupils to benefit the less able ones. Dividing pupils within one school into streams or sets according to ability is argued by some to create greater divisions between children than existed in the selective system. Finally, proponents of grammar schools argue that they had developed fine traditions, worthy of conservation.

The extent to which the proposals in Circular 10/65 were implemented varied throughout the country. This was because local education is controlled by local authorities in the absence of legislation. In 1976, legislation was introduced to make comprehensive schools compulsory, but this was repealed in 1979. In the five years following the issue of Circular 10/65, 35 per cent of schools turned comprehensive, and by late 1980s over 85 per cent of all children were educated in comprehensive schools.[9] In 1998, regulations were passed by the Labour government to allow for local ballots which would compel schools to admit children of all abilities. This could mean the end of the few remaining grammar schools.

However, for two reasons, many comprehensive schools are not fully 'comprehensive'. The first involves the continued existence of voluntary and independent schools, which select pupils. As a result, comprehensive schools do not take all the children in a particular area. Second, most comprehensive schools stream or set pupils in some way, on the basis of the school's perception of their ability. Recent years have seen a further drift away from the idea of comprehensive education as schools opt out and some move towards selection for entry, and with the development of City Technology Colleges (described below).

City Technology Colleges

The 1988 Education Act also proposed the establishment of 20 City Technology Colleges (CTCs). These were originally to be located in deprived inner-city areas. CTCs are independent schools taking children from 11 to 18 and charging no fees. Children are selected on the basis of their interest in technology and CTCs offer a broad education with a special bias towards technology. They should have better science and technology facilities, more specialised staff and close links with industry. In the words of the government, they should be 'beacons of excellence'.

The original plan was that the CTCs would be set up with money from industry and the running costs met by grants from the government. However, industrial sponsors have not shown the interest that the government hoped for. Most have preferred to continue with existing schemes spread over a wider number of schools and potentially benefiting more children. In response, the government was forced to put in more money than was originally intended. By 1993, 15 CTCs had been established around the country.

In 1993 the CTC idea took a new direction when it was announced that voluntary or grant-maintained secondary schools could apply to become CTCs. Schools had to raise a sum of money from industry and would then receive up to £250,000 in extra funding from the government. However, again sponsors from industry have been hard to find. Many of the larger firms are already involved with schemes such as Compacts (outlined below). The head of educational services at BT, Peter Thompson, commented:

> We would prefer to maintain our consistent relationship with a significant number of schools in the way we have done rather than select one or two of them for substantial funding.[11]

Specialist schools

The specialist schools programme was launched in 1993. Specialist schools are state secondary schools which teach the full national curriculum but also specialise in technology, modern languages, sport or the arts. Schools need the backing of private sponsors and are then eligible for government grants. In September 1998 there were 330 designated specialist schools.

Education Action Zones

Education Action Zones are aimed at improving education in deprived areas. The original idea was for clusters of 15–25 schools in a local area to join together as a zone, run by a partnership of businesses, parents, schools, local authorities and community organisations. An action plan sets targets for improvements and proposals for new ways to provide education. The proposals supported by the government include:

- rewarding good teachers through incentives for success;
- strengthening leadership through pay incentives for heads who turn around failing schools;
- improving standards of literacy and numeracy, especially for pupils who are under-achieving;
- using the support of business and other partners to provide school services;
- providing opportunities for work-related learning;
- reducing truancy and exclusions;

- changing the school day or school year to provide before and after school clubs, weekend and holiday classes, reading clubs and nursery facilities;
- using parents to support teaching and learning.

Twenty-five Education Action Zones were established. A £350 million package announced under the banner of *Excellence in Cities* announced new, smaller education action zones based on individual secondary schools offering schemes to improve teaching and learning. Successful schools receive extra funding from the government for up to 5 years. They are also encouraged to raise money from private organisations which will then be doubled by the government.

Changes in the curriculum

Other developments in secondary education concern the curriculum and its assessment. In the summer of 1988, the first students took the GCSE examinations which replaced the old GCE 'O' levels and CSEs. This meant that all students entered the same examination, instead of there being two types of exam (although later developments brought in tiered GCSE exams, restricting the grades which could be achieved). Most GCSEs included coursework assessment in addition to more traditional examinations. Although most teachers and students were pleased with this broader form of assessment, the change meant a lot of work for both teaching staff and students. The principle behind GCSEs is that they should be *criteria-referenced*, which means students' work is measured against a set of criteria stated in advance, rather than against the overall standard of the work. In the early 1990s, the School Curriculum and Assessment Authority (SCAA) became responsible for approving GCSEs and all other aspects of the curriculum. With later developments, a new agency was set up as the Qualifications and Curriculum Authority (QCA). From 1994, GCSEs have been used to test pupils on the national curriculum (see above) at age 16 and the structure of the exams has been adapted in line with the requirements of the national curriculum.

Vocational initiatives

In 1983, the government established the Technical and Vocational Education Initiative (TVEI). This initiative set out to change the curriculum for 14–18-year olds, making it more relevant to work. By 1987, many local education authorities were running pilot schemes in schools and colleges, with funding from the Manpower Services Commission (now abolished). The national extension of TVEI was announced in 1986, extending the initiative to all LEAs. All courses were to adapt to meet the criteria of TVEI. These criteria include a practical, problem-solving approach to learning, the use of new technology, avoidance of sex-stereo-typing, and the development of links with industry with various schemes for work experience and work shadowing. Although not achieving its aims in full, work experience is now a part of secondary schooling for most pupils. Pupils in school can study General National Vocational Qualifications (GNVQs) in any of seven vocational areas: art and design; business; engineering; health and social care; information technology; leisure and tourism; and manufacturing.

Education Business Partnerships consist of representatives from industry, education and the community. They are funded by TECs and LEAs and aim to link education and industry and make sure that the right attitudes and skills are taught in schools to make pupils attractive to employers. Under this scheme, teachers have spent time in business settings to update their knowledge of the world of work and improve the careers advice they pass on to pupils. Compacts are schemes which involve employers and others in encouraging pupils to achieve more at school and continue in education beyond the minimum leaving age. Under these schemes young people agree to work towards certain goals – perhaps in terms of attendance and punctuality, or staying on another year – and in return employers offer incentives, including in some areas, jobs with training.

7.4   Further and higher education

The 1944 Education Act states that local authorities have a duty to provide education up to the age of 19 for all those who want it.

Organisation of provision

The way in which education for the post-16 age-group is organised varies from area to area. The traditional pattern was for young people wishing to take 'A' levels to remain at school in the sixth form, and for others wanting more vocational courses to attend a college of further education. In some areas this system continues. Most schools have however widened their provision for people staying on and offer courses other than 'A' levels, perhaps working in partnership with the local college. In other areas there are sixth form colleges which take students from the local schools and provide 'A' level, GCSE and possibly other courses. The further education college will continue to provide vocational courses. A third variation is a tertiary college which provides all education for those over 16, in one establishment. Schools and colleges are funded differently, with further education colleges very much the poor relation: there are suggestions for a more coherent system in the future.

Colleges of further education usually provide some GCSE and 'A' level courses for people re-sitting examinations, or for those who wish to continue their studies, but do not want to remain in a school environment. Colleges also offer full-time courses related to specific areas of work such as nursery nursing, hairdressing and secretarial work. In addition, colleges provide day-release courses for local employees, varying to suit the needs of local industry. Finally, colleges provide part-time recreational classes in such subjects as modern languages and crafts. Since 1993, colleges have been self-governing, independent of the LEAs, and are funded by the Further Education Funding Council. In 1990s charters were produced for students, parents and employers – these set out the standards of service and complaints procedures.

The National Council for Vocational Qualifications (NCVQ) was set up to provide an overall structure for the many different courses and qualifications offered in further education. This work is now part of the role of the Qualifications and Curriculum Authority (QCA). Levels of achievement are set so that the different courses can be compared with each other more easily. General National Vocational Qualifications (GNVQs) provide an education based on broad vocational areas such as Art and Design, Business, and Health and Social Care. Courses are available at Foundation, Intermediate and Advanced levels. Advanced levels, are equivalent to 'A' levels and a route into higher education. Developments in the year 2000 allow young people to combine academic and vocational courses and follow broader educational pathways. Examining bodies also provide other vocational alternatives to GNVQs.

Numbers staying on

Recent years have seen an expansion of the numbers of young people entering colleges for full-time courses. In 1997, around three-quarters of young people between 16 and 18 were in education and training. This is a big increase since the 1980s, when around half of all young people stayed in education.[12] This is partly a reflection of government policy which is to encourage young people to stay on in education or training. The expansion in numbers of young people staying on is however also a reflection of the lack of choice available at 16. There have been few job openings for young people and their rights to benefits have been cut.

There has also been an expansion in the number of mature students attending further education courses. Access courses have proved especially popular, offering an alternative route into higher education and some areas of professional training. These include study skills training, counselling and guidance, as well as academic study at advanced level, and are usually assessed through coursework rather than examinations.

Although there are increased numbers of full-time students, there has been a reduction in day-release students, as fewer young people have been taken on by employers.

Grants for students attending further education courses are discretionary and therefore vary from area to area, depending on the policy adopted by the local education authority. Discretionary grants are means-tested and paid to parents or mature students on low incomes. Fees are free to all full-time students under 19 and some colleges do not charge fees to older students on full-time courses. In 1999, proposals were set out for a grant of up to £40 a week to encourage young people from less well off families to stay on at school or college. Students have to sign a learning agreement and those who miss classes or do not complete work set risk losing their allowance.

Work-based education

National Vocational Qualifications (NVQs) recognise work-based skills and knowledge. They are available at Levels 1 to 5. Level 1 awards cover routine tasks done under supervision and Level 5 NVQs involve complex roles with technical knowledge and high levels of responsibility. These levels are the same as those used in further and higher education where 'A' Levels and Advanced GNVQs are at Level 3 qualifications.

Specifically for young people, Modern Apprenticeships offer NVQ Level 3 qualifications and training for jobs at craft, technician and management levels. National Traineeships offer NVQ Level 2 awards. Proposals in 1999 provided 16- and 17-year-olds who are working with a right to paid time off for training.

Adult education and lifelong learning

Adult education refers to non-vocational study ranging from subjects such as philosophy to recreational classes in pottery or art appreciation. Classes are run by local education authorities in colleges of further education and by the Workers Education Association (WEA). In 1973, the Russell Report recommended expansion in this area of educational provision but provision decreased in the 1980s and early 1990s and cuts in funding resulted in increases in fees for classes.

In 1998, the DfEE announced proposals for a new initiative for continuous development of skills and knowledge under the banner of 'lifelong learning'. One of the proposals is for a University for Industry *(UfI)* providing open and distance learning. This will begin in the year 2000 and co-ordinate a national network of multimedia learning centres run by various organisations and partnerships. *Individual Learning Accounts* are proposed to help people save and borrow for investment in learning.

Higher education

Higher education consists of degree and degree-equivalent courses taught in universities and colleges of higher education. Colleges of further education have also increasingly begun to offer degree and degree-level courses, and there has been an expansion of vocational courses which lead to a degree. Examples of these are in nursing and occupational therapy.

Until 1992 there was a binary system within higher education – with polytechnics and universities offering broadly similar provision. Universities tended to have a higher status in people's minds than did the polytechnics. In 1992, polytechnics and some colleges of higher education were allowed to become universities and most did so.

Numbers in higher education

In 1963, the Robbins Report reviewed higher education. The Report recommended expansion in its provision to allow all qualified young people access to higher education. At the time of the report, 8 per cent of young people entered universities and the report recommended that this should increase to 17 per cent of the age group by the 1980s. The Robbins report was remarkably successful and almost immediately the government allocated a large sum of money for the expansion of higher education. The number of universities increased again in 1992 when the polytechnics were allowed to become universities. In 1994 there were 83 universities, including the Open University. The proportion of 18-

year-olds in higher education increased in the late 1980s and early 1990s, reaching about around one in three by the mid-1990s[13] There has also been an expansion in the numbers of mature students going to university and in 1997 over 50 per cent of students were over twenty-five.[14] However, numbers of mature applicants fell in 1998 and 1999, probably as a result of the introduction of fees and the abolition of grants, although falling rates of unemployment may also have affected applications.

Universities are self-governing and are funded by higher education funding councils, with the exception of Buckingham University, which is a private university.

Students on first degree courses have in the past been eligible for mandatory grants from their local education authorities and discretionary grants for non-designated courses. These were assessed according to parents' or spouse's income. The grant covered fees and a maintenance allowance to live on. In the 1990s grants did not increase in line with inflation and students were eligible to apply for loans to help pay their living expenses. The loans were not means-tested and repayments started in the April following the end of the course. The loans are administered by the Student Loans Company in Glasgow.

In July 1977, the National Committee of Inquiry into Higher Education, chaired by Lord Dearing, recommended further expansion of higher education over the next 20 years. The government decided that further expansion needed a new form of funding and in 1998 introduced a tuition fee of £1000 a year, about a quarter of the full cost of fees. Students from lower-income families continue to have their fees paid. The following year maintenance grants were abolished and fully replaced by loans, means-tested against parental income and repayable by students when they have graduated and are earning a high enough level of income. In response to falling numbers of mature applicants to higher education in 1999, loans were extended to include part-time students.

7.5 Private education

In 1997/98, 615,000 pupils were in fee-paying independent schools. This is about 7 per cent of the school population. The proportion of children in private schools rose through the 1980s but fell in the early years of the 1990s.[15] The majority of these pupils come from middle-class homes. A MORI poll in 1994 showed that 54 per cent of parents sending their children to private schools earned more than £40,000 a year.[16] Children who have attended private schools are most likely to gain places at the high-status universities, for examples, Oxford and Cambridge. A large number of the people who occupy powerful and well-paid positions in society attended private schools.

Independent schools range from small kindergartens to large boarding schools. They include experimental schools such as Summerhill where pupils are allowed greater freedom than is usual in school in making their own decisions. Some of the schools have been set up by religious orders and ethnic minorities. About 500 of the 2500 independent schools are known as 'public schools'. These are prestigious and usually larger and older schools for secondary-school-age pupils.

In 1968, the Public Schools Commission was set up to look into public schools and consider their integration into the state system. Two reports were published, one in 1968 and one in 1970. The 1968 report focused on the small number of schools classified as public schools. The report recommended a number of changes such as the inclusion of girls in public schools and the abolition of certain traditional features, such as the beating of boys, and 'fagging' (a system whereby younger boys acted as unpaid personal servants to older boys). The second report concentrated on independent day schools and direct grant schools. The direct grant schools received a grant from central government, on condition that they reserved 25 per cent of places free for children educated for at least two years in maintained schools. The 1970 report recommended that the direct grant system be ended.

These reports caused a great deal of controversy, although little was done at the time of their publication. In 1975, however, the government announced that the direct grant system would stop. As a result, many of the direct grant schools changed their status to that of independent schools. The 1980 Education Act established the Assisted Places Scheme to enable children who would not normally have been able to attend independent schools to receive assistance from public funds to do so. From 1997 the Assisted Places Scheme began to be phased out, although pupils already holding places were allowed to continue.

Source: Bob Watkins, Photofusion
A minority of children attend private schools and even fewer go to public schools such as Eton

Should there be private schools?

Activity 7.6

Some people believe that private schools should be abolished. What are the arguments for and against this proposal in your view?

There are several arguments against the existence of private schools alongside the state education system. First, the very existence of private schools means that comprehensive schools cannot be said to be truly comprehensive, since some children in a particular area will go to a separate school. Second, state education is based on the idea of equal opportunity for all children. Private education operates against this principle, in that richer parents can buy a private education for their children. Whilst it is difficult and probably impossible to evaluate and compare in the field of education, most private schools have smaller classes than state schools and are more successful in terms of examination results. Third, private schools are said to perpetuate an elitist system. This means that people in the most privileged group in society are able to buy a separate education for their children, which leads into positions of power and prestige. This has the effect of dividing society into distinct and separate groups. It also means that people in positions of power are not necessarily those with the greatest ability. Finally, private education is state-subsidised through tax relief. Private schools have charitable status which gives exemption from income tax, corporation tax and capital gains tax on income or profits. Gifts to private schools are also partly exempt from capital gains tax and private schools benefit from a 50 per cent reduction in rates. The sum of money lost to the government has been estimated to be around £38.5 million.[17]

The arguments presented in favour of private education include the belief that parents who choose to educate their children privately should be able to do so. Also, some important educational innovation and experimentation have taken place within the private sector; for example, at the school set up by A. S. Neill at Summerfield, where children were given much greater freedom and choice about their education, including the right to choose whether or not to attend classes.

7.6 Special education

The 1944 Education Act required local authorities to make provision for children with special educational needs. Such children were to include those with disabilities and those who were confined to bed, either at home or in hospital. One of the continuing problems of special education has been the difficulty of defining the children in need of special help. In 1959, the categories of children with special needs were legally defined in regulations issued by the government. The groups listed were: the blind, the partially-sighted, the deaf, the partially-hearing, the delicate, the educationally sub-normal, epileptic children, maladjusted children, the physically handicapped, and those with speech defects. In 1971, the list was extended to include severely subnormal children, children who are both blind and deaf, those with autism and other psychoses, and those suffering from acute dyslexia. Now a child is defined as having special educational needs (SEN) if he or she has a learning disability which requires special teaching. In 1997/78, 116,000 children received full-time education in special schools in the UK.[18]

The Warnock Report

In 1978, the Warnock Report on children with special educational needs was published. The report attempted to move away from the idea of special categories of children, since the categorisation of needs had come to be seen as a restriction on provision. The report saw children with special needs as making up some 20 per cent of the school population, as distinct from the 2 per cent receiving education in special schools.

The Warnock report stated that a range of provision was required to meet varying needs. Some children would require extra help and support whilst remaining in ordinary classes. For others the best way of meeting their needs would be to provide for some periods of withdrawal to special classes. For children placed in special classes, some would benefit from periods in ordinary classes, others would need social contact with the rest of the school. Children in special schools might have some classes in an ordinary school or might participate in social activities. The report also said that there was a need for long- and short-term provision of education in hospitals and other institutions. Finally, some children would require home tuition.

Priority areas indicated in the Warnock report were: provision for the under-5s, further education, and the need for teachers to be trained to meet special educational needs.

1981 Education Act and 'statementing'

The 1981 Education Act is based on the recommendations of the Warnock report, although no government money was made available to improve special education. The 1981 Act defines special educational needs as:

'learning difficulties, greater than those experienced by the majority of children, or which hinder the child in benefiting from education.'

The Act states that as far as possible the local education authority must educate children with learning disabilities in ordinary schools, whilst taking into account the views of parents, the needs of the child, the needs of other children and the efficient use of resources.

It is a requirement of the Act that, in the case of a minority of children, the authority carries out a formal assessment, consulting parents as well as medical, psychological and educational experts. The parents must be told that the child is to be assessed, allowed to give evidence and informed of the authority's plans for the child. This process has come to be known as 'statementing'. In addition, parents must be given the name of a local authority officer from whom they can obtain information.

Although the 1981 legislation improved parents' rights with regard to special education, some problems have remained. One has concerned the distinction which has arisen from so-called 'statemented children' and others with learning disabilities. Around 2 per cent of children have statements and a further 18 per cent are thought to have some degree of learning disability. The effect of the statementing procedure has been to concentrate resources and attention on 'statemented' children and for the needs of the rest to slip into the background. Also processes have been very slow. In the worst cases, children have moved on to a different stage in their education by the time the authority has made a decision. Many parents have felt they have had to fight every inch of the way to get a satisfactory deal for their child. Such a system works very much to the disadvantage of those who are less articulate, less confident and less knowledgeable about how to get things done.

1993 Education Act

As a result of concerns over the working of the 1981 legislation, a new law was passed. The 1993 Education Act requires that:

- The local education authority carries out procedures for assessments and statements within a set statutory time limit.
- The education authority fits in with the parents' choice of school unless this is not appropriate for the child or involves an inefficient use of resources.
- There is an independent tribunal for appeals against decisions by the education authority.

The law also now states that a state school named in a statement must take a child. There is a code of practice for schools in identifying and assessing special needs. Finally, schools must give details of their policies for treating children with special educational needs who are not 'statemented'.

In 1997, a review of SEN and a process of consultation was started by the government. The main themes were:

- the importance of early identification and action to tackle problems;
- increased inclusion of children with special needs in mainstream schools;
- better partnerships with parents.

Provision in mainstream education

Activity 7.7

The 1981 Act says that, where possible, children with learning disabilities should be provided for in ordinary schools. What advantages can you see in this policy?

There are advantages both to children with learning difficulties, and to other children, in educating the largest possible number of children in mainstream education. From the point of view of ordinary children, the removal of children with disabilities does not encourage young people to learn to accept those who are in some way different.

Local authorities cannot afford to provide a large number of special schools, for example there may be only one school for blind children for the whole area. This means that many children are unable to travel daily and are obliged to attend school as boarders. The standard of academic education in some special schools is not as high as that provided in ordinary schools. As a result, children may become educationally disadvantaged as well as disabled. The segregation of children may have the effect of increasing any social difficulties they experience (see also Chapters 11, 12 and 14).

Problems with children's learning and behaviour at school can be difficult to assess and there can be unfair biases in assessment. Cultural biases can operate against working-class and black children, especially in cases where the child's use of language is different from that of the teacher. In 1969, Haringey Education Committee admitted that errors had been made when it was discovered that 50 per cent of children in the borough's special schools were black, compared with 18 per cent of the local population. Whilst this problem has now been recognised, there are people who believe that the biases persist. The organisation MIND reports a case of a 13-year-old West Indian boy who had been in a car accident in which his uncle was killed. As a result he was emotionally disturbed and the misinterpretation of his behaviour led to his being wrongly placed in a school for children with learning difficulties.[19]

The advantages of special schools are that they can provide specialised aids, equipment and teachers who fully understand the problems of children with a particular disability. Also they shield disabled children from the cruelty of other children.

Fears have been voiced that the requirement for secondary schools to be measured against each other in performance or 'league tables' will discourage schools from taking children with learning disabilities, worrying that these children will do less well in examinations.

7.7   Education and welfare

Special services

Local authorities employ Careers Officers who interview young people and provide advice and information on employment and opportunities for further education. In 1993, the government began a gradual programme of competitive tendering to provide careers services. The winning contractors came under the control of the Department of Employment (now part of the Department for Education and Employment). Youth workers are also appointed by local authorities to make contact with young people in their areas and to organise social activities.

Child guidance clinics are usually run by the education authority and the health service. They are staffed by a multi-disciplinary team of psychologists, psychiatrists and social workers. Referrals to the clinic may come from the school or other sources. The team make a study of the child and the family and look at the child's school record. Various recommendations can follow and the clinic can provide long- or short-term therapy to work on emotional problems.

Education welfare officers visit schools and families to investigate non-attendance and entitlement to benefits. They also work with families with problems.

Educational welfare benefits

School meals

Until 1980, local authorities were obliged by the 1944 Education Act to provide meals at a standard price and of a prescribed nutritional standard for all children, and free for some children. Entitlement to free school meals was later defined in terms of low income or receipt of family income supplement (now family credit) or supplementary benefit (now income support/income-based Jobseeker's Allowance). The 1980 Education Act changed this, allowing local authorities to provide school meals, but not requiring them to do so. Education authorities had to make some provision, the nature of which was left to them to decide, for those children whose parents received family credit or income support. When the social security benefits were reformed in 1988, family credit no longer entitled children to free school meals. So it is now only income support or income-based Jobseeker's Allowance which is a passport to free school meals. In grant-maintained schools, it is the school rather than the local authority which has the duty to provide the meals.

After the 1980 Act, prices of school meals rose in most areas. The numbers of children eligible for free meals fell, since parents on a low income, but not claiming benefits, are not automatically entitled to free meals for their children. A further result of the new legislation is that provision of school meals varies considerably throughout the country. Some local authorities only provide a cold snack at mid-day for those children claiming free meals.

School milk

Since 1971, school milk has been limited to children under 8, or attending special schools. The 1980 Education Act allows authorities to provide milk for any category of children and to charge for it, if they wish. As a result, some authorities do not provide milk for children under 8, whilst others continue to do so.

Discretionary grants

Grants can be made to allow pupils to participate in educational activities. This means that local authorities can help parents in paying for school outings, holidays and extra lessons.

Uniform and clothing grants

Most local authorities have schemes for providing clothing for school to less well-off families. Again, there is regional variation, as it is for the authorities to decide what they will provide.

Transport

Local education authorities are bound by law to provide transport for children under 8 whose school is more than 2 miles from home, and children over 8 who travel more than 3 miles to school. The authority can provide free transport or give a grant to cover the cost of fares. It is left to the discretion of authorities to provide more than this – that is, to shorten the distances or help low-income families even if their children live nearer to the school.

Maintenance allowances

Local education authorities pay allowances to some young people who continue their education beyond the age of 16. This is a discretionary allowance, normally decided on the basis of the income of the parents.

7.8   Inequality in education

Equality in education is believed to be important, both as a goal in itself and because society cannot afford to waste talent. Therefore an important aim in education has been to discover and develop abilities in every individual, regardless of their background. A considerable amount of research has focused on the extent to which this has been achieved.

The early research in this area focused on inequalities relating to social class. More recent work has examined the achievement and treatment of ethnic minorities and looked at gender inequalities in education.

Education and social class

A great deal of research has investigated social class and educational achievement. The evidence produced shows that social class is more significant than ability in determining educational attainment. At each stage in their educational careers, children from middle-class homes are more successful than working-class children.

Statistics show that it is children from the upper social groups who are more likely to benefit from education before they are 5.[20] Reasons for this were given earlier in this chapter, in section 7.2 on pre-school education. A major research project, known as the National Child Development Study,[21] demonstrated significant differences in attainment, according to class, in children in infant schools. The study found that, by the age of 7, the chances of an unskilled manual worker's child being a poor reader were six times as great as those of a child of a professional worker. A later study which tracked 5000 children from the age of 4 found that social class continued to be a crucial factor determining how well or badly the children did at school. Performance was measured in assessment test for reading, writing, speaking and maths.[22]

Douglas, in 1964, found that children from upper-middle-class homes were five times as likely to go to a grammar school as children with working-class parents. Success in 'O' levels was also found to be related to class, rather than ability. Several studies have found that early learning is statistically linked to class.[23] The Robbins Report found that few working-class students entered universities.

Table 7.1 Participation rates (percentages) in higher education, Great Britain – by social class

	1991/2	1997/8
Professional	55	80
Intermediate	36	49
Skilled non-manual	22	32
Skilled manual	11	19
Partly skilled	12	18
Unskilled	6	14
All social classes	23	34

It was partly as a result of such research findings that comprehensive schools were introduced. Many people believed that the abolition of selection at 11 would lead to greater equality of opportunity. However, more recent research shows that policies intended to reduce inequality have had little effect. Two studies published in the 1980s found that class-related inequalities were as great as in the period before the war.[24] New research shows a continued gap in achievement in GCSEs. By 1996, eight out of ten state school pupils from professional families were getting at least five good GCSEs, compared to just a fifth of those from families where no-one has a paid job. The results for children from better-off families have improved over the last ten years and the gap between poorer and richer children is widening.[25]

Table 7.1 shows the percentages of people from different social classes in higher education.[26] Although participation in higher education has grown overall, the experiences of people across the socio-economic groups has been different. Other figures also show a class divide in terms of which universities people attend. The universities with the highest proportion of students from professional or managerial backgrounds are Oxford and Cambridge, followed by Bristol, Edinburgh, Nottingham and Imperial College, London. Students from working-class backgrounds are more likely to go to the universities which were originally Polytechnics, such as East London, South Bank and the University of Central Lancashire.[27]

Explanations for class differences

- The child's progress in school may be affected by the home environment. Overcrowding, for example, will make it difficult for a child to find a quiet space in which to do homework. The presence of books in a middle-class home perhaps encourages a child to want to learn to read. Money may also be a significant factor, in that children from poorer homes might be encouraged to leave school and bring home a wage.
- Other explanations concentrate on different attitudes to education. It is believed that the amount of interest parents take in their child's education is important. Some studies have found that working-class parents are less keen to visit their child's school.[28] This may not be because of lack of interest, but

rather that the parents are more easily intimidated by the school. Middle-class parents may feel more at ease with teachers, since they are themselves middle-class. Research carried out in the 1950s discovered a feeling among working-class people that the grammar schools were not really for 'people like them.'[29]. It may still be the case that working-class parents do not put as much value on education and do not expect their children to stay on at school and go to university.

- More recent studies suggest that the values of school are middle-class and cause conflict in working-class children. An example of this might be the idea that it is better to stay in and do homework than to go out having fun, because sacrifice now will produce rewards later. The values of the school, including examination results and further education, are rejected by some working-class children.

- Another approach to the same problem argues that middle-class and working-class people use language in a different way.[30] Two mothers might mean the same thing, when one says 'Shut up', and the other says 'I'd rather you made less noise, darling'. This does not matter, except that the language of school teachers is middle-class. The working-class child has to translate what the teacher says in order to make sense of it. There may be cases where the child is not able to translate what is being said, and will be left feeling puzzled.

- Finally, it is suggested that teachers and pupils can be involved in a self-fulfilling prophesy. The way this works is that the teacher believes that certain children are more intelligent and will be more successful. The teacher then treats the children as if they are more intelligent and communicates to them his or her belief in their abilities. As a result, the children believe in themselves and do better. Teachers do not expect working-class and black children to succeed at school and, as a result of this expectation, they do not. This could also be relevant in explaining why boys do better than girls in science subjects, for example.

Activity 7.8

Which of these ideas make the most sense to you? Try to think of any other reasons why social factors such as class, gender and race may affect educational achievement.

Gender and education

There are differences in the educational achievement of boys and girls. For most of this century it was girls who were under-achieving, particularly in subjects like mathematics and sciences and at higher levels of education. Many of the women who have returned to education as adults through Access and other courses provide examples of the wasted ability of girls. This situation reversed in the early 1990s when achievements of all pupils improved but girls began to out-perform boys at all levels of compulsory education, including achieving slightly higher rates of success in GCSEs in the traditionally male-dominated subjects of Mathematics and Science. At advanced level, more girls are achieving two or more GCE 'A' levels. Choices of subjects at 'A' level continue to be different for boys and girls. Although more girls get grade C or above in GCSE Mathematics, three-fifths of entrants at 'A' level are boys. Men continue to outnumber women in higher education courses in engineering and sciences.

Why did girls under-achieve?

There are various factors which could explain girls' under-achievement, although little investigation was done until the revival of feminism in the 1970s. Before this time, girls' education was seen as unimportant, since their 'natural' role in life was believed to be marriage and motherhood. There were even ideas earlier in the century that women's brains were not suitable for study, particularly of 'unfeminine' subjects like science. Untangling the reasons why girls under-achieved is made more complex by the relationships which existed between education and other areas of society, such as industry. For example, girls were likely not to choose scientific and technical subjects, believing that they had little chance of gaining employment in these areas. This meant that careers in science and engineering remained restricted to males, since females lacked the necessary qualifications for entry.

It is only relatively recently that girls have been allowed to take certain subjects. The 1975 Sex Discrimination Act made it illegal to restrict educational opportunities by sex but more subtle factors still intervened to limit choice. Subjects were often blocked together on a timetable in such a way as to prevent pupils combining arts or science or offering the choice between domestic science or technical drawing. This had the effect of continuing to push boys and girls into stereotyped choices. Teachers and friends may have been influential in persuading girls that arts subjects were more appropriate – perhaps more 'feminine' – than sciences and engineering. The fact that science teachers have tended to be male discouraged girls from seeing science as a female interest. The influence of the home may also be of relevance, giving girls less familiarity and interest in technical matters.

It is interesting to note that research found that in single-sex schools, girls are more likely to opt for mathematics and science subjects than are girls in co-educational schools.[31] This indicates the influence of social factors on girls' choice of subjects for study.

The national curriculum now requires all children to cover certain subjects in school. The national curriculum means that boys and girls will study the same subjects up until age 16. This has contributed to the reversal in achievement levels in traditionally male-dominated subjects at GCSE level, described above.

The reasons why fewer girls than boys enter higher education may have related to lingering attitudes holding that girls only need a basic education since they were expected to marry and spend their lives as housewives. Teachers may have been influenced by this kind of approach to girls' education. Surveys found that in mixed classes, boys receive more attention than girls from teachers.[32] This is partly because boys' behaviour is noisier and more potentially disruptive, also girls in a mixed group are less assertive in asking questions and seeking help.

Activity 7.9

Talk to women of different ages about their experience of school. Were some subjects available only to one sex? Did they feel teachers treated girls and boys differently? Were there any influences from home which led to girls being discouraged to succeed in some areas? Compare the experiences of women of different ages and from different backgrounds.

Boys' under-achievement

A huge amount of publicity and attention has been focused on boys since girls overtook them. Various explanations have been offered:

- 'Girl power' – feminism is thought to have increased girls' confidence at the expense of boys who suffer from low self-esteem.
- 'The future is female' – changes in employment, especially the loss of manual unskilled jobs, in areas like manufacturing and the growth of service jobs have made education seem pointless to boys who feel they won't get a job anyway. Opportunities for work for women, in contrast, have expanded.
- 'School is uncool and girlish' – 'lad culture' is anti-school and sees learning and academic success as 'girlish'. Boys can hide their failure in a macho male self-image.
- Projects suit girls – it has been suggested that GCSEs have benefited girls more than boys. Girls are thought to be better at working on and presenting projects which are now assessed (although providing a smaller proportion of the marks than originally).

Race and education

Disadvantage and bias

Black children have been disadvantaged in school in several ways. At the beginning of the 1990s, the Commission for Racial Equality found:

- In one school in the North, fewer Asian children were entered for GCSEs than white pupils. More Asian children were put in the lowest set and they weren't moved up, even when their grades were as good as those of pupils in higher sets.
- Black children are more likely to be encouraged to do 'soft', less academic subjects – and sport – and are scoffed at when they want an academic career.
- In some schools, Afro-Caribbean children were four times more likely to be suspended than white children, and often for the same sort of behaviour.[33]

A decade later, the number of exclusions for all children was falling for the first time since national records began to be kept. However black children continued to be up to 13 times more likely to be excluded from school.[34]

Other problems occur for children whose first language is not English. Knowing another language should be seen as a skill but children have been categorised as having learning difficulties and placed in special groups. In the following quotation a Pakistani girl talks about how she felt about this:

> On starting school we were put into the 'immigrant' class along with other Asian children for the first year. We had special reading sessions with the headmaster a few times a week, for which the group was termed 'backward readers'. A few years later I can remember feeling resentment at having been called a 'backward reader'.[35]

There is also racism built into the content of lessons, which affects the way black and white children view the world.

Activity 7.10

How do you think a school curriculum could be biased in terms of race? Discuss your own experience at school with other members of the class.

Many of the lessons in school contain an implicit message that white people are superior and other cultures are of less value. European culture predominates and children are not taught about achievements of black people. History tends to be biased in the sense of presenting only a 'British' point of view, for example in teaching about the time of the British empire. In 1990 the then Prime Minister Mrs Thatcher made this bias very clear, saying:

> From our perspective today, surely what strikes us most is our common experience, for instance, how Europeans explored and colonised and yes – without apology – civilised much of the world.[36]

In geography, there is a tendency for countries like Africa to be shown as primitive jungle-lands, whereas in fact there are large cities very like those of Europe. Cookery lessons ignore different cultures and religious instruction assumes the superiority of Christianity. Also schools, even in areas with large Asian populations, ignore the bilingual abilities of many children.

Black children also face racism from other pupils and sometimes from teachers. This operates in many different ways: from making a child feel odd and different, as the extract below describes, to bullying and violence in some schools. In the extract, Rifat Malik explains why her 11-year-old brother does not want to go to the same predominantly white school as she attends:

> Like countless Asian children before him, he fears being treated like some kind of alien life-form. He fears he will be ridiculed for silly things, such as his name being deemed unpronounceable. Then of course there is the aggravating fact that he dares to have six siblings! This is undoubtedly a capital offence in a society where it is *de rigueur* to have 2.2 children.[37]

As a result of all the factors described above, many black children underachieve at school.

The Swann Report, published in 1985, collected statistics on educational achievement.[38] Although these have been criticised, they appear to show that West Indians in particular under-achieved throughout their educational careers. Later statistics showed a similar pattern. In 1996, 23 per cent of black young people compared with 46 per cent of white pupils got at least five Grade C GCSEs and 23 per cent of children from ethnic minorities left school with no qualifications compared to 19 per cent of whites.[39]

Activity 7.11

What measures are schools or local education authorities in your area taking to improve the situation for black and white children, leading to greater equality and a recognition that Britain is a multi-racial society?

Multi-cultural understanding

There have been several initiatives by local education authorities to introduce what is termed *multi-cultural education*. Multi-cultural education involves a recognition of different cultures in the content of lessons and in the school environment. These moves have, however, been criticised for not going far enough to combat racism. An anti-racist policy in a school involves a commitment to opposing racism in pupils and teachers and in the running of the school. It also means greater involvement of black parents and of the community as a whole.

The Swann Report argued that society was faced with a dual problem: eradicating discriminatory attitudes of the white majority and evolving an educational system which ensures that all pupils achieve their full potential. The title of the report was *Education for All*, meaning that the problem for schools is not how to educate children of ethnic minorities, but how to educate all children. The report argues that:[40]

- Britain is a multi-racial and multi-cultural society and all pupils must be enabled to understand what this means.
- This challenge cannot be left to the independent initiatives of education authorities and schools; only those with experience of substantial numbers of ethnic minority pupils have attempted to tackle it, though the issue affects all schools and all pupils.
- Education has to be something more than the reinforcement of the beliefs, values and identity which each child brings to the school.
- It is necessary to combat racism, to attack inherited myths and stereotypes and the ways in which they are embodied in institutional practice.
- Multi-cultural understanding has also to permeate all aspects of a school's work. It is not a separate topic that can be welded on to existing practices.

The Report also made a large number of specific recommendations for implementation of 'education for all'. These include the need for more language teaching, although not in separate centres; the need for teacher training to include experience in teaching in multi-racial classrooms; and the need for more black teachers in schools.

Activity 7.12

Several government reports have been mentioned in this chapter. Find out about *one* of the reports listed below, including the recommendations, and what happened as a result. Report your findings to the class.

Government Reports on Education
The Early Leaving Report (1954)
The Crowther Report, 15–18 (1959)
The Newsom Report, Half Our Future (1963)
The Robbins Report, Higher Education (1963)
The Plowden Report, Children and their Primary Schools (1967)
Public Schools Commission (1968, 1970)
The James Report, Teacher Education and Training (1972)
The Bullock Report, A Language for Life (1975)
The Taylor Report, A New Partnership for Our Schools (1977)
The Warnock Report, Special Educational Needs (1978)
The Swann Report, Educational for All (1985)
The Elton Report, Discipline in Schools (1989)
The Dearing Report, The National Curriculum and its Assessment (1993)
Dearning, Review of Qualifications for 16–19 Year Olds (1996)

Note: Two books will help in this exercise – A. Corbett, *Much to do about Education,* 4th edn (London: Macmillan, 1978) and R. Rogers, *Crowther to Warnock* (London: Heinemann, 1980).

For more recent reports see the summaries provided in the *Education Yearbook,* which is published annually by Longman Community Education, or contact the Department for Education and Employment.

Activity 7.13

The Department for Education and Employment has told your local education authority that there is some money to spend on education locally. In groups of three or four, decide how the money should be spent, explaining why such an area is a priority.

Activity 7.14

Make sure that you understand the following expressions used in this chapter. Check in the Glossary at the end of the book if you need to.

binary system
central government
City Technology Colleges (CTCs)
community schools
comprehensive school
curriculum
direct grant school
discretionary
dyslexia
education action zones
education welfare officer
elite
equality of opportunity
foundation schools
General National Vocational
   'A' levels
grant-maintained school
independent school
IQ
league tables
lifelong learning
local authority

mainstream education
maintained school
mandatory
national curriculum
non-accidental injury
parity of esteem
positive discrimination
pre-school education
psychiatrist
psychologist
public school
segregation
selective education
special school
specialist schools
speech therapy clinic
'statementing'
tertiary college
therapist
tripartite system
universal
voluntary school

Further reading

There is a vast literature on education, which makes it difficult to choose one or two books to list. The Department for Education and Employment is a useful source of statistical information, although not always in a very digestible form. Most Sociology textbooks contain useful sections on education and inequality.

Useful addresses

Department for Education and Employment
DfEE Publications
PO Box 5050
Sudbury
Suffolk CO10 6ZQ
tel. 0845 602 2260

The Pre-School Learning Alliance
69 King's Cross Road,
London WC1X 9LL
tel. 0207 833 0991

Websites

Department for Education and Employment: **www.dfee.gov.uk**

Qualifications and Curriculum Authority: **www.qca.org.uk**

The Advisory Centre for Education provide advice and information for parents on issues such as bullying, exclusion, special needs education. Their website is at **www.ace-ed.org.uk**

☑ **8** Personal social services

This chapter looks at the origins and work of the local authority personal social services department. This work has taken a new direction as a result of the NHS and Community Care Act in 1990. Community care is the subject of the next chapter and therefore the two chapters go together to some extent. The following five chapters are also relevant since they focus on the needs of groups with whom social workers are likely to be involved.

8.1   The origins of social service departments

Nineteenth-century services

The present system whereby each local authority has a social services department has only existed since 1970. The origins of social work can however be traced back to the nineteenth century. Services were originally concerned only with poor people and the only government-run provision was the workhouse for the destitute set up under the 1834 Poor Law (see Chapter 3). There were also a number of charitable organisations to help people in poverty and need, and it was fashionable in the nineteenth century for middle- and upper-class women to visit and help the poor. Some women took this further and were more systematic in their attempts to work with needy people. Octavia Hill renovated and built housing for poor people in the slum areas of London. She developed a kind of casework approach to her tenants, offering advice and support as well as a home to rent. She trained her rent-collectors, mostly young women, in the same skills and approach. Although these activities can be considered as the origins of present-day social work, the help was often given in a very condescending and patronising way.

1920s–1960s

The next important development came at the beginning of the twentieth century when hospitals began to employ 'almoners' or social workers. These were initially concerned only with assessing whether the patient deserved and needed free treatment, but soon widened their role. Training courses were set up and in 1920 the Institute of Almoners was established.

After the Second World War, at the time that the Welfare State was being established, local authorities began to provide welfare services for some groups of people. In 1948 Children's Departments were set up to provide services for children deprived of a normal home life. The work of these departments was the most professional of local authority social work. The 1946 National Health Service Act gave the local authorities the responsibility for maternity and baby welfare, for the after-care of mentally ill people, and for home services for elderly people and some other groups. The 1948 National Assistance Act required that local authorities provide accommodation and some other services for elderly people, handicapped people and homeless families. Although all these services were provided by the local authorities they were not organised in a coherent way, but were fragmented.

These fragmented services and divided responsibilities were thought to be unsatisfactory for a variety of reasons. The focus on particular client groups such as the mentally ill had the effect of isolating people in need from their families and the community. There were both gaps and overlaps in provision and a confusion over responsibility for meeting needs. Also, the services operated primarily on a casualty basis, only becoming involved when problems arose. The need for preventative help was increasingly recognised, as was the need for community alternatives to residential care.

Seebohm Committee (1968) and afterwards

As a result of these misgivings over existing provision, the Seebohm Committee was set up by the government to look into local social services. The Report of this committee was published in 1968, recommending that a *unified* and *family-orientated* service be established. The report argued for:

> a new local authority department, providing a community based and family orientated service, which will be available to all. This new department will, we believe, reach far beyond the discovery and rescue of social casualties; it will enable the greatest number of individuals to act reciprocally giving and receiving service for the well-being of the whole community.[1]

The proposals of the Seebohm Committee were incorporated into the Local Authority Social Services Act 1970, which came into force on 1 April 1971. The 1970 Act required local authorities to appoint a Director of Social Services and set up Social Services Committees. The new social services departments would be responsible for the welfare of all sections of the community. This was the beginning of *generic social work*, whereby social workers deal with all kinds of people and problems, instead of specialising in one area, such as mental illness or deprived children. The training of the new generic social workers was to be the responsibility of the Central Council of Education and Training in Social Work (CCETSW) which was set up in 1971. The central government department to which local authority social workers are responsible is the Department of Health.

The NHS and Community Care Act

This Act is discussed in detail in the next chapter. It was important in changing the role of the local authority social services departments from a *provider* of services to that of a '*purchaser*'. Instead of providing services for local people, social services staff have become *care managers* who co-ordinate services provided by a mix of statutory, voluntary and private organisations.

8.2 Social work

There is no clear and simple definition for the term '*social work*'. It is often used in a broad sense, for example by people working in education or the police force, who may see their work as including aspects of social work. In this chapter, social work is discussed in the more limited context of people employed by the local authority as social workers.

Activity 8.1

Use library resources to collect a number of different definitions of social work. Decide on the definition which seems most appropriate to you.

Social workers are involved in a broad area of work, although there is a tendency for caseloads to concentrate on problems such as old age, disabilities of various kinds, low income and family relationships. Working with children also takes up a large part of social work time and this is dealt with separately in Chapter 10, in conjunction with a description of the role of the courts involved with young people. Some of the duties of the local authority social services department are statutory, that is, services required by legislation. Other provision is at the discretion of the local authority and therefore varies from area to area.

Activity 8.2

What services do you think are provided by the local authority social services department?

This summary of services is divided in terms of the different client groups with which social workers are involved.

Children

Statutory responsibilities for children include those for children who have got into trouble with the police as well as those for children whose parents are thought to be unable to provide adequate care. The legal responsibilities of social services towards children are set out in the 1989 Children Act which is looked at in Chapter 10. Social workers organise foster-parents and provide supervision for children living at home. Where residential care is needed, it may be provided in social services-run homes. Alternatively social services place children in privately-run homes or those provided by voluntary organisations. These homes are inspected by social services and placements are monitored and reviewed.

Other local authority duties concerned with children include acting as an adoption agency and registering child-minders in the area. Day-care is also provided for children in need, as described in Chapter 7. The Children Act also requires that social services monitor all day-care for children up to the age of 8. Since 1999, some of the work of regulating child-care provision has passed to the education watchdog OFSTED.

There is a tendency for work with children to dominate field social work. This is partly because of the number of statutory responsibilities which personal social services departments have for children. There has also been a rise in the number of child sexual abuse cases since the publicity given to this issue. The various enquiries involving children and social workers have also caused a great deal of anxiety, and meant other areas of social work have tended to be seen as less pressing. (See also Chapters 2 and 10.)

Older people

Social workers are also involved with the needs of older people in a variety of ways. Social workers may be needed as care managers sorting out a package of care for older people living at home. The package of care might include meals-on-wheels, home helps or home carers and the provision of adaptations for homes, ranging from small items such as kitchen equipment to help people with severe arthritis, to stairlifts for those unable to get upstairs. Some of these services are organised within social services departments and others are provided by outside agencies, with social services monitoring and reviewing the services. There will be charges for these services in many cases, although services are usually free for the very poorest people. Day centres for older people are sometimes provided by social services, offering recreational and social facilities. Social services can also intervene to help older people who are unable to remain at home. Increasingly however residential care is in private or voluntary homes rather than in homes run by the social services department. Private homes are inspected and registered by social services. About half of social services expenditure is on older people.

People with disabilities

Social services departments also have responsibilities to people who are sick or disabled and to those with learning disabilities. Sheltered workshops are run to provide opportunities for rehabilitation for people with disabilities, through employment and recreation. In these and other areas of work, social workers work in conjunction with voluntary organisations. Social workers are also based in psychiatric and general hospitals, providing advice and working with therapists.

People with mental illnesses

Social workers help patients and their families with the problems caused by mental illness. Social services departments work with health services and voluntary organisations in the provision of preventative care and after-care for mentally ill people in the community. Services include drop-in and other day-care centres and hostels. Specially qualified social workers are involved in compulsorily admitting people with mental illnesses to psychiatric hospitals.

Families

Social work with families involves providing counselling, putting people in touch with other agencies, both statutory and voluntary, and guiding people through the complexities of housing or social security provision.

Activity 8.3

What skills and personal qualities do you think are required for social work?

8.3 Social workers

Very different sorts of people can be successful in social work, so different qualities can be useful in different ways. However, at a general level, social workers need a considerable degree of self-awareness, including an understanding of their own motives in their work. They should be people who are able to get along with a wide variety of other people without falling back on stereotyped notions. Understanding and sympathy are important qualities for social work, as is patience. Social workers need to be able to cope with conflict and to be able to make difficult decisions, perhaps against the will of their clients. At the same time, where possible social workers should allow clients to make their own decisions and encourage self-determination.

Social workers need skills in assessing situations and needs. They need to be organised in record-keeping and filing information. Finally, social workers need knowledge of resources which may be useful to clients and an understanding of the working of society and individual psychology.

Training for social work aims to develop skills and abilities in all these areas, through development of personal skills and the teaching of psychology, sociology and social administration. Pre-service training combines theoretical knowledge with supervised practice in a variety of placements. As mentioned earlier, social work training is organised by the Central Council in Education and Training in Social Work (CCETSW). CCETSW validates courses of social work training in universities and colleges. The basic professional qualification for social workers is the Diploma in Social Work (DipSW). Since this is quite a recent development, many social workers currently working have other qualifications. In the past, social workers, working in the community trained for a Certificate of Qualification in Social Work (CQSW) while those in residential work qualified with a Certificate of Social Service (CSS). Now the two qualifications are combined and all social workers whatever their area of work, train for the same diploma. CCETSW also runs courses for qualified social workers to update or further develop their knowledge and skills.

Following a review in 1997, the government plans to replace CCETSW with a General Social Care Council which will combine the regulation of professional social work training with overseeing standards of conduct and practice in social work.

The social-work profession is made up of field workers and residential and day-care workers. Field workers are involved primarily with families and individuals in the community. Family and individual casework involves providing information and counselling and support to help people to understand and cope with their problems. Field workers may be involved in a combination of individual and family casework, and group work and community work. Residential workers are employed in the various types of residential accommodation provided by the local authority. The Barclay Report on social work, published in 1982, saw residential social work as the 'Cinderella' service within social work. Residential workers suffer low pay and the stigma attached to institutions. Demoralisation results from the tendency for residential care to be seen as 'undesirable' and only to be used 'as a last resort'.

8.4   Organisation of social services departments

Generic approach

Social services departments vary in the way the work is organised. The Seebohm Report recommended that all social work take a generic approach. In the early days, most social services departments were divided into teams covering a geographical area. Each social worker in the team would have a generic caseload, including all types of clients. However, there was a trend towards specialisations within the teams. For example, intake workers would deal with all new enquiries and referrals, before passing them on to other social workers. Social workers began to specialise in particular areas such as welfare rights or the needs of older people. Now it is common for departments to be organised into teams, dealing with different types of work or clients.

Activity 8.4

List what you think are the advantages and disadvantages of generic social work. How will a department decide what policy to adopt on this issue?

Frustrations and satisfactions

There is some feeling among social workers themselves against the generic approach, as is illustrated in the view of this social worker:

Why we can't have social workers for people with disabilities, people with a learning disability, and so on, I don't know. I think it will come. If you are going to work under stress, you should work in a field you know something about.[2]

There are obviously arguments on both sides of this debate and it may be that the best situation is that which exists at the present time, where teams have a generic approach, whilst allowing individual social workers a degree of specialisation.

Social workers have a very difficult and demanding job which can put them under considerable stress. Whilst the work has many satisfactions, it can also be depressing as the comments of this social worker demonstrate:

> I sometimes get depressed when I think of all the things I'd like to do for my clients but can't. I've worked with some of them for the last two years and, with some, it's the same sort of situation now as it was then – particularly with adolescents in trouble. You don't see results like you do with other jobs. If you do ever finish a case there's always another one to take over. A lot of the time you're physically tired, and there's always the paperwork.[3]

Violence is a growing problem for social workers. A survey carried out by the British Association of Social Workers found that the threat of violence had become part of the job for most social workers. Although a great deal of publicity has been given to the dangers of people with mental illnesses in the community, social workers working with children were found to be at highest risk.[4]

Many social workers express frustration over the hierarchical organisation of social work. Promotion takes workers away from the job for which they were trained and into a management role. There is little opportunity for experienced social workers who wish both to further their career and to retain contact with clients. Many social workers experience feelings of demoralisation in the face of the difficulties of their work, criticisms from outside and cuts in expenditure.

Barclay (1982) and Griffiths (1988) Reports

In 1982, the Barclay Report was published, following the establishment of a committee by the government to examine the role of social work. The report emphasises the importance of the role of local people in providing care in the community. In this context, the report recommends that social work develops in the role of providing support for carers in a community-orientated service. The report itself contains criticisms of this approach to social work and is intended as a guide to ideas and possibilities rather than as a blueprint on which to base legislation, requiring local authorities to follow particular policies.

Partly as a result of the Barclay Report, some social services departments have developed a 'patch system'. This means that small groups of social workers move out of the area office and set up in a house, shop or Portakabin in the neighbourhood in which they are working. This way it is hoped that they can have better links with the community and develop local resources.

In 1988 the Griffiths Report on community care was published. This is discussed in detail in Chapter 9 on community care. The Report criticised the lack of organisation between all the different agencies and people involved in providing community care services. The Report recommended that the position of local authorities be strengthened to allow them to take a lead role in organising and overseeing community care provision. These recommendations of the Griffiths Report were accepted by the government and became law in the 1990

NHS and Community Care Act. This was finally implemented in 1993. The changes broaden the range of social work to include working with some people who were previously the responsibility of the health services (such as people with mental illnesses leaving psychiatric hospitals). It has also meant a change in role, further towards managing services provided by other agencies, for example in the private and voluntary sectors (see Chapter 9 for more detail on this).

Criticisms of social work

Considerable criticism of social work is made by social workers themselves, by clients and by academic writers. Scandals reported during the 1990s in the fields of child protection and community care included the following three cases: [5]

- A man who had been allowed by six different social service departments to foster 19 children over 18 years – despite an earlier conviction for sexually assaulting a boy – was sentenced to six and a half years in prison after admitting ten charges of indecent assault.
- An independent inquiry into the handling of the case of Rikki Neave, who was killed in 1994 at the age of 6 while on the 'at risk' register of Cambridgeshire social services, confirmed earlier reports of 'demoralisation, internal wrangles, unbearable case-loads and poor management'.
- The director of two private homes for people with learning disabilities in Buckinghamshire was convicted of wilful neglect and ill-treatment of residents. The homes had been inspected every six months over a 'ten-year regime of terror'.

Chapter 10 looks at some of the problems which have occurred in residential care for young people.

Activity 8.5

How would you criticise social work in the light of recent press reports about the handling of child abuse cases, etc.?

Clients or customers

Social workers have had a tendency to see people as *clients*. Clients are then thought of as people who are unable to take rational decisions and live independently of social workers. Being seen as a client has a stigmatising effect and can lead to resistance on the part of the person who needs help, or an acceptance of the label, resulting in increased feelings of inadequacy and dependency. The social worker–client relationship rarely includes any notion of mutual needs and support. For this reason, many people feel that they gain more from the support of friends, or of self-help groups, as described in Chapter 16. This stereotyping of people as clients probably helps social workers to cope with the pain and demands of their work and is common also to the nursing and teaching professions, where people are seen not as whole people, but as *patients* or *pupils*. In recent years, social work has tried to tackle this problem, substituting the term 'client' with a range of terms such as *user* or *customer* and emphasising 'empowerment'.

Empowerment

Empowerment is not an easy term to define since it is used in a number of different ways. Generally it involves service-users taking or being given more power over decisions concerning their welfare. The notion of empowerment includes the 'user-led, customer-oriented' services, particularly in community care. However the tensions caused by lack of resources, discussed below, have severely limited choice for customers of social services. A move in the direction of empowerment came in 1997, when legislation allowed local authorities to give physically disabled people under 65, needing care and support, the money to pay for and manage their own services.

Counselling not practical help

Social workers are also subjected to criticism because they are often unable to provide practical solutions to problems. Many clients see their problems as essentially practical, such as the need for a job, extra money or better housing. Social workers have very limited power to solve these problems and instead offer counselling and social work support. Both clients and social workers experience frustration as a result. Clients may reject counselling in situations where they feel they should be given practical help.

Role conflict

The job of social workers involves several roles which can come into conflict. On the one hand, they are expected to befriend clients, whereas at other times they have to carry out statutory duties without the agreement of the client. This conflict can be particularly acute when social workers have to take children into care against the wishes of the child or the parent. In situations such as this, many people come to see the social workers' role as being more like that of the police than that of friends.

In the 1960s and 1970s, there was a move towards *community work*, instead of individual casework. Community workers aim to encourage and help groups of people in the community to get together to solve their own problems. Community work sometimes leads social workers into difficulties over loyalties and obligations, in situations where the community groups oppose the decisions of the local authority. This dilemma also arises in other forms of social work and many social workers experience conflict between their commitment to the people they are supposed to help and that to their employers. Community work tends to be vulnerable in times of cuts in expenditure and increasing demand. The following quotation from a social worker illustrates one view about the role of social work in society and the feeling of frustration over the limitations of casework:

> It's all very depressing if you come to think about it. Society uses social workers to appease its conscience about the poor ... I was idealistic when I

started but it's brought home to you with a jolt how it really is when you have to say to someone, 'Sorry there's nothing we can do for you except, perhaps, take the children away'. We are not caring for the community, helping a community to cope with its own problems. We're dealing with individuals, and have no time to invest in community projects.[6]

Resource-limited services

A study of the impact of the 1990 NHS and Community Care Act found that the biggest problem for social services departments was balancing resources against needs.[7] There has been enormous pressure on budgets at the same time as changes in life expectation have increased needs. The assessment of clients' needs is limited by awareness of the need not to raise expectations that cannot be met and to ration resources.

A no-win situation

Particularly in the area of child protection, many social workers feel they are 'damned if they do, and damned if they don't'. Social workers have been criticised both for removing children from family homes and for not doing so. Here social workers are placed in an impossible situation as they are expected to protect children without intruding on the privacy of families.

Social control and individual failure

Radical criticisms of social work focus on two related aspects, social control and the emphasis on individual problems and casework. Expressed very briefly, those who see social work as a form of social control look at the way in which social workers, as state employees, go into people's homes, criticising and keeping records on life-style and activities. Social workers have the power to take away children if the way people are living their lives is thought to be unsatisfactory. In this way, social workers, mainly middle-class themselves, impose standards of behaviour and family life on their working-class clients. The second line of attack emphasises the way in which social work is a way of individualising problems, which are social and economic in origin. Many clients are poor and living in bad housing conditions. Individual casework can do nothing to solve these problems. By treating the victims of problems in society as people with personality problems, social workers help to maintain the *status quo* and distract attention away from the wider issues. People are thus encouraged to see structural problems in society in terms of individual failure.

8.5 Race and social work

In recent years, attention has been paid to the issue of race in the context of social work. Problems have been noted such as the lack of black people in social work professions, lack of knowledge of social workers of black cultures, and inadequate understanding of the nature of racism in social work and in society.

The following extract makes a number of proposals for improving social work practice in this area. It is written by a social worker in a children's home in London:[8]

Many of the black people and those of other ethnic communities living in this country were born here, and are second or third generation. Notwithstanding, we are providing a home to many people for whom the English language is a second one. Social services departments could channel communication skills into producing a range of leaflets about provision for elderly, mentally and physically handicapped people, or children and families, written in various languages, reflecting and recognising the needs of certain ethnic groups within an area.

Included in the information provided could be details about sheltered housing, home help and other domiciliary services. In a leaflet about child care, information could be included about the juvenile court system and the way care orders are awarded, explaining at the same time clarification about parental rights regarding access and appeal. A list of useful addresses could be included, indicating details of lawyers experienced in handling complex child care law. Where appropriate for example, a Turkish Cypriot social worker in an area team, or a Nigerian Yoruba-speaking home help, could be in some way identified, so that people could seek appropriate help or even interpretation.

Field and residential social workers need to be aware of different cultural values, and should not make judgements on people's parenting skills for example, based on what is an acceptable norm in our white European society.

There is a need to recognise that Afro-Caribbean families are usually very close and there is a large extended network within them. It is quite natural for an African child to be looked after by older more responsible siblings and these children can be brought up by any number of different relatives while the natural parents continue their education or undertake some commercial business.

When receiving black or other children from ethnic groups into care, social workers need to be aware of these extended family networks, and of the need to explore other members of the family if possible, before taking a child away from its natural family, and putting a child into an unnatural environment of foster-parents or a residential care home.

Regarding qualifying training there could be changes on the horizon, but a dipstick survey carried out on students who are taking part in a CQSW [now DipSW] course or who have just completed one, reveals that many students feel that their courses are not equipping them for working in a trans-cultural society.

One student said that she had spent only half a day on her CQSW [now DipSW] course looking at cultural issues. It would be unfair to blandly accuse the course of not covering cultural issues sufficiently, as already too much has to be crammed into the [social work] courses …

Again if change is to be truly effective, wider representation from ethnic groups is needed on bodies like the Central Council for Training and Education in Social Work, and at the Department of Health. This is not to undervalue the work of sitting members, but unless there are more people from ethnic groups involved, such an important body is not in a position to truly reflect the needs of the various communities.

Two more practice issues are relevant, firstly in terms of adopting an acceptable anti-racist dialogue within social work. We need to get rid of redundant and often offensive terminology. As a fundamental basic it is offensive to refer to black or brown people as 'coloured'. They are black or brown people and are proud of that fact and as a matter of courtesy should be referred to likewise. Equally, children born of black and white parents should never be referred to as of 'mixed-race'. This again is quite offensive and these children should be addressed as being of 'mixed-parentage'.

The second practice issue is in terms of placement of children, and some of these comments apply equally to all children who are placed away from their respective community and links. For some inner-city children being placed away from home in some country area can be a tremendous shock. It cannot be doubted however that for some children a period away from the inner-city can prove a valuable experience. However in general for black and other children from ethnic groups, this has led to some appalling experiences.

Living away from their families and their natural culture only serves to further isolate many of these young people. Most of the towns outside major urban areas are in predominantly all white areas. Here the young people lose touch with their cultural identity, and for many it is only in their late teens that they come into contact with their own black community.

We should think really hard before condemning a black or other ethnic child to cultural isolation, and instead concentrate on seeking a placement either directly in the individual's own locality or in the immediate surrounding area.

The role of professional associations to support and direct moves within social services towards trans-cultural provision is enormous. The record of some of these bodies on this issue has not always been good. Some years ago many black social workers formed their own professional association, and they may need persuading that these organisations are relevant to their needs.

8.6   Home-care services

This chapter has focused on field social workers but the work of others in social services departments is also very important. Home helps in particular provided a service much valued by clients but somewhat unrewarded in terms of pay and status. The work of the home-help service extended far beyond the traditional image of housework and cleaning. Home helps offered support and counselling as well as practical services. In some areas they have become known as 'family aids' to stress their changing role. The policy of care in the community has placed great pressure on the home-help services as more elderly and disabled people are maintained in the community instead of in residential care.

Home-care services have changed a great deal. Home helps are now known by a range of titles such as home carers. Many of the services have been

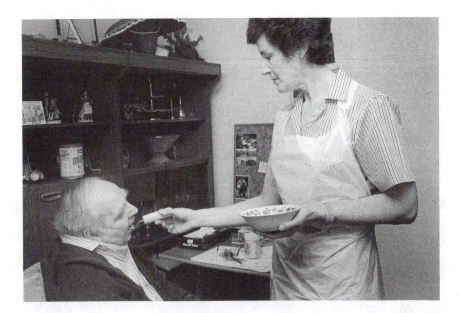

Source: Sam Tanner, Photofusion
Services are available to enable people to remain in their own home

privatised and contracted out to private organisations. Attempts to cut the costs of a growing area of need mean that home carers are less likely to spend time on housework and are more involved with personal care. Many clients have to pay a contribution for the service.

Activity 8.6

Find out about home-care services in your area. Is it possible to interview a home carer or to accompany someone during their work to find out what the job involves?

Activity 8.7

Make sure that you understand the following expressions used in this chapter. Check in the Glossary at the end of the book if you need to.

care manager	patch system
care package	personal social services
'Cinderella' service	provider
community care	purchaser
community work	self-help group
domiciliary service	statutory duty
field social worker	stereotype
foster-parent	stigma
generic social work	voluntary organisation

Further Reading

Community Care is a useful source of up-to-date articles on issues relating to social work. Details of careers and training in the personal social services can be obtained from the CCETSW Information Service (see below). A very detailed and useful source of information on legal aspects of social work is Hugh Brayne and Gerry Martin, *Law for Social Workers* (6th edn) (London: Blackstone Press, 1999).

Vivienne Coombe and Alan Little (eds), *Race and Social Work* (London: Tavistock, 1986) also has many useful articles concerning race.

Useful addresses

For Department of Health publications:

Department of Health
PO Box 777
London SE16XH
Tel. 0800 555777

CCETSW Information Service
Derbyshire House
St Chad's Street
London WCIH 8AD
tel. 0207 278 2455

British Association of Social Workers (BASW)
16 Kent Street
Birmingham
B5 6RD
tel 0121 622 3911

Social Care Association
Thornton House
Hook Road
Surbiton
Surrey K76 5AN
tel. 0208 397 1411

Website

The Department of Health is responsible for social services. Their website is at **www.doh.gov.uk** This website is designed for people involved in health and social care provision and is perhaps less helpful to the general user than some of the other government department websites.

▾ **9** Community care

In 1990 the NHS and Community Care Act was passed. This introduced a radically new system of care for many different types of people: older people, people with disabilities, people with a learning disability, and those with mental illnesses. Since the legislation, changes are continuing to be made to the system and will no doubt continue as new problems and solutions emerge. This chapter describes the history of the idea of community care, outlines the procedures introduced by the 1990 Act and looks at some of the problems being encountered. The chapters on mental illness, disability, old age, learning disability and children in trouble also cover aspects of community care in relation to these groups. (See also Chapter 2 on the family.)

9.1 What is 'community care'?

The term 'community care' is notoriously difficult to define. As will be described later, it has gone through a series of changes in use and is still used differently by different people in different contexts. The idea behind community care is that it is better (and perhaps cheaper – although this is debatable) for people to live in their own homes than in institutions. Nowadays community care is generally taken to mean the provision of services for those needing some support to live independently.

Key aspects of community care

Aspects of community care include the following:

- The closure of large psychiatric and (to use the old-fashioned name) 'mental handicap' hospitals.
- The development of new jobs for people working with clients or patients in the community, for example community psychiatric nurses or home carers (different terms are used in different areas).
- The development of services to support informal carers (relatives or perhaps neighbours).
- The development of smaller-scale residential units.

Enablers and service 'packages'

The NHS and Community Care Act encourages local authority social services departments to take the role of 'enabler' or 'manager' of services rather than that of provider. This means that the local authority will be less likely to own and run their own homes, day-centres and other services and more likely to refer people to services run by voluntary or private organisations (the independent sector). Social services are responsible for providing a 'package' of such services and for inspection and monitoring of homes. This change in the role of the social services is not necessarily a part of the philosophy of community care. It reflected a wider desire by the Conservative government of the time to privatise services, widen choice and reduce the role of local authorities. Because the two ideas have coincided, private provision of services is inextricably bound up with the development of community care in the 1990s.

9.2 The history of community care development

Problems of total institutions

Community care first began to be talked about in relation to people with mental illnesses. The traditional treatment was in large hospitals built in the nineteenth century on the outskirts of most towns. Patients who went into these hospitals often did not come out again. In the 1950s and 1960s people began to question whether this was the best way to deal with mental illness. It was however to be nearly 40 years until a real response was made.

Living their whole lives within the institution led to patients becoming 'institutionalised'. People's original symptoms may have disappeared but they had become dependent on the routines and ways of the hospital and could no longer function outside its walls. The majority of the population would be unlikely to enter their local hospital but everyone was aware of the large brick-built buildings in spacious grounds. Lack of knowledge and fear led to stigmatising of the hospitals and this extended to anyone who had been a patient. The stigma of having been in the hospital created further difficulties for a patient seeking to re-integrate into the community.

Concern over these issues led to a search for alternatives. Community care was first mentioned in the 1954–57 Royal Commission on Mental Illness and Deficiency. The Commission recommended a 'general orientation away from institutional care in its present form and towards community care'. Then, in 1961, Enoch Powell, then Minister for Health, announced the run-down of the mental hospitals. At the conference at which Powell made his speech it was argued that the motives for this change were primarily in terms of saving money and that there was no commitment to building up community resources in place of hospitals. This was a comment which was to echo throughout the next 35 years (and probably beyond). The community care policy was developed further in the 1963 government publication, *Health and Welfare: the Development of Community Care*, known as the 'Community Care Blue Book'.

The arguments for community care were strengthened by sociological critiques of institutions. Goffman's book '*Asylums*', published in 1961, introduced the concept of a *total institution*. Total institutions included mental hospitals, army barracks and prisons and were characterised by several features. In a total institution the barriers usual in our society between areas of work, play and sleep are broken down:

all aspects of life are lived in the same place, under the same authority and with a number of others, all doing the same things. The activities are subject to routines and schedules, designed by the authorities.

Finally, according to Goffman:

the various enforced activities are brought together into a single rational plan purportedly designed to fulfil the official aims of the institution.[1]

Other characteristics of total institutions are the split between the 'managed' group and the staff, who have stereotyped views of each other and between whom there is no social mobility. This means that a member of staff could not become an inmate and an inmate could not become a member of staff. There is also a barrier on information and inmates are discouraged from finding out why decisions are made. Other distinguishing factors include the role of work (for which incentives for work outside do not exist) and the lack of any notion of family life.

Activity 9.1

Try to visit a local institution, for example a home for older people. To what extent did you find it a 'total institution'?

Other writers looked at other areas of care, providing further evidence of institutionalisation. In 1962 Peter Townsend carried out a survey of homes for old people.[2] He found that many of the residents did not really need to be in a home and were there for reasons of poverty or homelessness or because they had no relatives. He also found that people were isolated and lacked freedom of choice and power over their own lives. In 1969 Pauline Morris looked at the 'mental subnormality hospitals' as they were then known.[3] She had found a similar situation to that reported by Townsend: many of the residents did not need to be there and they were poorly cared for by an inadequate number of staff.

In the late 1960s and 1970s publicity was given to a series of scandals concerning cruelty and neglect in institutions. Reports followed on these and a series of government White Papers suggested improvements in services for people with mental illnesses and learning disabilities (then known as mental handicaps). The reports argued for services to be provided to support people in their own homes or in smaller residential settings in the community. Still, however, progress was slow.

Moves toward community care

The 1980s saw greater impetus towards community care with the closure of many residential institutions and the encouragement of community care for all groups previously thought to need residential care. However there was a tendency for the development of services in the community to lag drastically behind the closure of institutions. This meant that ex-patients were often isolated and uncared for in bed-and-breakfast accommodation or that great strain was placed upon relatives. Existing community services, such as home helps, were stretched to breaking point, without any expansion in resources to meet the need. Increasingly, publicity began to be given to these issues and there was growing public awareness that something needed to be done.

One of the problems with the development of community care concerned funding arrangements. Hospitals are part of the national health service (NHS) and the NHS is funded from national government with tax payers' money. Social services, however, are part of local government and therefore financed by the council, mainly with money from rates in the past, and now from council tax. The closure of hospitals in effect meant a saving for the NHS but an increased cost to the more limited budgets of the social services departments and the councils who became responsible for people in the community.

In 1976 a system was set up to allow joint-funding of projects by the health authority and the local authority. An example of a joint-funded scheme is the Neighbourhood Resource Centre at Elm Tree Close in Frinton, Essex. Elm Tree Close is an Elderly Persons' Home with the Neighbourhood Resource Centre attached. The work of the centre is as follows:[4]

> This will be a joint venture between Social Services and the North-East Essex Health Authority. Elm Tree Close will provide the centre from which a team of Health and Social Services Department staff will support elderly people in the Community. The tasks of that team will be to identify those people 'at risk' in the surrounding area, to design and deliver 'packages of care' for such vulnerable clients, including the provision of relief for carers, and to determine which elderly people need to live in Elm Tree Close on a permanent basis. The team will include a Social Worker, a Home Help Organiser, a Health Visitor, a Nurse, an Occupational Therapist and some Physiotherapy treatment. The Neighbourhood Resource Centre will have its own tail-lift vehicle and driver. We will be able to provide maximum planned support for elderly people to remain in their own home, but if and when the time comes that there is no alternative to permanent admission to an Elderly Persons' Home, the Home will not be strange and alarming, but a known and trusted environment.

The Audit Commission – an organisation which monitors local government and health – produced an important report on community care in 1986. The report pointed out other financial anomalies. In the case of elderly people, the system of financial support was working against the development of community care. Social security payments were available for residential care (up to a certain amount) but there was no equivalent to pay for care in the community. Social services were therefore likely to want to place people in homes rather than providing expensive services for them to remain in the community.

The Griffiths Report

Following the Audit Commission's report, the government asked Sir Roy Griffiths to look into community care and make recommendations for change. The

Griffiths Report, *Community Care: Agenda for Action,* was published in 1988.[5] This became the blueprint for the White Paper which followed and the resulting 1990 legislation. The terms of reference for Griffiths were:

> to review the way in which public funds are used to support community care policy and to advise on the options for action that would improve the use of these funds as a contribution to more effective community care.

The Report argued that the system whereby community care was shared between the health authorities, the local authorities, voluntary and private organisations and informal carers with no overall lead given was ineffective. Griffiths believed that an overall responsibility should lie with the local authorities as 'arrangers and purchasers – not monopoly providers' of community care services. This would require some clarification and strengthening of local-authority powers. The report also recommended that the government should appoint a Minister with overall responsibility to set standards and to oversee provision. This Minister would also distribute central government grants to help local authorities with about half the costs of community care projects.

The Wagner Report

In the same year as the Griffiths Report, the Wagner Report on residential care was published. This Report argued that residential care should be seen as a positive choice. People should not have to go into a residential home purely in order to receive the level of care they needed. This should be provided for people at home by the local authority. Gillian Wagner made many recommendations to improve care for various different groups of people. The underlying philosophy she set out in five principles – five Cs: [6]

The Wagner Report – five Cs to improve residential care

- Caring
  This should be personal and residents should feel valued, safe and secure.
- Choice
  Each resident's right to exercise choice over their daily life should be respected.
- Continuity
  This includes both consistency of care from staff, and the maintenance of links with a resident's previous life.
- Change
  For residents, the opportunity for continued development; for staff, a commitment to respond to changing needs.
- Common values
  Ensuring that practice is based on a shared philosophy and values.

Caring for People

Nearly two years after the Griffiths Report, the government published the White Paper *Caring for People.* This adopted many, but not all, of Griffiths' recommendations. Instead of social security payments only for residential homes, social services would receive additional money to use for care – either in a residential home, or in the community.

The White Paper set out six key objectives:

- Services should be targeted on those in most need.
- Carers should be supported.
- There should be assessment of need and good care management.
- Authorities should make use of the independent sector.
- It should be clear who was responsible for what.
- The social security money previously used to pay for homes should transfer to social services.

The 1990 legislation and afterwards

The 1990 NHS and Community Care Act gave local authorities the duty to draw up a plan for community care, to assess people's needs and to inspect all provision of community and residential services. The implementation of the Act was delayed and the date for the beginning of community care was finally April 1993.

As from April 1993 the system of community care works as follows:

- The local authority has lead (but not sole) responsibility for care.
- The local authority has the duty to plan the overall *pattern of care* in the area. The plans must be publicised and available for people to see.
- People who appear to need community care services are *assessed*. How exactly this is done varies according to the situation and different procedures adopted in different areas of the country.
- A *care plan* for the individual is drawn up, taking into account their wishes and needs and those of their relatives.
- For more complex cases, a *care manager* is allocated to supervise, monitor and review the care.
- Services provided include those of the independent sector (voluntary or private organisations) to provide a wider choice.
- The local authority is accountable for the services they provide and there is a complaints procedure.

In 1994 the Health Secretary announced the introduction of *charters for community care*. These are locally prepared documents to allow for variations in areas, but all include standards for the speed and quality of services and set out which services must be paid for by users.

In a book on community care, written for Age Concern, Barbara Meredith gives the following example of a community care package:[7]

Mr O'Malley has tripped on the sill of the back door and fractured his hip. He is in hospital recovering, learning to walk with a frame, and contemplating returning home.

His family live 200 miles away. They are concerned that he might fall again and feel guilty that they can't visit more frequently. They feel that he might be safer in a care home.

But Mr O'Malley is determined to remain at home, if necessary moving the bed downstairs. An assessment is arranged in the hospital, to sort out his care needs. The social worker, physiotherapist, occupational therapist and doctor all agree on the services which will help him remain at home, and a care manager takes responsibility for arranging this support.

An arrangement is made with a neighbour to shop and do other errands for him. Mr O'Malley will contribute to the cost of this service. A home from hospital scheme will help with other care in the first few weeks. A physiotherapist and home gardening scheme will also offer support.

From time to time Mr O'Malley's 'care package' will be reassessed. If his needs have changed or increased, he and the care manager may need to readjust it.

Mr O'Malley reassures his family that he would rather be at slight risk of another fall than move to a care home, away from his friends and neighbours.

Activity 9.2

Get a copy of your local community care plan (you could write to the county council or to the local social services office). Study it carefully and try to identify the following:

- The process of consultation with local people.
- Examples of use of the independent sector to provide services.

Select a particular group and look at the provision for them. What is available? Where are the gaps? What is planned for the future?

In 1996 the Community Care (Direct Payments) Act was passed. This gives physically disabled people under 65 the possibility of receiving money to arrange their own care services rather than receiving them directly from the local authority.

9.3 Can community care work?

Most people agree that community care is a 'good thing' and there has been a remarkable level of agreement among the politicians on this issue. There have, however, been problems with the implementation of the policy and a number of criticisms of the basic thinking and of the practice of community care have emerged.

The nature of communities

Through the development of the idea of community care there has been a continued ambiguity over the role of the 'community'. Some writers have argued that there are two different ideas: care *by* the community and care *in* the community. Government documents have varied in their emphasis. The quotation below from the 1981 White Paper *Growing Older* shows how the government of the time expected the community itself to provide care:

Whatever level of public expenditure proves practicable, and however it is distributed, the primary sources of support and care are informal and voluntary.

These spring from the personal ties of kinship, friendship and neighbourhood. They are irreplaceable. It is the role of public authorities to sustain and, where necessary, develop – but never to displace – such support and care. Care *in* the community must increasingly mean care *by* the community.[8]

Expectations of care *by* the community contain a number of assumptions. The word 'community' has itself a tendency to mislead. It is a cosy, romantic sort of word: one that conjures up images of friendliness and caring. Perhaps it makes you think of villages in the countryside where everyone knows everyone else and people are constantly popping in and out of each others' houses, borrowing sugar and offering lifts to town. Or maybe of the sort of communities portrayed in television soap operas: in *East Enders* they may not always get along but people of different races and classes all mix together, spending time in the local pub, all knowing each others' business. There has been very little research carried out on modern-day communities but it seems unlikely that many of us live in the type of communities imagined above or shown in television fiction.

Activity 9.3

Think about where you live. What sort of contact do you and your family have with others in the locality? What kind of favours could you ask of your neighbours, and what do you do for them? Compare your experience with those of others in the group. What factors could explain any differences and similarities?

For most people the idea of 'community' has little meaning. In an article on community care, Nigel Derricourt argues that increased social mobility has meant that people are less likely to have links with others in their immediate area. Instead people are likely to have various networks of relationships through work, hobbies and interests and family members. Some of these will be in the neighbourhood and some not.[9] Within social networks, some relationships will be more limited than others: some will be based on a particular area of life only, some will be very superficial. For many people, relationships with immediate neighbours are not close. Most of us live in 'communities of limited liability': we can ask our neighbours to feed the cat when we go on holiday or to take in a parcel, but this is just about the limit of 'community caring'. Also it is very important to note that some people will have very limited networks – if any at all – and these may well be the people with the greatest needs.

Activity 9.4

1 Make a list of all your relationships with people. Categorise these in the following way:

- *Near/distant*, depending on the geographical distance between you – your grandmother, for example, may live far away.
- *Strong/weak*, depending on the strength of the relationship. You probably have stronger relationships with your immediate family and a few close friends than with your neighbours.

- *Specific/general*, depending on the nature of the relationship. You may know people through a sports club with whom you share an interest. Perhaps you could ask them favours related to this – a lift to a competition maybe – but the relationship does not extend beyond your shared interest. You may have a similar type of relationship with people at work, or work-based friendships may have developed further.

2 Attempt to draw a diagram to show your networks of relationships.
3 How effective would your support be if you or someone in your family were seriously ill or disabled and needed a lot of help? How many of these people would be able and willing to support you, and in what ways?

Of course it is true that, in some areas, a real sense of community does exist and members do support each other. This is more likely to be the case in rural areas where communities are smaller. Also the population is often more stable with families staying on the same farms for several generations, although increasingly young people move away to find work and cheaper housing as richer commuters move into rural areas. Another factor which makes a difference is the number of women at home. Where women are working outside the home, it is unlikely that strong community relationships will develop. Areas with predominantly young families – such as new estates – commonly provide mutual support for parents caring for small children. The school may provide a meeting point as parents drop and pick up their children. However such communities are not necessarily willing to extend their support to others more needy and less able to offer anything in return. In fact, communities such as these are more likely to oppose housing for people with learning disabilities or mental illnesses. More anonymous city areas where people are at work all day and out pursuing interests in the evenings and week-ends are also more tolerant.

Activity 9.5

Discussion question:
Is community care possible in this society? To what extent are people prepared to tolerate and give to others who may be able to offer little in return and whose behaviour and appearance may be different?

The role of families

Despite romantic ideas of caring communities, research has found that most care is provided by family members, and within the family it is usually women who provide care. In 1982 the Equal Opportunities Commission stated:

A growing body of evidence suggests that 'community care' has in reality meant care by individuals on an unpaid and often unaided basis in the home ... They will often find themselves badly supported by statutory services and without any real choice as to whether they will care or not. Far from the community carrying the costs, the allocation of caring responsibilities has major implications in financial, social, and emotional terms for the individuals involved.[10]

The idea of the family taking a greater role in caring as the welfare state shrinks is at the centre of the Conservative Party's philosophy.

There is an assumption that family members are willing and able to care for relatives. But at the same time as the family has come under increasingly pressure to provide care, changes in both the structure of the family and the wider society have made this increasingly difficult. These changes include:

- increasing numbers of women in paid employment;
- increasing trend to cohabitation instead of marriage;
- higher divorce rate;
- increasing re-marriage and step-parenting;
- increased number of single parents;
- a tendency for families to move apart in search of work;
- smaller numbers of children.

Trends such as cohabitation, divorce and re-marriage may serve to weaken ties between people. Janet Finch has researched the role of the family in caring and she found that one of the things people think about is what they *ought* to do in a particular situation.[11] It may be that people are less likely to feel they ought to care for a parent who left as a result of divorce, or for a step-parent. Where people do not marry they may not feel the same sense of obligation to their partner's parents.

Also it cannot be assumed that everyone has relatives. A significant proportion of people in residential care do not have relatives at all. There are also cases where people have no desire for contact with their relatives.

Carers

The term 'carers' did not exist in the 1980s. Now it has come to describe people who care for a relative or friend, without pay. Since the 1980s there has been a growing interest in carers – both in research and government statements. Janet Finch's research on carers found the following:

- few people care for non-relatives;
- single, never-married women are the traditional carers, but there are fewer of these than in the past – they do however provide a disproportionate amount of care;
- men care for wives, but women care for husbands, parents, children and other relatives;
- carers receive little support from other family members;
- caring often dominates the carer's life.[12]

Carers face a variety of problems. All situations are different but several common themes emerge from accounts by carers. Many feel isolated and lonely. Many carers are themselves elderly or have a disability and may find the physical work involved in caring very difficult. For anyone, caring is exhausting. The hours are long and there are no week-ends or holidays. For some the personal care aspect is embarrassing and difficult – perhaps especially so if you are caring for a parent. The symptoms of Alzheimer's disease can be particularly difficult to cope with. The disease involves loss of memory, often to the point that the sufferer will not know his or her own relatives, and people in the later stages of the disease are likely to develop bizarre, anti-social and distressing habits. Spending long periods of time with someone with Alzheimer's disease tests the patience and good nature of even the most tolerant and caring nurse. Many carers feel guilty. There is the guilt of feeling sometimes cross and tired, perhaps even of wishing at times that the person would die. There is guilt if a carer feels he or she is neglecting others – especially children. Of course it is not all gloom and doom and there are many sources of satisfaction in caring, but most carers report themselves to be very tired and many experience periods of depression.

In many cases people want to care for their relatives but want some support to enable them to do so. This might include respite care which gives the carer a break for perhaps a week-end or longer, or a sitting or day-care service to allow people to shop or enjoy some time alone. A common theme in research on carers is that such help has not been available. A study sponsored by the National Institute for Social Work on people looking after a confused relative found that 45 per cent of heavily incontinent people were never visited by a community nurse and lacked other support services. They had never been offered the services. 83 per cent would have liked short-term respite care.

Activity 9.6

Imagine you are a carer. Write a letter to a newspaper describing your situation and the sort of help and support you need to receive, and how far local provision is likely to help you.

The 1990 NHS and Community Care Act makes a commitment to supporting carers and social services departments have emphasised this in their plans for community care. But the help still does not seem to be reaching the people who need it. The Carers' National Association (Carers) is a voluntary self-help group for carers. In a survey of 426 carers in touch with a voluntary organisation they found that one in four carers had not even heard of the system of community care introduced in 1993. Almost three in four of the carers had had no assessment carried out on the person they cared for. 79 per cent said the new law had made no difference to them and 8 per cent believed that services had in fact got worse.[13] Below is the 10-point plan drawn up in 1994 by a group of organisations involved in caring.

Carers' needs: a 10-point plan for carers

A group of organisations involved in caring, including Age Concern, the Alzheimer's Disease Society and the Carers' National Association have produced the following list of carers' needs:

1. Recognition of their contribution and of their needs as individuals in their own right.

2. Services tailored to their own individual circumstances, needs and views, through discussions at the time help is being planned.
3. Services which reflect an awareness of differing racial, cultural and religious backgrounds and values, equally accessible to carers of every race and ethnic origin.
4. Opportunities for a break, both for short spells (an afternoon) and for longer periods (a week or more) to relax and have time to themselves.
5. Practical help to lighten the tasks of caring, including domestic help, home adaptations, incontinence services, and help with transport.
6. Someone to talk to about their own emotional needs, at the outset of caring, while they are caring, and when the caring task is over.
7. Information about the available benefits and services, as well as how to cope with the particular condition of the person being cared for.
8. An income which covers the costs of caring and which does not preclude carers taking employment or sharing care with someone else.
9. Opportunities to explore alternatives to family care, both for the immediate and long-term future.
10. Services designed through consultation with carers, at all levels of policy planning.

(*King's Fund Informal Programme*)

In 1995 the Carers (Recognition of Services) Act was passed, giving the right to a separate assessment to carers of sick, elderly or disabled friends or relatives. Social services are required to take carers' views and the results of their assessment into account when deciding what services to provide for the person being cared for.

This was followed in 1999 by the announcement of a national support package recognising the needs of carers. The proposals included extra funding for flexible forms of respite care to allow carers to have a break and support for young carers whose school work often suffers as a result of their responsibilities.

Young carers

It is only recently that young carers have been recognised. The Department of Health defined a young carer as:

a child or young person who is carrying out significant caring tasks and assuming a level of responsibility for another person, which would usually be taken by an adult. The term refers to children and young people under 18 years caring for adults (usually their parents) or occasionally siblings.[14]

Exact numbers are unknown but there are thought to be between 20,000 and 50,000 young people caring for relatives. Many are afraid to be identified, fearing being taken into care if their situation comes to the attention of the authorities. Young carers may face emotional problems as a result of the role reversal situation in which they find themselves and they are often disadvantaged in educa-

Source: Debbie Humphry, Photofusion
Hostels provide some support while allowing people to lead independent lives

tion owing to poor attendance and the lack of time left for studying. Young people caring for parents with mental illnesses or who are substance abusers face particularly stressful emotional problems.

Life in the community or life in a hospital or home?

It is not possible to make any general or conclusive statements about the best form of care. Individual needs and desires have to be taken into account and everyone's situation is different. It is also important to note that none of the points made below about residential care are bound to be the case. The problems with institutions in the past could have been tackled within institutions and changes made. To some extent this has happened and much more flexible and sensitive practices have been adopted. It is also true that many of the problems of community care are not intrinsic to community care. Better resources and facilities could vastly improve people's lives in the community. Education could shift public attitudes.

The section below sums up this chapter by considering some of the pros and cons of residential care and community care for the people most directly affected. The focus here is on people with mental illnesses: some of the points are relevant to other situations, some are not. These issues are also covered in the chapters on mental illness, disability, learning disability and old age.

If we take the situation of people with mental illnesses, it is undoubtedly true that many people were in hospital who did not need to be there. Many people stayed much longer than necessary and it became impossible for them to leave. (Nowadays this would not happen and people are treated and then leave – only returning if things get worse.) Within institutions, there is a strong tendency for the needs of the organisation to take precedence over the needs of the individual. In one large hospital in the 1970s it was the practice for everyone to be got up by the night staff who went off duty at 7.30 a.m. This meant that patients were woken around 6 a.m. The day staff would have everyone in bed before they went off duty – this was at 8.30 p.m. and patients would start going to be bed around 7 p.m. The day was built around other rigid routines with everyone having drinks, baths and meals at set times – even going to the toilet at particular times in the day. There was no choice over food and little choice over clothes for most people.[15] Institutions have a tendency to be authoritarian in these sorts of ways, minimising choice, freedom and power over one's own life. Residents feel inferior, lose confidence in their abilities and become dependent. Many of the buildings were unsuitable: too large and too old. It is probable that acts of cruelty did occur and quite commonly – either in deliberate acts of violence and deprivation or in the form of insensitivity to suffering. Residential care takes people away from the community and usual patterns of living and carries a stigma.

On the other hand the hospital is a safe environment for people in trouble. There are no responsibilites to worry about and bizarre behaviour is tolerated. The community can be a cruel place for people who do not fit in. Large psychiatric hospitals formed communities in themselves in which people with mental illnesses had a social life – visiting the cafe, attending occupational and other therapy centres, going to organised social events and outings, visiting other wards and roaming in large grounds. Many people with mental illnesses have left hospital only to be lonely and isolated in bed-and-breakfast accommodation with none of the social facilities they had in hospital.

Activity 9.7

Think about each of the following situations. Imagine that you are the person or that he or she is a close relative. Would community or residential care be best? In each case explain your reasons, thinking through the pros and cons of each.

- May is 80 and living alone. She has a large house which she lived in with her husband (now dead) and her family. She has become frail and cannot move about very well. She is unable to shop or cook and feels insecure – worrying that she will be burgled or robbed or worse.
- Sue is 25 and has quite severe Down's Syndrome. She has lived most of her life in institutions.
- John has schizophrenia. He is 40 and has long lost touch with his relatives. For quite long periods he feels fine. Every so often however he is tormented by voices. Sometimes the voices tell him to hurt himself.

- Balwinder is 18 and is unable to walk following a riding accident. She has been living at home but does not get on very well with her parents.
- Andrew is 50 and has multiple sclerosis. Gradually his condition has deteriorated, affecting all movements and balance. He is a widower and his daughter lives some 200 miles away. He is lonely and increasingly unable to look after himself.

Activity 9.8

1 *Discussion question*:
   What is needed to make community care work?
2 Write a report setting out a strategy for a policy of community care for people with mental illnesses in your area.

Activity 9.9

Make sure that you understand the following expressions used in this chapter. Check in the Glossary at the end of the book if you need to.

Audit Commission	independent sector
care manager	informal carers
care package	institutionalisation
care plan	joint-funding
carer	learning disability
charter	respite care
cohabitation	stigma
community care	targeting
community psychiatric nurse	total institution
enabler	voluntary organisation
home carers	White Paper

Further reading

There are a number of government reports and White Papers in this area: most make for dry and difficult reading. An exception to this is the Wagner Report on residential care – its full title being *Residential Care: A positive choice* (London: HMSO, 1988). This was written to be helpful to staff working in this area and it is full of information and ideas for all types of residential care. Robin Means and Randall Smith provide a well-organised and readable review of all the issues relating to community care in *Community Care Policy and Practice*, 2nd edition (London: Macmillan, 1998). A lot of useful articles are included in Joanna Bornat, Charmaine Pereira, David Pilgrim and Fiona Williams (eds), *Community Care: a reader* 2nd edn (London: Macmillan, 1997). Finally it should not be difficult to get local documents on community care: try the council or social services departments.

Useful addresses

Carers' National Association
20 Pentonville Road
London N1 9XB
tel. 0207 837 7345

The King's Fund is an independent organisation which researches health and social care issues:

11–13 Cavendish Square
London W1M OAN
tel. 0207 307 2400

Website

The Kings Fund: **www.Kingsfund.org.uk**

10 Children and young people in need

Social welfare has long been interested in the well-being and upbringing of children, mainly because children have been seen as society's investment in the future. However this society has seen children's needs, in general, as being most appropriately met by their families. Only when something went wrong would the state intervene. Chapter 2 on the family has already looked at the issue of child abuse. This chapter focuses on procedures by which children come into the care of the local authority, perhaps because they have been abused, but also because their parents cannot look after them, either temporarily or permanently, or because they have broken the law in a serious way. Child-care law is very complicated and only an indication of the main points can be given here, together with a discussion of some of the key policy issues. The chapter finishes by examining the various ways in which young offenders are treated by the courts and social services.

10.1 The historical background

Young offenders were treated in exactly the same way as adults until the beginning of the nineteenth century and punishments for even trivial crimes tended to be very harsh. In 1838 a prison was opened to deal specially with children, so that they would not be locked up with adults. Then in 1854 Reform Schools were started as an alternative to imprisonment. Also around this time, in 1847, magistrates were allowed to deal with children for some offences instead of sending them to a trial with a jury. Over time, it became the custom for magistrates to hold separate sessions for juvenile offenders and in 1908 an Act was passed saying that such cases must be heard in separate sessions. The same Act abolished imprisonment for children under the age of 14. The 1920 Juvenile Courts (Metropolis) Act stated that only specially selected magistrates could work in the children's courts.

Children without parents or whose parents could not or would not look after them were looked after under the Poor Law in institutions or boarded out with families. In both cases life could be very hard and families usually expected a child to work hard in return for food and a roof. Charities such as Barnardo's also ran orphanages and boarding-out schemes. Here the treatment was usually of a higher standard. The attitude taken towards deprived children at this time was less that they needed love and a caring family, as it is now, than that they would best be helped by being offered training to enable them to find independent employment. Some charities paid fares so that older children could go out to Australia and Canada to work.

The 1933 Children and Young Persons Act gave magistrates in the juvenile courts the power to remove children believed to be in need of care and protection from their parents. They would then be looked after in foster-homes or in children's homes run under the Poor Law.

The Curtis Report on child care was published in 1945 and its recommendations became law in the 1948 Children's Act. This important Act attempted to bring together all the responsibilities for homeless children. Local authorities were to employ Children's Officers who would draw on expert knowledge and be managed by a Children's Committee of the local authority. Local authorities would receive children into care voluntarily if the parents were unfit or unable to provide adequate care. They would supervise children who were boarded-out and register adoption societies. The Children's Department would also provide magistrates with information and be responsible for children sent to remand homes, committed to the care of the local authority by the courts or sent to approved schools. The act stated that local authorities must seek to return the child home wherever possible and to try to board-out children who could not be returned home. Reception centres were to be set up to assess the child's needs on coming into care.

As mentioned in Chapter 8, the work of the Children's Officers was highly professional and set the scene for the future development of family casework in the Social Service Departments created in 1970.

10.2   Care and protection of children

In 1991, the 1989 Children Act was implemented. The Act pulled together lots of older Acts and aimed to simplify the law. Under the Act, local authorities have a duty to protect children in their area. This duty is carried out by the social workers in the social services departments. Although the law does not say how local authorities must organise their service, they are bound to provide services which prevent children from being the victims of ill-treatment or neglect. If it is suspected that a child may be in danger, the local authority is bound, under law, to investigate the situation.

The main principles of the Act are that:

- The welfare of the child must come first.
- Children are best looked after by their own families and should only be removed if absolutely necessary.
- Decisions must be made quickly and without the courts if possible.
- Local authorities must work in partnership with children and their parents.
- Parents have a right to have a say in decisions about their children.
- Parents keep responsibility for their children, even if someone else is looking after them.
- Families must be helped to keep in contact with their children.
- Services to children and families must take account of race, religion, culture, language and any disability.

The law provides for a number of different court orders which give social workers powers to intervene in families. Cases involving children are dealt with in the Family Proceedings Court. Magistrates in these courts have special training in children's cases. The courts are more informal than others and no-one wears a wig or a gown. The public are not allowed into the Family Proceedings Court.

In a situation where social workers are concerned for the welfare of a child, they do not have to take the child into care. The social worker may feel that it is damaging for a child to be taken from his or her home. If the child is not felt to be in danger, he or she may be left at home. Social services can provide support in the home – perhaps the services of a family home help, or the support of a social worker. They can also provide money if this will help the situation. The law also provides that help – perhaps in the form of different housing – could be given to someone else in the household, for example someone who is suspected of abusing the child. But these decisions must always be made with the child's interests and safety as the main consideration.

Child assessment order

If the social workers feel that a child is at risk in their home they must investigate the situation. They can then apply for one of the court orders available or decide to review the situation at a later date. There have been situations in the past where social workers have not been able to get access to examine a child they were worried about. To stop this happening again, there is now a *child assessment order*. The court will give this order if they feel that there is a suspicion of significant harm to the child, but no immediate emergency. A child assessment order lasts for 7 days. It can include the child being taken from the home for examination if this is thought to be necessary.

Emergency protection order

An *emergency protection order* can be granted if the court feels that the child is likely to suffer significant harm if he or she is left at home or allowed to go home. It lasts for 7 days and can be extended for a further 7 days.

Police protection powers

The police have the power to remove a child straightaway, but they must then inform the local authority. This is for a period of 72 hours and the parents must be allowed to see the child.

Care order

Care orders bring the child into the care of the local authority. A care order gives parental responsibility for the child to the local authority. With a care order the child would normally be removed from home to live with foster-parents or in a community home run by the local authority or a voluntary organisation. The fact that the local authority has parental responsibility does not remove responsibility from the parents (or people looking after the child). It is a *prime* responsibility only that goes to the local authority. The law encourages parents to continue to be involved with the child and local authorities are expected to look for ways to share responsibility. The grounds for a care order are:

- that the child is suffering or is likely to suffer significant harm; and
- that the harm is because either,
  - (i) the care given by the parents is not what it is reasonable to expect, or
  - (ii) the child is beyond the control of the parents.

Supervision order

With a *supervision order*, the child remains at home and has a social worker whose role is to advise, help and befriend. The child and the parent must make sure the social worker is aware of any moves of house, and can meet the child. It may be that the child is required to live at a particular place or has to join in some organised activities. The grounds for a supervision order are the same as those for a care order.

Interim care order

It is also possible for an *interim care order* to be made, if the full hearing cannot take place for some reason. This lasts for up to 8 weeks but a second one can only last for 4 weeks.

Guardian *ad litem*

There is a system whereby an adult is appointed to represent the interests of the child in court. This person is called a 'guardian *ad litem*'. It is the duty of the court to appoint such a person unless the court is satisfied that it is not necessary to do so. The guardian *ad litem* carries out an investigation, interviewing various people such as the child him or herself, social workers, parents and relatives. A report is then presented to the court which tries to state what actions are in the best interests of the child.

Case conferences

As was mentioned earlier, the law does not state how the social services departments must act to prevent child abuse. The usual system is through multi-disciplinary committees and case conferences. These bring together all the different people who might be involved with a particular child. Knowledge is shared and a decision made as to the best course of action. The people involved are likely to include social workers, police officers, a member of staff from the school, GPs and other health care workers such as health visitors. There may also be workers from the National Society for Prevention of Cruelty to Children (NSPCC), if they are also involved with the case.

'At risk' registers

All areas keep a register of children who have been abused or who are suspected of having been abused. This is either looked after by the local authority or by the NSPCC.

Children looked after by the local authority

It is possible for a child to be looked after by the local authority without being in care. This happens in situations where the local authority is providing a home for a child without there being a court order. Social services must provide for children who have no-one to look after them, who are lost or abandoned, or whose carer is unable – temporarily or permanently – to provide care. The child's wishes in such a situation should be considered and the parents are allowed to take the child back without any notice. The local authority have a duty to facilitate contact between the parents and the child. This can include paying the costs of visits to the child. There must also be regular reviews of the situations of all children being looked after by the local authority.

The numbers of children looked after by local authorities (previously described as being in care) have gone down through the 1980s and 1990s. In 1980, 95,300 children were in care.[1] In 1996, 51,000 children were being looked after by local authorities. About 65 per cent of these are in foster placements, 13 per cent in residential homes and the rest living with parents or others.[2]

Practical problems

Although the 1989 Children Act has done a great deal to improve the legal situation and to extend more rights to parents and children, problems remain. The section below looks at some of the problems which researchers have identified.

Rochdale Area Child Protection Committee commissioned a research study to look at parental participation in case conferences. The study found that many parents left feeling confused. Reporting on the study in the *Guardian*, Kathy Batt writes:

> You are sitting at a table, surrounded by a dozen people. You know the health visitor and the teacher. You recognise the social worker, just. She was the one that came to the door a fortnight ago to tell you that your child's welfare was 'causing concern'. But there are other people you have never seen before – health managers, psychologists, social service managers and a policeman. They are all there to talk about your family and to decide whether your child is 'at risk'. You are now taking part in a Child Protection Case Conference.
>
> Everyone says they 'want to work in partnership with you'. That's all right then. A partner is an equal and if you don't agree with their decision you can say so and they will have to change their mind. Won't they?
>
> Well, no. Most local authorities now invite parents to case conferences, where a skilful chairperson will ensure that the parental viewpoint is given due consideration. But if parents disagree with the conference's recommendations,

there is not a lot they can do about it. No wonder so many parents leave the conference feeling confused.[3]

The survey also found that 25 per cent of parents did not turn up. This was due to many factors. Sometimes the problems were practical, such as difficulties to do with work, child care or transport. Sometimes however it was their feelings about the system which stopped them attending. Some parents felt too angry. Others felt too much of an outsider from the powerful system that was making decisions about their lives. In other cases parents were simply terrified. Parents who did attend the meeting felt they were inadequately prepared. They did not fully understand who was who and what was going on. The majority of parents were however glad they had been able to attend, even if they left feeling somewhat angry or bewildered.[4]

Problems of liaison and co-ordination

A common theme in the reports which have been published on child abuse has, as we have seen, been the lack of communication and co-ordination between the various services involved. These can include: social services, schools, doctors, health visitors, the police, voluntary organisations, nurseries, hospitals, child guidance clinics, and educational welfare officers. Many reports have recommended closer links between the various agencies. In 1991 a government document, *Working Together Under the Children Act 1989*, stated that Child Protection Committees should be organised in each area to set up, monitor and review procedures to ensure inter-agency communication. These committees have been established. However a report commissioned by the National Children's Bureau argues that these sort of strategies have a very limited effect. Setting up new structures and new committees is not an effective method of making children the primary concern. The organisations involved with children – the police, social services, the health services etc. – have too many other issues to deal with. Children are not 'centre stage' among all the various concerns of the organisations. What is needed, the report argues, is a small team of various professionals solely concerned with children's needs.[5]

To intervene or not?

Whatever new laws are brought in, whatever procedures are set up, it seems that social workers face an impossible task in protecting children. They carry an enormous and unrealistic burden of responsibility for the safety of children. They work with the fear of public exposure hanging over them: knowing they will be damned by the press and the public if a child is hurt, but similarly damned if children are taken into care wrongly. It is not surprising that social workers cannot usually work very long in this type of work before they 'burn out'.

Research in Britain and Australia has demonstrated the impossibility of predicting which parents will hurt their children and which will not. The research shows that the families in which children die are just like any others. Yet social workers have often been trained to look for key factors which singly or in combination indicate a risk of abuse. The Australian study found that social workers were too influenced by moral standards on how families should live – focusing their attentions on families whose houses were dirty, parents whose children were not clean or well-dressed and those who had unusual life-styles. Families under investigation were more likely to be poor, headed by lone parents or Aboriginal. In Britain the emphasis was on families with a history of violence of some sort. The head of the research in Britain, Jane Gibbons, agreed that the child protection system cannot identify children at risk. She said:

> It is probably quite impossible to pick out children who are going to be killed or seriously injured. Common sense may tell us that a child living with a man with a conviction for violence is at greater risk, but we don't actually know that.[6]

A sociologist, Nigel Parton,[7] believes that child abuse demonstrates the impossible situation in which social workers are expected to work. On the one hand, society expects that social workers will protect children and intervene in families. But on the other hand, the family is seen as a very private area. We believe that parents should have the responsibility for bringing up their own children and no-one should interfere with this. Therefore it is only when things go wrong that social workers can legitimately intervene. By which time it may be too late and the social services department will get the blame. In other words the social worker involved with children is always treading a very fine line between interfering too much and not doing enough.

10.3 Provision for children and young people

Foster-parents

At the present time the trend is away from residential care for children, to care in the community. Two explanations for this lie in the fact that care in the community is cheaper and in the widespread belief that children benefit from a family home. Whilst there is much to be said for these points of view, there are dangers in the situation. For example, there is a tendency for residential homes to close before sufficient resources in the community have been established. Second, some disturbed children, especially adolescents, have difficulty coping with the emotional pressure of family life and benefit from the less demanding atmosphere of an institution.

The following quotations from a young person illustrate the danger of assuming that foster-parents provide the best care for all children. The first extract recalls experience of being fostered:

> The most striking feature of the boarding out was the loneliness – I was one child, a stranger with a family. The family had been going on for years and could not really be expected to adapt itself to me, and yet I was not old enough to adapt myself to people – not really. It was rather like a tug-of-war and in turn they expected that, 'I am doing so much for you, surely I deserve something

in return!' and that something in return always seemed to be far more than I could give.[8]

The same young person goes on to compare fostering and life in a children's home:

I can't think why there is so much controversy about foster-parents versus Children's Homes, institutions versus foster-parents – there is no comparison. In a Children's Home there is nothing except good behaviour demanded of a child – no loyalty and they don't have to fight their way into the circle – it is accepted on its terms. There is no fighting inside the family circle, because each child is there on its own merits. No one has more right than another, there is no feeling that you have to be loyal to the houseparent and forsake your own. It is a neutral sort of place where you can go and recover from whatever has happened to you, or get ready for the next step.[9]

Social workers spend a lot of time looking at the suitability of people to foster children. In spite of this, breakdowns are common. Often as described above, the foster-parents expect too much of the young person and of themselves. Fostering is a cheap way of providing care for children as the majority of foster-parents are not paid, but given an allowance towards the cost of the child. There is however a move towards paying 'professional' foster-parents, who take older and more difficult young people into their homes.

Activity 10.1

Discussion questions on fostering:
1 What are the advantages and disadvantages of foster-parents, as opposed to institutional care, for children and young people?
2 Should foster-parents be paid?
3 Should single men and women, or those who are lesbian or gay, be allowed to foster children?

Publicity has recently been given to the needs of black children in foster-care. It has been argued that children must be placed with parents of the same race and living in black communities. There are two basic reasons for this viewpoint. First, it is believed that black or mixed race children brought up by white parents in white areas will grow up confused about their identity and will tend to deny that they are black. Secondly, it is argued that black people need to grow up in black communities and to have the support of each other in order to cope with the racism they will experience in British society. In other words of John Small, assistant director of social services in Hackney:

Black and ethnic people need to develop survival skills, and this means not denying their racial origin. There are many white liberals around who don't accept that we have racial problems in Britain today.[10]

The following two case studies illustrate the problems faced by black children raised in white foster-homes in white communities.

Harry

Harry is the illegitimate West Indian child of a brief alliance between a widow who already has six children of her own and her deceased husband's brother who is also married with six children. Harry had never been accepted by either of his parents who freely expressed their hatred of him. The situation reached a peak following the birth of the mother's latest baby while Harry was living with her. In her over-wrought condition she threatened to kill Harry and the Social Services department had no choice but to take him into care for his own safety. He was placed with the only foster-mother available. This foster-mother happens to be white and lives in an all-white neighbourhood. There are only about two or three other black children at the school Harry attends, but he shows no particular affinity with them. Harry has never expressed any desire to see any member of either side of his family and for a time called the foster-mother 'mummy'. He is very concerned about the difference in the colour of her skin and often asks why he can't be white like her. Occasionally he makes secretive attempts at whitening himself. For some time, for example, the foster-mother has been finding white powder on the bathroom floor, only to discover later that Harry was rubbing Harpic on his skin. There is no doubt that Harry has received more love from his foster-parent than he has ever received from his own parents. However, the foster-mother is worried that this may still not be sufficient to help him later in life, after he has passed the stage of childhood.[11]

Perlita

Perlita Harris went into care at birth, and was later fostered then adopted by the same couple. Her parents were Christian and specified Christian foster-parents.

Her foster-parents, however, are white. Perlita is Pakistani. Growing up in Gloucestershire she never saw another black face. She was the only black child in her primary school and she didn't meet an Indian until her natural father tracked her down when she was 17.

He introduced her to her Pakistani family, but her grandmother didn't speak a word of English, and Perlita spoke no Urdu.

It left her with an irreparable feeling of disorientation. She studies sociology and anthropology at university and has since chosen to live within the black community where her feminist views cause conflict with her Pakistani family, exacerbated by the cultural differences which she was totally unprepared for, and which she feels is a common experience of black children in care. 'White people see you as black, treat you as black, black people want to know why you behave so white. You're always answerable to somebody.'[12]

A problem in the past has been the lack of black people to foster black children. As a result, many local authorities have mounted special campaigns to attract black and mixed race foster-parents.

Residential care

Social services provision includes small family group homes, community homes and specialised provision such as observation and assessment centres. Some homes are run privately with the aim of making a profit and some are run by charitable organisations. Social services pay to send children to these private and voluntary institutions. During the 1990s the trend was for social services departments to close their residential accommodation and rely on other organisations when children could not be placed in foster homes. This was part of the wider idea that departments should be 'purchasers' of care, rather than 'providers'.

Community homes vary a great deal in the sort of atmosphere and regime provided for children and young people. Homes with a high reputation often maintain this by operating a selection policy and only taking young people whom it is argued will benefit from a stay in the home. The inclusion of offenders along with other children leads to a situation where many community homes treat children as in need of treatment of some sort. There is also a tendency for people to think of children in community homes as delinquents. In the words of one young person:

> People think that if you're in care you must have done something wrong. The first question they ask is 'What did you do?' It's not just teachers and other kids at school but it's the kids and staff in children's homes. When you go to a new place, before you've got your feet in the door they say 'Hey, what are you in for?'[13]

There is undoubtedly a stigma attached to being in care, no matter how good the provision is.

Social services must hold review meetings to make plans for children in care. The first review must be 4 weeks after the child is placed in care, the second after 3 months and then reviews must continue every 6 months. Children do not have a right to go to the review but will often be invited for some or all of the meeting. Exclusion is sometimes resented, as is shown by the view of a young person who says:

> What happens, you see, they talk about you, what you are trying to think. Well, how do they know what you are thinking if you are not there?[14]

Another issue concerned with care involves the use of secure units in residential accommodation. Authorities have had the discretion to lock up the children who commit offences or who are difficult to control, although some have rejected this approach and have no secure accommodation. Since April 1983, local authorities are no longer allowed to lock up young people for more than 72 hours without a court hearing. Under the Children Act, children under the age of 13 must never be locked up in secure units in children's homes unless special permission is first given by the government. In all other cases children cannot be locked up unless they have a history of running away or are likely to hurt themselves or someone else.

Institutional abuse

There have been an increasing number of scandals regarding children's homes. Some of these have involved cruel and unacceptable systems of discipline such as that known as 'Pindown', used in homes in Staffordshire. There are now stricter national regulations regarding what is allowed in children's homes and more attempt is made to inform children of their rights. The following is an extract from a booklet written for children and published by the Department of Health:

Some kinds of punishment are not allowed in children's homes. You should not be punished in any of the ways listed below:

- Hit, slapped, pinched, squeezed, shaken, dealt with roughly or have things thrown at you.
- Stopped from having food or drink.
- Stopped from seeing your parents, family or friends, stopped from getting or sending letters or from getting or making phone calls.
- Stopped from getting in touch with your social worker, guardian *ad litem* or solicitor.
- Made to wear clothes that draw attention to yourself, things like punishment badges or pyjamas during the day time.
- Stopped from having your usual medicines or from going to the doctor or dentist when you need to.
- Given any other form of medicine, such as drugs to keep you quiet, or given medical or dental treatment when you do not need it.
- Deliberately stopped from going to sleep.
- Made to pay a fine (unless it is a court fine) but up to two-thirds of your pocket money can be kept from you.[15]

In various parts of the country, there have been disturbing exposures of abuse of children in homes. Some of these have taken twenty or thirty years to come to light. It is almost unbearable to think of vulnerable, powerless and perhaps already damaged children being further abused by the very people entrusted with their care. In one example, paedophiles, Gordon Knott and Brian Maclennan, ran two homes in Scotland through the 1970s and 1980s, routinely abusing children in their care. Some of the victims reported the abuse, but no-one believed them. One child wrote a harrowing poem about how no-one would listen. It was not until 1998 that the men were convicted of a catalogue of sexual assaults and an investigation launched. A member of staff from one of the homes told the inquiry: 'At the end of the day I wish we could get together with these kids and say we are really sorry we let you down'...[16]

The Utting Report looked into the problems of institutional abuse for the Department of Health in 1997 and found a number of loopholes and inconsistencies in the inspection system. Some smaller homes and schools were not registered or inspected at all. The Department of Health and the local authorities have focused on tightening regulations and inspection processes. Other recommendations for change include tougher vetting procedures for staff and a clearer system for complaints. Critics of this administrative approach to reform have emphasised the underlying powerlessness of both the children and the staff in residential care which makes it far from easy to expose abuse. Residential staff are underpaid, undervalued and often unqualified. Children are made silent and powerless victims by a combination of directly exploitative relationships and indirectly dis-empowering structures, policies and practices. [17]

Leaving residential care

A major problem with care comes when young people are expected to leave and suddenly adjust to looking after themselves, having been used to living in an institution. Some local authorities attempt to help with this problem by providing independence and life skills programmes, perhaps in a self-contained flat within the home. These policies are not always successful as is demonstrated in the following example, taken from a placement report written by Heather Roberts on her experiences as a student on a Preliminary Course in Social Care. The community home had a programme to prepare young people for leaving care. In spite of this, one ex-resident had a habit of visiting the home at meal-times, obviously wanting to be fed. When the staff limited the times of the visits, other residents began to pass food out of the window to the boy. Heather identifies two reasons for the seeming failure of the home to prepare the young people for independence. The first is related to institutionalisation and the second to the often unrealistically high standards set by social services. She says:

> a person who seems unwilling to be independent at de Bouvoir House [not the real name] and so is assumed to be incapable could simply be quite pre-pared to let someone else do things for him while they are there to do it but is more than able to cope on his own. Added to this is the difference between the standards set at de Bouvoir House, 'ideal' standards, and those by which many of the young people will live. Ideal standards of cleanliness, tidiness and diet are actually achieved by only a minority of people – especially people living alone. So if a person doesn't seem to be up to expected standards at de Bouvoir House it could quite possibly be irrelevant as he would not live by those standards anyway.

In addition to these factors in explaining the 'failure' to achieve independence, it should be said that many young people who have left their parents' home return for food, washing of clothes, loans and other forms of support. Leaving home is rarely an abrupt cut-off from sources of help. This issue is particularly important if the situation is to be avoided where being in care is the beginning of a life in institutions. In the words of a young person with experience of care:

> For the first time in your life you are making real decisions about yourself, and as you are not used to this, it is truly survival of the fittest. It's easy to see why so many of us get into trouble with society. We can very easily become lost souls. [18]

The 1989 Children Act attempted to improve the situation for young people leaving care. When a young person of 16 or over stops being 'looked after' by the local authority, he or she is entitled to help up to the age of 21.

The social services department have a duty to befriend and advise and may provide financial or other practical help. However since the implementation of the Children Act young people leaving care can still have difficulties in making their way in the outside world. A national survey published in 1994 found the safety net for young people to be 'small and full of holes'. Problems were found in benefits, grants and training and in the social services' implementation of their duty to befriend and advise. Although not all young people leaving care get into trouble, more than 40 per cent of homeless teenagers in London have been in care and many end up in trouble with the police. The report says:

Young people who have been in care are amongst the most vulnerable people in the country ... But they need support and encouragement to achieve.[19]

The following account describes how young people's needs are not receiving the priority they require:

Owen has spent his early years in care, experiencing that nomadic existence which sadly characterises young people caught up in the care system. He vaguely remembers eight children's homes and two sets of foster-parents and now waits until he can move into independent living. But he has been failed by the education system, has a number of medical problems which have never been satisfactorily resolved because of his constant moves, and is now not regarded as a high priority by the local housing department. Despite the clear responsibilities which the 1989 Children Act puts on all the local authority departments – rather than solely upon social services departments – where Owen lives little provision is made for young people leaving care and needing accommodation.[20]

Proposals put forward in 1998 emphasised the need to improve the educational achievement of children looked after by the local authority, to prepare young people for leaving care and to provide more support after young people have left care. Too many end up unemployed and sleeping rough.

Charter of rights for young people in care

The following is a charter of rights drawn up by a group of young people in care and reproduced in the book *Who Cares?*[21] It was written before the Children Act extended the rights of young people in care, but it is still relevant even after the implementation of the Act:

We have drawn up this charter for 'young people' because we feel it is the responsibility of the residential worker and social worker to make sure that younger kids get a good deal.

1 The right to be accepted and treated as an individual member of society. Also the right to be treated with the same respect given to any other valid member of the human race.
2 The right to know who we are. To know our parents and brothers and sisters. To have factual information about our family origins and backgrounds.
3 The right to be able to make our own decisions and to have real influence over those decisions we are sometimes considered too thick to participate in.
4 The right to privacy. We understand that in care it is not always possible to choose who we are going to live and share our lives with. But we are still

human beings and are still entitled to the essential amount of privacy needed before cracking up.

5 The right to be given an insight into the use of money by handling it, using it and paying the consequences if we misuse it, for example, being given the money in our hand to buy the clothes our clothing allowance will allow.

6 The right to choose those who will represent us whether it be legally or otherwise, for example, social workers. Also the right to choose who we wish to confide in.

7 Finally, the right to be as much a part of the society as the next person and not to be labelled in any way. In short, to live.

These rights can be interpreted how you like. But don't misuse them or distort them for your own devices.

Activity 10.2

Do you agree that young people in care should have the rights listed in this charter? Are there any other rights which could be included? What specific rights should people in care have – for example, should they be allowed to attend reviews, to have visitors and to have access to contraception on the same basis as other young people?

Activity 10.3

In small groups, design a residential setting for children or young people. Think about how many residents there should be, and of what age. Consider the physical lay-out, the staffing, the rules and obligations for residents and workers. Discuss your ideas with the whole class.

Workshops on children in care

A conference was held to discuss issues relating to black children in care. Some of the participants were social workers, but the majority were young black people in care or recently out of care. Five workshops were held, producing the following resolutions for the future:[22]

Workshop on culture, health, hair and skin
(a) Social workers should learn about black health and the needs of black children and young people for hair oils and skin creams in relation to hair treatment and skin care.
(b) Young black people should be educated about and tested for sickle cell anaemia.

Workshop on mixed parentage
Social workers must not use the term 'half caste' and 'half breed', etc. when addressing young people from mixed parentage families. Instead the term 'mixed parentage' must be used.

Workshop on racism in the care system

(a) Disciplinary action must be taken on those social workers who make racist remarks or comments to young people.

(b) Young black people should be provided with references to their cultural history and backgrounds.

(c) Funds should be made available for young people to visit their origins.

(d) Black people should be encouraged to take residential and field social work posts.

(e) Black people should not be split up when going into care – they must be kept together.

(f) Young black people should be placed in the black community and not sent out to areas where there are no black people.

Workshop on fostering

(a) Young black people and parents must have a say as to whether they are fostered in a black or white family.

(b) At least one black person must be involved in fostering procedures when a black child is to be fostered.

(c) More foster homes should be found within the black community.

Workshop on leaving care

Young black people should be prepared for leaving care and returning to the black community, through social services ensuring that they experience their own culture in care – e.g. through weekly 'black activities' courses, positive black image books, posters, videos and cooking experiences in the home. Also encouraging contacts in the black community would help.

The Children Act states that children and young people must have their language, cultural and religious needs met.

10.4 Treatment or punishment for young offenders?

For a long time there has been uncertainty in society and in social policy as to how best to deal with young offenders. Are young offenders to be seen as unfortunate victims of their backgrounds, needing help and support, or are they to be held responsible for their actions and punished accordingly?

Social workers have tended to take the first approach – seeing the causes of crime in terms of social and emotional deprivation and offering support to young offenders. The strongest argument against locking young people up is that it does not prevent re-offending – the reconviction rate for those who have been in detention centres is very high. Sending young people away breaks their links with families, education, work and communities and makes it difficult for people to fit back in when they are released. They will be labelled and stigmatised by neighbours and potential employers. The idea of custody does not seem to deter people from starting to offend, even when they know friends who have been in custody.

The police tend to take a more punitive approach to young offenders, believing that crimes must be punished. Through punishment it is hoped that offenders will be put off from offending again. (Although, as has been suggested above, the evidence does not show this to be the case, especially when young people are sent away in detention.) The popular press and the majority of the public seem generally to line up with the view that young offenders should be severely punished for serious offences. Sometimes the motive here is a desire for revenge rather than a belief that any good will be done to the criminal.

The James Bulger Case

The tragic case of the two 11-year-old boys who, in 1993, killed the toddler James Bulger, illustrates these points very clearly. The boys, John and Robert, were brought up in an inner-city area of Liverpool characterised by poor housing and poverty. The unemployment rate in the area was twice the national average and both boys' fathers were out of work. Both John and Robert had experienced their parents' separation. Both families were poor and Robert in particular was always conscious of the pressures of poverty. Neither child was successful at school and Robert was a persistent truant. The children regularly watched horror videos.

Opinions on the case varied. The policeman who headed the investigation was not impressed by theories of the effects of inner-city deprivation. He believed the children were 'evil'. Another policeman, a religious man, said, 'you could look into the eyes of Robert and know you were looking at evil'. Others explained their behaviour in terms of the absence of an adult male role model. A psychotherapist said:

> I think it has something to do with a hatred of vulnerability and babyness in themselves which they projected onto this toddler. If, in their own lives, they have had it so extremely tough and been bullied and neglected and abused then they end up having to prove themselves to be extremely tough and invulnerable ... In this state it is quite painful to see a normal relationship between mother and child. There is hatred and envy directed at the baby – a wish to see it suffer in the same way they have suffered. They probably weren't out to kill someone, but they were probably out to ruin someone else's happiness.[23]

The international press told the story to its fullest extent and generally the public bayed for blood. Public opinion was that the boys should be locked up for a long time and should suffer for what they had done.

Activity 10.4

Discussion questions:
1 At what age are children aware of right and wrong?
2 At what age should children be held responsible for their behaviour?
3 Are criminals born or made?
4 Do children who break the law need help or punishment?

10.5 Provision for young offenders

The various forms of provision for young offenders reflect the uncertainty which exists as to the best way to deal with juvenile crime. The idea that young and adult offenders should be dealt with separately has been accepted for some time, as has the notion of reform. However, the ways of achieving, or attempting to achieve, reform are varied and at different times, some approaches have been more popular than others. There have been a confusing number of changes in recent years to the juvenile justice system. This reflects the highly political nature of this issue. Politicians, from all political parties, often liven up their party conferences with promises to 'crack-down on crime'. The policies which then follow are often re-hashes of previous policies. This section will describe some of the types of provision available for offenders, bearing in mind the debate between principles of punishment and treatment. As has been remarked earlier, this debate is confused and often measures which are designed to treat rather than punish may be seen as punishment by the young people concerned.

Youth justice

Criminal proceedings cannot be brought against children below the age of 10 years old. However the 1998 Crime and Disorder Act (described below) allows for intervention with children under 10 at risk of offending or involved in anti-social behaviour. A child between 10 and 14 cannot be convicted of a crime unless it is first proved to the court that the child knew he or she was doing wrong.

The Criminal Justice Act was passed in 1991, affecting children over 10. Children up to the age of 17 are dealt with in *youth courts* (previously known as juvenile courts and taking children up to 16). The magistrates are especially selected for these courts and must include a woman. For young people aged 10–15, parents must attend the court. Parents can be bound over by the court to exercise proper control over their child and their financial circumstances are looked at in making decisions about fines.

The 1998 Crime and Disorder Act attempts to keep young offenders out of the criminal justice system and to prevent re-offending. Partnerships between the police forces and local authorities are responsible for producing annual youth justice plans for each area of the country and setting up a multi-disciplinary team. The Act introduced a *statutory final warning* to replace the practice of repeat cautioning. Young people receiving this warning will be referred to the youth offending team who will draw up a rehabilitation programme to examine and attempt to deal with the factors that caused the offending. The Act also introduced new orders which the court can use (included in the list in Activity 10.6 near the end of the chapter). Radical new interventions include *local child curfew schemes* to prevent children under 10 in a particular area from getting into trouble, *parenting orders* which require a parent or guardian to attend counselling and guidance sessions and to comply with specific requirements, and *child safety orders* place a child under 10 who is at risk of being involved in crime or who is behaving in an anti-social manner under the supervision of a youth justice officer. A child safety order can include particular requirements such as attendance at a homework club or not visiting certain areas unsupervised. An example of this order in use might be:

> an eight year old girl is found shoplifting with a group of older girls in the local shopping centre and has been referred by the police to the social services. The local authority then applied to the court for a child safety order. The order required her to stay away from the shopping centre, not mix with the older girls and (with the agreement of the organisers) attend a local youth pro-gramme to make constructive use of her leisure time.[24]

Youth custody

In the case of very serious crimes or, more commonly, repeated crime, young people can be sent away to custodial centres. Over the last 15 years or so, there have been a series of name changes and changes in regulations regarding lengths of sentences and age limits. This section traces some of the changing ideas on youth custody and details some of the institutions which have been used.

Detention centres

Detention centres used to take young people aged 14–21 for a short period, reduced under the 1982 Criminal Justice Act from a minimum of 3 months to a minimum of 3 weeks. Detention centres aimed to give young people a 'short, sharp shock' to deter them from committing further crimes. The regime was one of strict discipline, involving highly structured routines and physically demand-ing activities. A typical day involved rising at 6.30 a.m. with physical training on the parade ground, cleaning cells and dormitories, inspection, work from 8.00 a.m. to 4.30 p.m., more physical education and, in the evenings, classes in subjects like English and time for reading and writing letters.

Detention centres provided a punishing routine and it is interesting to note that when the Conservative Party sought to increase the deterrent effect of detention, most of their proposals for a hard system were already in existence. In terms of preventing crime, detention centres were not particularly successful, since many people who had been in a centre committed further crimes. The reasons for this are not fully understood and certainly not agreed by everyone working in the area of juvenile crime and justice. One possible explanation for the failure of detention centres to provide a deterrent is provided in the follow-ing quotation from an ex-inmate:

> Three months' detention was a shock. However, all of us began to adapt very quickly to this, and it was no time at all before the shock became routine frus-tration. Any treatment of this kind is moderately successful in breaking habits and behaviour, but in replacing the offender in his environment, with no change in him or that environment, it seems to defeat what would be the real object.[25]

In addition to this explanation of continued criminal activity which focuses on the inability of detention to change the young person or the environment, other reasons might be the way in which detention leads a young person to identify with the criminal way of life and to learn from others in this situation. Also, the chances of securing employment are reduced by a period in a detention centre.

Youth custody orders

From May 1983, magistrates were able to impose a youth custody order on boys and girls over 15 and under 21, under the Criminal Justice Act of 1982. The youth custody order replaced Borstal training. The Criminal Justice Act stated specifically that youth custody orders were only to be used as a last resort, although 6 months after the introduction of the sentence, concern was being expressed at the numbers of young people serving such sentences. This reflected a tendency for magistrates to make use of any sentence available and to fail to reserve them for use as a last resort. Most of the youth custody centres were old Borstals and there was pressure on the Home Office to establish new centres, possibly by making use of detention centres. Youth custody centres aimed to reform young people through discipline and training. The daily life was similar to that described for detention centres. Reconviction rates show that they achieved little in terms of reform. The discipline and structured life can make it more difficult for young people to cope with life outside an institution, rather than showing them a better way to live.

Young offender institutions

Following the 1988 Criminal Justice Act the terms detention centre and youth custody centre are no longer in use and the law simply refers to young offender institutions. For young people aged 17 or under, detention may be in a secure local authority residential unit (as was the case for the boys convicted in the James Bulger case), a centre managed by the Youth Treatment Service or a young offender institution (for those over 18). Offenders aged 18–20 are sent to a young offender institution. The 1991 Criminal Justice Act again tried to ensure that young people are only sentenced to custody for very serious offences. A young person can only be put in custody if the offence will result in imprisonment for an adult and one of the following conditions apply:

- the offence is violent or sexual and only a custodial sentence will protect the public from serious harm;
- the crime is so serious that an alternative cannot be justified.

The minimum period for custody is now 2 months. The idea of this is to stop the courts from using sentences of a few weeks for less serious reasons.

In 1999 conditions at the largest young offender institution, at Feltham in West London, were criticised by inspectors. The inspectors found inmates locked in cold and dirty cells for 22 hours a day with no opportunities for outdoor exercise. Prisoners had infrequent changes of clothes and dirty bed linen and blankets. In one unit there was no food between tea at 4.30 p.m. and breakfast at 8.00 a.m. the next morning. Boys were eating in dirty cells with filthy toilets. One boy said:

> I have nothing to do. I get hungry and there's nothing to distract me. If I get depressed, I talk to the chaplain and ask him to pray for me. Most of the time I sleep. My mum's not at home during the day and I'm not allowed to phone in the evenings. [26]

Thorn Cross, near Warrington in Cheshire became the first institution to pilot a project called High Intensity Training, more colloquially known as a 'boot-camp'. The course consists of a physically demanding 16-hour day with starts at 6 a.m. with cleaning, inspections and drill training. Inmates also undergo courses to help them understand the impact of crime on victims and life skills training. The last part of the sentence is spent in work outside the institution. A year on, the scheme was being judged a success. Another scheme at the military-run corrective centre in Colchester was closed after only one year because the costs – at £31,000 per inmate per year – were judged too high by the Labour Government. Both schemes were started under the Conservatives.

Secure training orders

The 1993 Criminal Justice and Public Order Act introduced secure training orders. These are to be in units providing 'high standards of care and discipline' for 12- to 14-year-olds who are seen as persistent offenders. 'Persistent offenders' are defined as children who have been found guilty of three or more imprisonable offences or who have re-offended during a supervision order or broken the rules of a supervision order. The secure training order is for a maximum of 2 years, half of which is spent in custody and half under supervision in the community. The Act provides for five new secure training centres, each with 40 places. The institutions can be provided by public, voluntary or private organisations and the government hopes that in fact the centres will be provided by the private sector.

A study by the independent Policy Studies Institute has questioned the logic of this approach. Many imprisonable offences are petty and the three offences could have been committed at the same time. It is not easy to decide who is a 'persistent offender' and who is not, in any way which is fair and objective. The study could not identify a group of children committing a large number of offences over a period of time. To put some children into secure units will not have a noticeable effect on crime rates. According to a report of this study in the *Guardian*:

> The study paints a detailed portrait of seven frequent re-offenders, in which their lives and early backgrounds emerge as chaotic, peppered with school failure, home breakdown and children's home admission. John, aged 12 at the beginning of 1992, had 15 known offences on his record for that year, including theft from shops, causing actual bodily harm and criminal damage. He was shuttled from one children's home to another, to his father, back to a children's home, then another, then to his mother and back to his father. At 13, he

escaped from one home and spent three and a half months living rough on the streets. The interviewer commented: 'He looked to have the world's sadness in his eyes … I wish I knew what had happened to cause such pain'.

Yet most of the youngsters stressed the importance of family members, particularly mothers, in helping them break out of the cycle of offending. Placing such children in five isolated centres without regional catchment areas, up to 250 miles from their home base, is hardly designed to strengthen their perceived reliance on what remains of their fragile families.[27]

Non-custodial orders

Attendance centres

Alternatives to sending young offenders away include making them report to *attendance centres*. These are run by the police, usually on a Saturday morning and take people aged 12–21. The sessions commonly include drill and some form of craft work. The police see themselves as impressing on people that their activities will lead them into further trouble.

Community service orders

Since the 1982 Criminal Justice Act, *community service orders* can be made on offenders aged 16, whereas previously the age limit had been 17. Community service orders are intended to be an alternative to custody and require the offender to do a specified amount of supervised community work, such as gardening or working in an old people's home. In 1989 minimum national standards were set to, in the words of the Home Office Minister, 'toughen up' community service orders. At least 21 hours of manual work must be done and a weekly report of the work compiled. The intention of the 1991 Criminal Justice Act was to further make sure that community options for sentencing of offenders were tough and thought of as a punishment.

Supervision orders

Supervision orders can be made on children aged 10–17. This puts the young person under the supervision of the local authority social services department or the probation office. Various requirements can be added by the court to a supervision order. These include:

- living in local authority accommodation (a number of circumstances must apply for this to be required, more usually a young person under a supervision order would live at home);
- living with a particular person;
- taking part in supervised activities;
- reporting to the supervisor at certain times (maybe Saturday afternoons if the offence was connected with a football match);
- a curfew, meaning that the offender must not be out at certain times in the evening or night;
- attending school or college;

- agreeing to requirements set by the supervisor, for example participating in certain activities.

Probation orders

Probation orders can be made on young people over 16. This involves supervision by a probation officer and again requirements may be attached to the order.

Therapy schemes

Various other schemes exist for offenders and include group therapy sessions to enable people to gain insight into themselves and others, and recently-devised schemes for offenders to meet victims and make some repayment by doing tasks such as repairs.

The following report from the *Guardian* illustrates an innovative community-based scheme for children under 17 found guilty of taking and driving away cars. The treatment is designed to fit the needs of the young people:[28]

> Normally those under 17 convicted of joyriding – taking and driving away in police-speak – will be sentenced to custody, but recently the Home Office has been experimenting with alternative community-based schemes. One – the first of its type – is the Inderton Road Motor Project in Deptford, South London.
>
> At IMP ex-joyriders are encouraged to get old cars ready for banger racing. Every evening in a chilly warehouse 20 boys can be found hard at work on rusty Cortinas and Datsuns – all generously donated by a local scrap dealer. The boys (and one girl, who recently left the project) rip out seats; insulate the petrol tank to lessen the chances of explosion if the car crashes during a race; fix steel rods through the middle to act as a support in case of somersaults; and paint the exterior in jazzy designs.
>
> Everyone at IMP must attend at least two nights a week. Then, if they keep out of trouble with the police the boys are allowed to race against professionals at a local banger track.
>
> Inderton Road may not sound like punishment but, as project leader Peter West argues, 'prison does not work for joyriders. Here we actually confront the reasons why people steal cars in the first place.'
>
> The results so far support his argument. Very few attenders at IMP leave and re-offend. Mark, 21, has 'done a couple of turns in prison for driving without a licence' and says that before coming to the project he was always in trouble.
>
> Now, he believes, 'I'm on the right track.'

As mentioned above, the 1998 Crime and Disorder Act introduced counselling and guidance for parents of offenders. There are also proposals for schemes which use responsible adults as mentors or role models for young offenders with the aim of preventing re-offending.

Youth justice centres

In some cases, youth justice centres have been set up to provide alternatives to custody for young offenders. Essex County Council has set up a number of such centres. They describe the work of the staff in the centre as follows:[29]

Staff within the Centres will be responsible for the provision of a range of programmes suitable for juveniles subject to Supervision Orders. Programmes will be made known to the Courts in social enquiry reports, with the agreement of the offender and the offender's parents being sought to the recommendations made. Programmes will include intensive contact between the offender and supervising staff and introduction to additional constructive activities in order to deter further offending. For example, where an offender has broken into a house, repair of damage and apology to house occupier in certain circumstances may be the correct course to pursue. Involvement in group work to improve life and social skills, a requirement to give service to the community or the opportunity for the individual juvenile offender to consider how he or she can use their time and energy usefully may be offered. It will be expected that the offender subject to such a programme would have already been cautioned, conditionally discharged or fined and be at serious risk of removal from home to care or custody. *A wilful failure to comply with the conditions attached to a Supervision Order would result in the juvenile being brought back before the Court.*

Centre staff will keep local Courts fully informed of the range of facilities available for juvenile offenders and an annual report will be published. Local support from volunteer helpers will be encouraged and it is anticipated that measures aimed at crime prevention and deterrence will be developed.

Activity 10.5

What are the arguments for and against taking young offenders into custody? Make a list of points and decide what sort of approach you think is most useful.

It is difficult to reach a conclusion on the best way to deal with young offenders, since the issues are so complex and the evidence conflicting. Arguments that punitive measures such as detention centres act as a deterrent and prevent crime are not valid as re-conviction rates are high. Whilst the more liberal methods of dealing with young offenders cannot be conclusively shown to be more successful, they are certainly no worse. At a purely practical level, community-based schemes are cheaper than custodial provision. There is also the argument that crime is predominantly a young person's activity which will be grown out of unless the person is locked up and begins to identify with the criminal world. It does however seem to be true that society seeks revenge for crime and wants people to be punished. This can be seen in the popular press's calls for harsher punishment and longer sentences. The balancing of these views by the government has, at times, as much to do with politics and votes as with looking at evidence on the effectiveness of various measures and at the needs of young people.

Activity 10.6

Working in pairs, write a brief account of an imaginary young offender. Describe the offence, the history of offending and any punishment, and give brief details of the home environment. Pass this on for the next pair to decide what action they think the youth court should take if the person was found guilty. Use the summary of possible actions given below, some of which have been described in more detail in the preceding section.

You could show your understanding of approaches to youth justice by providing two answers: one which you thinks fits with a model of youth justice committed to punishment and deterrence, and one which fits with a model which sees the offender as a victim of deprivation in need of treatment. Explain the reasons for your decisions. Add ideas of your own for new ways of dealing with offenders if you want to.

Bind over – the person agrees, on a sum of money specified by the court, to keep the peace for a certain period. Parents can be bound over to exercise proper control.

Absolute discharge – no action at all.

Conditional discharge – if a further offence is committed within a certain period, the person may be punished for the original offence.

Deferred sentence – no action for a period of up to 6 months whereupon the person reappears in court and the decision will depend on the person's behaviour during the period of time.

Fine – of offender.

Fine – of parent or guardian.

Compensation order – up to £1000 can be ordered to be paid to the victim.

Disqualification – young people charged with motoring offences can have their licence endorsed or be banned from driving when they reach 17.

Attendance centre (10–21 years).

Supervision order – can have conditions attached such as participation in activities or a night restriction condition, whereby the young person must remain in a certain place, usually at home, between 6 p.m. and 6 a.m. for up to 30 days. Other conditions can be made such as an order to refrain from attending football matches or to undertake particular activities devised by the local authority or probation service.

Probation (16 and over).

Community service orders (16 years and over).

Combination orders – include community service and probation.

Curfew order.

Action plan order – requires the offender to comply with an individually tailored action plan intended to address their offending behaviour.

Reparation order – the offender is required to make non-financial reparation to the victim or community.

Parenting order – this requires the parent or guardian to attend counselling and guidance sessions and to agree to certain requirements for the offender.

Child safety order (under 10) – places a child at risk of being involved in a crime or behaving in an anti-social manner under the supervision of a specified responsible officer.

Child curfew (under 10).

Detention in a young offender institution (15–21).

Secure training order (12–15).

Detention and Training Order – combines custody and community supervision

Detention under Section 53 of the 1933 Children and Young Persons Act – for 'grave' crimes, the magistrates can commit 10–17-year-olds for trial in the Crown Court

Activity 10.7

This chapter has included a lot of terms which may be unfamiliar. Make sure that you understand the following expressions used in this chapter. Check in the Glossary at the end of the book if you need to.

at risk register	foster-parent
attendance centre	group therapy
bind over	guardian *ad litem*
Borstal training	institutionalisation
care order	legal aid
care proceedings	multi-disciplinary
case conference	probation officer
community home	rehabilitation
community service order	secure unit
detention centre	social inquiry report
	supervision order

Further reading

There are a number of guides to the 1989 Children Act available. One is Nick Allen, *Making Sense of the Children Act*, 2nd edn (London: Longman, 1992). This is detailed and covers all aspects of the Act. At a much simpler level the Department of Health have published guides written for children and young people.

Children and Social Policy by Paul Daniel and John Ivatts (London: Macmillan, 1998) provides a more wide-ranging review of social policy which relates to children than has been provided in this chapter. Areas covered include poverty, health and education, as well as child welfare and protection.

Although not written at an introductory level, a review of sociological and social policy issues relating to young offenders can be found in *Youth and Crime* by John Muncie (London: Sage, 1999).

Useful addresses

For Department of Health publications:

Department of Health
PO Box 777
London SE16XH
tel. 0800 555777

NSPCC
42 Curtain Road
London EC2A 3NH
tel. 0207 825 2500
Child Protection Helpline: 0800 800 500

Barnardo's
Tanner Lane
Barkingside
Ilford
Essex IG6 1QG
tel. 0208 550 8822

Voice for the Child in Care
Unit 4
Pride Court
80–82 White Lion Street
London N1 9PF
tel. 0207 833 5792

National Children's Bureau
8 Wakley Street
London EC1V 7QE
tel. 0207 843 6000

Websites

The Department of Health is the government department responsible for social services provision for young people. Website address **www.doh.gov.uk**

The Home Office deals with the juvenile justice system. They are at **www.Homeoffice.gov.uk**

The Children's Society **www.the-childrens-society.org.uk**

⊻ **11** Mental health issues

This chapter, together with the three which follow, concentrates on the needs of a particular group of people and the welfare provision which exists to meet these needs. People suffering from mental illnesses are the subject of this chapter, while the following three look at learning disability, old age and physical disabilities. In many ways there is nothing special about the nature of the needs of these people. For example, the needs to be accepted and to have a place in society are shared by all human beings. Similarly, everyone needs suitable housing, an income and care in times of ill-health. However, there are people for whom meeting these needs requires additional help. The problems which may be experienced by groups like those who are elderly and those with a disability are problems for the whole of society, since it is not so much old age or learning disability which is a problem, but society's attitude to people who are old or have some disability.

There are several problems in discussing this area of social need and social policy. First, there is a danger of implying neat distinctions, which do not exist in reality. For example, there are no clear-cut definitions for terms like learning disability and physical disability and categories often overlap: some elderly people also suffer from disabilities. Finally it should be emphasised that many people who are physically disabled, elderly, mentally ill or have a learning disability manage their lives without needing any special provision.

11.1 Attitudes to mental health problems

There is considerable misunderstanding about mental illness. Many people have stereotyped, prejudiced or old-fashioned ideas.

Activity 11.1

Note down any thoughts which come into your head about mental illness. Start with some statements like: 'If someone is mentally ill, it means that ...'

Working in small groups, compare your ideas and feelings. Try to sort out which are true and which are not. Check out your ideas with those in the rest of this chapter. Compare them with those of anyone in the group who has had a relative or a friend suffer from a mental illness.

A survey carried out by the Department of Health found that nearly a third of the people surveyed believed it was a simple task to spot the difference between someone with a mental illness and a 'normal' person. Only 19 per cent would allow a woman who had been in a mental hospital to babysit for them. However, on the positive side, most believed that society should adopt a more positive attitude, would be happy to live next door to someone with a mental illness and backed the policy of caring for people with mental illnesses in the community.[1]

Mental illness is a complex area, difficult to define, and definitions of normal and abnormal behaviour vary over time, from society to society and in different contexts. Mental illness is much more common than people usually realise with 1 in 10 people experiencing it and more than six million people seeking help for mental health problems at some point in their lives.[2] Even though mental illness is so common, it carries a stigma. Glyn Jones, who suffers from depression writes:

> Depression should have a blacker name. It is a disease which shrinks the spirit and sucks the colour from life. I know because I am a depressive, now mercifully stabilised with drugs, one of the 11 million people in Britain who will experience some kind of serious mood disorder in their lifetime.
>
> Not that it is wise – save in really enlightened circles – to admit publicly that you are a sufferer. You might become known as a bad risk. There is no limit to the social stigma. However frequently depression strikes, society still winces and walks away.[3]

Many people are reluctant to believe that a person who has been mentally ill can ever be fully recovered. The stigma is probably greatest for those who have been in hospital and to admit this can cause problems with employers, landlords and credit agencies.

Activity 11.2

Consider the following list of activities and decide if you would consider a person doing such a thing to be mentally ill.

1 Going for a walk in a thunderstorm.
2 Joining a demonstration against nuclear arms.
3 Parading London with a sign warning of the end of the world.
4 Checking the door is locked three times before leaving the house.
5 Having three baths every day.
6 Being a Communist.
7 Wearing a Nazi uniform.
8 Betting £1000 on a horse.
9 Having hair dyed pink with green stripes.
10 Living in a commune.
11 Becoming pregnant without being married.
12 Being scared of spiders.
13 Getting anxious before an examination.
14 Writing an extra statement because 13 is an unlucky number.

The line between normal and abnormal behaviour cannot be clearly drawn. Not too long ago women who had children outside marriage could end up in mental hospitals and there are still some elderly patients who entered hospital for this reason. In some countries, certain types of political behaviour have been treated as symptoms of mental illness. There is a tendency to see people who do things of which we disapprove as mad. Compulsive behaviour such as washing over and over again and checking that doors are locked is common, but can, in extreme cases, become debilitating and prevent people from living a normal life. Behaviour which is considered eccentric in some people is labelled as mental illness in other contexts. For example, there is a tradition of tolerance of eccentricity amongst the very wealthy. Anxiety can be useful at times of examinations or interviews, or can become a totally incapacitating condition.

Neuroses and psychoses

For purposes of definition, mental illnesses are usually divided into two categories. There are *neuroses* and *psychoses*. *Neuroses* are less serious and more common, although illnesses in this category still cause a great deal of suffering to victims and their families. Neuroses typically involve an exaggeration of usual emotions, for example, sadness becomes *depression*, which is the correct term for the illness that many people call a 'nervous breakdown'. Other neuroses are *phobias* which are irrational fears as in the case of *agoraphobia* which is a fear of open spaces, and *obsessions* where actions are repeated over and over again.

Depression is thought to be increasing amongst young people. The director of Young Minds, a research organisation looking at mental health of young people says:

> We live in particularly difficult times for a growing youngster. There are huge cultural pressures, a lot of uncertainty and many broken homes; kids may have difficult relationships with parents and may lack a supportive centre to life. [4]

Steve Austin was in his late teens when a close friend died. It was as though all his confidence was shattered in a moment. He says:

> I stopped believing anything could be good any more. I became very aggressive, I snapped at my parents all the time and I lost my friends. Things were very bad for a year until – fortunately for me – a teacher spotted that things were wrong. [4]

Psychoses affect people's ability to think and to act in a rational way. People with psychotic disorders lose touch with reality as a result of their illness. *Schizophrenia* is a psychotic illness, although it is a descriptive term for a collection of symptoms rather than a clearly defined condition. It does not mean split personality, which is a very much less common mental illness. Schizophrenia typically involves a split between feelings and actions, and a schizophrenic may suffer from hallucinations and delusions. People who suffer from *paranoia* wrongly believe they are being persecuted. *Psychotic depression* is a more serious type of depression, totally incapacitating the sufferer who experiences feelings of self-hatred and worthlessness. *Manic depression* is an illness in which the person experiences swings of mood from elation to deep depression.

Personality disorders

A separate category covers people suffering from a *personality disorder*, sometimes described as *psychopaths*. Such conditions are more likely to be permanent and involve a lack of social development resulting in anti-social behaviour.

All the terms in the field of mental illness are used loosely and are open to dispute and disagreement. There is a tendency in some hospitals and amongst some psychiatrists for diagnoses not to be made, as the terms can become labels which lead to further suffering and perhaps to a loss of hope. For example, to be labelled a schizophrenic can have adverse consequences since there exists a false belief that such a person cannot be helped and can never again live a normal life.

Activity 11.3

Create a mental picture of a person suffering from a mental illness and describe your image of that person.

The portraits in fiction and myth of mental illness affect the way we think of psychiatric disorders. Such images include Mrs Rochester in *Jane Eyre* who was thought to be 'mad' and the scientist with the split personality in *Dr Jekyll and Mr Hyde*. The power of these images is unfortunate since they have little in common with reality and lead to unnecessary fears and misapprehensions. The following account of a person, whose illness posed no threat to others and could easily have gone unnoticed, is far more realistic:

Take James Wilkins. Twenty-one-years old, in his final year at university. Intelligent, but not brilliant, he has to work hard to keep up with his Modern Languages course. He is not bad-looking, quiet, enjoys playing and watching football, and is also interested in politics and films. Three months before final exams, his girl-friend dropped him. His revision suffered immediately. A week later he heard that his father had to go into hospital for an exploratory operation to find out whether a tumour was cancerous or benign. His work stopped completely for a week, he went home but was urged by his parents to return to university and prepare for his finals. He tried, but was totally unable to concentrate. He got some pills from the university medical centre but by now, well into a state of anxiety and depression, he was beginning to contemplate suicide.

James was referred by a friend to the university counselling service which resulted in his receiving psychiatric treatment as an out-patient and deferring his examinations.[5]

11.2 The causes of mental health problems

The causes of mental illness are not fully understood and there is considerable disagreement among doctors and others on this issue.

Activity 11.4

What factors do you think may be causes of mental illness?

It is likely that any one person's illness results from a combination of factors, difficult to isolate and identify. Stress is one possible cause of illness, resulting from examinations, pressure of work or the need to appear successful or to be coping with problems. However, different people react differently in different situations and stress does not lead to breakdown in everyone. Social factors are relevant in understanding mental illness in a variety of ways. Statistics show that women are more vulnerable than men to psychiatric problems; it may be that women's lives are more stressful or it may be that it is more acceptable for women to define their feelings in terms of an illness such as depression and to seek medical help, where men perhaps turn to alcohol and express their emotions through violence rather than introverted depression. There is also a perspective which seeks to explain the higher incidence of mental illness among women and working-class people in terms of social control. Mental illness, according to this viewpoint, is a means of controlling less powerful groups in society and dealing with behaviour which does not conform.

Environmental factors such as poverty and inadequate housing may lead people to become unable to cope and cause them to sink into illness. Much of the psychology of mental illness is concerned with relating experiences in childhood to later symptoms and breakdowns.

11.3   The law and mental health

Current mental health legislation is based on principles established by the 1957 Royal Commission on the Law relating to Mental Illness and Mental Deficiency. The recommendations of the Commission became law in the *1959 Mental Health Act*. Several important principles were established in the Act. Where possible, care was to be provided without compulsion, on a voluntary or informal basis. Admission for treatment would be on the same basis as admission for a physical illness, with no special forms to fill in and no loss of rights. In cases where compulsion was necessary, this would be at the discretion of the medical profession. Finally, tribunals were established to review medical decision-making.

The 1959 legislation remained essentially unchanged until 1982 when the Mental Health (Amendment) Act was passed. In 1983, the legislation in the 1959 and 1982 acts was brought together in a new Mental Health Act. The *1983 Mental Health Act* covers most aspects of mental health law, retaining much of the 1959 Act, but including changes fought for by pressure groups such as MIND. Like most aspects of the law, legislation concerning mental health is complex. A summary of basic points is provided here, but this does not constitute a guide to the law.[6]

Section 1 of the 1983 Mental Health Act defines mental disorder as 'mental illness, arrested or incomplete development of mind, psychopathic disorder and any other disorder or disability of mind'. The Act begins with the legal position of informal patients. In hospitals in Britain, 90 per cent of admissions are informal,[7] although there is often pressure to enter hospital voluntarily, perhaps under threat of compulsory admission, so this figure is misleading. Informal patients are legally free to leave hospital and can refuse treatment in the same way as any other patients. However, 'holding powers' are available to medical practitioners in the event of a patient wishing to leave. A doctor can hold a patient for 72 hours and, where the doctor is not available, a nurse can detain a patient for 6 hours.

Part II of the Mental Health Act 1983 deals with compulsory admission to mental hospital in various categories, allowing detention for differing periods of time. Applications for admission are made by the nearest relative or a social worker approved by the local authority as being competent in working with the mentally disordered. Emergency 72-hour admissions can be made on the written recommendation of one doctor in cases of urgent necessity. Admissions for assessment for up to 28 days can be made on the recommendations of two doctors, one of which must be a doctor approved by the Secretary of State for Social Services as having special expertise in diagnosis and treatment of mental disorder. On the same basis, a patient can be detained for 6 months, renewable for a further 6 months and then for periods of 1 year at a time.

Mental Health Review Tribunals hear applications from patients concerning decisions made by medical practitioners. There is a tribunal for each Regional Health Authority. A tribunal usually has three members – a lawyer, a doctor and a lay person experienced in administration or social services. The 1983 Act covers other areas of law such as patients' rights regarding treatment, the role of the Mental Health Act Commission in reviewing the working of the law and the position of the criminally insane.

In 1999 a Department of Health commissioned review of the 1983 Mental Health Act was published so changes are likely to result in the new millennium.

11.4 Treatment of mental health problems

Provision for people who suffer from a mental illness is the responsibility of the NHS and the local social services departments. In less serious cases, treatment has always been provided in the community, by GPs with support and help given from social workers. Hospital-based psychiatrists were also seen by out-patients. More serious cases involved hospitalisation. Unfortunately many of the psychiatric hospitals are large and old-fashioned, dating from the Victorian era when the solution to the problem of mental illness involved locking people up away from centres of population. Even in more recent times it was too easy for people to be admitted to hospital and to remain there longer than necessary, sometimes even a life-time.

For some time, it has been believed that these out-of-date buildings are not the best form of provision. Doctors and others began to be aware of the problem of institutionalisation (see Chapter 9). This happens when people become dependent on the routines and structure of the hospital and get used to people doing things for them, to the extent that they are unable to cope for themselves.

Source: Gina Glover, Photofusion
Old-fashioned psychiatric hospitals are being closed down

Institutionalisation can happen in any institution such as a prison, Borstal or hospital. Many hospitals try to overcome the situation by running rehabilitation programmes which attempt to get people to take responsibility for their lives and teach coping skills, such as budgeting, and social skills. However, there remain a number of elderly people in hospital who have been there for many years and who have no symptoms of illness but who would find it impossible to live in the community.

A government White Paper *Better Services for the Mentally Ill*, published in 1975, recommended a move towards community care and day-hospital provision. In the 1980s patients began to be moved out of the hospitals and into the community. The 1991 NHS and Community Care Act, implemented in 1993, has given further impetus to this policy (see Chapter 9 for more details on this area). Where the large psychiatric hospitals have closed, new units have often opened within district general hospitals.

Services in the community

- Some areas have *mental health centres*, which act as a kind of gateway for all mental health services. These are multi-disciplinary, with a number of different workers based at the centre. These might include a psychiatrist, a psychologist, community psychiatric nurses and perhaps a social worker. In other cases, these services might be based at a hospital. The mental health centre will provide some services and treatments itself and in other cases refer people on to other services.
- *Social workers* help people with mental health problems. They can provide information and advice. They offer support for individuals and families. *Approved social workers* (ASWs) can also be involved in admitting someone to a psychiatric hospital.
- *Community psychiatric nurses* (CPNs) also provide support and counselling for people in the community. They can also administer drugs.
- There are *residential homes* and *hostels* for people with mental illnesses. These may be run by the social services department, perhaps together with the health authority, or by private or voluntary organisations. Generally the trend is towards smaller homes in which residents are involved in decision-making. Voluntary organisations such as the Richmond Fellowship run therapeutic communities providing a supportive environment, preventative care and rehabilitation for people with emotional and psychiatric problems.
- In many areas there are *day centres* and *clubs*. These provide recreational facilities and also help in training and preparation for work.
- *Counselling* and *psychotherapy* are available privately for those who can afford to pay and in some cases are available free through the health service or a voluntary organisation such as MIND.

Looking at the list of services described above, it appears that people with mental illnesses are well catered for in the community. Sadly, this is not the case in all areas of the country. There have been many reports on television and in the newspapers of people dumped in bed-and-breakfast or other accommodation and left much to their own devices. In some cases people with mental illnesses end up in prisons. The following extracts from an article in the *Guardian* illustrate the inadequacies of care in the community for some people. The article is written by a neighbour.[8]

His name is Clifford – a huge black panther of a man – he has been my neighbour for four years now, since he was released from a mental institution under the euphemism of 'care in the community' to be housed on a large rundown South London estate.

The council gave him a flat on the top floor of my block which they probably thought would keep him out of the way.

…

We grew used to his ways. We had to. Several petitions were put together in the first couple of years when he continually tormented, abused and assaulted those in his immediate vicinity. But the petitions were misplaced by the housing officer. Some learnt to face up to him, others, like myself, just scattered when he came too close.

…

This was care in the community. Nobody came to check on him or to see he was taking his medication. No one ever contacted us, Clifford's neighbours, to explain, reassure, warn us of what to expect and how to deal with it. As far as I could see, the only care involved was that with which we, his immediate community, took to avoid him. Then the police would arrive every few months to make a forcible arrest and haul him away in a straitjacket.

Activity 11.5

What is the local availability of community provision for the mentally ill and people leaving mental hospitals?

Chapter 9 looks in more detail at the advantages and disadvantages of community care for people with mental illness.

Fear of violence

Since the expansion of community care, a great deal of publicity has been given to cases of violence involving people with severe mental disorders. One case involved a paranoid schizophrenic who stabbed and killed his social worker with a kitchen knife. Anthony Joseph was convicted of manslaughter and sent to Broadmoor maximum security prison indefinitely. After spending time in psychiatric hospitals, he was living in a half-way hostel where staff knew he had stopped taking his medication, but could not do anything about it. He believed he was the son of God. His social worker, Jenny Morrison, should have visited him in the presence of the hostel manager, but was late when her car broke down, and saw him alone.

Cases like this are tragic and terrifying. New procedures are needed to reduce the risk of such incidents, but there is a danger of over-reaction when so much publicity is given to a minority of people. In the words of a newspaper editorial:

Everyone knows the high risk of being killed by a mental patient suffering from schizophrenia. The news media never stops reporting such events. Like a lot of things that everybody knows, the truth is not quite so straightforward. Fewer than 10 homicides a year – less than 2 per cent of all killings – involve patients with schizophrenia. Another 30 have had some contact with mental health services, usually for alcohol or drug dependency or a personality disorder. Statistically you are far more likely to be killed by a sane than insane person. The biggest threat which mental patients pose, as the release of the biggest study ever carried out demonstrated, is to themselves. Researchers examined 10,000 suicides over two years and concluded about one quarter had had contact with mental health services.[9]

Proposals to decrease the risk of violence as a result of mental disorder include new powers to force people to accept treatment in the community and the detention of around 2000 people with personality disorders, who have not committed a crime, but who are judged to be high risk cases. There is no treatment for these people and they would be detained indefinitely. This presents problems with civil liberties, where it is argued that people who have not committed a crime should not be locked away without treatment. Also doctors have warned that assessment of risk can never be an exact science.

Clinical treatment

There are several types of treatment available to the medical profession for treating mental illness. Since the illnesses are so little understood, the treatments are in a sense experimental and may or may not produce results.

Chemotherapy

Chemotherapy – or treatment with drugs – is probably the most common form of treatment. The use of psychotropic drugs, which affect emotions, began in the 1930s and expanded rapidly in the 1950s. Drugs are useful insofar as they can bring emotions to a level where problems can be tackled. The danger of drug therapy is that people can become dependent on the drugs and lose the motivation to deal with problems. The drugs may bring feelings of numbness and lack of energy, making it more difficult to take on real problems. Many drugs also have unpleasant side-effects, some of which are quite serious.

Critics of physical treatment argue that drugs are over-used in hospitals and at times are given, not to help the patient, but to enable the ward to run more smoothly. As one doctor writes:

> For a time I studied the use of sedatives in a hospital practice, and discussed with the nurses the events which led up to each act of sedation. It ultimately became clear to me and to them that no matter what the rationale was, a nurse would give a sedative only at the moment when she had reached the limit of her human resources and was no longer able to stand the patient's problems without anxiety, impatience, guilt, anger or despair.[10]

It is a small step from this observation to the suggestion that it is nurses and doctors instead of patients who should take sedatives and tranquilisers!

Electro-convulsive treatment (ECT)

Shock treatment has a long history in psychiatric medicine; for example, at one time patients used to be immersed in cold water as a form of treatment for mental illness. The modern version of ECT was developed in the 1930s. ECT is used in cases of depression and schizophrenia. It involves the passing of an electric current through the brain to produce a seizure; this is done while the patient is under anaesthetic and no pain is involved. Usually the treatment will be repeated in a course of three or six 'doses'. While some people believe that ECT has no side-effects, others recognise that it can cause loss of memory and feelings of disorientation.

ECT can produce dramatic results, especially in cases of severe depression, although the explanation for such cures is unknown. It was originally thought that people who were epileptic were never also schizophrenic although this has since been disproved. ECT sometimes produces no results at all and there is a story of a hospital where the machine in use was found not to have been working for two years, and no-one had noticed. ECT is much criticised for its dubious value and punitive use but continues to be a popular form of treatment in hospitals.

Psychosurgery

This form of treatment is less popular than it used to be although it is in use. It is based on the unproven idea that certain parts of the brain are responsible for certain sorts of behaviour. There are various types of psychosurgery, also known as *lobotomy*, including removal of part of the brain, severing connections between areas of the brain, and destroying parts of the brain. Psychosurgery is not especially safe and cannot be proved to be effective.

Psychotherapy

Psychotherapy covers treatment by talking, either one-to-one with a specialist or in group discussions. The aim is to uncover reasons for illness and to get well through this new understanding. Other forms of treatment which may be available in hospitals include drama therapy and therapy through art and music. All these types of therapy aim to increase self-understanding, build up confidence and introduce the patient to new ways of releasing emotions.

Activity 11.6

Imagine you have a friend who is very depressed and has been told that she must go into hospital. She is very worried about this. What could you say to her, and how could you help her?

Activity 11.7

Role-play:

The situation

A voluntary group in the town has proposed setting up a half-way house for psychiatric patients. The council is considering donating premises and social services could provide a grant for a full-time worker. There is some local opposition to the plan so a public meeting has been called to discuss the project.

The characters

1 A psychiatric hospital patient who experienced loneliness on leaving hospital and had difficulty in finding a job and a place to live.

2 A team-leader from the social services department who is prepared to give special responsibility for the residents to one of the social workers in the area team.

3 The local vicar who believes the idea should be supported in a Christian spirit of charity and community support.

4 A member of the voluntary group who believes that mental health is the responsibility of the whole community and should not be left to paid professionals only.

5 A local resident who has young children and is concerned for the safety of children in the area.

6 A Labour councillor who supports the idea and believes the council could easily allocate a house bought for a redevelopment scheme which was abandoned.

7 A local resident with experience of voluntary work in a psychiatric hospital who believes that the fears of local people are based on misunderstandings about the nature of mental illness.

8 A local resident concerned about the reputation of the area and fearful that house prices will fall if the scheme goes ahead.

9 The headmaster of a private school near to the house which is rumoured to be a possible home for the project, who believes that the safety of the children means that the half-way home should be located elsewhere.

10 A psychiatrist at the local hospital who believes that people who are mentally ill need professional help from trained people and that the volunteers, whilst well-meaning, are naive in thinking such a project is feasible.

11 A conservative councillor who sees health as the concern of the NHS and is anxious about the costs to the council.

12 An elderly local resident suspicious about the sort of people who will live in the home and fearful of an increase in violence and crime in the area.

Activity 11.8

Make sure that you understand the following expressions used in this chapter. Check in the Glossary at the end of the book if you need to.

approved social worker	paranoia
community care	phobia
day hospital	pressure group
depression	psychiatric social worker
district general hospital	psychiatrist
ECT	psychopath
half-way hostel	psychosis
informal patient	psychosurgery
institutionalisation	psychotherapy
learning disability	psychotropic drug
lobotomy	senile dementia
manic depression	stigma
multi-disciplinary	tranquilisers
neurosis	tribunal
obsession	voluntary organisation

Further reading

The organisation MIND produces an excellent range of clear and straightforward leaflets on most aspects of mental health. They also recommend books. A list of publications together with the leaflets are available from MIND at the address below. The Department of Health also have some free booklets – see below for address.

Useful addresses

MIND
15–19 Broadway
London E15 4B4
tel. 0208 519 2122

For Department of Health leaflets:
Department of Health
PO Box 777
London SE1 6XH
tel. 0800 555777

The Richmond Fellowship
8 Addison Road
London W14 8DL
tel. 0207 603 6373

Mental Health Foundation
20/21 Cornwall Terrace
London NW1 4OL
tel. 0207 535 7400

Websites

MIND **www.mind.org.uk**

Young Minds **www.youngminds.org.uk**

The Department of Health **www.doh.gov.uk**

⌄ 12 Learning disability

12.1 Defining 'learning disability'

What does the term 'learning disability' mean? Mencap – the organisation which works for people with learning disabilities – uses the following definition:

> Someone is described as having a learning disability if they have considerably more difficulty in understanding and managing their day-to-day lives than other people of the same age, and their social skills are also deficient. In general, someone with a learning disability will not learn as quickly as other children, and will not attain the full intellectual capacities normally associated with an adult.[1]

Mencap go on to stress however that all people are individuals and the use of a category such as 'learning disability' should not lead us to lose sight of people's individuality. People with a learning disability need to be seen as people first. They should not be defined purely in terms of their disability.

A section in Chapter 1 discussed the importance of language in creating and reflecting attitudes. 'Learning disability' has now long replaced the older term 'mental handicap'. Occasionally in this chapter, the older term is used where there is a reference to provision in the past, or where quotations date from earlier years.

More than 1 million people in the UK have some form of learning disability. The degree of disability varies widely from a person who lives a normal life but is perhaps regarded as not very academic, to someone who needs a great deal of care and cannot cope with simple tasks such as dressing. There are 190,000 people in the UK with severe learning disabilities. Learning disabilities cannot be cured but care and education can do a great deal to allow a person with a learning disability to reach his or her full potential.[2]

There is no single cause of learning disability. In many cases people are born with their disability, although it can result from a severe injury affecting the brain or from certain infections. Not all the causes of learning disability are known, although the most common condition, Down's Syndrome, is known to be genetically caused. While the risks of a child being born with a learning disability increase if the mother is over 40 at the time of the birth, anyone can have a child with a learning disability.

Many people with learning disability are quite capable of coping with life in society and their problems are sometimes solely related to the reactions of other people. Here a man tells of his longing to be treated as a normal person:

I don't see why people don't treat me as a normal person instead of some kind of – well, you know, some kind of crazy person. I try so hard to act like a normal person.[3]

In the following quotation, the writer explains that people with a learning disability may lack skills in communication but that this is not a one-sided problem:

You [the one non-disabled person] will be embarrassed, you won't be able to think of anything to say, you will tend to talk in an inappropriate tone of voice, you will tend to have a wide grin on your face and ask questions without being really interested in the answers. The handicap is thus a mutual one.

However there is a difference in the position of the two people, both unskilled in communicating with each other:

The trouble is that you have lots of opportunity to go off and form relationships more easily. We don't. You can deny your handicap. We can't – we live with it all the time.[4]

There is a tendency in our society for anything which is different to be seen in a negative way, as something to be avoided and feared.

Many people with a learning disability look after themselves or are cared for by relatives. This can put strain on a family and such families need support and help in coping.

Activity 12.1

Imagine you are a child and you have a brother or sister who has a learning disability. Write about your life.

12.2 Provision for people with a learning disability

'Mental handicap hospitals'

As was stated at the beginning of the chapter, 'mental handicap' is now an old-fashioned and unacceptable term. The old institutions in which many people with a learning disability lived were however known as 'mental handicap hospitals' – so this term will be used in talking about these institutions.

The last few decades have seen a huge decrease in the numbers of people living in hospitals. In 1993, some 21,000 people lived in mental handicap hospitals – half the number of 20 years ago.[5] By the end of the decade most of the English long-stay hospitals had closed, although there were still some 8000 learning-disabled people in NHS.[6] The closure programme was slower in Wales and Scotland.

Some of these hospitals provide a high level of care but problems of finance, shortage of staff and general lack of interest in the needs of handicapped people have led to a number of scandals being reported.

In 1967, allegations of ill-treatment led to an enquiry at Ely Hospital in Cardiff. The report found some incidence of ill-treatment and much to criticise in terms of standards of facilities and care. As a result the Hospital Advisory Service was set up in 1969 to visit hospitals, assess facilities and make constructive criticisms. Pressure continued for a reappraisal of the policy for people with a learning disability in hospitals, and in 1971 a government White Paper *Better Services for the Mentally Handicapped* expressed a commitment to community care. However, it is not possible simply to close hospitals without the establishment of alternative forms of care and support.

In 1978 the Committee of Inquiry in Normansfield Hospital found the physical environment unsatisfactory, the standard of nursing poor and a lack of clothing and facilities for patients. The Jay Committee, set up by the DHSS, reported in 1979 and recommended that nursing staff be replaced by holders of a new social work qualification, staff numbers be doubled and hospitals be replaced by homes. In the financial climate of the time with cuts in spending and learning disability not treated as a priority need, these proposals were unrealistic. In 1975, a Development Team for Mentally Handicapped had been established. The team carried out a survey of 50 hospitals and 30 homes between 1976 and 1982. The confidential findings were printed in the *Guardian* in July 1983,[7] and revealed that previous inquiries and reports had resulted in a deterioration of staff morale but little improvement in services.

A report published in 1999 found that learning-disabled people enjoyed a better quality of life away from residential campuses in smaller dispersed housing in the community (see section below on community care).[8]

Problems with institutional provision

Hospital never were appropriate accommodation for people with a learning disability. Typically, the hospitals were large, old, and located away from towns and cities. Learning disability has always had a low status in medicine, since the medical profession is geared towards the idea of cure and is frustrated by conditions for which there is no cure. Hospital life had a tendency to take away individuality – in the opinion of the resident quoted here this was the worst kind of deprivation:

> The real pain came from always being in a group. I was never a person. I was part of a group to eat, sleep and everything. As a kid I couldn't figure out who I was. I was part of a group. It was sad.[9]

Lack of privacy and forced group life made it very difficult for people to form relationships. There is a theory which suggests that humans need a territory of their own and without this people are too insecure to be able to relate to others.[10] It is certainly true that a large number of people in institutions were socially isolated despite the fact that they were constantly surrounded by others.

Another basic need, the need for sexual relationships was denied by hospitals. This did not mean that sexual liaisons did not occur:

> 'us never got caught once' remembers one woman who has since married the man she met in an institution, 'we used to get out night times in the wood, and then if we heard someone coming, I'd run one way and he'd go over the hedge'.[11]

In hospitals there is a tendency for routines to dominate the lives of the staff and the patients. A nurse describes how the residents in the hospital where he worked always had to get up at 7 a.m. and follow a strict routine and order of events. The nurse says:

> Imagine a 'normal' person at home being told that for the next thirty years he must get up at seven o'clock sharp every single day ... The prospect of a patient ever being allowed the privilege of staying in bed until eight or even nine o'clock and still getting his breakfast when he wakes up is a remote dream.[12]

The rationale for the strict following of routines was in terms of the shift system, the argument that any variation would create more work, and of course the idea that things must be the way they always have been.

The shift system, unavoidable in hospitals, also creates problems where shifts are rigidly separated and operate in quite different ways. It is astonishing at times how well patients coped with such confusing aspects of hospital life. In institutions, the standards of behaviour expected are often higher than those met by people living at home. There is further a tendency for all behaviour to be monitored and analysed in terms of symptoms. The nurse already quoted tells how he observed that ordinary people could make mistakes or be clumsy, but similar behaviour in patients would lead to criticism or punishment. Similarly, the same behaviour could be classified as normal or abnormal, depending on who was doing it:

> Some of the lads spend hours on end twirling pieces of string and gaining enormous pleasure from this. It is classified as 'self-stimulating' behaviour and considered to be a characteristic of the severely subnormal. The staff also twirl pieces of string. But this is considered normal because there's a key on the end of it.[13]

In many hospitals needs like food and clothing were met in the most basic way. Food was often served lukewarm and may have been spoiled in the course of the journey from the kitchen to the ward. Many hospitals did not use clothes which were individually owned by the patients but which form the ward stock of clothing. Such clothes were frequently washed and became shrunk and soiled. Staff who were overworked failed to ensure that clothing fitted and looked presentable. In the following extract the patient is allowed no say in what he wears:

> 'This'll do. He'll never know the difference.'
> A coat covered in stains with no buttons. The coat in question would fit someone a foot taller and several stone heavier. Simon looks a terrible sight.

'I'd like one with buttons,' he said.
'We've got no time to sort out one specially for you. Take this one.'
'It's too big.'
'Never mind that. It'll keep you warm.'[14]

As in psychiatric hospitals, drugs may be given to patients not for their benefit but to keep them quiet and facilitate the smooth running of the ward.

This description of life in mental handicap hospitals has focused on the worst aspects and obviously there were some hospitals where standards are very high. However, those staff who were committed to helping people to get the most out of life battled against problems of lack of funds, inappropriate buildings and staff shortages. In these conditions it was easy for staff to become demoralised and begin to treat residents cruelly, providing for physical existence but failing to treat people as human beings with rights. As the numbers of people in hospitals have been reduced, improvements have been made and staff are now rather more aware of the need to preserve individuality and self-determination. But there will always be a tendency within an institution for the needs of the institution to become dominant over the needs of individuals.

Community care

For some time now community care has been the accepted official policy for people with a learning disability. The 1971 White Paper *Better Services for the Mentally Handicapped* emphasised the importance of community care and set a programme for the next 20 years. This programme turned out to be rather optimistic and initiatives in the community were slower to develop than was anticipated. (See Chapter 9 for more details on the development of community care.) Other government documents followed but the real impetus for community care came with the Griffiths report in 1988 and the resulting White Paper *Caring for People*. This became law in the 1990 NHS and Community Care Act, implemented in April 1993 (see also Chapter 9).

The 1990 Act makes local authorities responsible for assessment and provision of care in the community. Where someone needs a lot of help to live in the community, a care manager will be appointed to put together a mix of services providing support and care. These services will be organised into a care plan and will be monitored and reviewed by the care manager. It is government policy that increasingly the services should be provided by the independent sector – private and voluntary organisations – rather than by social services themselves.

The following extract is a case described by Mencap to illustrate how families can use the assessment provision of the 1990 Act to obtain an assessment covering all aspects of need:[15]

M is a young man who is described as severely mentally handicapped. He has a diagnosis of autism and attended special schools for many years. When he was 15 he was diagnosed as suffering from a psychiatric breakdown and was admitted to hospital. He was prescribed anti-psychotic medicine and spent several periods in hospital as an in-patient. A residential placement was secured for him which was funded by the Local Authority. He has continued to live in community care placements for the last 10 years. He is now 25 years old. M's parents are concerned that his medical needs have been poorly managed over the last 10 years and that he has now become extremely dependent on his anti-psychotic medicine which is beginning to show quite serious side-effects. They have asked the Local Authority responsible for his care to conduct a full assessment to include education, housing, medical and social needs. They are unhappy that their son's needs have not been addressed in previous assessments. They are planning to go to his next review meeting with a request that all aspects of his care be assessed. They have also asked the Local Authority to liaise with the health and housing authorities, to consider a more appropriate placement for him. In their view his current community placement is one of containment not of care. The medical aspects of his programme are minimal. They are concerned that his behaviour needs are not being treated but are simply being suppressed by medication. They are now looking to the NHS and Community Care Act to get a comprehensive assessment with targeted services for their son's needs.

Research published in 1999 found that learning-disabled people living in smaller units in the community had a better quality of life than those in larger more institutionalised accommodation.[16] They had more social contacts and access to facilities, lived in more homely environments, enjoyed more control and choice in their lives, took less medication and were less likely to be overweight.

Education and housing

Since 1971, education authorities have been obliged to provide education for all children. Many children with learning disabilities are educated in special schools by teachers trained in meeting special needs. The emphasis in these schools is on teaching children to communicate, to develop social skills and to learn how to survive and function in society. The merits and dangers of special education are discussed in Chapter 7. Some colleges offer further education for people with a learning disability, although there is a need for expansion of such provision.

Social education centres (previously known as adult training centres and originally based around work activities) are increasingly focused on helping people with a learning disability to find supported employment, training and educational opportunities. This is done by sharing courses outside the main centre with non-disabled people. Centres usually provide recreational and skill programmes and may have care facilities for people with severe learning disabilities.

Social clubs are provided sometimes by social services and sometimes by voluntary organisations. Some integrate people with a learning disability better than others. An example of this approach is the Gateway clubs.

There are various types of *residential accommodation.* Many areas have hostels which provide a sheltered environment but allow a considerable measure of self-determination and do not segregate people with a learning disability from the rest of society. Many small residential care homes are privately

Source: Helen Stone, Photofusion
Children with learning disabilities benefit from leisure activities

run and cannot be distinguished from ordinary houses. Some 35,000 people live in residential homes run by the NHS, local authorities, voluntary bodies or private home owners. However the majority of adults and nearly all children with a learning disability live with their parents.[17] For people living at home, respite care is available. This involves a temporary stay in a residential home either in an emergency or on a planned basis. There are also in many areas schemes for lodgings or placements with families. Landlords or landladies are especially selected and supported in providing a home for a person with a learning disability. Family placements are more commonly found for children and involve a child being placed with another family for an agreed number of days each year. This scheme, as with respite care, allows carers a break.

There are employment schemes providing work in sheltered workshops and in sheltered placements in ordinary workplaces. These may be organised by a voluntary organisation such as Mencap and are supported through government schemes (some of which are described in Chapter 4). The disability working allowance is a means-tested benefit to help disabled people in work.

12.3 Advocacy

A relatively new concept in this country is *advocacy*. Advocacy simply means someone speaking up for someone's needs. The term is used in a number of different ways. Citizen advocates are independent people who speak up for someone unable to do so for themselves, staff advocates defend the interests of people they are paid to look after, legal advocates are lawyers. Self-advocacy can mean people speaking up for themselves – perhaps with support and preparation in a self-advocacy group – but is also used when people with a disability speak up for another person with a disability.

In the following quotations, some people with learning disabilities write about what self-advocacy means to them:[18]

To me, self-advocacy means that I can speak out for myself and tell other people to speak out for themselves. It means to help them to speak out to better themselves in the world. Part of it is to get other people to listen to us, to see what we want.

To me, self-advocacy means learning to speak out for what you believe in and having a good life. Since I got involved an awful lot of good has happened inside of me. I've gotten better at helping other people by listening to their problems, and I'm better at listening to people to get advice from them. I'm also better at speaking up for myself.

To me, self-advocacy is getting out, getting everything going and getting things done. It's helping out other people. I like to help the handicapped who can't do as much for themselves. Now I'm better at speaking up for other people. If I see someone being mean to a handicapped person, I jump in and say: 'Hey! If you don't know how to treat him, leave him alone and find someone who does!' I believe everyone should have their rights, and they should get out and do it for themselves. If they can't do it for themselves, they can try to learn.

Activity 12.2

Make sure you understand the following expressions used in this chapter. Check in the Glossary at the end of the book if you need to.

advocacy	learning disability
care manager	respite care
care plan	sheltered workshop
community care	social education centre
further education	special school
independent sector	voluntary organisation

Further reading

Mencap is the best source of information on learning disabilities (see below). They have a number of useful publications of their own and can supply others from their bookshop.

Useful addresses

Mencap
Mencap National Centre
123 Golden Lane
London EC1Y ORT
tel. 0207 454 0454

The King's Fund is an independent organisation which researches health and social care issues:

The King's Fund
11–13 Cavendish Square
London W1M OAN
tel. 0207 307 2400

Websites

There are several excellent websites on disability.

www.disabilitynet.co.uk provides an Internet-based disability information and news service.

Disability Now at **www.disabilitynow.org.uk** provide links to a range of other websites. An excellent starting point.

The King's Fund is at **www.Kingsfund.org.uk**

◪ **13** Old age

The chapter on elderly people in Muriel Brown's *Introduction to Social Administration in Britain* begins with the statement, 'Simply to grow old is not in itself a problem.'[1] Ageing is a natural process which happens to everyone. In some cases it brings particular needs and it is the failure of society to recognise and meet these needs adequately which causes problems for older people. As a group, elderly people have limited political power; they are not organised and cannot go on strike for better pensions. Pressure groups such as Age Concern are active in campaigning on behalf of elderly people, but to a large extent, meeting needs relies on the goodwill and commitment of society.

In this chapter, the terms 'older' and 'elderly' are used synonymously to refer to people over retirement age. Whilst there is a tendency for these terms to carry negative connotations, this is not the intention in this context. This section first examines population trends with regard to age and then looks at feelings and needs of elderly people in relation to poverty, housing, health and segregation from the rest of the community.

13.1 Population trends

Statistics on population show there to be an increase in the number of elderly people. The 1901 census counted 1.7 million people in Britain over the age of 65, now there are over 10.5 million people in this age category.[2] This increase is not simply an increase in the population as a whole, but represents an increase in the proportion of elderly people in relation to the rest of society. In 1901, 5 per cent of the population were aged 65 or over, compared with 18 per cent in 1996 and a predicted 26 per cent by 2031.[3] A distinction is sometimes made between 'young elderly' people aged 65–74 and 'older elderly' people aged 74 plus. This is partly because the needs and situations of the two groups can be very different but also because the statistics show a significant trend towards a higher proportion of 'older elderly' in the elderly population. Figure 13.1 and Table 13.1 show the details.[4]

Whilst the figures showing the increase in the number of elderly people are in one sense a cause for celebration, the lack of provision for elderly people means that they are also a cause for concern.

Britain

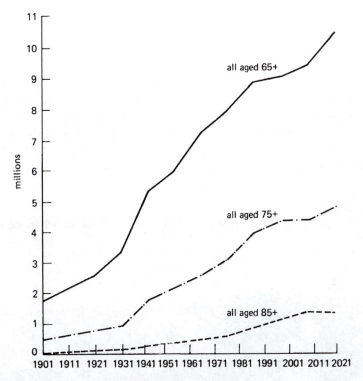

Source: Population projections by the Government Actuary, 1985–2025, OPCS PP2, 15
(London: HMSO, 1988, © Crown copyright)
Figure 13.1   The elderly population, Great Britain, 1901–2021

TABLE 13.1   The elderly population, Great Britain, 1901–2025 (000)

	65+	%	75+	%	85+	%
Historical trends 1901–1981						
1901	1734	4.7	507	1.4	57	0.15
1931	3316	7.4	920	2.1	108	0.24
1951	5332	10.9	1731	3.5	218	0.45
1961	6046	11.8	2167	4.2	329	0.64
1971	7140	13.2	2536	4.7	462	0.86
1981	7985	15.0	3053	5.7	552	1.03
Projections (1985 based)						
1985	8371	15.2	3544	6.4	671	1.22
1991	8847	15.8	3925	7.0	865	1.55
2001	8995	15.7	4320	7.5	1146	2.00
2011	9404	16.3	4374	7.6	1301	2.30
2021	10562	18.2	4678	8.0	1300	2.23
2025	11013	18.9	5177	8.9	1331	2.28

Sources: 1901–81 Census data OPCS, Population projections by the Government Actuary
1985–2025, PP2, 15 (London: HMSO, 1988, © Crown copyright).

Activity 13.1

Why do you think a greater number of people are living longer?

There have been two basic reasons for increased life expectancy since the beginning of the century. The first and most important has been improvements in general living standards: less poverty leading, in particular, to better housing and better nutrition. This has meant that very many more people live to retirement age and beyond. Secondly there have been improvements in medical science, the availability of medical provision and in welfare. This means that some health problems can be cured and that elderly people are better cared for than previously.

Activity 13.2

What problems with health, housing, etc. can occur when people get older?

Growing old and staying fit

13.2 Attitudes to old age

Some of the problems associated with old age are practical in nature, relating to increased frailty. There are also emotional difficulties in coming to terms with various kinds of change. Finally negative attitudes towards ageing people can cause problems which are not found in societies in which elderly people occupy a position of prestige and power.

This society is not one in which the experience of older people is respected and their continued contribution to society encouraged, although there are exceptions to this idea – for example, judges and politicians are predominantly older people. However, most people do not look forward to old age and the images held of old age are rarely attractive ones. With a few exceptions, such as the Queen Mother, images of elderly people in the media tend to focus on negative characteristics such as vulnerability, for example, in showing people as victims of crimes.

The psychological problems of growing older include adjusting to retirement which, as well as involving a reduction in income, may require getting used to loss of status, and to living an active life without the structure and routines of the working week. There are courses designed to help people to prepare for retirement, sometimes provided by companies and sometimes by colleges of further education. Many older women have given over their lives to child-rearing and it may be equally hard to adjust to the loss of this role. There are no courses laid on to help women deal with the 'empty nest' syndrome, equivalent to those provided for people leaving paid employment.

Some older people find it difficult to keep up with the rapid process of change which is a characteristic of modern society. In addition, old age may be a time of loneliness and bereavement as brothers, sisters, wives and husbands are lost. A person who lives to be 80 will probably experience the loss of a number of relatives and friends. These emotional challenges have to be met in a context of increasing practical difficulties.

13.3   Elderly people and poverty

Several studies have found a high proportion of elderly people live in poverty.[5] In 1995/96, 1,764,000 people aged 60 or over were receiving income support because of their low incomes. The Department of Social Security has estimated that between 34 per cent and 40 per cent of older people eligible for income support do not claim it. Older people spend a higher proportion of their income on housing, fuel and food (basic necessities) than do others in the community.[6]

Pensions and benefits

Women are particularly vulnerable to poverty in old age. The basic reason for poverty among elderly people is that almost universal compulsory retirement prevents people from working and an adequate replacement for earnings is not provided. The reasons for the number of people living below the poverty line include the fact that many people are unaware of benefits they could claim and others are reluctant to claim their rights since they feel benefits are a form of charity.

The provision of pensions is complex and only a brief summary of the main points can be given here. Women over 60 and men over 65 who have stopped work and paid sufficient contributions are entitled to receive a national insurance pension. (Legislation has been introduced to equalise the age limits for men and women; this will affect women retiring in 2010 who will no longer receive a pension at age 60.) In the year beginning April 1999, the rates were £66.75 for a single pensioner and £106.70 for a couple (claiming on the husband's contributions). People who live on the national insurance pension alone are likely to fall below the poverty line. In this case income support can be claimed.

Some people receive a second pension because they have paid into an occupational pension scheme whilst in work. Governments have made a number of attempts over the years to introduce second pensions for people without occupational schemes. Between 1961 and 1975 the national insurance contribution included a graduated scheme and people who paid into this receive an extra sum of money. The amount payable is small and often occupational pensions are relatively small. In 1975, the government produced a White Paper called *Better Pensions*. This introduced a new pensions scheme which began in 1978 and became fully operational in 1998. The new government pensions scheme was for people who are not already adequately provided for by an occupational scheme. These people pay extra national insurance contributions and receive a second pension under the *State earnings-related pension scheme* (Serps) at a rate determined by their contributions. The amount is based on the best 20 years of the person's working life. This improves the position of women since the scheme recognises that many women leave work for a period to care for young children and does not penalise them for this. New proposals at the end of 1998 are for the abolition of Serps and its replacement by a *state second pension* for people earning under £9000 a year. This gives credits to people who are looking after dependent relatives or children under five and long-term disabled people with broken work records. Thirdly, there will be the opportunity to make contributions to a *stakeholder pension* – this is intended to provide a low-cost and flexible pension for those without an occupational pension. There is no compulsion to join.

Whilst there are likely to be improvements in the financial situation of some elderly people in the future, the problem of people who are now retired remains, and there will always be people who are excluded from any scheme based on employment, because for one reason or another, they have not paid sufficient contributions.

Activity 13.3

Are the financial needs of older people likely to be greater or less than those of the rest of the community? Why is this?

Living costs

Comparative financial needs cannot be evaluated in any definitive sense. Whilst elderly people are less likely to have dependants and those who are home-owners may have paid off their mortgage, full use of the extra leisure time provided by retirement requires adequate income. Fuel costs can be a major problem for older people. Costs have risen sharply in recent years and elderly people are more inclined to feel the cold than young people. Old houses are also often hard to heat. Hypothermia is a serious problem, particularly in a severe winter.[7]

13.4   Housing

The majority of older people live in their own homes. However, many live in unsuitable housing which is too large for their needs and not adapted to take account of increasing infirmity. Gardens can become a worry instead of a pleasure if the owner is no longer able to work in a garden and has no source of help. Old people tend to live in older properties which are hard to heat and difficult to maintain. Townsend found that, particularly in the case of the older elderly, many lived in housing lacking basic amenities.[8] A government survey on housing revealed the following:

- 473,000 (43 per cent) of all unfit properties were occupied by elderly households.
- 500,500 (55 per cent) of all properties lacking amenities were occupied by elderly households.
- 223,000 (47 per cent) of unfit properties and those in serious disrepair were occupied by elderly households.
- 283,000 (27 per cent) of all properties requiring at least £7000 of repairs were occupied by elderly households.[9]

More recent figures do not reveal any significant improvements to the situation. In 1996, 18.7 per cent of single older people in England lived in poor housing, increasing to one in four of people over 75 living alone.[10]

Care in the community

About a third of people over 65 live alone. The statistics for women and people over 75 are higher.[11] This can lead to problems of isolation, loneliness and practical difficulties when people are unable to manage for themselves because of ill-health or infirmity. Social isolation is greater in redeveloped areas where communities do not exist to provide support.

Most older people living at home do not require or receive any special services. Provision varies from area to area and may include some or all of the services described below. Care in the community is the responsibility of the local-authority social services (as has been explained in Chapter 9). Following the 1990 NHS and Community Care Act, services have increasingly been provided by the independent sector – private and voluntary organisations – rather than by social services. Social services are however responsible for monitoring service provision.

In 1997, 79,000 people aged 65–74, 178,600 people aged 75–84 and 155,100 people over 85 received home help or home care services.[12] The 1990s saw a number of changes in the home help service. Most people are now expected to pay towards the service and the emphasis has shifted from help with housework to personal care. The old-style home help service was a particularly popular service, providing company as well as practical help and many people have regretted the changes, which have been motivated by increasing costs and demands for savings in public expenditure. Some older people receive meals delivered to their homes. The meals-on-wheels service may be provided by the local authority or by a voluntary group. This is a good example of a service initially provided on a voluntary basis and then taken over by social services, or run jointly by social services and volunteers. Day-centres provide company and help for those who do not require residential accommodation or for whom no accommodation is available. Some local authorities offer holidays for elderly people which provide a valuable break for both the older people and the caring relatives. Social workers and health visitors are involved in the support of elderly people in the community, although both have many other demands on their time. Other forms of provision include luncheon clubs which offer company and a mid-day meal, voluntary visiting services, laundry facilities, social clubs and home nursing.

When older people do need help to remain at home, most of the help they receive is provided by their family, neighbours and friends. Many carers are husbands or wives, but there are also children who look after their parents. As was discussed in Chapter 9, where people are cared for by grown-up children, the carer is more likely to be a daughter than a son. Many carers are themselves elderly. In 1995, 27 per cent of carers who devoted over 20 hours a week to caring were over 65 themselves.[13]

Sheltered or residential accommodation

Some elderly people move into sheltered accommodation. This enables people to live independently, usually in a flat, with the security of a warden on hand if needed and without the whole responsibility of upkeep and maintenance of a house. There is some local-authority sheltered accommodation but not enough to meet the need. Some sheltered accommodation is provided by voluntary organisations such as housing associations and there was a boom in the building of private sheltered accommodation for sale in the late 1980s and 1990s. Sheltered housing usually offers limited levels of support from a warden and problems can arise if residents begin to need higher levels of support. A solution which provides a viable alternative to residential care is found in 'extra care' or 'very sheltered' schemes which still allow elderly people to have the independence of living in their own homes with the support of round-the-clock nursing.

Activity 13.4

Is there sheltered accommodation locally? Who is it provided by? What services are offered? What are the costs to residents?

A minority of older people – around 209,000 in 1997 – live in residential homes. These can be provided by local authorities, voluntary organisations or privately. In 1997, 46,000 people over 65 were in local authority homes, 37,000 in homes run by voluntary organisations and 127,000 in privately owned homes.[14] In the 1980s the overall numbers of older people in residential care increased, partly because income support was available to pay for fees of residential and nursing care but money to pay for care at home was not easily available. This situation was however changed as a result of the NHS and Community Care Act and since then numbers have fallen as more people are able to receive care services in their own homes. The largest growth in the 1980s was in private residential care and this increase has continued whilst there has been a massive reduction in the numbers of people in homes run by the local-authority social services departments. This again is an effect of the NHS and Community Care Act and also part of the overall switch in social policy from statutory provision to the independent sector. This is another example of the idea of an 'internal market' in which the organisation paying for care is not the provider of the service.

Standards in elderly persons' homes vary considerably, but many of the local authority homes were old, too large and unable to offer a sufficient degree of privacy. It was common for people to have to share rooms. There is also a tendency for life in residential care to become routine and lacking in stimulation and for residents to become institutionalised. Staff in homes are extremely low paid and often lack training. Social services are responsible for inspecting all residential homes for elderly people. As has been said, in the past they also provided homes, but this is now discouraged by the government. Social services are encouraged to take the role of purchaser of services from others, no longer as provider. The social service inspection units are expected to work at 'arms' length' from the provider of the services, in this case residential home owners.

The question of who should fund residential care became controversial as government attempts to save money required people to spend their savings and sell their houses to pay for care. People with assets over £16,000 were required to pay the full costs while those with between £16,000 and £10,000 received a contribution from the local authority. Care was free for those with less than £10,000. Costs are very high – in 1999 the average bill for a year in a nursing home was £18,720 and £13,260 for a residential home. The means-test was resented by older people who felt that those who spent their money benefited from free care whilst those who had been frugal and saved lost their life savings. It was more widely unpopular with those who stood to lose an anticipated inheritance. It also seemed unfair that a cancer sufferer would receive free care in a hospital whereas someone with Alzheimer's disease would pay for care in a residential home. Very few people in Britain take out long-term insurance to pay for care in their old age, believing that they have paid National Insurance and taxes in order for the state to care for them or that they will be one of the majority of people who do not require care.

In 1999 a Royal Commission reported on this issue. The commissioners rejected ideas of private insurance and proposed that nursing and personal care should be free, in the same way as for people in hospital. Living and housing costs should continue to be means-tested, but with the threshhold raised from £16,000 to £60,000. Two of the eleven members of the Commission did not agree with these proposals, arguing that the end of means-testing allows better-off people to benefit from inheritance from their parents, while the state has met the cost of their care. Shortly after the report was published, the health secretary for the government rejected the proposal that long-term nursing costs would be provided free of charge.

In the account below, Rebecca Leathlean describes how her mother suffered the impact of changing ideas about the care of elderly mentally ill people:[15]

> During her 19 years in care, my mother was buffeted by the forces of social policy. In the early 1980s she was moved out of a large NHS asylum in Margaret Thatcher's drive to privatise the care system. In the unregulated free-for-all that followed, my mother suffered shoddy care in a succession of sub-standard homes. The first good one was closed down just one year after Mum moved into it: the council turned it into flats.
>
> Finally we found James House, a beautiful old home on the edge of Dartmoor run by enlightened managers and caring staff. This wonderful place was her home for eight years, but then the whole sorry saga started again. This time the upheaval was due to the care-in-the-community policy, under which state funding for care is cash-limited and controlled by local authorities. There is no longer enough to fund private as well as state homes.
>
> I travelled down to Devon to see the new home that had been chosen for my mother. Sadly, I noted the identical chairs lined up around the walls, the televisions playing loudly in the communal rooms. On the positive side, I was glad to meet kind staff, and relieved the new place was clean, apparently efficient and less than a mile from the old one.

Less than a month after the move, Rebecca Leathlean's mother fell victim to a chest infection and died. Another of the residents forced to move died just before her. Rebecca Leathlean concludes:

> The people of James House and all the other homes being closed to save money may seem 'no more' than old, mentally ill bodies of little consequence; but each in their time was a vibrant, vital individual – they still have feelings and they still matter. Many have suffered hugely. Surely they deserve to end their days in peace and security – regardless of the cost.

Activity 13.5

Draw up a design for an ideal development for elderly people and decide how the accommodation will be managed. Include ideas about the admission policy for the housing.

The shrinking family

Some 12 per cent of old people live without a spouse in the homes of relatives.[15] Although this can bring benefits, it is not always a happy situation either for the elderly person or for the relatives. Changes in society have made it more difficult for relatives to provide care, although the trend towards community care, examined in Chapter 9, is increasing expectations that families will care for elderly relatives.

Activity 13.6

What changes in society may mean now that people are less able to provide care for elderly relatives?

Several social and economic changes have reduced the abilities of families to provide care. Families are smaller than they used to be, so there are fewer relatives to help out in time of need. Changes in the position of women – for example, in employment – mean that many women are unable to be carers. The tendency for people to move to find work is another factor leading to difficulties in supporting elderly relatives. Finally, housing patterns reduce the possibilities for care – for example, estates of three-bedroomed houses mean that housing is too large for an elderly person alone, but too small to accommodate a family and an old person comfortably.

The issue of elder abuse was first raised some twenty-five years ago but is still often ignored and unrecognised. Abuse includes neglect, violence and sexual abuse of elderly people by informal and formal carers. Elderly people in the homes of relatives are often isolated and may be afraid to tell of their suffering. They are financially, physically and emotionally vulnerable.

Activity 13.7

Role-play:

The situation
The Browns live in a four-bedroomed house in the suburbs of a large town. The family consists of John and Sylvia Brown, their three children and their dog. John's father, Harry, lives alone (since the recent death of his wife) in the village he has lived in all his life. The village is about 30 miles from the Brown family's home. Since the death of his wife, Mr Brown Senior is finding it increasingly difficult to cope.

The decision
Should Harry Brown move in with his family or should he move to a residential home?

The characters
Harry Brown, aged 70, suffers from arthritis which means that he has difficulty in dressing and cooking as he cannot grip properly. Most of his friends in the village are also elderly, although he enjoys their company and visits to the local pub. He doesn't want to be a burden on his son's family, but neither does he want to go into a home.
John Brown, aged 38, is sales director in a job he enjoys and which means quite a lot of travelling. He does not feel happy about his father going into a home and would like him to move in with the family. He gets on well with his father when he sees him, which, at the moment, is most weekends.

Sylvia Brown, aged 35, has a good job in a local nursery, which she started after the children were in school. In a year or two, she expects to be promoted to deputy head. She knows of a good private home for elderly people quite near which the family could just about afford.

Jane Brown, aged 15, is afraid she will no longer have a bedroom of her own if her grandfather moves in. She is doing GCSEs at school and plans to stay on into the sixth form.

Susan Brown, aged 11, has just started at a new school which she likes. She is fond of her grandfather, but has a friend whose grandfather lives with the family and she always has to be quiet and can never have friends round to play music.

Peter Brown, aged 9, is very fond of his grandfather who always plays with him. He would love his grandfather to come and live with the family.

The dog has no opinion on the subject.

13.5   Health

Many older people are perfectly fit and some extremely so. In sports such as running, show-jumping and swimming there are many examples of older people who can put youngsters to shame. However, it is also true that, as a group, older people are in poorer health than the rest of the population. This is especially the case with the older age group – those over 75. In 1996, 66 per cent of people aged 75 and over in a government survey had a long-standing illness, compared with 35 per cent of people of all ages; 52 per cent said that they had a long-standing illness which limited their lives.[16] Older people rely more on the services of doctors and district nurses.

A growing problem which affects a minority of people in later life is Alzheimer's disease. This is a physical disease which causes a progressive decline in the ability to remember, to learn, to think and to reason. The prevalence of dementia (Alzheimer's disease is the most common form of dementia) is as follows:

Age	40–65	Less than one in 1000
	65–70	Two in 100
	70–80	Five in 100
	Over 80	Twenty in 100[17]

The causes of the disease are not understood and it occurs equally in all social groups and areas of the country. The symptoms of the disease vary but the commonest early sign is loss of short-term memory. Disorientation and confusion are also common. The course of the disease also varies: for some people decline is quicker than others and for some people the pace of decline is uneven.

Alzheimer's disease, especially in the early stages, causes great distress to the sufferer. Enormous stress is also placed on relatives and friends. In the later stages the sufferer may be unable to recognise close relatives and may develop anti-social behaviour. Wandering is common and can be dangerous. This short account is taken from one of the leaflets of the Alzheimer's Disease Society:

Ron is suffering from dementia caused by Alzheimer's disease. Although he can remember events which happened 20 years ago, sometimes he can't recall what he did two minutes ago. He forgets whether he had breakfast, whether he dressed, even where the kitchen is.

At first Ron's wife thought he was merely getting forgetful. Then one day he forgot the way home. Yesterday he was so confused he didn't know who she was.

13.6 Segregation

In the past it was common for elderly people to end up living on hospital wards. This is less likely to happen now as a result of changes in policy within the NHS and the move to community care. In fact things have turned around so much that, instead of concern about older people staying too long in hospital, the worry is now that patients are discharged too quickly into situations where convalescent nursing care is not available. The two poems which follow are both said to have been written by elderly residents in hospital settings. Even if the messages regarding the inappropriateness of hospital as a place to live are not so relevant today, the points about dignity and humanity are still just as important:

That I should come to this strange place
To finish up my days
O God I've prayed for help that I
May fit in with their ways.

I've washed, I've dressed, I've stood, I've sat
I've learned to toe the line
My mouth is washed, eyes swabbed, nails cut
To suit the nurses' time.

I've smiled at 'Pop' and 'Dad' and 'Dear'
They mean well, I know
But will I ever hear my name
Before I have to go?

The Staff are few, and they are rushed
And mostly they are kind
They walk me, bath me, feed my frame
But do not feed my mind.

Deaf ears, dim eyes imprison me
Just memories remain
But they are not enough, Oh Lord
Please take me, whence I came.

I have been, I am, grateful
For food and warmth and light
But now I have no dignity
No privacy, no right.

We even have our bottoms wiped
In full view of the wards
I used to say 'please screen me off'
My words were never heard.

The patients say a nurse was blamed
For letting someone fall
So now the screens are stored away
And they can watch us all.

Today I soiled my pants and chair
Is this the end of me?
The lost control
Was it a sign of my senility?

No, it was not my fault at all
I called the nurse for sure
But she was busy, said to wait
She'd see me to the door.

Was I so helpless, burdensome
The family sent me here?
I only asked to share their home
To feel my loved ones near.

The first time when Dot was gone
They seemed to want me there
I smoked outside
I held my tongue and never took his chair.

But soon their feelings changed for me
Their eyes said, 'In the way'
We can't go out, the car's too small
No friend can come and stay.[18]

The writer of this poem was unable to speak, but occasionally wrote. Again the poem was allegedly found in a locker, after her death:

What do you see nurses
    What do you see?
Are you thinking
    when you are looking at me
A crabbit old woman
    not very wise,
Uncertain of habit
    with far-away eyes,
Who dribbles her food
    and makes no reply?
When you say in a loud voice
    'I do wish you'd try'
Who seems not to notice

the things that you do,
And forever is losing
  a stocking or shoe,
Who unresisting or not
  lets you do as you will
With bathing and feeding
  the long day to fill,
Is that what you're thinking
  is that what you see?
Then open your eyes nurse,
  You're not looking at me,
I'll tell you who I am
  as I sit here so still,
As I use at your bidding
  as I eat at your will.
I'm a small child of ten
  with a father and a mother,
Brothers and sisters who
  love one another,
A young girl of sixteen
  with wings on her feet,
Dreaming that soon now
  a lover she'll meet:
A bride soon at twenty
  my heart gives a leap,
Remembering the vows
  that I promised to keep:
At twenty-five now
  I have young of my own
Who need me to build
  a secure happy home.
A young woman of thirty
  my young now grow fast,
Bound to each other
  with ties that should last;
At forty my young ones
  now grown will soon be gone,
But my man stays beside me
  to see I don't mourn:
At fifty once more
  babies play around my knee,
Again we know children
  my loved one and me.
Dark days are upon me,
  my husband is dead,
I look at the future
  I shudder with dread,

For my young are all busy
  rearing young of their own,
And I think of the years
  and the love I have known.
I'm an old woman now
  and nature is cruel
'Tis her jest to make
  old age look like a fool.
The body it crumbles,
  grace and vigour depart,
There now is a stone
  Where once I had a heart:
But inside this old carcase
  a young girl still dwells,
And now and again
  my battered heart swells
I remember the joys,
  I remember the pain,
And I'm loving and living
  life over again,
I think of the years
  all too few – gone too fast,
And accept the stark fact
  that nothing can last.
So open your eyes nurses,
  Open and see,
Not a crabbit old woman,
  look closer – see ME.[19]

Activity 13.8

Discussion questions on the two poems.
1 What complaint is made by both writers?
2 What improvements in care could be made in the light of the feelings
   expressed in the first poem?
3 What are the needs of elderly people, whether or not they are infirm?

Ellen Newton lived for part of her life in homes for elderly people, where she
kept a diary which was later published. This book captures much of the suffering
felt by an older person forced to live away from the community. Ellen Newton
writes:

The sense of segregation is so palpable, you feel as if at any moment you will
be tightly enclosed in a cocoon of isolation. Except for the milkman, before
dawn, there's no sound of traffic passing by. Everything is negative. You never
hear young people singing, speeding recklessly home from late parties, or
even the stereophonic calls of philandering tomcats. Never the sound of

children's voices, laughing and calling to each other as they race down the street.

Later in the book she writes: 'Very soon you know that the complete human being that you still hope you are, is slowly beginning to perish.'[20]

The segregation of elderly people results in a loss for all, although it is more keenly felt by the elderly people. This point is illustrated in the following extract from a report by Julie Winters, after a placement undertaken as part of the Preliminary Course in Social Care. Julie states honestly: 'I did not make it a secret that I was not looking forward to my old people's placement. It was something that I had to do.' She goes on to describe how she benefited from the experience:

However, I not only feel that it helped me, I thoroughly enjoyed it. The things that I have learnt through this placement could be put into practice at any time, not only through a job but in society. There are lots of old people that we meet, on buses, in the street, etc. and a lot of them love to talk to young people. When this happened before I sometimes found myself embarrassed or I did not know how to react to them ... The placement has given me insight into the needs and emotions of elderly people and I feel that now I know what to do and how to do it. My professional and personal development has progressed.

This extract shows how much people have to learn from each other in breaking down barriers between different groups of people.

Activity 13.9

Imagine you are 80. Describe how you are living and look back on your life.

Activity 13.10

Make sure you understand the following expressions used in this chapter. Check in the Glossary at the end of the book if you need to.

carer	occupational pension
domiciliary service	pressure group
housing association	segregation
hypothermia	sheltered accommodation
life expectancy	status
national insurance contributions	voluntary organisation

Further reading

Age Concern is the best source of up-to-date information on issues to do with ageing (see below). There are now a good range of books covering most aspects of the subject. A useful collection of articles on age and social policy can be found in *The Social Policy of Old Age*, edited by Miriam Bernard and Judith Phillips (London: Centre for Policy on Ageing, 1998).

Useful addresses

Age Concern
1268 London Road
London SW16 4ER
tel. 0208 679 8000

Centre for Policy on Ageing
25–31 Ironmonger Row
London EC1V 3QP
tel. 0207 253 1787

Website

Age Concern England have a very informative website which provides statistical and other information and includes links to other organisations. The address is **www.ace.org.uk**

⊻ **14** Disability

14.1 What is a 'disability'?

There is no clear dividing line between disabled people and the rest of society. Everybody experiences disability to some extent at some point in their lives and most people are 'able' in some situations and not in others. The line from 'normality' to 'abnormality' is a continuum with no sharp cut-off point. Labelling some people as 'the disabled' is part of the problem of disability.

As has been discussed in Chapter 1, language is important is determining how people feel about themselves and how they react to others. Michael Oliver and Colin Barnes write:

> the disabled people's movement has realised that definitions and terminology play a significant role in their individual and collective disadvantage. Terms such as 'cripple', 'spastic' and 'mongol' are offensive when used to refer to a disabled individual. Others which depersonalise and objectify the disabled community are also considered unacceptable. Examples include 'the disabled', 'the deaf' or 'the blind'. Further, in an effort to overturn traditional negative assumptions and attitudes surrounding disability, organisations controlled and run by disabled people have developed definitions and terminology of their own. [1]

Several writers and organisations have tried to make a distinction between physical aspects of disability and socially created limitations. Ann Shearer uses the terms 'disability' and 'handicap' in this way, suggesting that disability must be taken as given, but handicap 'is something that is imposed on that disability to make it more limiting than it must necessarily be'.[2] The extent to which a disability is a handicap depends on a number of factors such as the type of job a person has, the services which exist to help, the attitudes of society and the personality of the person with the disability. Ann Shearer illustrates this point by arguing that not being able to run for a bus would not be a handicap if buses waited for their passengers. However, many disabled people find the term 'handicap' offensive because of its historical association with begging and charity. A similar distinction can be made using the term 'impairment' to refer to the physical dimension and 'disability' as the term which incorporates the socially created aspects.

These distinctions are important because they reflect differing ways of thinking about disability. On the one hand there is a medical model of disability which focuses on the individual and physical conditions (impairments). A social model of disability takes the focus away from the individual and looks at disabling environments – ways in which society creates disabilities. Disability now becomes a political issue. Here, Kevin Donnellon, who is without limbs as a result of the thalidomide drug, talks about his experience of attending a conference and hearing about the social model of disability:

> It was like a bolt from the blue, a bombshell. They were talking about the social model of disability, that the real problem for disabled people is out there, not in us. For years, whenever people carried me into a building, I was grateful. But I should have been angry instead, angry that there wasn't a lift.[3]

In considering which terms are most appropriate, members of the disabled people's movement have been concerned to emphasise the social and political dimensions. Oliver and Barnes adopt a slightly adapted version of a definition put forward in 1975 by the Union of the Physically Impaired Against Segregation. This definition suggests that the term disability refers to:

> the disadvantage or restriction caused by a contemporary social organisation which takes no or little account of people who have … impairments and thus excludes them from the mainstream of social activities.[4]

Oliver and Barnes do not like the term 'people with disabilities' which some have used to emphasise the fact that people with impairments are people first. They argue the expression implies that disability is the property of the individuals and not of society. They suggest that the terms 'disabled person' and 'disabled people' give a better sense of a disabled identity and the social and political dimensions of disability. This chapter will follow these authors and use 'impairment' to refer to a medical condition and 'disability' as the term which encompasses externally imposed disadvantage and social restrictions.

The disadvantage and discrimination experienced by disabled people means that it makes sense to bring people together under this collective identity. However you need to be aware that the term covers many very different types of impairment with different causes. People also live in differing situations with different needs. There is a tendency for the notion of disability to create a stereotyped image in people's minds. In many respects generalisations about disabled people do not make sense (this is a problem with a chapter such as this which does attempt to discuss disability in a general way).

Using the definition of disability offered above, it is not possible to estimate the numbers of disabled people, since disability is dependent on the environments in which impaired people live. The number of people in this country who have impairments is unknown, partly owing to problems of definitions, and partly because no comprehensive survey has been carried out. Without this information, it is more difficult to assess the adequacy of provision. Registers of people with impairments are maintained by local authority social services departments, but registration is voluntary and these figures do not provide a complete picture. The duty of local authorities to maintain registers was initially established in the 1948 National Assistance Act. The 1970 Chronically Sick and Disabled Persons Act gave local authorities a statutory duty to inform themselves of the needs of local people. However, the procedure for the implementation of this duty was vague and few local authorities carried out comprehensive surveys. Various surveys have produced differing figures – probably depending on how they have defined disability. Government statistics at the end of the 1990s put the figure at 8.6 million people.[5]

Activity 14.1

Can you identify any common areas of need for disabled people? To what extent are disabled people's needs being met?

14.2 Acceptance

Needs vary but may include financial support, special educational facilities, sheltered employment, support, help in making social contacts, and aids and help in the practicalities of daily life. However, the greatest need for many people is to be accepted and not rejected as somehow 'abnormal'. Often the greatest problem is not the impairment itself, but other people's attitudes which may then be internalised by the sufferer. Christopher Reeve is the actor best known for his role as *Superman*. After he was paralysed by a fall from his horse he wrote a book describing his life. It is called *Still Me*.[6]

This society is one of ideals, for example the ideal of slim 'perfect' women, and to be noticeably less than ideal brings suffering when society is intolerant and rejecting of those who fail to meet the standard. Reactions which hurt and damage include fear, withdrawal, embarrassment, pity and low expectations. In the following extract, a woman with multiple sclerosis explains how she felt about categories of normality after the onset of the disease:

I was confused, I still felt fundamentally the same. My body was different, I know that all right, but inside it was me. Normality is after all what you know. The male who is very short is normal to himself, it is other people who make him aware of an 'abnormality'. The ugly female is 'normal' to herself (try denying your own being), it's the others who make her 'abnormal'. After all if we were all very short and ugly (decide for yourself what that means) a person unlike that would be 'abnormal'. 'Normality' and 'abnormality' are socially defined. It also has to be a relative concept, we are all normal/abnormal to the social norm, in varying degrees. Disability can and sometimes does interfere with the practical running of a life, but it is the reaction of and non-action of society which causes disablement. There is no such thing as THE DISABLED, there are just people.

The woman goes on to tell how powerful an effect the reactions of other people have on the person:

On leaving hospital and finding the mantle of 'disabled' placed firmly upon my unwilling shoulders I entered a world which was alien, absurd and ultimately defeating. My weak grasp on my identity was no real match for the massed forces of society who firmly believed themselves as 'normal' and myself just as firmly as 'abnormal'. I found myself inhabiting a stereotype. I became my illness.[7]

There are many ways in which people make others feel abnormal. The woman quoted above tells how she and her problem became public property such that strangers approached her to discuss it, whilst at the same time friends were incapable of talking about her disability without embarrassment or joking. Various expectations of their limitations and their feelings are placed on people with a disability. Many people with a physical disability complain of assumptions made about their mental abilities, and the BBC radio programme *Does he take sugar?* is aptly titled, referring to the tendency for people to refuse to address a person who has a disability directly.

Attitudes to disability can be clearly seen in attitudes to sexuality. The experience of the woman told in the following extract is echoed in many other accounts of similar experiences. Angie has cerebral palsy and is unable to walk:

> One day while Tony was at work the gas man came to read the meter … As he was leaving the flat he turned and asked if I was married? I told him I was, then a funny look came into his eyes and he asked if I had sex? I was shocked at his question and at first stuck for words. Then I was angry and said the first thing that came into my head, 'Yes, do you?' He look embarrassed and turned away. During the rest of the day I kept thinking what a cheek he had asking me such a question. Since then I have been asked that question several times in different ways, most often by men, and I answer them in the same way.[8]

Attitudes to people with disability who want to have children are similarly misinformed and hurtful. There is no reason why the right to have children should be denied to people with a disability. The idea that it is wrong for such people to have children cannot be connected to fear of a disability being passed on, since cerebral palsy and many other disabilities are not hereditary. The basis for such attitudes can only be denial that people with a disability are human beings in the same way as everyone else and only different to the extent that they suffer from a particular condition.

Activity 14.2

What can be done to improve attitudes to disability? How would you set about educating people's attitudes?

Fear and prejudice are often based on ignorance and unfamiliarity. Many fears would be eliminated if disabled people were further integrated into the community. The media could play a role in changing attitudes by portraying people with a disability in everyday situations, leading a normal life. There is a tendency for the media to overdo the 'tragedy' aspect of disability. Schools could help young people by extending community projects and encouraging young people to get to know disabled people.

14.3 Taking control

Organisations for disabled people have traditionally been run by able-bodied people and invoked images of weakness, pity and charity. Since the 1980s a disability movement has arisen, giving disabled people their own voice. In similar ways to earlier Women's Liberation, Gay and Lesbian Liberation and Black Power movements, the Disability Movement has been a focus for disabled people to create their own definitions of their situation, express anger instead of gratitude, and challenge patronising attitudes in welfare, traditional disability organisations and the whole of society. Disabled people have found a new identity through solidarity with each other. Some have become involved in direct action and protests on a variety of issues concerning the representation and treatment of disabled people.

In 1981 the British Council of Disabled People (BCODP) became the first umbrella organisation run by and for disabled people. It represents a wide range of local and national organisations covering varying disabilities. Ten years later the Direct Action Network (DAN) was set up. DAN uses tactics of non-violent civil disobedience such as handcuffing to buses, occupying transport offices and crawling into Parliament to draw attention to the need for accessible transport and buildings and other civil rights issues. The existence of the disability movement has radically changed the traditional organisations which are now more political in their demands and much more likely to include disabled people in ruling bodies as members of staff.

Things are also changing on an individual level as disabled people demand the right to control their own lives. Here Bonnie Chamberlain who is 18 years old and has cerebral palsy, talks about the way others have tried to exclude her from decisions about her own needs and her fight to make her own decisions:

'People seem to think of you as incapable of having an opinion or making a decision,' explains Bonnie. 'I've spent much of my life being "assessed" for various aids and adaptations, but they never ask you what you want to do with the equipment when you get it and so you end up with something that's not what you need.'

'They talk about a team approach but the person in the wheelchair has to have an equal place in that team.' ... 'All my life I've tried to make the professionals realise that I know what I'm talking about. But they always think they know what's best for you. I may be in a wheelchair but I still want to do a lot of the things that other people do. But you have to fight every step of the way to be allowed to do that.'[9]

As was discussed in Chapter 8, there is now more awareness amongst social workers and others of the issue of empowerment and the need to involve people in decisions. Other developments on this front include the introduction of direct payments (discussed in section 14.8 below) which allow people to manage their own care services.

14.4 Finance

Some disabled people are unable to work, others have limited earning power and many have extra costs. These include wear and tear on clothes caused by appliances, costs of special equipment, and money to pay people to do tasks such as decorating which other people are able to do for themselves.

In the last decade, several new benefits have been introduced, reducing the number of people dependent on income support. Benefits for disabled people include contributory benefits such as incapacity benefit. Non-contributory benefits include the severe disablement allowance, the invalid care allowance (for carers), the disability living allowance and the disability working allowance. The rates for benefits are not especially high and have been given in Chapter 3. State provision of benefits is patchy and, as the above list demonstrates, complex. It has been criticised for creating distinctions based not on the extent of the disability but on the source of the condition. For example, disabled people whose impairment results from an industrial accident or a war injury receive superior provision to those with an impairment from birth or caused by a non-industrial injury. These distinctions are based on value judgements about different people's contribution to society, and on a tendency to reward the able and penalise those with a disability. The emphasis on contribution to society through employment can be criticised if a consideration is given to the amount of time spent at work and the nature of many jobs. There are many ways in which people contribute to society through activities outside employment.

Other criticisms of provision for disabled people include the kind of tests people have to pass or fail in order to qualify for benefits. The mobility allowance was fenced in with rules and regulations. A man with one leg was refused the benefit and decided to appeal:

> To do that, he had to go to an office set up for the purpose. And to reach the office, he had to take himself and his crutches, slowly, with difficulty, up no fewer than twenty-eight stairs. And when he at last got to the top, he eventually lost his appeal, because he had, slowly and with difficulty, made his way up twenty-eight stairs to lodge it.[10]

The old mobility allowance is now incorporated into the disability living allowance but the rules are still strict and sometimes can seem unfair. The account below concerns a woman who has suffered a hernia and had an operation, after which two months' convalescence were recommended. She works as a self-employed arts administrator:

> Bea stood in the street looking for some sign that she had come to the right place. It had been a long, slow haul from the bus stop through an unfamiliar part of town. Her scar and stitches were still painful two months after the operation.
>
> She spotted Cambridge House but there was no indication that the benefits agency examination centre was to be found here.
>
> Bea saw an entry phone and reaching up, she pressed the buttons and stated her name and business. … Finally she made herself heard. With a click she was admitted. A steep flight of stairs lead to the first floor. There was no receptionist, no lift, no one to greet or advise. Bea stood at the foot of the stairs, wondering how she was going to climb them.
>
> Reflecting that the benefits agency must have searched long and hard for office accommodation located above ground level and without a lift, Bea noticed, hidden away in the corner, a cumbersome wheelchair lift and a

notice: press for assistance. Ringing a bell to announce that she was incapable of climbing a flight of stairs was just too much. So, despite considerable pain, fuelled by mounting anger at this shoddy treatment, Bea embarked on the stairs, her progress watched by a woman sitting behind a glass partition at the head of the stairs. The woman did not smile nor offer help. After all, if you wanted assistance, you had to ring the bell.

The medical assessment was conducted at a brisk pace and began to feel increasingly, 'like a game where only the doctor knew the rules,' she said.

After 25 minutes of interview and physical examination, Bea was told that, in the doctor's opinion, she was fit for work. Still in pain and by now, close to tears, Bea protested that she was far from fit to work, that she had no work arranged for the following month and therefore no money coming in. The doctor said that was not his concern. Bea left the consulting room torn between rage and despair. She took the stairs very carefully, fearing a fall.[11]

The costs of disability benefits increased hugely in the 1980s and 1990s. There were three probable reasons for this. People were made more aware of their entitlement to benefits, take-up rates improved and greater numbers of elderly people increased demand for benefits. Also people made redundant, perhaps who had always suffered health problems but managed to work, were put on incapacity benefit by sympathetic GPs (some politicians were of course happy to see the numbers classed as unemployed reduced in this way, particularly around the time of an election). Alarm over fraudulent claims resulted in the Benefits Integrity Project in which people claiming benefits were further questioned to check their eligibility for benefits. This caused considerable anxiety amongst disabled people and did little to reduce the numbers on benefits. The latest proposals are to further restrict eligibility for incapacity benefit and to make disability benefits means-tested.

The Family Fund is a source of finance for families with a child with a severe disability. The money is from the government but is administered by the Joseph Rowntree Memorial Trust.

The complexity of the benefits system causes suffering as the following extract, from a woman with multiple sclerosis raising a family alone on benefits, shows. She experienced many difficulties in claiming her rights and had to fight all the way:

My main feelings about my experience are anger and frustration. Anger because not only do I have to cope with the physical and mental difficulties of being a person with a disability, but I have to use precious energy struggling to make ends meet. Frustration because there seems very little prospect of improvement in this situation. The long-term effects of this social security system are extremely detrimental to families. The children, in particular, suffer as they are unable to compete with their friends on any level. Not only do they have a disabled parent but they are also poorer than anyone else.[12]

The Disability Alliance campaigns for three long-term policy objectives. The first is to eliminate poverty, the second to bring the incomes of those with disabilities up to the level of the non-disabled and the third to have funds distributed equally, not on the basis of the cause of the disability or the place where it happened. A common feature of campaigns on disability is the demand for a single comprehensive benefit paid as of right.

Source: Vicky White, Photofusion
This cycle mechanic has no sight or hearing

14.5 Employment

Employment is very important in our society as a source of income, status and a way of meeting people and feeling part of society. A woman who had to give up work because of her disability tells how she felt:

> It was the most shattering experience I had had, because going out to work, you felt part of society, you were contributing, you were earning your own money. You also had your friends that you went to work with, and then suddenly you were cut off, you were in the house alone. Also of course financially you were worse off. You were lonely, you felt useless, on the scrap heap, finished, and it really was a very bad time.[13]

Disability Service Teams work within the Employment Service to provide specialist advice to disabled people seeking work and employers. Disability Employment Advisors (DEAs) provide advice and practical help in finding a job. Through Access to Work, work premises can be adapted to meet special needs or a support worker provided. The Job Introduction Scheme allows people to try out a job. Disabled people are entitled to join any of the schemes for unemployed people, such as the New Deal (see Chapter 4), without waiting for the qualifying period of unemployment. A disability symbol identifies employers with a positive attitude to disabled people. For people with severe disabilities, there are supported employment schemes to help people find and keep jobs. Supported placements allow people to work at their own pace alongside able-bodied colleagues. Remploy is a national organisation which operates a similar scheme with employers. Remploy also have factories of their own, although plans were announced in 1999 to close these, and there are a range of workshops run by local authorities and voluntary organisations, all providing supported employment for people with severe disabilities. Within Training for Work, training providers can provide special equipment and make adaptations to workplaces. For people with more severe disabilities, there are residential training courses and customised local training which provide extra support, longer training, with social and medical care.

In October 1999 a Disabled Person's Tax Credit replaced the disability working allowance which was a means-tested benefit for disabled people in low-paid work. Disabled Person's Tax Credit is available to all disabled people. The amount received depends on the level of income and number and age of dependent children. Child-care costs are also taken into account. Payments are received through the person's wage packet and mean a guaranteed income of around £150. Plans for the future include more encouragement for disabled people to work, including compulsory job advice interviews.

Sheltered workshops have been criticised for a number of reasons. They have tended to be biased towards industrial work, which may not be the most suitable type of employment. It may be more helpful for disabled people to be trained to work in areas where their experience is an advantage, for example in counselling or welfare rights work.

Disabled people are more vulnerable to unemployment, especially in times of recession. Following the Second World War and the consequent increase in disability, the 1944 and 1958 Disabled Persons (Employment) Acts provided a system of special help for disabled people. A voluntary register of disabled people was set up, although for a variety of reasons many disabled people chose not to register. The 1944 Act established a quota system whereby employers with a staff of 20 or more people were required to employ 3 per cent of registered disabled people. Many employers ignored the quota and few were prosecuted: government departments and nationalised industries were no more likely to keep to the law than employers in the private sector. The Act also provided for occupations to be designated for disabled people, but only two were named, those of lift operator and car park attendant. In 1995 the quota systems were abolished when the Disability Discrimination Act was passed.

14.6 The 1995 Disability Discrimination Act

After a decade of campaigning by disabled people, the government brought in anti-discriminatory legislation in 1995.

The 1995 Disability Discrimination Act is designed to prevent discrimination against disabled people in a range of areas of life. In the Act, disability is defined as long-term physical or mental impairment which substantially affects the ability to carry out normal day-to-day activities. This includes physical and sensory impairments, learning disabilities and mental health conditions lasting 12 months or more, or likely to recur. 'Severe disfigurements' and progressive conditions such as cancer, HIV and multiple sclerosis are also included. The Act means it is against the law for employers with twenty or more staff to treat disabled people less favourably than others and requires employers to make 'reasonable adjustments' to work practices and premises to overcome barriers to employment. The Act also makes it unlawful for providers of goods, services and facilities to discriminate against a disabled person either by refusing to serve disabled customers or providing them with second-rate services. All goods and services provided to the public are covered, including health, insurance, legal services, and sport and leisure facilities. Policies and practices which have the effect of excluding disabled people have to be changed, for example a restaurant cannot refuse a person with a guide dog because they do not allow animals. If a disabled person needs a helper, a shop must change a policy of only allowing one person in a changing room at a time. People who sell or let properties cannot unreasonably discriminate against disabled people. Schools and colleges must provide information on their facilities for disabled students. The law also provides a right of access to railways and bus stations and allows the government to set minimum criteria for disabled access to new buses, trains and taxies. Finally, the 1995 Disability Discrimination Act set up a National Disability Council (NDC) to advise the government on how the measures are working and to recommend new developments.

Although wanting legislation to stop discrimination, this Act was opposed by disability organisations who felt it did not go far enough. The Royal Association for Disability and Rehabilitation (RADAR) objected on a number of grounds. The

Act divides disabled people and discriminates against disabled people in its definition of disability. By focusing on an individual's impairment rather than the social restrictions and stigma which are placed on the person, the definition of disability in the Act is unhelpful and unnecessarily complicated. RADAR argued also that all employers should be included and the quota system for employment should be retained until it could be shown that the Disability Discrimination Act was working. Other aspects of the Act are weak and unlikely to greatly improve access to services and housing. The use of the term 'reasonable' throughout the act makes it too easy for employers and providers to avoid inclusive practices. The enforcement procedures are weak and ineffective.

Whilst in opposition the Labour Party disagreed with the exemption of small employers from the provisions of the Disability Discrimination Act. Many expected changes when the Labour Party were elected in 1997. In power, however, disabled people were disappointed when the new government compromised and made only a limited change to the law – including employers with 15 or more staff. This still leaves nine out of ten companies and 75 per cent of employees outside the scope of the act. The beginning of the twenty-first century will see a Disability Rights Commission aiming to work towards eliminating discrimination and promoting equal opportunities and good practice. Disability organisations welcomed the idea of the Commission, but hoped it would have sufficient finance and enough 'teeth' to make a difference.

Activity 14.3

Look in newspapers for any examples of cases which have been brought under the Disability Discrimination Act. Have they been successful or not?

Look around as you go about your life. Is the Act having an impact on the places you visit – schools, colleges, sports centres, workplaces?

Are attitudes changing as a result of the legislation? Perhaps you could carry out a survey to see if people are familiar with the requirements of the Act.

14.7 Education

The provision of education for disabled children was reviewed by the Warnock Committee and legislation was introduced in 1981. The Warnock Report encouraged integration of disabled children into mainstream schools, but also allowed for a variety of other methods of education (see Chapter 7).

There are disadvantages and advantages of educating children and young disabled people in separate schools. A girl with restricted movement in one side tells how the cruelty of other girls in school led her to ask if she could attend a special school. She says that in the special school:

It was much easier to make friends and I didn't feel an outsider any more. Everyone had a disability and no-one was self-conscious about it. They treated each other as human beings and you could be friends with anyone.[14]

This young woman is however aware of her loss of contact with the outside world. Another woman who suffered from a disease called brittle bones tells of her isolation until she went to a boarding school for girls with disabilities. Here she learned the joy of sharing doubts and fears:

> Our boarding school had rows of adjacent loos. One day, very soon after my arrival at the school, I was sitting in one loo whilst a new friend was sitting in the loo next door. 'Micheline' she said, 'Do you think you will ever get married?' A flood of relief came over me then. I knew the question was coming from someone who had asked herself the same question many times already. There were other people who had gone through all that doubting too! Nice people! Other young women who had had their self-image as women so severely damaged that they too had wondered if they were entitled to anything life had to offer.[15]

These women were lucky in that they attended schools which set high academic standards and provided an education equal to that of ordinary schools. Others are not so lucky and go to schools where little is expected of disabled children and where the teaching is of a lower academic standard. This is part of the 'cycle of expectation' whereby little is expected of people and, as a result, they achieve little. It takes great personal strength and confidence to overcome such a handicap. Another disadvantage of special education is the way in which it segregates people with a disability from the rest of society. This is as much a loss to the able-bodied as to the disabled people. Finally, there is a need for greater provision in further and higher education for disabled people.

The 1981 Education Act set up procedures for disabled children to be assessed in order to decide if special provision should be made. If it is thought that special educational provision is required, the local authority must make a statement of special educational needs. This process is known as 'statementing' and must involve the parents of the child (see page 191).

14.8 Care and support services

If people with a disability are to lead a full life in the community, practical help and support are needed. These services are provided either by health authorities or by local social services departments. The duty to make provision was strengthened in the 1970 Chronically Sick and Disabled Persons Act. The Act gave local authorities the responsibility of informing themselves of the number of such people in their area and providing for their needs. There was a great deal of optimism about the potential of the Act but the implementation of the legislation has been disappointing and provision remains inadequate, fragmented and patchy. Local authority social services departments may provide aids to households such as telephones and can finance adaptations to homes, although there may be a requirement for the recipient to meet part of the cost. Other services include home helps, holidays and day-centres. These services have been vulnerable to cuts in expenditure in recent years. A survey by the Disability Alliance found that the number of telephone installations had fallen and fewer council homes had been adapted.[16]

The duties of the local authorities have been strengthened by the 1986 Disabled Persons Act and the 1990 NHS and Community Care Act. Under these Acts the local authority must make an assessment of needs if asked to do so and decide what provision, if any, to make. In complex cases requiring the co-ordination of a number of services, a care manager will be appointed to work on a care plan and to monitor and review the provision. Services vary from area to area but are likely to include the following:

- social workers providing advice, information and counselling;
- home care staff to help with personal care at home;
- meals-on-wheels;
- occupational therapists who provide advice on the practicalities of daily living and organise aids and adaptations for the home;
- day-centres offering a variety of educational, therapeutic and recreational facilities.

All of these services may be charged for, although usually on a means-tested basis. Again this varies from area to area. As the following account shows, these charges are resented by many people:[17]

> To get in and out of bed, Joanna Buckle needs the assistance of two home helps. Multiple sclerosis prevents her from standing alone and she is unable to dress herself to get to work.
>
> For this help Ms Buckle is now expecting to have to pay more than £500 a month. 'I will have to pay all this money just to get into and out of bed each day which is pretty obscene to me,' she said.
>
> 'I did not ask to have multiple sclerosis – now I am being penalised for being disabled.'
>
> ...
>
> She has held down a professional job with neighbouring Waltham Forest council for almost 10 years. Now she faces a stark choice – either to sit in bed or in a wheelchair all day, or to carry on with her job and make severe economies in her budget.
>
> ... Ms Buckle does not want people to think of her as a tragic victim. All she wants, she says, is some simple help at an affordable price so she can lead a normal life.

The Independent Living (1993) Fund works in partnership with local authorities to fund 'joint care packages' for severely disabled people between the ages of 16 and 66 who need extensive help in order to live in the community.

The 1996 Community Care (Direct Payments) Act came into force in 1997. The law allows local authorities to give funds to disabled people between the ages of 16 and 65 who want to make their own care arrangements. Direct payments are popular with service users but local authorities have been slow in setting up schemes and people with learning disabilities have tended to be excluded. Graham Thody lives in Burgess Hill, Sussex, and has cerebral palsy. After he left residential care and moved into a bungalow, he was supported by six staff employed through an agency. He always resented the agency getting a cut of the money earmarked for his care and felt he could do a better job himself:

As one of the first to join the council's direct payments scheme, Thody is now in control of his budget and, he believes, getting better value for money and more hours of care. Each week he receives £200 from the local authority and a further £300 top-up payment from the Independent Living Fund. With this he can employ someone to help him to go out or tend his garden, as well as feed, wash and dress him and care for him at night.

According to Thody, the benefits of the new system are enormous: 'I don't have to put up with some patronising, inexperienced person sent by the agency who treats me as if I'm about 90.':[18]

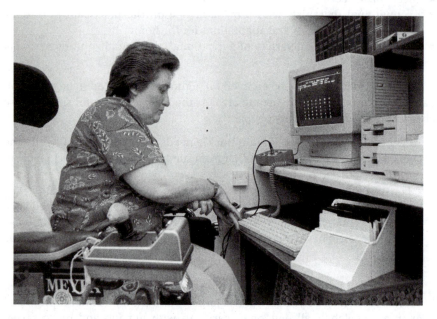

Source: Crispin Hughes, Photofusion
New technology helps disabled people

Wheelchairs are provided by the Artificial Limb and Appliance Centres. People who suffer from weakness in hands and limbs can be given electrically-propelled wheelchairs. Mobility is a key problem for many disabled people. In 1976, the policy of providing invalid vehicles ended and the mobility allowance was introduced (later changed to be incorporated into the disability living allowance). The introduction of an allowance initially posed some problems as it was difficult to use the allowance to buy a car. However, a scheme called *Motability* is now operated by a voluntary organisation. Under this scheme, the mobility component of the disability living allowance is paid to the organisation and a car can be hired or bought on hire purchase. There is also the well-known Orange Badge scheme which allows disabled people greater freedom in parking.

14.9 Access

The 1970 Chronically Sick and Disabled Persons Act included clauses concerned with making the community more accessible to people with a disability. The Act refers to buildings of public use and states that where new buildings are planned or old ones adapted, the building should be made accessible to disabled people. However, the Act allows that this should be done where it is reasonable or practical to do so. Words like 'practicable' and 'reasonable' weaken legislation and allow for the spirit of law to be ignored. Progress in opening up the community has been slow and there are many instances of ramps which lead into areas from which there is no exit and of special toilets which cannot be reached.

A further development came in 1981. The 1981 Disabled Persons Act gave planning authorities the duty of drawing people's attention to provisions relating to access. This must be done when planning permission is granted. These provision were later extended in 1985. Certain new buildings must now provide access and facilities for disabled people. These include offices, shops, single-storey factories, educational buildings and others which admit the public. Local authorities have begun to employ *Access Officers* to oversee these regulations.

The Disability Discrimination Act of 1995, discussed above, included access to bus and rail stations as part of its requirement that providers of goods and services do not discriminate against disabled people. This however only requires providers to make facilities accessible if it is reasonable to do so. The Act also empowered the Transport Minister to set minimum access requirements for new buses, taxis, trams and trains. The Act disappointed many in stopping short of making accessible transport a right and in excluding planes and ferries. Disabled people are angered by the long wait until 2020 before buses and coaches have to be made wheelchair accessible.

At present many problems remain. Disabled people sometimes have to stay on trains beyond their station, then take another train back, because they cannot get across to the other side of the tracks. The layout of many trains make it impossible for people in wheelchairs to use the toilets. Things have improved in some areas where local authorities have given grants for the introduction of low-floor buses. In Newcastle-upon-Tyne a pilot scheme using low-floor buses led to a 14 per cent rise in journeys. Parents with buggies were the biggest group of new users, showing that improvements in access for disabled people benefit the whole community. A survey by Scope highlighted the sense of exclusion felt by disabled people, particularly those without cars. One respondent commented: 'I find it difficult to get about – I tend to stay at home most of the time,' while another added: 'My dream is to be able to get on a train or a bus ... without having to make any special arrangements beforehand.'[19]

14.10 Residential accommodation

Residential homes for disabled people are provided by social services, voluntary organisations and by profit-making organisations. This form of provision shares the problems of institutions already described in other contexts (see Chapters 9, 12 and 13). As has been discussed in relation to elderly people (Chapter 13), the funding of long-term care is very muddled. NHS provision is free, while local-authority provision is means-tested. A legal case was brought to court by Pamela Coughlan, paralysed from the neck down after being hit by a car. Whilst taking a law degree, she brought an action against her health authority which, having promised her a home for life, threatened to close the rehabilitation centre in which she lived. The court of appeal upheld the high court ruling that the health authority had abused their power. Trying to sort out the issue of funding, the high court ruled that nursing care was health care and therefore the responsibility of the NHS. This would make it free to all. This could have cost the NHS around £220 million. The appeal court over-ruled this interpretation and said that local authorities could provide nursing services, but only those which formed part of the package of care expected to be provided by a local council. This would not be the sort of round-the-clock care needed by severely disabled people. The distinction between social care and nursing care remains unclear and creates inequalities between people with long-term care needs.

Activity 14.4

Make sure that you understand the following expressions used in this chapter. Check in the Glossary at the end of the book if you need to.

care manager	mainstream education
care plan	multiple sclerosis
cerebral palsy	non-contributary benefit
contributary benefit	quota system
cycle of expectation	rehabilitation
hereditary	sheltered employment
invalidity benefit	'statementing'

Further reading

There are many excellent books on disability. You could start with *Disabled People and Social Policy* by Michael Oliver and Colin Barnes (London: Longman, 1998).

Up-to-date information on all aspects of rights of disabled people can be found in the *Disability Rights Handbook*. This is updated each year and produced by the Disability Alliance ERA (see below).

Useful addresses

Disability Alliance ERA
Universal House
88–94 Wentworth Street
London E1 7SA
tel. 0207 247 8776

Royal Association for Disability and Rehabilitation (RADAR)
12 City Forum
City Road
London EC1V 8AD
tel. 0207 250 3222

Motability
Goodman House
Station Approach
Harlow
Essex CM20 2ET
tel. 01279 635666

The Family Fund Trust
PO Box 50
York YO1 1UY
tel. 01904 621115

John Grooms
50 Scrutton Street
London EC2A 4XZ
tel. 0207 422 2000

Websites

There are several excellent websites on disability.

www.disabilitynet.co.uk provides an Internet-based disability information and news service

Disability Now at **www.disabilitynow.org.uk** provide links to a range of other websites. An excellent starting point.

▼ 15 Health and the health services

15.1 Health, society and the environment

In this society, there is a tendency to see health as very much an individual issue. This leads to an emphasis on the biological causes of ill-health together with the recent stress on personal factors such as smoking and weight. Improvements in health are seen as resulting from intervention by doctors at the level of the individual, or changes in personal life-style. This chapter looks at health and health care from a different point of view, focusing on social, political, economic and environmental aspects of health. It will become apparent that health is not a purely personal matter, but an area of considerable national and social concern.

There are various ways in which the significance of this perspective on health can be illustrated. The meaning people give to the term 'good health' varies over time and from one society to another. One way of defining health was offered by the World Health Organisation in 1965. This definition sees health as a 'state of complete physical, mental and social wellbeing'. It is probably more common, however, for health to be seen as the absence of disease, although the definition of disease also varies.

Whilst the biological causes of ill-health are obviously important in combating disease, many health problems are social, economic or environmental in origin.

Activity 15.1

> What environmental factors affecting health can you think of? List them, and ways in which they can be overcome.

There are many ways in which health can be related to social factors. Working environments can cause health problems through industrial injuries and industrial diseases like asbestosis. Work can also be a cause of stress-related illnesses, as can unemployment. In addition, environmental factors such as pollution, transport and dangerous or damp housing are also important in relation to health. The analysis, later in this chapter, of the link between social class and health illustrates the significance of social and economic factors in any discussion of health.

Whilst individuals can improve their own health to a certain extent, national policies and programmes can achieve more significant results. For example, life expectancy at birth is now 74 years for boys and 79 years for girls, compared with 48 and 52 years respectively for those born around the turn of the century.[1]

Admittedly, it is difficult to isolate particular policies or factors which increase life expectancy, but variations between countries and over time indicate the importance of factors greater than the individual.

Health also has economic implications. The economics of health and health care are immediately obvious to people who live in countries where there is no public provision of health services. In Britain, the economic aspects are perhaps less apparent, but planners and policy-makers in the health service are very conscious that health is a commodity which has to be bought, and about which choices are made as to the allocation of limited resources. There are points at which a price is put on life itself, for example in deciding whether or not to offer a heart transplant operation to a dying patient. Other economic aspects of health can be seen in lost production through ill-health, or the costs to society of supporting people who cannot work because of disablement or sickness.

Health and health-care provision are both very much political issues. This can be seen in the way the two main political parties have differed in their policies and priorities for health. At the simplest level, the Conservatives have been more concerned to control public expenditure and to encourage private initiatives in health care. The Labour Party demonstrates a greater commitment to the original principles of the National Health Service (NHS), seeking to abolish charges and to increase funding. There has been however some blurring of these distinctions since the 1990s, with a shift in overall Labour Party philosophy and a re-emphasis of Conservative commitment to the NHS – the most popular part of Britain's welfare state.

15.2 The aims and organisation of the NHS

In Britain, most aspects of health care come within the scope of the NHS, and therefore this chapter is primarily concerned with the development, future and aims of this service. The NHS has been in existence for over fifty years, since its beginning on 5 July 1948.

Activity 15.2

Consult older relatives, neighbours and friends to find out about life in the period before the NHS was established. Report your findings to the class.

Before the NHS

There were some state-provided services prior to 1948. For example, public health, in the form of water and sewage systems, was provided under the 1848 Public Health Act. Services for pregnant women and young children were introduced at the beginning of this century. From 1911, employment-linked insurance provided cover for doctors' services for people in work. Local authorities ran Poor Law infirmaries, public hospitals and mental hospitals. Hospitals were also provided by voluntary organisations.

However, there was great variation in the standards of care provided by these services, and considerable stigma attached to much of the provision. The insurance system only covered the person in employment and did not extend to the families of workers. The following quotations based on accounts of people living in Sheffield give some indication of the quality of life in the period before 1948:

[In] Attercliffe in Sheffield's East End which housed the heavy industry of the Don Valley and the workforce which operated it – bronchitis was a way of life. People expected to live with it, suffer from it and eventually die from it, with only their weekly bottle of medicine for relief.[2]

Two women described their memories as follows:

Bills from general practitioners were always hard to meet ... Kay remembered especially a doctor in the Crookesmoor district of Sheffield who employed a debt collector ... The effects were particularly severe for working-class women, who due to a policy of not employing married women in Sheffield always tended to fall outside the insurance scheme. 'Mother never had the doctor.' 'You just didn't go to the doctor until you were on your last legs.' Kay recalled how her own mother hadn't gone to the doctor even though she was in bed with asthma. And Jessie likewise how her mother continued to suffer with high blood pressure, even though she knew that tablets were available which could have helped to lessen her condition.[3]

Looking at health from the other side, the extracts below are from a doctor who worked as a GP before the beginning of the National Health Service.[4]
Dr Arnold Elliot remembers:

I ran my practice from a small house in Ilford, but most surgeries were lock-up shops in industrial areas. On the whole, most of them were awful, with no running water, heat, lighting or toilets, some with no couches.

I knew one East End doctor who had a cigarette machine in his waiting room. Many doctors had two doors; one for 'panel' patients (the insured workers) and one for private patients, who weren't kept waiting.

Doctors didn't speak to each other, because they were deadly enemies. They went in for head-hunting the breadwinning panel patient, who would often bring in the rest of his family.

Various private arrangements were set up for his dependants – so-called 'clubs' – where they paid a small amount a week for a doctor and medicine. For the destitute, there were dispensaries, which engaged the services of a doctor for a small annual payment ... Doctors used to dispense their own medicines too. The pharmaceutical firms came round and filled up the big 'Winchester' bottles every week. Many of the medicines were placebos; aspirin, for instance, which was available in a red or yellow mixture. You had to give the same colour to a patient every week, and sometimes there'd be trouble when you had a locum in and he gave out the wrong one. It sounds immoral, but that was trade.

From another perspective, Sir George Godber was involved in setting up the National Health Service. In 1942, before the NHS, he surveyed hospitals in Britain. He tells what his survey found:[5]

You must remember hospitals in those days were very different from today. An isolation hospital might only have five beds. There was a hospital for scarlet fever in the Prime Minister's [Margaret Thatcher's] home town of Grantham that was housed in a wooden hut on the top of a hill without sewers or water – the water was delivered by cart once a week. The system in 1942 was incapable of delivering modern medicine. There were dilapidated buildings, insanitary conditions on the wards, inadequate space for radiology and laboratory services.

There were casual wards where tramps stayed overnight and even more depressing house wards where elderly residential patients waited to die in the most uncivilised conditions – the nights spent in narrow and dark dormitories of 20 to 30 beds and the daytime sitting on hard benches in a different room looking at their feet.

The start of the NHS

The National Health Service Act was passed in 1946, for implementation in 1948. Aneurin Bevan is seen as the individual politician responsible for designing the health service, but it is important to understand that the system was not created by Bevan alone, but formulated as a result of bargaining and compromise between the government and various interest groups. Doctors were, and are, a powerful and well-organised group and were able to get what they wanted to a considerable extent. The doctors won a number of concessions, which continue to influence the running and development of the NHS. For example, doctors are not salaried workers in the health service, but retain an independent status, contracting to provide services. Also, the option of private practice was included in the service, and access allowed to pay-beds within NHS hospitals. Further, doctors won for themselves a major role in the administration of the NHS.

The idea behind the NHS was that it should bring together all aspects of health care in one organisation in an attempt to achieve certain aims. The most important principle was that health care should be available to all, irrespective of ability to pay. National planning of resources was intended to reduce overlaps in services and ensure that there were no gaps in provision.

The organisation of the NNS

The government department responsible for the health service is the Department of Health (the Department of Health and Social Security until 1988, and originally the Ministry of Health). The NHS is a massive and highly complex service. It is not surprising that planning, managing and organising such an unwieldy service has been a continuing issue. The sections below describe the various changes in administration which have taken place.

In the beginning

Originally, the administrative structure for the NHS consisted of three parts. First, GPs, dentists, pharmacists and opticians were administered by executive Councils, appointed by local professionals, local authorities and the Ministry of Health. Second, personal and environmental services, including maternity and child welfare clinics, health visitors, midwives, health education, vaccination programmes and ambulances, were controlled by the local authorities. The third part of the administrative structure was concerned with hospitals. Regional Health Boards were appointed by the Ministry of Health. The Boards in turn appointed Hospital Management Committees. The prestigious teaching hospitals had a separate status and were managed by Boards of Governors.

1974 and 1982 changes

In 1973 a new National Health Service Act was passed to come into force on 1 April 1974. This aimed to reorganise and unify the NHS, to increase co-ordination between health services and related local authority services, and to improve the management of the service. The first aim was only successful to a limited extent, since GPs continued to remain outside the main structure. As a step towards achieving the second objective mentioned, the area boundaries for the health service were made the same as the new local authority boundaries which were also implemented on 1 April 1974. With regard to improving management, management experts were consulted, although the system was later criticised for relying on an over-theoretical approach to management.

The new structure consisted of three tiers organised in a hierarchy. First, *Regional Health Authorities* (RHAs), appointed by the Secretary of State for Health, were responsible for the planning of services and resources. The next tier was the *Area Health Authorities* (AHAs), appointed partly by the RHAs, partly by the local authorities and partly by non-medical and nursing staff. AHAs were responsible for planning and management, and were expected to work with local authorities to improve co-ordination of services. Alongside AHAs in the hierarchy, *Family Practitioner Committees* (FPCs), appointed by the AHAs, local professionals and local authorities, were to administer GPs, dentists, pharmacists and opticians. Most areas were then split into districts, and the third tier was the *District Management Teams* (DMTs).

At the district level, *Community Health Councils* (CHCs) were set up and given the task of representing the views of consumers. CHCs each consist of about 30 members, appointed by local government and chosen by voluntary organisations. The role of the CHCs includes obtaining information and visiting local health facilities. They are also consulted by the district authorities before major decisions are made. While performing an important role, CHCs have been criticised for their inability to represent public opinion adequately or to exercise any real power in the system.

Almost as soon as the new organisation began to work, it was subjected to criticism. It was said that the structure contained too many tiers and administrators, and led to unnecessary delays. It was also argued that the organisation was undemocratic, allowing too much power to professionals (a continuing problem within the NHS). The attempt at establishing a unified structure was said to have failed. After these attacks, a second new system came into being on 1 April 1982. This consisted of Regional Health Authorities and District Health Authorities, the middle tier having been abolished. CHCs continued to operate at the district level of management. Family Health Service Authorities (previously Family Practitioner Committees) were further separated from the main administrative structure, becoming employing authorities in their own right, responsible directly to the Department of Health.

Activity 15.3

Contact your local Community Health Council. Find out how this organisation works and what its tasks are.

Activity 15.4

Construct diagrams to show the three earlier management structures of the NHS. You may like to consult Christopher Ham's book, listed in the 'Further reading' section at the end of this chapter.

1991 changes – 'internal markets'

Major changes in the working and philosophy of the health service were implemented in April 1991, as a result of the 1990 NHS and Community Care Act. The key aspects of the Act were the creation of *independent trusts* – hospitals and other units which opted out of the control of the District Health Authority – and the possibility for doctors to hold their own budgets for spending on hospital and other services. The main theme of the reforms was that there should be a separation between the *purchasers* and the *providers* of health care. The health authorities and fund-holding doctors became purchasers from the hospitals and other units (the providers). Another way of talking about this is to use the term 'internal market'. This refers to the fact that the purchasers have a choice as to which provider to use and will therefore choose the hospital or other provider unit which offers the best value for money (as in a marketplace). Purchasers can purchase health care from private hospitals or voluntary groups if they wish to.

By the end of the eight-year period in which the internal market in the NHS was operating, all hospitals became trusts and 57 per cent of the population had a fund-holding doctor. Few members of the public however understood the idea of the internal market and most people did not know whether their doctor was fund-holding or not.

Debate over the internal market

It was believed that the internal market would increase efficiency and be more responsive to patient needs. Financial incentives and penalities would mean more efficient development would be encouraged and flourish while less sucess-ful practices would stop. Patients' views would be paid greater attention and there would be more auditing and assessment of the effectiveness of provision and procedures.

An important argument against the introduction of markets into health care is that decisions about health care are too important to include concerns about budgets. In reality, there has always been some element of thought to cost some-where along the line in health-care decisions, but the 1990 reforms made costs more of a central issue. Anxieties were also voiced that standards in hospitals would fall as hospitals tried to cut costs to make themselves more competitive to win contracts from the health authorities and doctors. GPs with an eye to their budgets could be reluctant to take on elderly or chronically sick patients, who might be anticipated to be a greater drain on funds. Overall planning of health-care services is difficult to achieve where hospitals and other units make inde-pendent decisions for financial reasons rather than in the interests of the health needs of the whole population. Competition can also lead to pointless duplica-tion of services, instead of more fruitful co-operation in meeting local, regional and national needs. The internal market also increased variations and inequali-ties across the country and between patients as different purchasers defined need in different ways.

Activity 15.5

Make a table in which you list arguments for and against the idea of an internal market in health care.

Labour reforms

Six months after its landslide election victory, the new Labour government pub-lished a White Paper outlining a ten-year plan for reforms to the NHS. The White Paper proposed to abolish the internal market, considering that its business ethos did not fit with the goals of state-run health care. The separation between planning and provision continues but without the need to compete.

Hospitals remain as Trusts but are encouraged to work in partnership with other health organisations. In 1999 the Labour government abolished fund-holding for GPs, returning the purchase of health care to the health authorities. In England, this power will be gradually devolved to new primary care groups (PCGs). Each PCG covers an area of about 100,000 people, initially acting as an advisory body to the health authority, then becoming a trust, commissioning and providing community-based health care and taking over the budget from the health authority. The members of the PCGs are mainly doctors, with com-munity nurses and a representative from social services. Similar groups will be set up in Wales, where they are known as 'local health groups', and in Scotland, as 'local health care co-operatives'.

1999 saw the introduction of *Health Improvement Programmes*. The lead role in drawing these up goes to the health authority, in consultation with local NHS Trusts and Primary Care Groups. Local authorities, voluntary organisations and

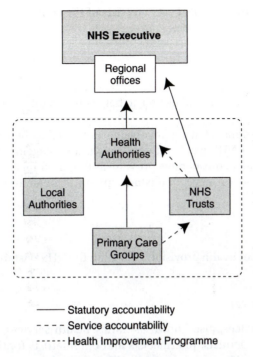

Statutory accountability
---- Service accountability
------ Health Improvement Programme

Figure 15.1   The present structure of the NHS

educational and research institutions share in the process of identifying needs and targets for improvements.

Eleven *health action zones* were set up in 1998 and a further 15 in 1999 in more deprived areas of the country. They aim to break down barriers between the NHS, social services and other agencies and set targets to improve health and reduce inequalities in health.

A summary of the present structure of the NHS

(see Figure 15.1)

The person who is ultimately responsible for the health service in Parliament is the Secretary of State for Health in the Department of Health. In Scotland, Wales and Northern Ireland there are separate Secretaries of State. Within the Department of Health, the NHS Executive with its eight regional offices, is responsible for developing and implementing policies for the provision of health services.

There are 100 health authorities in England, 5 in Wales and 15 health boards in Scotland. The health authorities are responsible for identifying the health-care needs of people living in the area. They secure hospital and community health services and arrange for the provision of services by doctors, dentists, pharmacists and opticians. The trusts – hospitals or other services which have opted out of health authority control – are responsible directly to the NHS Executive.

Community Health Councils cover all parts of the country and represent local opinion on health-care services.

Activity 15.6

Create a map to show the local organisation of services in your area. Your Health Authority should be able to help you with information.

In all organisations, changes involve costs as well as benefits. The pace of change within the NHS has been very fast, and management and other staff have been put under considerable pressure as they attempt to keep up with new developments and to meet a constant stream of objectives set by national governments.

Activity 15.7

What areas of health provision fall within the NHS? List them.

Primary health care

Primary care services, also known as family health services, include general practice doctors, dentists, pharmacists and optometrists (opticians). All these practitioners are self-employed people, independently contracted to the health service, receiving fees and allowances for their work. Working alongside them are community health staff who are employed by the health service.

The role of the GP

The first point of contact with the health service for most people is the local general practitioner or GP, who is the main person responsible for primary health care. Everyone has the right to register with a GP and health care is free. The role of the GP has changed since 1948, with group practices becoming more common and a move towards the concept of a *primary health care team*, including health visitors, nurses and sometimes social workers. There has also been a trend towards health centres, bringing together a variety of services. In rural areas, GPs may have permission to dispense drugs. As practices have become larger and more complex, practice managers have commonly been employed to run the practice.

Between 1990 and 1997, more than half of GPs became fund-holders as a result of the 1990 NHS and Community Care Act. Fund-holding GPs were allocated a budget with which to buy services for their patients. These services included hospital treatments, drugs, mental health counselling and chiropody. As a result of a change of government, fund-holding was abolished in 1999.

Problems with primary health care arise from the shortage of good GPs and the tendency for some areas of the country to have a better ratio of doctors to patients than others. The lack of GPs is related to the higher status and better pay prospects given to doctors working in hospitals. As with all aspects of health

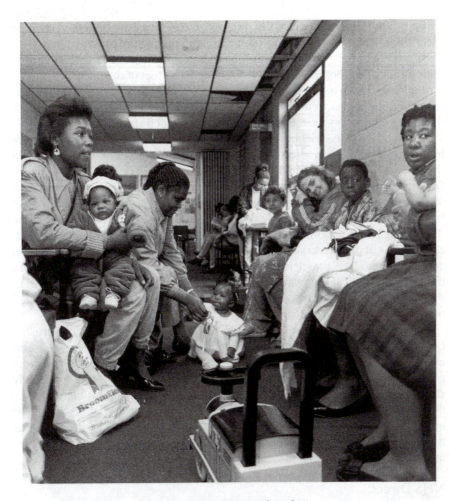

Source: Crispin Hughes, Photofusion
Long waits to see the doctor at some health centres

(see sections on inequalities) there are inequalities in GP provision. The areas in the country with the greatest health needs have the lowest proportions of GPs. Areas like East Anglia, which have the best health, have the highest numbers of GPs per head of the population. The overall tendency for this to happen is known as the 'inverse care law'.

Pharmacists, dentists and optometrists

Pharmacists receive fees for dispensing prescription drugs. More and more pharmacies are part of chains and the opening of pharmacies in supermarkets has further threatened small independently owned pharmacies. Prescriptions are free to people on a low income or receiving means-tested benefits, under 16 (19 if in full-time education), aged 60 or over, or those who suffer from certain chronic conditions. Others with long-term illnesses can buy pre-payment certificates. In 1997–98, it was estimated that 85 per cent of prescriptions items were supplied free.[6] People who are not exempt pay a set fee for each item in their prescription. Sometimes this is more than the cost of the drug, but often it is much less. There has been a problem with people claiming free prescriptions who are not entitled to do so, and this is to be made a criminal offence, with computer technology used to make it easier to detect fraud.

New contracts were negotiated with dentists in 1990, followed by a dispute between the profession and the government over the level of fees. As a result there has been a reduction in the number of adults accepted for NHS treatments. Only three-quarters of patients are now treated under the NHS, compared with 90 per cent in 1990. Although only 3 per cent of dentists do not give any NHS treatment, in some areas of the country access to an NHS dentist has become difficult. In 1997 a scheme called Investing in Dentistry aimed to improve dental care in areas of poor access by offering grants to dentists in return for a long-term commitment to NHS practice. Free treatment is available for people under 18 (18 if in full-time education), women who are pregnant or who have given birth in the last 12 months, and people on a low income or claiming means-tested benefits. Others pay 80 per cent of the cost of the treatment.

Optometrists have the weakest link with the NHS. Since the 1980s, advertising has been allowed and glasses can be bought 'over the counter'. 1989 saw the end of free eye tests, except for people on low incomes, under 16 (19 if in full-time education) or over 60, with diabetes or glaucoma, registered blind or partially sighted. Optometrists opposed the ending of the free eye test as problems can be diagnosed and treated. Evidence suggests that more better-off people have their eyes tested. Some people are entitled to a voucher which can be used towards the cost of glasses or contact lenses. Since 1999, free tests have been re-introduced for people over 60.

NHS Direct

NHS Direct began in March 1998 when three pilot 24-hour telephone advice services, staffed by nurses, were set up. The scheme covered the whole country by 2000. In 1999 a pilot scheme established twenty walk-in centres attached to existing NHS premises, open between 7 a.m. and 10 p.m. and offering advice, information and treatment for minor conditions.

Hospitals

In terms of financial resources, hospitals are a very important part of the NHS, taking up about two-thirds of all expenditure. It is possible that hospitals play too important a role in the NHS, and that the overall balance of the health service could be improved by a shift of resources to community-based services. One of the reasons why hospitals take up so much of the money available to the NHS is that they quickly become out-of-date, as well as having high costs for maintenance and staffing. When the NHS was set up, it was intended that new hospitals should be built, to replace obsolete and run-down buildings and to ensure that provision was available in all areas of the country.

In the first decade of the NHS, little hospital building was done and in 1962 the Hospital Building Plan was published. The plan recommended that for every 100,000–200,000 of the population, there should be a district general hospital with 600–800 beds. The hospitals would be located near the centre of the population to be served and would provide beds for all types of patients except those suffering from rare diseases. The idea of district general hospitals was approved, although there were problems of finance, or finding land at the centres of populated areas, and some local opposition to the closure of specialised hospitals, especially the small cottage hospitals. A considerable amount of hospital building was completed in the period following the publication of the plan.

Hospitals were originally run by local health authorities. Under the NHS and Community Care Act, implemented in 1991, hospitals could opt out of the control of the health authority and become Trusts. The first Trusts came into operation in 1992 and by 1995 all hospitals were Trusts. The idea was that NHS Trusts would compete to receive funds for treating patients, although since 1997 partnership between health organisations has been encouraged. NHS Trusts are self-governing organisations run by a board of directors. They have considerable freedom in planning and using resources – they make their own decisions about buying and selling land and about employment of staff. Outside the NHS there are also private hospitals, some of which are run by organisations for private health care such as BUPA. People can pay as individuals or through health insurance. Health Authorities can also decide to buy services from private hospitals.

Other changes affecting hospitals in the 1990s have been the policy of community care (discussed in Chapter 9) which has led to the closure of many facilities providing care for long-term conditions, and a new system of management of hospital staff and services.

The major issue for hospitals over the past decade has been that of waiting-lists. Despite a limit of 28 weeks set by the Patients' Charter, introduced in 1992, waiting-lists have continued to increase in some areas. In 1998, out-patient statistics showed that 126,000 people had been waiting more than 28 weeks for a first appointment with a specialist. Publicity was also given to acutely ill patients who wait more than 24 hours in corridors and on trolleys for a bed to be found for them. A snapshot survey of casualty departments in 1999 found an improvement on the previous year but an unacceptable situation. The worst cases identified included the following:

- Birmingham City Hospital: An 84-year-old man with diarrhoea and vomiting, waited 28 hours 43 minutes for a side room.
- Kent and Sussex Hospital: A 33-year-old woman with abdominal pain waited 23 hours 30 minutes for a bed.[7]

Waiting-lists have become a highly political issue. Attempts to pressure hospitals to reduce lists can result in stretched resources being moved around to reduce lists in one area of care and creating problems in other areas. Political pressure can also result in administrative attempts to disguise situations and make apparent improvements for statistical purposes, without making any real changes.

Hospitals have also experienced problems with staffing. A national shortage of nurses has led to various schemes to import nurses from other countries, use agency nurses to fill gaps and to demands for increased pay and improved conditions to attract and keep nursing staff in NHS hospitals. Another staffing issue has been the long hours worked by junior hospital doctors. In 1999 the European Union working time directive set a limit of 48 hours, which the British government had seven years to meet.

Community health services

Other important areas of NHS work come under the heading of the 'community health service'. These areas include district nursing, health education, health visiting, screening and vaccinations, ante-natal and child health clinics, family planning and school health services. Local authorities can also provide home services such as sickroom equipment, help with laundry and home nursing. The planning of these services is the responsibility of the community physician. Since 1990, community health services are incorporated into NHS Trusts.

Activity 15.8

In pairs, choose one aspect of community health and find out, either by writing to visiting local clinics or organisations, or by using the library, the work done by the service. Report your findings to the whole class.

15.3   Policy issues

Resourcing the health service

Many of the issues concerning health and the NHS are related to problems of finance. There is a tendency for both the public and governments to support the NHS, but to be reluctant to want to provide sufficient resources. When the NHS was established in 1948, it was believed that there would be an initial backlog of demand for services, which would then eventually stabilise and possibly even decrease. This assumption has turned out to be false and demand has continually increased. In the first year, the cost was £433 million; by 1996–97 total spending was £34,727 million.[8] There are a number of different reasons for this escalation in cost. First, rather than health-care demands decreasing as services are made available there is a tendency for expectations of health and health care to rise as needs are met. Also scientific and medical innovations have introduced new and often expensive possibilities for treatment. Finally, the increase in the numbers of elderly people, discussed in Chapter 13, has meant increased demands on health services.

Most of the money for the NHS comes from general taxation, with a smaller amount from national insurance contributions. A very small proportion comes from charges – 2 per cent only in 1995–96.[9] In 1992, the Private Finance Initiative (PFI) was launched to promote partnership between private and public sectors. In the health service it involves the use of private finance in NHS building schemes. This was extended in 1997 and a new hospital building plan announced, under which 25 hospital schemes in England and 11 in Scotland began. The hospitals are built and owned by the private sector and then leased back to the NHS.

In 1988, an all-party Commons Committee published a report on resourcing the health service.[10] The report suggested that resources had suffered a shortfall over the past few years totalling £1896 million. The report expressed concern about the ability of hospitals and other services to maintain levels of care. The MPs made the following recommendations:[11]

- An immediate £95 million to make up the shortfall in funding of pay and price inflation in the current financial year.
- An additional sum of at least £1 billion over 2 years to pay for specific developments, including information technology, building maintenance, and replacing essential equipment and community care.[12]
- A commitment to fund the coming pay awards in full, enabling health authorities to plan their budgets rather than make cuts in anticipation of underfunding.
- A guarantee to fund a 2 per cent rise in services in 1988/89.
- Urgent development of systems to measure the performance and effectiveness of the health service.

There are many examples reported of the effects of under-funding and cuts on health services. The following three examples illustrate the nature of the problems:

- In Reading, local doctors paid for a full-page advertisement in the local evening newspaper warning that 3000 operations would be cancelled as a result of a deficit in funds in their area.
- In Doncaster, 1000 non-urgent hospital admissions would be cut and 69 beds closed.
- In Mexborough, two new wards and operating theatres would not be opened.

The issues discussed next are the role of charges in the NHS and of private insurance, the NHS drugs bill, the allocation of resources to different client groups, and finally inequalities in health between regions and social classes. All these issues can be related to finance, although the last section examines social factors, some of which are wider than the scope of the NHS.

Charges

The original idea of the National Health Service was that services should be free to people at the time of use and financed wholly through taxation and national insurance contributions. However, it was not long before this principle was eroded and charges were introduced. Bevan resigned from the government in 1951 when the Labour Party proposed to introduce charges for glasses, drugs and dental care. Bevan believed that this threatened the most basic principle of the NHS and would be the beginning of an irreversible trend. The policy of charging for particular services was extended by later governments, although a system of exemptions was introduced in 1968.

The current situation is that charges are made for prescriptions and for services provided by dentists and opticians. In 1999, prescriptions cost £5.90 per item, with exemptions available for children under 16, older people, expectant mothers, people suffering from certain illnesses such as epilepsy where continuous treatment is required, and people on a low income or in receipt of family credit, income support or income-based Jobseeker's Allowance. There is also a system whereby people can obtain a pre-payment certificate for prescriptions. In 1999, these cost £30.80 for four months or £84.60 a year. Dental treatment is no longer free and the system introduced in 1981 means that people pay up to a maximum figure for a course of treatment. Free dental treatment is available for people under 18, or 19 if they are in full-time education, expectant mothers, and mothers with children under one year of age. As with prescription charges, those receiving Family Credit, Income Support or on a low income also receive free dental treatment. Eye tests are similarly free to those groups mentioned above, with the exception of women who are pregnant or who have small babies. Free eye tests have been extended to people over 60. People entitled to free eye tests may also receive vouchers towards the cost of glasses.

Visits to GPs continue to be free for everyone, although there has been discussion about the feasibility of a £10 charge, with exemptions for less well-off people.

Activity 15.9

Should there be a charge for health services? List reasons for and against.

There are two sets of arguments to look at here. The first concern the role of charges as a contribution to NHS costs. The second debate is bigger, looking at the pros and cons of a system like that in the USA, where there is no national health service. We will look at charges within the NHS first. The first basis on which to argue against charges in the NHS is that charging for services goes against the basic idea that money should not be a barrier to access to health care. The NHS, despite its limitations, has achieved a great deal in improving the health of the nation and was introduced partly as a result of hard campaigning by people in the 1930s and 1940s. The introduction of charges can be seen as a betrayal of the principles of the NHS and the efforts made to achieve a free and comprehensive service. Health is too important for money to be a barrier to seeking help. Illness creates enough anxiety without the additional worry of the costs. The high standards within the NHS are a result of its nature as a universal service, free for all. Where some people are charged for services, this nearly always results in a two-tier system, as people who pay feel they should receive superior services.

However it can be argued that charging those who are able to afford to pay means more money for health care and therefore a benefit to those less well-off. Also, when the NHS was first introduced, it seemed that the rush for glasses was created by people who thought they should have something just because it was free. Maybe people would think about their need for health care differently if they had to pay a contribution.

Looking at the bigger issue of a wholly private system of health care, the full costs of many types of treatment and care are simply too expensive for the vast majority of people to be able to afford. Costs are also highly unpredictable and a visit to a doctor may result in treatment costing a few pounds or several thousand pounds. Charging involves administrative costs, so some of the financial saving to the country is lost. Few patients are knowledgeable about medical matters, and this means that unscrupulous doctors are in a position to recommend expensive or unnecessary treatment in order to increase their profits. The following story from the USA illustrates the danger in this situation.

> The *New York Times*, in an article on medical costs, recently told of an elderly woman with a temperature and bronchitis, who could have been treated in a surgery with antibiotics. Instead she was admitted to hospital for nine days and ended up with a bill for $9065.[13]

Other problems in charging for health care concern the fact that an important part of NHS work is preventative care for which few people would be prepared to pay. A full system of charges is not feasible, since there will always be people, often those most in need of services, who are unable to pay. Examples of groups of such people are elderly people, people with chronic illnesses and disabled people.

Private medical insurance

There has been a recent expansion in the number of people subscribing to private insurance schemes. This expansion was supported and encouraged by the Conservative Party. There are currently three main private companies operating in the UK. These are the British United Provident Association (BUPA), the Private Patients Plan (PPP) and the Western Provident Association. The way the schemes work is that people subscribe, paying a premium, and receive money for treatment when they need it. There are, however, several restrictions – for example, BUPA will not accept new subscribers over the age of 65, payments are made up to a maximum figure and are only for certain types of health care.

Activity 15.10

> Contact a private medical insurance company and find out the details of their schemes. If possible, compare your findings with those of someone else in the class who has contacted a different firm.

By 1991 about 7.5 million people had private medical insurance.[14] The rise in numbers subscribing was particularly great at the end of the 1970s and at the end of the 1980s. The early 1990s saw a fall in subscribers, with the number down to six million in 1997.[15] Most people with private insurance join through group schemes, often provided by companies for employees as a fringe benefit.

There has also been an expansion in the numbers of beds available in private hospitals throughout the country. In 1971 there were 25,300 beds in private nursing homes, hospitals and clinics. In 1991–92 the number had grown to 147,200. The same period saw a drop in the number of private beds in NHS hospitals.[16]

Source: Vicky White, Photofusion
Some people choose to pay privately for health care

Activity 15.11

What are the advantages, and the disadvantages, to individuals, and to the whole society, of private medical insurance?

A major problem with private insurance companies is that, as profit-making organisations, they are reluctant to accept high-risk subscribers. Also, they do not provide a comprehensive service, but concentrate on acute illnesses which can be cured by a short stay in hospital and routine surgery. They do not cover pregnancy and childbirth, and normally limit cover to a certain number of days in any one year.

In common with other forms of private health care, insurance schemes distort the priorities of NHS, shifting the emphasis from need to the ability to pay. Insurance companies exploit inadequacies in the health service, as is shown in the following passage from BUPA publicity:

> Depending where in the country you live, you can wait months for treatment under the NHS for a condition not classified as urgent. Additionally, while waiting, you may be in considerable pain or discomfort. The assurance that treatment may be received without delay is attracting more and more people to the private sector.[17]

In providing the option of private treatment for those who can pay, private insurance has the effect of reducing pressure on the government to solve problems of waiting-lists. In the past it was common for NHS hospitals to have a number of pay-beds designated for patients paying privately. Although a few still exist, recent years have seen a decrease in pay-beds as private patients are increasingly treated in private hospitals. The existence of pay-beds in the NHS hospitals encourages queue-jumping and again leads to prioritisation on the basis of ability to pay instead of need.

Private patients are subsidised by the state in a variety of ways. Doctors, nurses and other trained staff who work privately have been trained at the expense of the state. The private sector does not contribute to post-operative health and social services home care. Private hospitals tend not to have very expensive equipment and instead use NHS facilities. Finally, private medical insurance is subsidised by the state through the tax relief given to employers providing insurance for their staff.

As was mentioned earlier, high-risk groups and those suffering from chronic illnesses are excluded from private insurance cover. With or without insurance schemes it would be impossible for all health care to be provided privately. Even in the USA, a country committed to private enterprise, a large public health sector exists to cater for the less fortunate and the elderly. Private health leads to a dual system of health care. People who pay expect to receive a better service, so dual standards develop. Means-testing leads to stigma in the public sector. The encouragement of the private sector in Britain could result in a system in which the principle of allowing everyone equal access to the best possible treatment and care is lost.

There is no evidence to support the idea that private hospitals can be run more effectively or cheaply than NHS hospitals. In the USA, the lack of central control together with the close relationship which exists between the insurance companies and the medical profession lead to high charges for health and large profits for both parties. The administration of private treatment involves complex and costly procedures. In the USA, 'admittance to hospital for a minor disorder involves an orgy of form-filling and medical insurance checking which makes filling in a car accident claim look simple.'[18]

The benefits argued to result from private insurance are a reduction in NHS expenditure and therefore in taxation. Individuals who can pay are said to benefit from greater freedom of choice and the option of paying for extra services, such as individual rooms in a hospital.

In conclusion to this section, it would seem that there are advantages to some individuals in allowing a private sector to co-exist with the NHS. However, the existence of such provision constitutes a serious threat to the future of the service set up to guarantee access to high-quality medical care regardless of ability to pay.

The NHS drugs bill

Whilst the NHS is a state-run and state-financed organisation, it relies on profit-making companies for drugs, equipment and some services. The multi-national companies which manufacture drugs count amongst the most profitable enterprises in the world. Drugs prescribed by GPs cost £3.6 billion in England and Wales in 1992–93. This is 10 per cent of the NHS budget.[19]

There are several explanations for the high profits of the drug companies. Patent laws are exploited by the large companies to control markets and prices. Several different names are given to the same drug to create 'brand loyalty', resulting in confusion amongst doctors and patients and an appearance of competition where there is none.

The drug companies spend enormous sums of money on promotion of their products. New drugs are particularly widely advertised, which has the effect of increasing their cost to the NHS. This promotion is aimed at doctors and takes a variety of forms:

> The general practitioner in Great Britain receives in an average month one hundredweight (1 cwt) of advertising literature and assorted free gifts including diaries, notepads and records, from which the drug brand-names beam out insistently. In addition, they will receive frequent visits from drug company representatives, of which there is one for every eight GPs in Britain; will be exposed to advertisements in the free medical newspapers and subscription journals; will be invited to films, drinks and conferences at home and abroad, all at drug companies' 'expense'; and will receive free samples of drugs given away at an annual cost to the industry of £2 million.[20]

Drug companies also provide much of the money for post-graduate research.

A final explanation for the success of the drug companies lies with the patients and doctors themselves. Patients tend to expect a prescription from a visit to the doctor. Doctors, often under pressure of time, are too willing to prescribe drugs as an easy way of dealing with patients' problems. This is particularly the case with tranquilisers and anti-depressants. Many drugs produced by the companies are ineffective or designed to meet a 'need' created by the drug company. More worryingly, many drugs have side-effects, varying from relatively minor irritants to the devastating and tragic effects of Thalidomide. A scheme to reduce the NHS drug bill was introduced in April 1985. For certain categories of drugs there are lists from which doctors must prescribe. The categories include cough and cold medicines, minor painkillers and tranquilisers. The drugs on the list are the cheaper, non-branded drugs. In 1993 it was announced that a further ten categories of groups would be reviewed for potential inclusion on the list. The first new category to be accepted for inclusion was drugs for the treatment of rheumatism.

In 1994 a government report published by the Audit Commission (which monitors public spending) claimed that doctors could save the NHS £425 million by more efficient prescribing.[21] The ways of saving money suggested by the report include prescribing smaller amounts of drugs such as antibiotics, fewer prescriptions for items of limited value such as cough suppressants, and the substitution of cheaper drugs with the same effect where this is possible. In 1999 a new deal was struck between the government and the drug companies to set profit margins on new drugs. The deal is estimated to save the NHS £200 million a year.

In the late 1990s, publicity was given to the issue of drugs-rationing within the NHS. Limited resources and the huge costs of new drugs have meant treatments have been refused to some people. In 1999 the National Institute for Clinical

Excellence (NICE) was set up to create more consistency across the country in the use of new treatments, including drugs.

'Cinderella' services

Analysis of resource allocation within the NHS shows that some client groups have been treated less favourably than others. Patients on acute and maternity wards received a greater share of NHS funds than did patients in psychiatric hospitals or those for people with a learning disability. These are the 'Cinderella' services, which attract fewer resources and have less prestige.

Explanations for this unequal situation can be found in different attitudes towards different groups and different types of medicine. People with disabilities and mental illnesses are groups who are unable to exert pressure on the government and who fail to attract public support. Medicine tends to focus on the idea of cure and treatment. Conditions like learning disability require care, since no cures are available, and therefore have less status within the medical profession.

In 1976, a DHSS document called *Priorities for Health and Personal Social Services in England* was published. The document set out guidelines for establishment priorities, proposing that priority be given to services for elderly people and people with disabilities and mental illnesses. A second discussion paper, called *The Way Forward* and published in 1977, re-emphasised the points made in the 1976 document and argued that chronically sick and disabled people should be included as priority groups. These consultative documents attracted general approval, but little has been done to rectify the situation of unequal allocation of resources to different groups.

Regional inequalities in health care

One of the aims of the NHS was to make health care equally available to everyone, as the following extract from the 1946 Bill shows:

> All the service or any part of it, is to be available to everyone in England and Wales. The Bill imposes no limitation on availability – e.g. limitations based on financial means, age, sex, employment or vocation, area of residence, or insurance qualifications.[22]

In spite of this, inequalities persist within the system. We examine variation between regions of the country here, and then look at inequalities between different social classes.

One way of comparing standards of health between different areas and different social groups is by looking at death rates. The infant mortality rate refers to the number of deaths of children under 1 year of age per 1000 live births, and can be used as an indicator of general standards of health. In 1990, the infant mortality rate for the whole of England was 8.4: the highest mortality rate was in the West Midlands with a rate of 9.9 and the lowest was in East Anglia with a rate of 6.4.[23] There are also variations in adult mortality rates.

There are variations throughout the country in expenditure on health and in the numbers of health-care workers. Looking at expenditure as a whole, the highest rate in 1988–89 was in the North East Thames Region and the lowest rate was in the Oxford region.[24] Different regions have different health needs, according to the local population. Areas where there are larger proportions of older people, for example, will need higher *per capita* spending on health.

Often in social policy there is a tendency for areas with greatest needs to have the least resources to meet these needs. This tendency is known as the 'inverse care law'. The inverse care law has operated in health-care expenditure where, for example, there are fewest GPs in areas where people had the greatest health needs.

In the 1970s this problem was recognised by the government and a working party was set up to investigate and make recommendations. The Resource Allocation Working Party (RAWP) published its report in 1976. The RAWP report recommended that resources should be allocated on the basis of regional populations, taking into account factors like age, sex, mortality rates and existing provision.

The proposal for a gradual introduction of this idea was accepted, but implementation proved difficult in a time of financial cut-backs. There was also opposition from areas which would lose resources, criticism of the use of mortality rates as an indicator of need, and criticism of the failure of the report to consider social deprivation factors such as housing standards and poverty. Despite these points, the RAWP report was important in reducing regional inequalities in health-care provision.

In 1988 a review of the RAWP report was published.[25] This recommended different criteria for allocation of resources, resulting in a shift of resources from the North and the Midlands to the South. The report was not immediately acted upon, but its recommendations were considered within the broader review of the health service taking place that year.

The reforms in the NHS in the 1990s have led to a new way of allocating funds, but the principles developed by RAWP are still in use. Health authorities receive an amount of money based on the age, sex and mortality rates of the population in their areas. However inequalities related to where people live have continued into the 1990s – some of these are related to social class (examined below) but some appear not to be. The following three examples were reported in 1998:[26]

A man with prostate cancer in Bexley and Greenwich, south-east London, has a 34 per cent chance of surviving for five years, while for someone living in Kensington, Chelsea and Westminster, the figure is 59.8 per cent. The figure for Kingston and Richmond, which is hardly a deprived area, is 38 per cent, well below the national average of 45.2 per cent, while that for Cambridge and Islington is 55.7 per cent.

If someone has a hernia repair in Kingston, Surrey, they have a greater than 95 per cent chance of making a complete recovery. Should the operation take place in most other parts of the country, their chances, on average, are less than 80 per cent.

A child living in Brent and Harrow, north London, with glue ear, a condition that usually clears itself, is eight times less likely than a child in East Kent to have an operation to fit plastic grommets, which help to drain the fluid but carry the risk of perforating the ear drum.

In 1999 the National Institute for Clinical Excellence (NICE) was set up to establish minimum standards and achieve greater consistency in treatments given to patients across the country. The Institute will collect data and examine doctors' performances, and try to explain and reduce variations in care.

Social class inequalities

Several surveys and reports have shown class differences in health and in access to health services.[27] In 1980, the DHSS published a report produced by a research group chaired by Sir Douglas Black. The report takes the name of the chairperson and is thus known as the 'Black Report'. The report used the Register-General's classification of social groups by occupation and found relationships between social class and all aspects of health. In the following passage, the statistical information was translated into an account of two imaginary families:[28]

Mr Smythe is the financial director of a large company. Mrs Smythe does not work and she is soon to give birth to her third child. They live in a pleasant suburb on the edge of the green belt with their two children, Emily aged five and Rodney aged 10. They own their own home and the area where they live is mainly populated by professional people. There are plenty of recreational and sporting facilities, good schools and a brand new health centre in the locality.

Mr Jones is an unskilled labourer at a factory. His wife supplements the family income by working as an office cleaner. They live in a high-rise block of flats in the centre of the city. The flats were built in the late 1950s and are poorly serviced with play areas and parks. The Joneses also have two children, Janet aged five and John aged 10. Mrs Jones is also expecting her third child. The family is registered with a local GP whose list of patients is already oversubscribed.

These two imaginary families are at opposite ends of the social scale in terms of occupation and income. In-between there are different shades of grey, but how are these two families likely to fare under the existing National Health Service arrangements? Based on the Black Report these are some of the likely outcomes.

There is a 60 per cent probability that Mrs Jones will not have consulted an obstetrician by the fifth month of her pregnancy. By that time it may be too late to diagnose congenital abnormalities like spina bifida or blood disorders in her unborn baby.

Mrs Jones's poorer living standards will probably mean her standard of nutritional diet is poor. She is nearly twice as likely as Mrs Smythe to die in childbirth, or her baby to be stillborn or die within the first few months of life. If her baby is a boy and survives at birth, he is still four times more likely to die before his first birthday than is Mrs Smythe's new-born son.

Like his brother John, the new-born Jones boy is ten times more likely to die, before he is 14, through an accident involving fire, a fall or drowning, than is his counterpart Rodney Smythe. John is seven times more likely to be knocked down and killed in a road accident.

Similar disadvantages will follow him into adult life. In only one case – asthma – is Rodney more likely than John to die at an early age.

Though the statistics show that Janet Jones is not as likely to be an accident victim as her brother, her individual health and life-expectancy will tend to follow the pattern of her mother and maternal grandmother.

Mr Jones's health and life-expectancy are also considerably poorer than those of Mr Smythe – and if his son also becomes a manual worker his health is likely to follow a similar pattern too.

Although the actual health of all families has improved since the setting up of the NHS, the relative gap between professional and unskilled manual workers has actually widened.

Contrary to popular belief, Mr Jones is much more likely to die of lung cancer or duodenal ulcer than Mr Smythe. He is twice as likely to die of a disease affecting the nervous system; three times as likely to suffer and die from a parasitic disease; four times as likely to incur a mental disorder or a respiratory disease and die.

In contrast, the Smythe family are more likely to follow a nutritionally satisfactory diet, to consult preventative services such as dentists, chiropodists and opticians. Mrs Smythe is more likely to have planned her family than Mrs Jones, or to have been screened to test if she might have treatable breast or cervical cancer. The Black Report comments that health facilities tend to be geared towards the middle-class consumer rather than the working-class.

Also the high-density urban areas where working-class people live tend to have a lower *per capita* expenditure than the suburban areas which are not so densely populated. The Smythe family are likely to have frequent medical check-ups as a matter of course – the Jones are more likely to use their GP after illness has set in, and consequently visit him more often.

Activity 15.12

Discussion questions:

1 Why might a family's health suffer if the mother works as an office cleaner?

2 Why are doctors' practices in working-class areas more likely to be oversubscribed than those in middle-class areas, and what effect might this have on the service?

3 Why are middle-class women more likely than working-class women to take advantage of ante-natal care facilities?

4 Why should there be a connection between level of income and standard of diet?

5 Why is it that some problems in childbirth can be traced to nutritional deficiencies in the mother?

6 Why are working-class children more likely than middle-class children to be victims of an accident?

7 There is a statistical connection between manual work and ill-health. Why should this be?

8 Why is lung-cancer more prevalent among working-class people?

9 Why are middle-class people more likely to use the preventive health service?

10 In what ways are the health services more geared to the middle-class consumer?

The Black Report made many recommendations for improvements which might help to reduce the inequalities between different social classes. These were rejected by the government, primarily on the grounds of expense. Evidence published since the Black Report has revealed that class inequalities have stayed the same and in some cases widened in the years following 1980.[29]

In 1998 the Acheson Report was published, reviewing health inequalities and recommending policy developments. The summary of the report states:

Although average mortality has fallen over the past 50 years, unacceptable inequalties in health persist. For many measures of health, inequalities have either remained the same or have widened in recent decades.

These inequalities affect the whole of society and they can be identified at all stages of the life course from pregnancy to old age.

The weight of scientific evidence supports a socioeconomic explanation of health inequalities. This traces the roots of ill health to such determinants as income, education and employment as well as to the material environment and lifestyle. It follows that our recommendations have implications across a broad front and reach far beyond the remit of the Department of Health. ...

We have identified a range of areas for future policy development, judged on the scale of their potential impact on health inequalities, and the weight of evidence. These areas include: poverty, income, tax and benefits; education; housing and environment; mobility; transport and pollution; and nutrition.[30]

Activity 15.13

The government is concerned to reduce inequalities in health and has earmarked some money for this purpose. Working in groups of three or four, make a list of policies to achieve this aim and decide the order of priority.

The main focus of this chapter has been on various aspects of the National Health Service in Britain. It is difficult to reach any final assessment of the impact of the NHS on the nation's health. Whilst there have been considerable improvements in health since the Second World War, particular factors cannot be easily isolated as causes. It may well be that improvements in the overall standard of living, in housing or in working conditions are of greater significance than developments in medicine and health-care provision.

Activity 15.14

Make sure that you understand the following expressions used in this chapter. Check in the Glossary at the end of the book if you need to.

acute illness	inverse care law
ante-natal clinic	life-expectancy
anti-depressants	mental disorder
Audit Commission	mortality rate
child health clinic	NHS Trust
chronic illness	obstetrician
'Cinderella' service	parasitic disease
client group	patent law
community care	*per capita*
congenital abnormality	preventative medicine
consultative document	primary care groups
fund-holding GP	provider
health education	purchaser
health visitor	respiratory disease
high density	social deprivation factor
infant mortality rate	stigma
insurance qualification	tranquilisers
internal market	

Further reading

There are a number of useful books which look at issues in health and health care. A readable review of all aspects of this area can be found in Rob Baggott, *Health and Health Care*, 2nd edn (London: Macmillan, 1998). Detailed analysis of the politics and organisation of the health service is provided by Christopher Ham in *Health Policy in Britain*, 3rd edn (London: Macmillan, 1992).

Useful addresses

For Department of Health leaflets:

Department of Health
PO Box 777
London SE1 6XH
tel. 0800 555777

Health Education Authority
Hamilton House
Trevelyan House
30 Great Peter Street
London SW1P 2HN
tel. 0207 222 5300

The King's Fund is an independent organisation which researches health and social care issues:

The King's Fund
11–13 Cavendish Square
London W1M OAN
tel. 0207 307 2400

Websites

The King's Fund: **www.Kingsfund.org.uk**

Department of Health: **www.doh.org.uk**

▪ Ṽ 16 The voluntary sector

Voluntary provision of services for people in need has a long history. In the nineteenth and early twentieth centuries, most health and social care provision was organised by voluntary organisations.

16.1 Statutory and voluntary organisations

The relationship between statutory and voluntary services has varied in different periods. For most of the twentieth century, the trend was for statutory organisations to take over the tasks of the voluntary sector in many areas of provision. Indeed, the expansion of state responsibility after the Second World War led to the expectation that voluntary organisations would shrink and ultimately cease to exist. However, recent years have seen a reversal in policy whereby voluntary organisations are increasingly encouraged to take responsibility for care.

The Griffiths Report and the 1990 NHS and Community Care Act had a major impact on the role of voluntary organisations (see Chapter 9 for more detail on these). A major theme in the Report and Act which followed was that there should be a separation between *purchasers* and *providers* of services in health and social care. Health authorities and social services departments would be the purchasers of services, not the providers. The providers would increasingly be the private and voluntary organisations, known collectively as the 'independent sector'. Local authorities would buy services from voluntary and other organisations on behalf of their clients.

Further development of the relationship between voluntary organisations and the state sector is encouraged through *Compacts* in England, Wales, Scotland and Northern Ireland. The Compacts establish principles for government support of voluntary organisations, stress the need for consideration of the impact of policies on the voluntary sector, and set standards for accountability and openness within the voluntary sector.

16.2 Definitions of voluntary organisations

Activity 16.1

> What do you think is meant by the term 'voluntary'? Write a definition of a voluntary organisation and list any examples you have learned about, and the work they do.

Aims, organisation and finance

It is difficult to establish a precise definition to cover all kinds of voluntary organisation. People who work in voluntary organisations may be paid, so the voluntary sector is not limited to groups staffed by volunteers. Voluntary provision is usually distinguished from statutory provision, although this distinction is not always clear-cut. For example, workers from local social services departments or health services may be involved in managing and running voluntary organisations. In many areas of work, there is close liaison between social services and non-statutory agencies. Some voluntary organisations work in areas which are also the concern of state-provided services. For example, the National Society for the Prevention of Cruelty to Children (NSPCC) will act in cases of child-abuse or neglect, overlapping with the responsibilities of social workers. Voluntary organisations cannot be distinguished in terms of being self-financing. Whilst many rely on contributions and fund-raising, a significant number of groups receive grants from central or local government to fund their work.

Financial support was first given to voluntary bodies by central government in 1914. Current funding from central government in the form of direct grants to voluntary organisations totals £957 million and tax relief to charities is worth a further £1800 million.[1] In 1971–72 local authorities grant-aided voluntary organisations some £1.3 million. By 1982–83 the figure was £29.5 million and by the 1990s had increased to over £250 million.[2] Despite this, voluntary organisations are different from statutory provision in the sense that they are not established through legislation and are not controlled by the government. Voluntary provision can also be defined as being non-profit-making, which distinguishes it from those aspects of provision which are independent of social services and health departments but run as business for profit. Whilst these two factors – non-profit-making motives and lack of state control – are common to all voluntary organisations, there is in other aspects considerable diversity, for example, in aims, organisations and sources of finance.

Since there is no clear definition of a voluntary organisation, estimates of the number of such groups vary. One researcher, using a broad definition, which includes voluntary schools, churches, sports clubs and trade unions, as well as charities, estimated that there were more than 350,000 groups in the voluntary sector. Of this number, some 40 per cent were registered as charities.[3]

The National Council for Voluntary Organisations (NCVO) is an umbrella organisation which provides links between voluntary organisations, local authorities, government departments, the European Union and the private sector. About one thousand organisations are members of NCVO. They receive advice and information.

Charities

Charities are organisations whose application for charitable status satisfies the Charity Commissioners in England, or the Inland Revenue in Scotland or Northern Ireland. Organisations wishing to become charities must show that their purposes fall within certain categories. These are the relief of poverty, the advancement of education or religion, and the advancement of purposes beneficial to the community. The last category is not an all-purpose clause into which any groups excluded from the other categories can fit, but is legally defined, such that, for example, improving the welfare of the unemployed was not accepted as a charitable purpose. The law on charity has been subjected to criticism since many anomalies have been found to exist. Religion, which includes groups like the Moonies, is 'charitable', but it was only at the end of 1983 that the promotion of racial equality, which could be argued to be part of Christian teaching, was allowed as a charitable purpose. When Amnesty International wanted to establish a fund for prisoners of conscience, this was disallowed when Mr Justice Slade ruled in the High Court that:

> The elimination of injustice has not as such ever been held to be a trust purpose which qualified for the privilege afforded to charities by British Law.[4] On the other hand, education is 'charitable', so public schools are able to establish themselves as charities.

To avoid the restrictions involved in charity law, some organisations split into two parts with separate funds and separate aims. In this way, they can engage in political activity which is not permitted to a charity. Organisations with charitable status can claim tax and rate relief, receive covenants at beneficial rates and apply for grants from charitable trusts.

The National Lottery

The introduction of the National Lottery in 1994 created a new source of finance for charities and voluntary organisations. By the end of 1998 the National Lottery Charities Board had given out 16,000 grants, totalling over £890 million.[5] Possibly because of the lottery, the amount of money given to charities by individuals fell in the period after 1994: fewer people gave money regularly and the amounts of money donated grew smaller.

16.3   The work of voluntary organisations

Whilst some charities and other voluntary groups work in areas where there is no statutory provision, others work alongside social workers and health teams. As was mentioned earlier, the 1990 NHS and Community Care Act increased the importance of voluntary organisations, so that in some areas of care they could be the major provider of a service.

Children

In the field of provision for children and young people in need, social service departments work with voluntary welfare groups. For example, social workers can place children in homes run by Barnardo's, the National Children's Home or the Catholic Rescue Society, and social services departments will contribute to costs and inspect the homes. Similarly, in family welfare, in addition to statutory provision, many large towns have Family Welfare Associations which provide financial assistance and social work for families in need. In the same field, Family Service Units are part of a national organisation founded in 1947 and based on the experience of the Pacifist Service Unit, originally concerned with problems caused by the war but continued when it was realised that problems existed not solely as a result of the war. Many Family Service Units have local-authority grants and their work is mainly that of intensive casework with families referred to them by other agencies. The caseworkers each work with a small number of families, visiting regularly and offering help and support. Volunteer families work in shared care schemes in which families look after a child with a disability for a number of days each year, to give the child variety and stimulation and the family a break.

Older people and disabled people

Provision for elderly people is also the concern of people in both statutory and voluntary organisations. Local voluntary groups provide clubs, recreational facilities and some residential accommodation. National organisations, such as Age Concern, co-ordinate the activities of local groups and also act as a pressure group trying to improve the position of elderly people in society. In the case of disabled people, the Royal National Institute for the Blind provides specialist facilities such as Braille literature, talking books, educational aids, and homes and schools for the blind. The Royal National Institute for the Deaf has a similar role, and many other organisations exist for the needs of specific disabilities or to campaign on behalf of all disabled people.

Mental health and learning disability

The voluntary sector is also active in the fields of mental illness and learning disability. In 1946, the amalgamation of existing groups led to the creation of the National Association for Mental Health. The Association is now known as MIND and is concerned with various aspects of mental health, including spreading information, promoting research, running training courses and providing homes for mentally ill people. Mencap does similar work in its area of concern. The Richmond Fellowship runs small community hostels for mentally ill people, while Rudolf Steiner schools are well-respected for their work with people with a learning disability and the same organisation runs colonies where people can live and work, sheltered from the wider society.

Status and role of volunteers

In 1969, a report was published by the Aves Committee, which had been set up by the National Council of Social Services and the National Institute for Social Work Training. The committee was concerned with the role of the voluntary worker in personal social services. The report emphasised that voluntary workers should not be used to replace paid staff. Other areas covered by the committee were the status of volunteers in public services, motivation and discussion of the type of people attracted to voluntary work. An important aspect of the committee's deliberation concerned the organisation of volunteers. It was recommended that voluntary bureaus be established to deal with recruitment and offer advice to potential volunteers. As a result of the report, the national volunteer foundation was set up in London in 1973, with the support of the Voluntary Services Unit, a statutory organisation, concerned primarily with co-ordinating government assistance to voluntary organisations. Volunteer bureaus now exist in most towns throughout the country and their work includes matching volunteers to needs in the community and running campaigns for voluntary workers for particular areas of work.

Voluntary groups

All the areas of provision described so far are also the responsibility of local health and social services. It would be impossible for a book, let alone a chapter, to describe all the voluntary groups which exist. In the following pages several examples of voluntary groups will be described to illustrate the diversity of organisations and demonstrate the work done by the voluntary sector. Some of the groups discussed here are mentioned in other chapters, for example, Women's Aid in Chapter 2, and Shelter in Chapter 5.

The National Society for the Prevention of Cruelty to Children (NSPCC)

Most people have heard of the NSPCC, although few are aware of the full range of the society's work. The NSPCC was started in London in 1884. It is a large organisation and NSPCC Children's Services work directly with 6000 children every day.[6] The NSPCC is a charity and 90 per cent of funds come from contributions from the public. The society is involved with helping families with problems in a variety of ways. The NSPCC has a Child Protection Helpline as a first point of contact for anyone who is concerned about the safety of children, including of course the children themselves. The NSPCC employs Child Protection Officers, who are qualified social workers, in around a hundred Child Protection Teams, Projects and Centres throughout the country. Cases may be referred by neighbours, relatives, local and other authorities, children themselves, or parents may themselves contact the society.

The work covers families in which children are deprived, neglected or at risk of abuse. The Child Protection Officers provide advice, support, counselling and practical help such as finding places for children in playgroups or nurseries. NSPCC staff can start proceedings in the family court when children are thought to be in danger. The work of the Child Protection Officers includes liaising with other organisations such as the police, social services and schools.

The following account from the NSPCC illustrates the type of work done by the organisation:

Every day after school, Michael, 5, and Paul, 7, crept home afraid of finding their parents drunk and fighting. Too ashamed to invite their playmates home, they wondered whether their parents drank because the boys weren't 'good' enough. At night they hid under their bed, terrified that their Mum and Dad would kill one another.

After the NSPCC became involved, the boys went to live temporarily with relatives. Skilled staff encouraged Michael and Paul to talk about their feelings, and helped them understand that their parents were addicted to alcohol and weren't drinking out of 'badness'. They also taught them what to do in an emergency, and set up a family network to support them.

On hearing about their children's distress, the boy's parents sought professional help. Now sober, they have helped Paul and Michael see that they weren't to blame for the drinking, and are fully involved in family activities with their sons.[7]

Most people are aware of the NSPCC's work in the field of child abuse and neglect. However the NSPCC is also involved in a wider range of schemes and projects, sometimes in conjunction with local authorities and other voluntary organisations. Many of these are new ideas in social care. The following are some examples of this work, showing the breadth of the NSPCC's work:[8]

- In Manchester – a new black youth counselling and advocacy service to help highly vulnerable and disadvantaged people, many of whom have been in residential care and have no family support.
- In London – a joint project with Centrepoint in a new refuge for homeless children. This is the first refuge for runaways under 16 set up since the implementation of the Children Act.
- In Surrey – a witness support scheme for children facing the trauma of legal proceedings.
- In Staffordshire, Warwickshire and Gwent – independent visitor services for children who are in local-authority care, using volunteers supervised by the Society's professional staff.
- In Derbyshire – the Dove project developed jointly with the probation service, to prevent the abuse of children by known perpetrators through working with known sex offenders in the community.

As well as providing immediate help for children and families, the NSPCC works as a pressure group, campaigning on behalf of children. This work involves running national campaigns to change attitudes and inform parents, giving information and evidence to the government on law and social policy matters which affect children, and generally promoting children's rights. The NSPCC is also active in training workers from other organisations and in research into child abuse.

The Citizens' Advice Bureau (CAB)

The CAB is another large and well-known voluntary organisation, providing a free and comprehensive information service. The CAB began in 1939 when it was recognised that people needed help during the Second World War conditions of ration books and bombing. During the war the CAB received funding from the government, although this was withdrawn after the war ended. The organisation continued without funds for some time until the government re-instated the grant, at the time of the housing crisis in the 1950s.

Currently, the CAB consists of a national organisation known as the National Association of Citizens' Advice Bureaus (NACAB), area organisations and some 700 local bureaus in England, Wales and Northern Ireland. Nationally the CAB deals with some 7 million enquiries each year.[9] NACAB decides the policy of the CAB, it collects and distributes information and is responsible for organising training. A government grant is made to NACAB and most local bureaus have full- or part-time paid organisers as well as volunteers. Each CAB is managed by a committee and applies to the local authority for help with day-to-day running costs. The CAB deals with many different types of problems, the most common being in the areas of debt, housing, employment, planning law and social security. As unemployment spread there was an increase in enquiries about social security. The CAB will refer people to other agencies if necessary and some bureaus are able to represent clients at employment and social security boards.

A new development in CAB is in *outreach*. This involves taking the service into health centres, hospitals and prisons.

The Relatives' Support Group

Some voluntary groups are small and locally based, existing to meet a particular need without the back-up service of a national organisation. In Coventry, the Relatives' Support Group is made up of professionals from Coventry's health and social services staff and people looking after senile relatives. The group has the support of the local authority who are aware that statutory provision for the old and senile is inadequate and that the burden of care falls on relatives. At group meetings, talks are provided to give information about the condition of senile dementia and problems are shared. The Relatives' Support Group also looks at problems which require practical solution – for example, the difficulty of leaving a senile relative prevents people from being able to attend meetings. The proposed solution to this situation is to set up a 'granny-sitting' service of people trained informally and given a telephone number to ring in the event of needing assistance.

Alcoholics Anonymous (AA)

Many voluntary groups operate through the principle of self-help. This involves people with the same problem helping each other. A well-known example of a self-help group is Alcoholics Anonymous, started in the USA in 1935. AA is a voluntary fellowship of alcoholics who want to stop drinking. Members meet once a week to discuss their problems and give mutual support to each other. In the UK there are about 3000 meetings each week and 40,000–50,000 members.[10] The basic idea of Alcoholics Anonymous is that alcoholics and recovering alcoholics are the best people to understand the problem and to provide help. There is no fee for membership, although the organisation is funded entirely from money collected from members. AA is not affiliated to any other organisations, including any religions, although the 'Twelve Steps' of the recovery programme include several references to God. The experience of Alcoholics Anonymous has led to the establishment of Al-Anon family groups which provide support for relatives of alcoholics.

Parentline

Parentline began as Parents' Anonymous which was a self-help organisation providing a telephone service for parents in danger of abusing their children. Janet's problems began when her son, later sent to a school for children with a learning disability, was born. He was put into an incubator and she was not allowed to breastfeed him. The baby was in hospital for several months by which time Janet says:

> Part of me was dying for him to come home and half was hoping for another relapse. Then within two weeks of when he did come home I'd beaten him.[11]

Janet tried to tell her husband and her doctor but both dismissed her problem. She then began to be secretive, keeping the child away from the health visitor. The situation was not recognised until the little boy went to school and a social worker put Janet in touch with Parents' Anonymous. Janet tells how her shame and fear prevented her from seeking help:

> 'I couldn't just go up to someone and say, "Hey, I keep bashing up my kid in fits of uncontrolled temper." 'They'd probably not have believed me, but if they had they'd probably have locked me up.' Janet felt that she 'was the only person, sort of isolated ... the only person who did this, the only person in the world.'[12]

Parentline grew from this beginning and now is an organisation that helps parents with any aspect of child-care. The organisation has a helpline run by parents and staffed by specially trained volunteers who are parents themselves. Confidentiality is an important feature of Parentline; people who phone in do not have to give their name or address or any other details usually asked for by health and social services staff. No criticism will be made of people's behaviour or feelings. The chief executive of Parentline, herself a single parent with three sons, says:

> Parents really struggle with admitting to having difficulties with bringing up their children. ... We don't live in a society where it's easy to talk about the problems we face, particularly with older children. It's perfectly acceptable to talk to other parents about the fact that your baby won't sleep, or that your toddler's having tantrums, but what about divulging the fact that your teenager may be a bully, is being rebellious or taking drugs?[13]

During 1998, Parentline received calls from 18,817 parents.[14] About half the calls were from parents worried about adolescent children's rebellious behaviour, possible drug-taking or sexual activity. Other worries included difficulties at school and the impact on children of divorce or re-marriage.

The Child Poverty Action Group (CPAG)

Whilst some voluntary organisations are concerned with providing immediate help to individuals in need, others are primarily involved with campaigning for change, putting pressure on the government to change laws and improve provision, and trying to change attitudes towards a particular problem. One such group is the CPAG which was established in 1965 by a group of Quakers who saw a need to draw attention to the plight of the millions of people living in poverty. CPAG does not give money to the poor but is an action group in the field of welfare rights and poverty. The three key aims of the CPAG are:

- To bring about positive income policy changes for families with children in poverty.
- To enable those eligible for benefits to have full access to their entitlement.
- To raise awareness about the causes and experience of poverty.[15]

CPAG activity in meeting these objectives takes various forms. The group produces information to influence opinion, putting pressure on MPs and public officials, and monitors changes in legislation. CPAG feeds information to the media in order to keep issues before the public. The group also provides a free information, advice and advocacy service through the Citizens Rights Office (CRO). The organisation specialises in test cases, where the law is unclear and the judgement will set a precedent for future cases. CPAG also runs courses, finances research and publishes guides to welfare rights and research findings.

The organisation is financed through membership fees, grants and donations, fees charged for courses, sales of books, and raffles. There is an executive committee which sets policy and a number of local branches which take up issues, provide advice and represent claimants at tribunals.

The National Campaign for the Homeless (Shelter)

Shelter is another organisation which has an important role as a pressure group. It started in 1966 when a group of people, mainly from the clergy, were concerned about the extent of homelessness, and the aim is to fight for the right of everyone to a decent home. In the early days, Shelter was mainly involved in funding housing associations and the campaign to persuade the government to take over this role achieved success with the 1974 Housing Act (see Chapter 5).

Currently, Shelter's work takes three forms. First, there are 50 housing aid centres throughout the country which provide advice and help to around 100,000 households each year.[16] Second, projects are initiated and supported in response to particular needs. For example, Shelterline was launched in 1998 to provide a free 24-hour national housing helpline. Another scheme – Homeless to Home – supports homeless families moving to a new home, providing practical help with moving in and decorating, advice on benefits, training, employment options and budgeting, and assistance with settling children into a new school. Third, Shelter campaigns for change. The group's analysis of homelessness leads to a view of the problem as one caused by the failure of the housing market, rather than personal inadequacy of people who are homeless. Shelter provides information to people in positions of power and makes suggestions for improvements in housing policy. Debates are initiated on areas of housing and Shelter produces pamphlets and books. Most of Shelter's finance comes from donations and fund-raising events.

Women's Aid

Clear-cut distinctions cannot be made among different types of voluntary groups since many combine different elements. For example, some are committed to the idea of self-help but allow people without personal experience of a problem to be involved. Also, some combine pressure-group activities with the provision of immediate help for individuals. Women's Aid is an example of an organisation which combines these different functions and philosophies. Women's Aid believes in the principle of self-help and encourages battered women to help each other. It does not however restrict involvement to those who have personal experience of marital violence. Women's Aid merges the functions of a pressure group and a provider of practical help and support. Refuges provide shelter for women and their children, while Women's Aid is also involved in fighting to improve the situation of battered women and the position of women in society generally. This more general approach to violence in marriage is explained by the early links between Women's Aid and feminism, and the organisation's support of the demands of the Women's Liberation Movement.

Women's Aid has a national organisation, Women's Aid Federation England (WAFE), which began, although with a different name, in 1975 when the 35 groups running refuges decided there was a need for a central organisation. At the present, some 100 local groups are federated in WAFE. Refuges in Scotland

Self-help in a refuge

and Wales are separately organised. Women's Aid sets out its objectives in five aims, listed as follows:[17]

1 Promoting the development of a network of autonomous locally-based groups to provide temporary refuge on request for women and their children who have suffered mental, emotional or physical harassment in their relationships, or rape or sexual harassment or abuse.
2 Encouraging the development of facilities which offer advice, support and practical help to any woman who seeks it, whether or not she is a resident of a refuge, and which gives continuing support and after-care to women and children after they have left the refuge.
3 Researching and campaigning for the provision of facilities which meet the emotional and educational needs of children of women who seek refuge.
4 Providing information and assistance to local groups who are members of the Federation and to create a forum for the exchange of information and ideas on all aspects of the objects of the Federation.
5 Educating and informing the public, the media, the police, the courts, the social services and other authorities with respect to the violence women suffer, mindful of the fact that this is a result of the general position of women in society.

The national organisation is a federation of local groups who decide for themselves how the refuges will be run. Local Women's Aid groups are made up of women living in the refuges, paid workers and volunteers. There are also regional organisations or refuges. WAFE provides information and support and unites local groups into a political movement, campaigning on feminist issues. Women's Aid has been successful in changing the law on injunctions for battered women and in getting recognition of the problems of battered women in housing law. Both these aspects of the law are discussed in Chapter 2. WAFE receives a grant from the government to run the national office. Refuge finances vary – some groups receive government grants, others have workers paid by the local authority, whilst some are self-supporting.

The Terence Higgins Trust

This work of the Terence Higgins Trust demonstrates how quickly voluntary organisations can spring up to meet new needs, ahead of slower-moving statutory provision. The organisation is named after Terence Higgins who died of AIDS in 1982. At that time, little was known about the disease. There were few services available to meet the needs of AIDS patients. Shocked by the lack of provision, Terence Higgins' friends decided to set up an organisation to provide support and help to people with AIDS and HIV infection. The Trust grew very quickly and is now the leading AIDS charity in the country. The Terence Higgins Trust has pioneered the 'buddy' system of support in this country. The Trust described buddying in the following way:

Buddies are trained and skilled volunteers who are committed to providing a consistent service of emotional and practical support to a person with AIDS on a one-to-one basis. The aim is to enable a person with AIDS to live well by leading a satisfying and fulfilling life based on personal decisions and choices. The role of the buddy is always determined by the wishes of the person they work with, their individual needs and the level of support they are already receiving. Needs may range from a listening ear, companionship and help in the home to advocacy, or just having someone available and there for them.[18]

Other services provided by the Terence Higgins Trust are 'helper cells' providing more practical support on a one-off basis, counselling, and various support groups for people with AIDS, their lovers and families.

Activity 16.2

Find out all you can about one of these voluntary organisations. The college or local library has various reference books describing their work and giving addresses and phone numbers. Many organisations will send information to you but you must send a stamped, self-addressed envelope, and in some cases you will have to pay for booklets.

16.4   The advantages and disadvantages of voluntary organisations

Activity 16.3

Why have voluntary groups continued to exist alongside statutory provision? Make a list of reasons, using the information already provided in this chapter and any other information you may know about.

Respond to need and specialisation

Whilst many people believed that the post-war expansion of social services would mean the end of voluntary organisations, others foresaw the continuation of such work, perhaps with a change in emphasis. Beveridge, who wrote the report which formed the basis of the social security system (see Chapter 3), believed that voluntary groups would continue to meet certain special needs and to act as 'society's conscience'. Both these roles are carried out by today's voluntary groups. Groups like Shelter and the CPAG keep homelessness and poverty on the agenda for debate, and educate the public and those in power. Considerable success is achieved; for example, the CPAG was influential in changing family allowances to child benefit, available for all children and not just the second child and subsequent children. Voluntary groups criticise state provision and make recommendations for change.

The state is often slow in responding to new needs and inflexible in adapting to meet changing circumstances. For example, Women's Aid was able to establish refuges in most parts of the country within a few years of recognising the need which existed. In many cases, the voluntary sector improves provision by experimenting with new forms of care and trying out ideas which are later adopted by statutory provision. It is probably true that, within the present structure of society, it would be impossible for the state to meet all needs and that voluntary groups fulfil an essential role in filling in gaps in state provision.

Voluntary organisations provide a specialisation in a particular area which may be lacking in state services. To take Women's Aid again as an example, its workers develop an expertise in law, housing and social security regulations relating to battered women. Similar specialisation can be seen from the experience of a woman who joined Kith and Kids, a self-help organisation for parents with children with disabilities. In the following quotation, Sheila explains how she was helped not only by being given an opportunity to share her feelings, but also by being given specialist advice from people who had developed detailed knowledge on the benefits available for parents with children with disabilities:

> Of course, you just speak and speak and if you've a few years of unspeakable things it all comes out and for the first time here was a group of people who were not only sympathetic but seemed to think the way I did. But after you spoke your heart out in a way then comes the practicalities. I remember Mavis saying to me straight away, 'Why, haven't you got a social worker?' And at that time I hadn't. Well I should have. 'Do you know all about practical things like attendance allowance, baby buggies', things like this. I mean I'd never heard of all this and it was really like opening the floodgates.[19]

Pressure groups like the CPAG are respected as the experts on poverty issues, and the quality of their information and research is recognised by MPs and government officials as well as the media.

Comprehensive and flexible response

In some areas of provision, the voluntary sector is able to offer a more comprehensive and flexible service than is provided by the state. Self-help groups provide support which is available for 24 hours a day, 7 days a week, without appointments, delay or payment. In many groups, help is offered without being asked for, in contrast to health service provision where it is extremely unlikely that a doctor would telephone a patient just to see how he or she is getting on. Self-help is also continuous; a member of CARE, an organisation for people who have or have had cancer, says:

> You see the lovely part of this organisation is that they don't drop you. Lots of things, hospitals or visitors, welfare visits, they care so long and then you're left entirely. They think, 'Oh well she's going to be alright' or on the other hand 'there's nothing more that we can do'. CARE is there until a person dies. They are not given up because they are terminal.[20]

There is a tendency for statutory provision to be available only in a crisis and this is not sufficient for many problems which need continuing support. A member of Alcoholics Anonymous explains this disillusionment with help provided by friends compared with that given by AA members:

> In AA I found I could talk to somebody and get a bloody answer or advice. AA and my sponsor followed it through. They saw me through the rough times.

They didn't drop me in the good times. Continuity. Somebody there all the time. I found this concern. I got let down so often while I was drinking. It was all little bits here and there. I never saw anything through.[21]

For many people having a social worker involves stigma, the stigma of being a client, taking help. Most voluntary organisations are able to provide help without this feeling of stigma as the staff do not regard themselves as professionals, especially where they are working in a voluntary capacity. Self-help groups are particularly successful in this respect, in that people with similar experiences help each other, no-one is in the role of helper and no-one is being helped, much in the same way as friends provide mutual support. As a member of Relatives of the Depressed (ROD) puts it:

It's the 'them' and 'us' situation and you've got to overcome it, because you get so humiliated if you're always on the receiving end.[22]

The interaction between a professional helper and a client can lead to increased dependency and feelings of failure. In the experience of a member of Depressive Associated, the professional–client relationship is:

one in which instead of being 'built-up' you are constantly being 'pulled-down'.[23]

As has already been stressed, self-help groups believe that particular understanding and acceptance are offered by people who have first-hand experience of a problem. This is especially true in the case of problems which carry a stigma, such as incest or family violence. Whilst it is not true that it is impossible to understand a problem without personal experience, the fear of disapproval and rejection is removed in the situation where the other person has the same difficulties. Self-help groups also remove the feeling of isolation, the feeling that the sufferer is the only person in the world with a particular problem and that there must be something terribly wrong with them to feel as they do.

Here, David Townsend, the Director of Croydon social service, writes about the advantages of voluntary organisations from his viewpoint:

Voluntary activity enhances local community development and adds to social cohesion. It helps shape community care plans and children's service plans. Harnessing voluntary activity to the local authority can be very productive. Croydon social services has over 1000 registered volunteers organised in teams led by paid organisers. They are active every day in a variety of ways, from visiting recovering psychiatric patients to ferrying outpatients around. These volunteers are 'vetted'; their altruism does not suffer as a result but an unsuspecting public is offered a safeguard. Their work 'value' to the department has been estimated at up to £750,000 per year.[24]

Activity 16.4

1 Why does the state encourage voluntary organisations?
2 What criticisms can be made of the way voluntary organisations help people?

The state makes a considerable investment in voluntary organisations, for example in the generous grant made to the CAB, although it should be said that such grants are given on a temporary basis and the future for voluntary groups is always uncertain. It is to the advantage of the state to fund organisations like the CAB, since a great deal of necessary work is done, mostly by volunteers, saving the state money. Statutory provision on a scale provided by the CAB would be very costly.

Criticisms

Whilst a great deal of valuable work is done by voluntary organisations, criticism can be made of the way in which such groups allow the government to avoid responsibilities, which perhaps should be included as areas of state concern. Organisations which arise from recognised inadequacies in provision allow the gaps and areas of neglect to continue. Self-help and other groups also provide help to individuals which may have the effect of distracting attention from structural causes of problems. For example, counselling a woman who has difficulty in coping with a child with a disability shifts attention from the problems of a system which expects women in isolation, without support, to manage families.

Even if it is accepted that voluntary organisations meet some needs which could not be met by the state or which are better provided for by more informal forms of care, there is cause for concern when the state begins to turn over areas of work to voluntary organisations. Finally, it can be argued that groups providing for accepted and established needs should not have to rely wholly on contributions from members of the public, or on temporary grants in a state of uncertainty about the future.

Other criticisms of voluntary organisations include the fact that many volunteers are untrained and may be using out-of-date methods in their work. Voluntary organisations may be unreliable and inconsistent in meeting need. Linked to this, they may provide an uneven service, available in some areas and not in others. Services provided by voluntary organisations may be a duplication of services already offered by statutory organisations.

As the role of the voluntary sector has expanded and the amounts of money involved have increased, more cases of mismanagement of funds and sometimes of fraudulent activities have occurred. There are few checks on staff in voluntary organisations and appointment of members of committees can be a haphazard affair. David Townsend, the director of Croydon social services writes:

> The appointment of those who become officers of voluntary organisations in a local setting is as much a matter of luck as careful choice. Once in office they may be responsible for spending grants of £25,000 per annum. The bad news is that there are often no prior checks on police records. In the case of services provided to vulnerable people that could be serious. Nor are there checks on the financial status of would be office holders. Yet they may have access to cheque books and cash. There are few questions asked about competence to manage staff or budgets, to understand employment law, or to support equal opportunities legislation. Finally the managers may have

no idea how to measure the quality of what is being done by the organisation.[25]

Changing roles

Some voluntary organisations have been concerned about the effects of their changing role since 1990. As part of the changes brought about under the 1990 NHS and Community Care Act, discussed earlier, voluntary organisations are expected to form contracts with local authorities for the provision of services. This takes the voluntary sector into a new more formal role which particularly the small organisations have found difficult to cope with. One study found that a voluntary group had spent £30,000 in staff time negotiating a contract.[26] There is also a concern that as groups take up a bigger role in the provision of services, they will be less involved in campaigning and pressure group work. Arthritis Care, for example, have taken a political decision not to get involved with contracting. Richard Gutch, the director, said:

> We aim to make sure that the voice of people with arthritis gets heard and that is what we want to continue to focus on, rather than trying to become a provider of home help services – which is what we often get asked to do.[27]

Activity 16.5

Make sure that you understand the following expressions used in this chapter. Check in the Glossary at the end of the book if you need to.

advocacy service	purchaser
casework	self-help
charitable status	statutory organisation
independent sector	stigma
injunction	test case
outreach	tribunal
pressure group	voluntary organisation
provider	volunteer

Further reading

In many cases, information on voluntary organisations can be obtained from the groups themselves. Understandably, some charge for leaflets and in all cases a stamped self-addressed envelope should be sent.

Useful addresses

There are several reference books which list names and addresses of voluntary organisations. Ask at your college or local library.

The National Council for Voluntary Organisations (NCVO)
Regent's Wharf
8 All Saints Street
London N1 9RL
tel. 0207 713 6161

Websites

For information on charities, try **www.charitynet.org.uk**

Many voluntary organisations have their own website. By using these you are not taking up the organisation's limited resources and time in your search for information. Some examples of informative websitses are listed below:

NSPCC at **www.nspcc.org.uk**

Shelter at **www.shelter.org.uk**

Citizens' Advice Bureaus at **www.nacab.org.uk**

Terence Higgins Trust at **www.tht.org.uk**

▪ ▼ 17 Policy issues in welfare

This concluding chapter provides a more general approach to the issues raised throughout the book. The aim is to examine the concepts and debates which influence social policy provision. Whilst issues are placed under a series of headings, they are, in many cases, interrelated and the separation is an artificial one, created for the purposes of analysis.

17.1 Perspectives on welfare

In making choice about social policies, politicians and others are influenced by a set of values about what is fair and right. The values are part of a world-view or perspective which we all use to justify what we believe. Because of this there are usually patterns to what people believe. If I knew your views about one aspect of welfare – for example whether child benefit should be increased or abolished – I might be able to guess your views on another aspect of policy – perhaps whether or not people should pay for care in residential homes. It is as if we can put people in boxes, label the boxes and say these people tend to have these sort of beliefs. I have written 'as if' because people never do fit neatly into boxes, the classifications below are more a way of thinking about ideas about welfare than an accurate reflection of the complexity of people's ideas. As you read the material below (which is more difficult to understand than the earlier chapters of this book), think about which of the categories best fits your thinking. Do you fit neatly into one box or are you a bit of this and a bit of that? Maybe you have different ideas about different aspects of welfare policy? – a lot of people think differently about health care, for example, than other aspects of welfare. People are often influenced by their personal experiences and situation, if you are a student, for example, this may affect your thinking about the introduction of fees and the abolition of student grants. You might also think about which political parties or particular politicians fit into each of the boxes.

Political Perspectives

1. Anti-collectivism

Various writers use different labels for similar sets of ideas. The category called here 'anti-collectivist'[1] is also sometimes described as 'market liberalism' or 'monetarism'. *Collectivism* means the belief that all members of a community have a responsibility towards each other, including sharing the costs of meeting other people's needs. The opposite to collectivism is *individualism*, which is the belief that individuals or families should be responsible for themselves. Anti-collectivists are against collectivism and strongly individualist. This view has its roots in the nineteenth century idea of '*laissez-faire*' (which was examined in Chapter 3 in the context of government responses to poverty) but is also that of the 'new right' which includes some sections of the Conservative Party. Anti-collectivism can be explained in terms of several key ideas.

Market forces

Firstly, the economy is seen as working best without any intervention from the government: it is believed that wages, for example, will find their own correct level through the workings of market forces. To understand the concept of 'market forces', imagine you are selling something – a car, perhaps. If the car you are selling is very rare, maybe is seen as a collector's item, and a lot of people want it, you can ask a high price. If, however, there are many cars like yours for sale and not very many people wanting to buy, then you will have to lower your price if you want a sale. This idea is at the heart of the philosophy of capitalist economies (although not always the practice, since sellers often get together to agree prices, or sometimes there only is one seller). It can be applied to any-thing, including wages, as in the comment above. Under market forces, high unemployment will have the effect of pushing wages down, since a lot of people are trying to find work. On the other hand, if there is a shortage of workers, people can demand, and get, higher wages. New right economists believe that nothing should be done by governments to interfere with this process. Jobs and wage levels should not be protected by social policy.

Self-reliance, competition and efficiency

Anti-collectivists believe that individuals should look after themselves and not rely on state help. They also think that services and goods, including welfare ser-vices, are best provided by private companies. In this way the firms will compete with each other and be efficient.

A speech given by John Moore as Secretary of State for Social Services, on the reform of social security, illustrates some of these points.[2] Moore explained the Conservative view of welfare as follows:

> We believe that dependence in the long run decreases human happiness and reduces human freedom. We believe the well being of individuals is best pro-tected and promoted when they are helped to be independent, to use their talents to take care of themselves and their families, and to achieve things on their own.

For the new right, state intervention is linked with many undesirable trends. There is a tendency towards over-centralisation – power and decision-making is concentrated too much with central government. Societies with a high degree of state intervention are seen as authoritarian – government bodies bossing people about and telling them what to do unnecessarily. Competition and individual freedom are restricted, so people are not free to find the best ways of doing things, especially in terms of building successful businesses and increasing profits. Moore goes on to argue in his speech:

> For more than a quarter of a century after the last war public opinion in Britain, encouraged by politicians, travelled down an aberrant path toward ever more dependence on an ever more powerful state. Under guise of compassion people were encouraged to see themselves as 'victims of circumstance', mere putty in the grip of giant forces beyond their control. Rather than being seen as individuals, people were categorised into groups and given labels that enshrined their dependent status: 'unemployed', 'single-parent', 'handicapped'.
>
> Thus their confidence and will to help themselves were subtly undermined, and they were taught to think only Government action could affect their lives.

For the anti-collectivists, welfare is ideally seen as having a residual role. This means the welfare state will deal only with any problems that cannot possibly be solved in any other way. The welfare state will be a safety-net only for a small number of people in very great need. The government is seen as having a duty to relieve poverty, but this is thought of as a necessary evil and provision should be kept to a minimum. This refers both to the level of benefits and to the categories of people receiving financial and other help. Most needs can be met on a voluntary and private basis. Moore says:

> The third important reform the (Social Security) Act makes is to focus help more sharply on people in greatest need. This is crucial as part of the long-term efforts to change the climate of opinion on welfare. The indiscriminate handing out of benefits not only spreads limited resources too thinly, it can also undermine the will to self-help, and build up pools of resentment among the tax-payers who are footing the bill, often from incomes barely larger than the money benefit recipients receive.
>
> By targeting our welfare resources we will be able to provide more real help where need is greatest.

'Targeting' and 'dependency culture'

Two concepts which have been talked about recently and which fit within this approach are 'targeting' of benefits and a 'dependency culture'. The idea of targeting is that benefits and services should be provided only for those in greatest need. Family credit is a targeted benefit in that it goes only to families on low incomes: child benefit, by contrast, is not targeted in that it goes to everyone looking after a child, whatever their income. This issue is looked at in more detail in section 17.6 on universal or selective welfare.

The notion of a dependency culture is that welfare encourages people to become dependent on benefits and to lose motivation to do anything to improve their situation. This term is used regularly by politicians in the Conservative Party. In the following quotation, Jonathan Aitken, Chief Secretary to the Treasury, is talking about the £80 million social security budget in 1994. He described the social security budget as 'enormously high' and said:

'I think most people will expect us to take a very close look at that.' He went on to warn against the creation of, in effect, a benefit dependence culture and society where people became too comfortable with benefits.[3]

2. Collectivism

The second approach can be termed 'collectivist' but derives from two strands of thought, that of the 'reluctant collectivists' and that of the 'Fabian socialists'. Another term used for the same ideas as described here is 'political liberalism'.

Reluctant collectivists

The first strand begins with the ideas of people such as John Maynard Keynes and William Beveridge. Keynes was concerned about the high levels of unemployment in the 1930s and believed that government economic policies could and should create work. Beveridge's report of 1942 set up the social security system after the Second World War (see Chapter 3). He saw welfare as an aspect of citizenship, since all would contribute to the insurance fund and all would receive benefits as of right.

These people are described as 'reluctant' collectivists because they see the market system as the best way for society to run and only believe in state welfare to put right minor or short-term problems. Reluctant collectivists believe that the inequalities between people created by capitalism are necessary and a good thing, because inequality promotes competition between people and preserves individual freedoms. However, people who go along with reluctant collectivist ideas believe that, if left unchecked, extreme inequalities lead to social divisions in society and eventually to conflict. The role of social policy and the welfare state is therefore to regulate the economy, but in a minimal way, in order to ease the smooth running of capitalist society. Because of these reasons, people sharing the ideas of thinkers like Keynes and Beveridge can be considered collectivist, but reluctantly so.

Reluctant collectivism is reformist. Supporters of this set of values do not see the role of social policy as being that of creating a different kind of society – one which is more equal for example. Rather they believe that society is harmonious, with a high degree of agreement over values and political beliefs. However the operation of capitalism, with its booms and slumps which create periods of high unemployment and poverty, may lead to pockets of extreme hardship which threaten this consensus and order. Piecemeal reforms are necessary to restore harmony without fundamentally changing the social and economic system.

Reluctant collectivism is part of a wider philosophy of liberalism, which holds that individual freedom is central to democracy and that in industrial societies there is a process of continual gradual improvement.

Fabian socialists

Fabian socialists date from the beginning of the century and put a more positive stress on the role of the state to create a fairer and more equal society, gradually working towards socialism. Equality is believed to be a more important goal than individual freedom, and a positive value is set on collective provision and central control. The welfare state, with comprehensive provision of national insurance, health services and education, is seen as an important part of a modern industrial society. When inequality is found to exist, collectivists believe the state has a responsibility to use social policy to bring about reforms. The role of the welfare state extends beyond the relief of individual suffering and the solving of problems to redistribution of access to services such as health and education through universal provision.

Activity 17.1

Try to link the options below with the perspectives outlined.

A. Help for unemployed people
1 People who have no other resources and are genuinely unemployed should be supported at the lowest level it is possible to survive on and people should be made to work without pay while they are unemployed. Where possible, people should be encouraged to take out private insurance against unemployment.
2 Everyone who is unemployed should receive a payment which prevents them from falling below the standard of living considered normal in society (see Chapter 3 on relative poverty).

B. Child benefit
1 This should be paid to all families at a rate which reflects the cost of looking after a child.
2 A small amount should be paid to poor families.
3 Child benefit should be abolished.

C. Hospital treatment
1 The best possible treatment should be available to all, free at the point of use, financed through taxation and run by the state.
2 The government should provide a minimal level of health care for poor people, whilst others use private care.

D. Housing
1 Good-quality housing should be provided by the state for low-cost rental for people who choose this option.
2 All housing should be within the private sector with no regulations limiting relations between lenders, landlords and occupiers.
3 State-subsidised housing should exist but only for those in special categories, such as people with disabilities or elderly people on low incomes.

New Labour and the 'third way'

In 1997 the Labour Party won a landslide election victory after eighteen years of Conservative government. The Labour Party determined to reform social policy and the welfare state. The new approach adopted by Labour has been termed the 'third' or 'middle' way. This is intended to suggest an alternative to both the collectivist thinking of the old Labour Party in the post-war period and the anti-collectivist approach of the New Right Conservatives through the 1980s and 1990s. The third way thinkers believe in a competitive capitalist economy and do not want to replace this with socialism, but seek to use social policy to create greater social justice and to tackle social exclusion. Although Labour want to keep public spending low, they believe in a modernised welfare state as a means of widening opportunities and supporting those in most need.

The key themes in New Labour's modernising agenda are:

- a commitment to a pluralist welfare system with partnerships between the state, private and voluntary sectors in the provision and funding of services;
- a determination to keep public spending on welfare as low as possible;
- a belief in the need for flexible welfare services which can adapt to changing economic circumstances and individual needs;
- a move away from universalism in welfare towards means-testing in order to target scarce resources on those people in greatest need;
- a belief in the need for individuals to take responsibility for their own welfare whenever possible or to share responsibility with the state, rather than relying on collective provision of pensions, for example;
- support for 'communitarianism' as a way of encouraging co-operation and collective action between people in local communities to create a wider sense of belonging and identity;
- rejection of equality as the goal of social policy and a belief instead in opportunities for individuals to better themselves, particularly through education, training and paid work;
- an emphasis on the obligation of everyone to contribute to society through work in order to achieve their rights and the need to punish those who try to avoid their obligations;
- a commitment to partnerships between those working in welfare services and those receiving the services in order to create flexible services which meet people's needs.

Some of these themes can be seen in the thinking behind the New Deal for unemployed people (see pages 112–13 and 115–6). This is one of the government's flagship policies. Initially for unemployed young people but later extended to other groups, the original scheme was financed with £5.2 billion raised from the new windfall tax on the privatised utilities. This high level of funding demonstrates Labour's commitment to use public money to widen opportunities for those presently thought of as socially excluded. In line with the emphasis on creating opportunities, rather than giving 'hand-outs' the aim of the New Deal is to improve the situation of long-term unemployed people by getting them into work. A particular strength of the programme is that all participants are dealt with by a personal advisor who gets to know them and treats them as a person, not a commodity to be processed. This has led to a change to a more 'client-centred' culture at the Employment Service. The New Deal offers unemployed people a set of options. In line with the idea that people must contribute to society and take responsibility for their own welfare, participation in the scheme is compulsory for young people and the Chancellor has said that there is no extra option to 'stay in bed watching television'. People not participating will have their benefit cut. This suggest the idea of conditional citizenship – the government will provide training but citizens have a duty to make use of the opportunities provided. They lose their rights if they do not do so. Finally, the New Deal emphasises partnership between government and the private sector, through the involvement of employers as well as voluntary organisations and colleagues, and the use of private as well as public agencies in providing New Deal Personal Advisors.

Critical Perspectives

The anti-collectivist and collectivist ideas described above can be related to Britain's history of social policy and ideas within political parties today. The ideas described below are a bit different as they are more useful as a way of thinking critically about the role of social policy in society. They are more radical and extreme than anything which has formed part of Britain's legislative history.

1. Marxism

Marxists see the economic system as the key aspect of society – influencing all other parts. The way goods and services are produced and distributed is referred to as the *mode of production*. Changes in the mode of production are the causes of other changes. In Britain the mode of production is capitalist. Capitalism is a system in which some people own the factories etc. and pay other people to work for them. Goods are then sold for a price higher than the cost of making them and the capitalists receive the profit. Where one group controls the mode of production, conflict is inevitable between this group (the employers who own the factories and must keep profits as high as possible by keeping wages low and prices high) and the group of people who work for them (employees struggling to live on the wages). Marxists believe that class conflict between these two groups is the inevitable result of capitalism.

Marxists see social policy in terms of actions by the state as a result of problems created by the structure and operation of capitalism. The state is not separate from capitalism, but is a part of it. The main function of the state is to maintain the conditions for the existence and expansion of capitalism.

To complicate matters further, there are several strands within a Marxist perspective which look at social policy differently. All however have the common starting point of focusing on the fundamental and inherent problems of inequality created by capitalism. The role of the welfare state is then seen in a variety of ways. Welfare provision can be characterised as a concession won by working-class people from those in power, a kind of ransom for the continuation of the capitalist system. More will be given in times of higher profits, but taken back at other times. Alternatively, welfare services are seen as a ploy on the part of those who rule to avert real political and economic change which would take the form of revolution. The welfare state serves to alleviate suffering and reduce inequality to the extent that tensions are removed without any real shift in power or redistribution of wealth.

With a slightly different emphasis, there is a Marxist critique of the welfare state which sees welfare as helping and maintaining the capitalist system by meeting some of its needs. For example, the national health service and state education provide healthy and educated workers at a relatively cheap price. Social security provides support for unemployed people when the capitalists cannot pay wages in times of recession; benefits like family credit enable low wages to be paid through state subsidy. The welfare state functions within capitalism as a form of social control and no real welfare can exist in an inherently unequal society.

Marxists believe that the welfare state has delayed the collapse of capitalism. This is by removing the worst aspects, by humanising it and making it more acceptable to the working-class. Reforms allow the same problems to continue. But social reforms are approved of insofar as they do improve working people's lives. Marxists do not believe that the welfare system can solve the problems of poverty, homelessness and deprivation, which requires the abolition of capitalism.

2. Feminism and anti-racism

There are also different views of society and social policy provided by feminists, who focus on the role of women, and anti-racists, who look at the racism which is a part of this society and its welfare provision. Feminists have pointed out that more women experience more poverty than men. There are several reasons for this: women are, on average, less well-paid than men; women live longer but, because of their role in the home, are more likely to have gaps in pension fund contributions and therefore have poorer pensions; and more women are single parents (see Chapter 2). Women's oppression is summed up in the concept of 'patriarchy' which is used to describe a society geared to the interests of men, rather than women.

Feminists have also studied the role of women in welfare. Women provide a crucial support to the welfare state. This is first in their role as informal carers. Women care for children, relatives who are sick and disabled, and for elderly people. As was shown in Chapter 9, women provide the mainstay of community care. Women also provide much of the labour for the welfare state, in low-paid jobs, in hospitals and as home carers, for example.

When the welfare state was set up after the Second World War, women were very clearly seen as the dependants of men and were rarely eligible for benefits in their own right. There were many examples of sexism in welfare provision, even in benefits added later. One classic example was the Invalid Care Allowance which paid a weekly income to someone caring for a person with a disability. This was payable to all except married women – presumably because this was thought to be their role in life anyway. This and many other discriminatory practices have now been removed, often as a result of cases taken to the European Court.

Anti-racist writers have studied the position of ethnic minorities in society. Black people are often in the least desirable jobs and more likely to be unemployed. They suffer more from poor housing and inner-city deprivation. They have also experienced problems in getting access to welfare services. These may be the result of language barriers or lack of knowledge or it may be that services are not geared to their needs. In the following quotations, Asian carers talk about why the services available are not helpful:[4]

> He used to have meals on wheels, but even though it was useful to have them delivered, because they were so appallingly bad … I don't think they had even heard of halal meat … it was just a waste of money.

> I see some of the old people in this area, they just sit and look out of the window all day. They have no rights. No Asian people that I know go to day centres. People have nowhere to go. In the day centres there is no food for them, culture for them, music … nothing … so they just stay as they are – housebound.

> There aren't many Asians working as home helps and my mum doesn't speak English. She doesn't want an English person who is a stranger to our ways in the house.

Activity 17.2

Apply each of these perspectives to a specific area of social policy, for example, housing, education or personal social services. Use the example of health care given below to help you.

Case study: applying the perspectives to health care policy

The *anti-collectivists* or *new right* thinkers believe that health care is best provided privately for most people. People should pay into private health insurance schemes to cover treatment from private doctors and private hospitals. Only for those who cannot afford such cover would there be a state system. This would provide a basic level of care only. This is similar to the system which has existed in the USA (although there are now plans for a national health service).

The *collectivist* philosophy on health is for a free national health service for all, funded completely by taxation. The NHS, as established in 1948, reflects collectivist thinking. Although there have been changes which have since moved the health service away from this philosophy, it remains an example of collectivist social policy.

The *Marxist* approach has several strands. One is to look at the causes of poor health in terms of the society in which we live and the way we work. Reluctance to take measures to prevent industrial accidents and diseases illustrates the priority placed on profit above the health of workers. The health service can also be seen as working in the interests of employers. Employers need healthy workers and under the NHS workers pay for their own health care. However another strand of Marxist thought would see the national health service as something hard won at a time when the ruling groups in society were ready to make concessions to workers. As such it should be defended.

Feminists look at the contribution made by women to health care. This is first in terms of informal care: much of the nursing of sick children, for example, is done by women outside the health service. Doctors do not actually look after sick people, women do this under their direction, and hospitals are only involved in more serious situations. Secondly, women provide most of the labour within the health service, especially in the less well-paid jobs. Another angle looks at the treatment of women by doctors. Women tend to have more needs for health care than men, partly because of their role in reproduction. Areas such as childbirth have been 'medicalised' and taken over by male professionals, often leaving women feeling a loss of control over their own bodies and a sense of frustration and bewilderment.

Anti-racists emphasise the role of black workers in the health service and the lack of provision geared to the needs of ethnic minorities.

17.2   Expenditure on social services

Expenditure on social services has increased rapidly since the Second World War. Maintaining an adequate level of social welfare is expensive but need not be seen as a luxury which can be discarded in an advanced society. Education and health services can be seen as necessary to production, and other areas of provision contribute to the quality of life.

Activity 17.3

Consider all the ways in which we use services and facilities which are provided by the state or state-financed organisations. Write an account to demonstrate what life would be like without state provision.

Activity 17.4

Why has the cost of welfare provision increased? Make a list of possible reasons.

It was believed that expenditure on areas like health would decrease or at least stabilise after the introduction of comprehensive services. However, there are cases where improvements in welfare lead to further demands. For example, as people live longer, more demands are made on services for elderly people. Also developments in medicine and increased expectations of health care result in ever spiralling costs. In times of economic growth, expansion in welfare costs can be met by an increase in public spending proportional to overall growth. In a recession, however, growth is rarely discussed as the emphasis is on cuts in public spending and defence of existing services.

The cuts began in 1976 under the Labour government and have continued since that time. Whilst it was initially argued that the standards could be maintained by more efficient provision, this has proved difficult to achieve in practice. Unfortunately, cuts often hit the most vulnerable sections of the community hardest. The 'Cinderella' services (see page 337) with low status are often the first to be reduced and people who have disabilities are least able to protest in defence of services.

A radical proposal concerning public expenditure involves a move away from services provided free at the point of use and financed through taxation. In some cases – for example, prescriptions – this has happened to some extent, although the exemption system shows the limitations of charging for services. The arguments about charging for health services have already been discussed in Chapter 15. At a general level, it is difficult to see why the distinction between public and private spending is a cause of such concern, since services are paid for in both cases, by different means. However, there is a tendency for both governments and the public to see public spending as undesirable. People tend to be reluctant to accept taxation whilst welcoming free provision of health and other services.

Activity 17.5

Discussion question:
Why do people complain about paying taxes? Are their complaints justified? How could you counter their arguments?

Activity 17.6

1 If cuts have to be made in public spending, how should choices be made?
2 Outline a policy document showing priority services that must be retained, giving reasons for your choices.

17.3 Social services: a redistributor of wealth?

The introduction, after the Second World War, of comprehensive health, education and social security services led to a belief that wealth was being redistributed from richer to poorer people. This idea continues and there is a widely-held belief that one sector of the population pays for welfare provision for the benefit of another group. This idea is based both on the belief that taxation is progressive – that is, takes a larger proportion of income from higher- than from lower-income groups – and on the belief that poorer people benefit more from social services.

Whilst there is disagreement among welfare economists on the subject, there is evidence to show that social services do not bring about a redistribution of wealth. Income tax takes the same proportion of income from most people and is only progressive in the case of very high-income groups. Since 1945, the burden of taxation has increasingly shifted to the poor. In 1949–50, a man with a wife and two children had to be earning 23 per cent more than the average wage before he started to pay tax. Today tax is payable on income well below the average and in some cases below the poverty line.[5] People with high incomes often benefit from loopholes in tax law and increase their resources by means of expense accounts and items such as health benefits schemes and company cars. Indirect taxes such as VAT are regressive, insofar as they take a greater proportion of income from poorer people. In one study of taxation, the author concludes that:

> The progressive effects of some taxes are largely offset by the regressive effects of others, and all taxes combined have little net effect on ... inequality.[6]

In terms of benefit, there is evidence to show that people from middle- and upper-income groups receive more from certain services and those which are restricted to poorer people are low-quality services. In the health services, the quality of care is better in more middle-class areas, and middle-class people are better at recognising symptoms and more effective in ensuring they get high-quality services. Similarly, in education, schools in middle-class areas are often better and the middle-classes make greater use of further and higher education facilities. In housing finance, tax relief subsidises home-owners. The only clear redistribution of wealth brought about by social services is that from childless people to families with children and over the life-cycle from younger to older people.

Activity 17.7

Discussion question:
Should social policy be concerned with a redistribution of resources from richer to poorer people? If so, how could this be achieved?

17.4 Administration of welfare

Central and local government control

A number of different agencies are involved in the administration of state welfare services. Central government, based at Westminster, makes laws and decides on spending on welfare. Central government departments such as the Department of Health, the Department of Social Security and the Department for Education and Employment are responsible for the implementation of policies in their areas of welfare. The European Union also has a role in welfare, particularly in ensuring equality of treatment. Although the central government departments have overall responsibility for welfare, the actual provision of services is delegated to other organisations. How this is done varies in different cases.

As was discussed in Chapter 15, the health service is run by health authorities, with NHS Trusts responsible directly to central government. Primary care groups will evolve into trusts responsible for community health services. Personal social services are run by the county councils or other local authorities. Social security was run by local offices of the Department of Social Security but is now run by the Benefits Agency which has greater independence from central government. Employment policies are carried out by local agencies, again with considerable independence. Housing is the concern of district or borough councils. Education policy has gone through a number of changes in direction. The decision to allow schools to opt out of local authority control resulted in separate funding agencies and self-governed grant-maintained schools. Since 1999, the reversal of this policy has brought previously grant-maintained schools back within local government control as foundation schools.

In some cases, local authorities have a legal duty to provide a particular service – this has been the case with education for children over 5; in other cases, laws give the local authority permission to provide services at their own discretion – this is the case with pre-school care facilities.

Central government control of local authorities is exercised in a variety of ways. There are circulars sent out to local authorities, inspections and of course laws setting duties for local authorities. An important source of control is through finance. Central government can send auditors into a local authority to check that money is being spent according to the intentions of central government. Central government can also control the amount of local authority borrowing. The largest part of local authority finance comes from a grant from central government – the amount of which is assessed by central government. The rest of local authority money comes from locally collected council taxes and central government can 'cap' this, that is set a limit to the amount which is asked for.

Source: Vicky White, Photofusion
Health care in the private sector

Changes in central–local relationship

Recent years have seen changes in the relationship between central and local government. Local authorities have less control over local services than was the case previously. This erosion of power has occurred in a number of ways. As has already been mentioned, schools and colleges have been allowed to opt out of the control of the local authorities and be financed from central sources.

Powerful new 'quangos' have been created. 'Quango' stands for 'quasi-autonomous non-governmental organisation'. It means a body set up by government but functioning with some independence from the government department to which it is responsible. Examples of quangos are the Funding Agency for Schools and the Further Education Funding Council, both of which carried out tasks previously done by local authorities. Members of quangos are appointed, not elected and, unlike local councils, meetings are not open to the public.

The financial controls described above date mostly from the 1980s, before which time councils could set their own rates and collect more money to provide a higher level of services if they wished. Now the Secretary of State for the Department for the Environment, Transport and the Regions can 'cap' councils which are thought to be spending too much money.

Activity 17.8

> List arguments for and against local freedom in how council tax is collected and services are managed.

The issue of the merits and limitations of management of services by local councils is of current concern, as many people perceive a move towards centralisation and control of the activities of local authorities. Where services are provided at the discretion of the authority there is a risk of too great a variation from area to area. On the other hand, this can be seen as an advantage, allowing flexibility in meeting local needs. Whilst local government may be weak, it provides a useful check on central government. However, turn-out at local elections is often low, perhaps showing a lack of interest in the activities of local authorities.

Activity 17.9

> 1 How can local authorities stimulate more interest and involve local communities in their work?
> 2 Draw up a report, with recommendations for local councillors and officers.

17.5 Privatisation

One of the key themes in social policy in the 1980s and 1990s, as we have seen in Chapter 8, was the transfer of responsibilities from state to private organisations. The means by which this policy has been pursued has included legislation, circulars to local authorities, encouragement of a belief that private provision is superior to public services, and physical conditions – for example, waiting-lists for health care – which create a demand for private services by those who can afford to pay.

Privatisation is not a single policy but takes place through a variety of changes and shifts in approach. Work which is paid for by the state and was traditionally carried out by state employees is being transferred to private institutions and companies. Examples of this include private provision of school meals and the contracting-out of hospital cleaning and laundry work. Second, state-owned property is being sold under a variety of schemes – for example, council houses to tenants, whole estates to housing companies in some areas, and hospital buildings sold and leased back. Third, the private sector received a boost with the 1990 NHS and Community Care Act. In terms of community care, local authorities are encouraged to use private and voluntary organisations as providers of care. Within the NHS, purchasers of health care (fund-holding doctors and health authorities) are free to choose private health services instead of those provided within the NHS. In both these cases, the privately provided services are paid for with public funds. Finally, there is the encouragement of the private sector in such policies as allowing tax relief on medical insurance.

The policy of privatisation is based on political ideology, although often justified in terms of efficiency and cost-cutting. Whilst complaints made of public services are in some cases valid, there is no evidence to support the view that private organisations are more efficiently run or can provide equal services more cheaply. The bureaucratic insensitivity which is often criticised in the public sector is a symptom of large-scale organisation rather than of state provision and could be reduced by policies of decentralisation.

Arguments in favour of state provision of welfare begin with the belief that state welfare is aimed at meeting social needs rather than making a profit and, in the fields of health, education and other aspects of welfare, this would seem to be a more appropriate approach. Services are provided for everyone, and policies such as removing regional inequality can be pursued whereas a profit-making organisation would not be concerned with such aims. State services are accountable to the government and subject to inspections. High standards can be maintained without pressure to cut corners to maximise profits. Conditions of work are usually better in the public sector and high standards of training are provided for professionals such as doctors. The state can provide a continuity of provision which could be lost if a firm closed down or decided an area of work was not worthwhile.

Activity 17.10

Use library resources and your own knowledge to make a list of facilities in welfare which have been provided privately since the 1980s.

17.6 Universal or selective welfare

This area of debate concerns the basis on which services should be provided. Services can be provided universally, for all irrespective of income, or selectively on the criterion of need. The arguments in this area are complex, operating on a variety of different levels and causing some confusion. Definitions of the terms 'universal' and 'selective' vary and it is sometimes argued that there are no truly universal services in the sense that all contribute and benefit equally. In terms of more commonly accepted definitions, universal provision includes health and education and, within social security, benefits like child benefit which are not subject to a means-test. Examples of selective benefits are those which are means-tested, such as income support and free school meals.

The importance of the provision introduced in the years immediately after the Second World War lay not so much in the services provided but in the universality of the provision. It was this aspect which gave rise to the term 'welfare state' to describe Britain. The debate concerning universal or selective welfare continues. At an ideological level it concerns the goals of social policy. For some, social policy is concerned with the creation of a just society and state provision is the best way of providing for needs. Others see the aim of welfare provision in terms of filling gaps left by the workings of the economy, acting in a residual role as a safety-net. At a political level, universal provision is seen as an attack on freedom of choice for the individual. For those more concerned with equality, the notion of freedom is seen as illusory, since it only exists for the better-off. For example, the freedom to educate a child in a private school is only meaningful to those who can afford such a choice. There are also arguments against universal provision based on the idea that high taxation, necessary to pay for services, leads to loss of incentive. This argument is refuted by the universalists.

At a more practical level, it is argued that universal benefits are wasteful, in that they provide for people who do not need state help and mean that provision for the needy is insufficient since the available resources are spread too thinly. Against this point of view it is argued that selective provision leads to double standards of care and greater social divisions and inequality. This is based on the assumption that people who are paying demand a higher standard of services than those who receive free provision. For example, in health and education, selectivity leads to two classes of hospitals and schools, in the state and private sector. Also selectivity leads to means of distinguishing those in need, and means-testing leads to stigma and low take-up. This can be seen by comparing child benefit, which is universal, with a benefit like family credit, which is selective.

The argument over universal or selective provision is intensified when new areas of need are discovered in a time of economic recession. These two factors lead to simultaneous demands for more spending and cuts. The trend in many areas at present is to move away from universal provision, examples of this being the selling of council houses and the increase in means-testing in social security benefits.

17.7 Positive action

Universalism is a policy of providing welfare for all. Whilst it avoids the stigma of the means-test, it does lead to resources being spread thinly over the whole population. In an unequal society, equal provision perpetuates inequality. A move towards equality and concentration of resources requires some form of positive action.

Focusing resources

Positive action is different from selectivity in that it involves the provision of extra resources or rights to areas or groups in special need. The focus on groups or areas avoids the stigma of assessment of individual need. Positive action policies which have been described in this book include Educational Priority Areas, the Urban Programme, Housing Action Areas and the Inner Cities Programmes. All these policies provide positive action on an area basis.

A further dimension to positive action is the extension of the policy to particular groups of people. This has been implemented to some extent in benefits for people with disabilities, where benefits are paid as of right, without a means-test. Arguments have been put forward for a benefit for single-parent families which is paid irrespective of income for all single-parents. Whilst this was rejected, increased child benefit for the single-parent was a small example of positive action. (New claimants no longer receive this additional benefit.)

Access to employment

Women and black people are discriminated against in many ways. Black people are disadvantaged in terms of income, housing, employment and education, caused by institutional racism. Although there is now legislation providing for equal opportunities in areas such as employment, it is illegal to discriminate in favour of previously disadvantaged groups. This is only allowed where being black or female is seen as a 'genuine occupational qualification' – this means a situation in which the job involves providing personal services and where the services can most effectively be provided by someone from that group. An example provided by the Commission for Racial Equality is of a counselling and information service on AIDS/HIV for African women. If a large proportion of the women do not speak English and would be embarrassed to talk to a male social worker, it would be acceptable for the health authority to seek to employ an African woman.[7]

The Race Relations Act allows positive action in providing access to training for particular work for ethnic groups which have been under-represented in that work at any time during the last 12 months. For example, a health authority has a very low proportion of Afro-Caribbean health visitors; the authority can encourage Afro-Caribbean nurses to apply for training as health visitors.[8] Employers are also allowed to select people from their employees and train them to do jobs in which members of that group have been under-represented in proportion to the local population.

Employers can encourage applicants from particular social groups to 'take advantage of opportunities' for work.

Access in education

An example of positive action in education is the provision of access courses which recognise educational disadvantage and provide a route into higher education for those to whom the traditional route is closed. Whilst little has been done as yet in terms of positive action, implementation of the policy may achieve the results which were sought but not realised in policies of equality of opportunity.

Activity 17.11

Should positive action be taken on racism? List arguments for and against.

Activity 17.12

Draw up a positive action programme for a particular aspect of local authority work, for example education or personal social services.

Activity 17.13

This chapter has used a lot of complicated language which is probably unfamiliar. Make sure you understand the following expressions used in this chapter. Check in the Glossary at the end of the book if you need to.

anti-collectivist	new right
'cap'	new right
capitalism	patriarchy
central government	positive action
centralisation	poverty line
'Cinderella' service	progressive tax
collectivism	quango
community care	regressive tax
dependency culture	safety net
individualism	selective
informal carer	selective benefit
invalid care allowance	stigma
laissez-faire	take-up
mandatory	targeting
market forces	Training and Enterprise Councils
Marxist	(TECs)
means test	universal
medicalisation	universal benefit

Further reading

A lot of the books covering the issues looked at in this chapter are quite difficult to read – they are suitable for dipping into but expect to have a bit of a struggle to understand the arguments. Such texts include Vic George and Paul Wilding, *Ideology and Social Welfare* (London: Routledge & Kegan Paul, 1976), which is quite old now but was the first to look at social policy in terms of perspectives. A much more readable introduction to some of these areas is found in Paul Trowler, *Investigating Health Welfare and Poverty* (London: Collins, 1991). There is also some useful material in Stephen Moore, *Social Welfare Alive!* (London: Stanley Thornes, 1993). As well as material on perspectives and other issues, there is quite a lot on the role of the European Union in this book. A review of feminist issues can be found in Gillian Pascal, *Social Policy: A Feminist Analysis* (London: Tavistock, 1986).

Researching and writing projects

Many courses, whether for academic or professional qualifications, require project work. Each project is a unique piece of work, chosen by the individual and worked on independently. To complete a good project is a very satisfying achievement. Starting a project can, however, feel very daunting, especially to those returning to study after some years out of school. The following pages offer some guidelines to writing and researching projects in social welfare.

Choosing a project

This is the first stage in beginning work on a project. It can be very difficult and is certainly very important. It is very hard to make a good project from a bad choice of topic. There are two starting points to choosing a project. The first and probably most important is the requirements set for the work and, if available, the marking scheme. It is likely that the project will be expected to demonstrate particular skills or types of knowledge. The topic should be chosen with these criteria in mind. The second starting point concerns subject areas. It is important to choose an area which is of sufficient interest not to become boring after a few days, weeks or months. On the other hand, it is necessary to be able to be objective about the information and this will be difficult if the topic is one on which the author has strongly-held and passionate views.

From these starting points, there are a number of other factors to be borne in mind when choosing a topic. Firstly, the subject chosen should be large enough to provide sufficient material for the project (whatever its length) but small enough to be manageable and to study in depth. It is more common for topics to be too large and to need narrowing down than for topics to be too small. It is much better to cover a small area in depth than to deal with a large area superficially. Secondly, the topic should not be too easy, but nor should it be too difficult. This point applies particularly to the research stage. Some areas are perhaps too easy to investigate: for example, a project which merely seeks to describe the work of the NSPCC can be done simply from the comprehensive and beautifully presented leaflets and Web pages which are easily available to anyone who contacts the NSPCC. On the other hand, it is important not to choose a subject which is too difficult to research. Such areas would include ones about which people are too embarrassed to speak, ones about which nothing has been written or where there are only articles in obscure journals in specialist libraries, or topics which require comparisons between factors which are very sensitive and difficult to identify and measure. For example, it would be very difficult to compare educational achievement with social class and intelligence in primary schools. Problems would arise in finding ways of identifying and measuring educational achievement and, even more, in measuring intelligence and social class. Such work has been done, but by professional researchers with thousand or million pound budgets and at least three years to do the research. Finally, better projects are those which seek to answer a question (even if failing to do so conclusively), rather than those which seek only to describe something. Projects based on questions are more likely to demonstrate higher skills of analysis and evaluation than those which merely describe. Another good way to demonstrate these skills is by comparison, perhaps comparing two types of provisions or by comparing what is provided with the needs of the clients.

It is important to keep a diary or log from the beginning of the project. This should start even before the topic is chosen. The diary will be vital in writing up the project.

Researching a project

Planning is an important part of project work. Once the subject has been chosen, strategies can be made for finding information and writing up. Plans should be recorded in the project diary.

A good place to start planning is by making a list of possible sources of information. These could include: books, either textbooks or more specialist studies; articles, either in magazines or newspapers; the Internet; interviews, with experts or others; visits and observations; minutes of meetings and other documents; leaflets and brochures; statistical sources from the government or from other agencies; and Websites. Whilst not all of these sources will be relevant for every project, it is good to have a variety of different types of research methods.

There are several short-cuts to finding information on particular subjects. The first and most obvious is the catalogues in the libraries which list books under subjects. Libraries also keep annual indexes which are the quickest and easiest way to find newspaper and magazine articles on particular subjects. Most catalogues are available on computer databases or CD-Roms which makes searching much quicker. Once one source has been found, the bibliography can be used as a guide to further material. Libraries also keep reference books which list names, addresses and brief descriptions of voluntary and other organisations. There are sometimes local directories of organisations as well.

It is rarely necessary to read a whole book. The contents and index should be used to find the relevant parts and pages should be skimmed rather than read.

All sources need to be read critically, looking for biases in the material. Organisations will always be presenting a particular point of view and all information is in some way limited. You must always bear this in mind and where possible compare more than one source of information. You need to be especially careful when using the Internet because anyone can publish anything they like on the Web. Ask the following questions:

- Is the information up-to-date? Good Web pages will state when the material was written and when last updated.
- Who is the author of the material? Why has the material been put on the Web? How reliable and trustworthy a source is this?
- Who is funding the site?

It is very easy to become overwhelmed by a huge amount of information. To minimise this problem, only information which is definitely relevant to the title of the project should be collected. This should be recorded in note-form and organised in some way. Notes kept on a computer disk or notebook PC take up a lot less space, and are easy to reorganise and to copy. By keeping back-up disks or copies of your work in progress on paper you will avoid the risk of losing your work.

For each book, article or leaflet, or Web page used, a note must be kept of the source. This must have all the details needed for the bibliography. Remember that downloading or copying information from the Internet and not giving the source is just as wrong as if you used a book in this way. Observations will also need to be recorded methodically. Interviews can be taped or notes can be taken during or immediately after the interview. Notes are easier than tapes to deal with, since tapes will have to be listened to afterwards and the information transcribed or noted. This stage is avoided if notes are taken in the first place.

Writing up a project

This is the final stage of the project and again it requires planning and organisation. Expect to write several drafts before you get it right. The process of drafting, re-writing and reorganising material is much easier on a computer where you can save one copy and edit another, delete material, add new ideas, move sections around – and always have a perfect version of your work. Another advantage of a computer is that at the end of all your hard work you can produce a very attractive and professional-looking document, something you can really feel proud of. The information needs to be selected for presentation and divided up into appropriate *chapters* and *sections*. The project is likely to include the following:

- a title page
- a contents page
- an introduction
- a description of the methods
- presentation of the findings
- a conclusion
- recommendations
- a bibliography.

The report should be written in such a way that the reader will find it easy to follow and should be presented as attractively as possible. A variety of methods of presentation should be used, including diagrams, tables, illustrations and photographs if these are appropriate to the title.

Probably the most important point about writing up the report is that it should be written in the author's *own words*. There is no value in copying out sections from other sources. Any quotations should be clearly referenced and kept short. Leaflets, etc. should not be included unless they have a definite purpose, for example demonstrating effectiveness or otherwise of communication, if this is what the project is about. Some items may be placed in the appendices, but again only for a particular purpose, not simply because they have been collected. Many projects are spoiled by the inclusion of material which seems to be no more than 'padding'.

When discussing information from different sources it is important to be aware of *biases* in the material. A pressure group, for example, is likely to present information in a particular way to best represent the cause it is concerned with. The same applies to leaflets or speeches from political organisations. Some sources are more objective than others and the project should show an ability to discriminate between these. It is good to set different viewpoints against each other, for example to compare the views of social workers and clients, of the Labour Party and the Conservative Party, or of council officials and residents. You could also compare information from different types of sources, for example the Internet and the books in the library.

The most important part of the report will be the *conclusion*. This is where all the information is weighed up and some conclusions drawn. These are likely to be tentative but are very important nevertheless. It may also be appropriate to make some recommendations about social policy and how things might change. The project itself should be evaluated and its strengths and weaknesses identified. A statement could be made about how the project could be improved if it were to be done again.

Finally, the report will end with a list of all the published *sources* you used. For books, this should include the author, the title of the book, the publisher, the place of publication and the date. For articles, the bibliography should show the author, the title of the article, the newspaper or journal in which it appeared, the date and the page number or numbers. Material from the Internet should show the address and, because Websites change, the date you accessed the material. Page numbers make less sense, so use paragraph numbers if this is possible.

Some projects will include *appendices*. Suitable contents are an interview schedule or a transcript of a tape. These are things which are necessary but which would interfere with the reading of the report if included in the main body of the project.

◪ Notes and references

I People in society

1. Amrit Wilson, *Finding a Voice: Asian Women in Britain* (London: Virago, 1978).
2. For example, Ivan Reid, *Social Class Differences in Britain*, 2nd edn (London: Open Books, 1981).
3. Terry Smyth, *Caring for Older People* (London: Macmillan, 1992).
4. Research by Margaret Mead, reported in Ann Oakley, *Sex, Gender and Society* (London: Temple Smith, 1972), p. 54.
5. Margaret Mead, quoted in Ann Oakley, *Sex, Gender and Society*, p. 55.
6. William Davenport, quoted in Ann Oakley, *Sex, Gender and Society*, p. 58.
7. *Community Care* (18 September 1986).
8. National Opinion Polls, Bulletin, 109 (1972).
9. Ivan Reid, *Social Class Differences*.
10. Quoted in *Times Higher Education Supplement* (4 December 1998), p. 6.
11. Office of Population Census and Surveys, *National Monitor* (Government Statistical Office, 1992), p. 20.
12. Office for National Statistics, *Social Trends 1999*, no. 29 (London: The Stationery Office, 1999), p. 32.
13. Salman Rushdie, 'The New Empire within Britain', *New Society* (9 December 1982), p. 418.
14. Amrit Wilson, *Finding a Voice*.
15. A. Bhalla and K. Blakemore, *Elders of the Ethnic Minority Groups* (Birmingham: All Faiths for One Race, 1981). See also Yasmin Gunaratnam, 'Breaking the Silence: Asian Carers in Britain', in J. Bornat, C. Pereira, D. Pilgrim and F. Williams (eds), *Community Care* (London: Macmillan, 1993).
16. Wilson, *Finding a Voice*, p. 106.
17. Berkshire County Council, *Education for Racial Equality*, Policy Paper, 1 (1983).
18. Jeremy Laurence, 'Should White Families Adopt Black Children?', *New Society* (30 June 1983), p. 499.
19. Remi Kapo, *A Savage Culture – A Black British View* (London: Quarter Books, 1981), pp. 7–8.
20. Amrit Wilson, *Finding a Voice*, p. 19.
21. Quoted in *The Guardian* (25 February 1999), p. 16.
22. Quoted in *The Guardian* (25 February 1999), p. 20.

23. Printed in *The Guardian* (24 February 1999), p. 5.
24. Salman Rushdie, *The New Empire*, p. 418.

2 Family life

1. Office for National Statistics, *Social Trends 1999*, no. 29 (London: The Stationery Office, 1999). p. 42.
2. Office for National Statistics, *Social Trends 1999*, no. 29 (London: The Stationery Office, 1999), p. 48.
3. Michael Argyle, 'What Makes Marriage Tick?' *New Society* (12 May 1983), pp. 217–19.
4. Quoted in Office for National Statistics, *Social Trends 1999*, no. 29 (London: The Stationery Office, 1999), p. 47.
5. EOC, *Facts About Women and Men in Great Britain 1998* (London: EOC, 1998).
6. EOC, *Facts About Women and Men in Great Britain 1998* (London: EOC, 1998).
7. *The Guardian* (21 December 1993), p. 6.
8. *The Guardian* (6 December 1993), p. 7.
9. Office for National Statistics, *Social Trends 1999*, no. 29 (London: The Stationery Office, 1999), p. 49.
10. *Teenage Mothers: Decisions and Outcomes*, in *The Guardian* (4 November 1998), p. 2.
11. National Council for One Parent Families, *The Child Support Agency's First Year: The Lone Parent Case* (London: NCOPF).
12. National Council for One Parent Families, *The Child Support Agency's First Year*.
13. *The Guardian* (29 April 1994), p. 4.
14. *The Guardian* (30 March 1994), p. 8.
15. *The Guardian* (13 September 1993), p. 4.
16. R. Emerson Dobash and Russell Dobash, *Violence Against Wives* (New York: The Free Press, 1979).
17. Marsden and D. Owens, 'Jekyll and Hyde Marriages', *New Society* (8 July 1975), p. 333.
18. M. Borskowski *et al.*, *Marital Violence: the Community Response* (London: Tavistock, 1983).
19. Reported in the *Observer* (25 February 1990), p. 21.
20. Dobash and Dobash, *Violence Against Wives*, pp. ii–iii.
21. *Domestic Violence, Home Office Research Study 191*, quoted in *The Guardian* (22 January 1999), p. 12.
22. Dobash and Dobash, *Violence Against Wives* (1979), p. 110.
23. Val Binney, Anna Harkell and Judy Nixon, *Leaving Violent Men* (Leeds: Women and Federation England, 1981) , p. 3.
24. Dobash and Dobash, *Violence Against Wives*.
25. Charlotte Rampling, *Daily Mirror*, quoted in *The Guardian* (May 1983), p. 10.

26. Binney *et al., Leaving Violent Men*, p. 14.
27. Women's Aid Federation England, *Written Evidence to the House of Commons Home Affairs Committee Inquiry into Domestic Violence* (Bristol: WAFE, 1992).
28. Women's Aid Federation England, *Written Evidence*, p. 17.
29. Binney *et al., Leaving Violent Men*, p. 15.
30. Binney *et al., Leaving Violent Men*, p. 79.
31. NSPCC, *A Good Year for Children? NSPCC Annual Report* (1986), pp. 4–5.
32. The Beveridge Report (London: HMSO, 1942), quoted in Gillian Pascall, *Social Policy: A Feminist Analysis* (London: Tavistock, 1986), p. 196.
33. Department of Health and Social Security, 1975, letter to National Council for Civil Liberties, quoted in Ruth Lister, 'Income Maintenance for Families with Children', in R. N. Rapoport, M. P. Fogarty and R. Rapoport (eds), *Families in Britain* (London: Routledge & Kegan Paul, 1982), p. 23.
34. See Pascall, *Social Policy A New Feminist Analysis* (London: Routledge, 1997).

3   Poverty and welfare

1. Michael Harrington, quoted in Ken Coates and Richard Silburn, *Poverty: The Forgotten Englishman* (Harmondsworth: Penguin, 1970).
2. Peter Townsend, *Poverty in the United Kingdom* (Harmondsworth: Penguin, 1979), p. 31.
3. Ruth Lister, 'First steps to a fairer society', *The Guardian* (9 June 1999), p. 2.
4. http://www.cabinet-office.gov.uk
5. Catherine Howard, Peter Kenway, Guy Palmer and Cathy Street, *Monitoring Poverty and Social Exclusion: Labour's inheritance* (Joseph Rowntree Foundation, 1998).
6. *Times Educational Supplement* (13 November 1998), p. 23.
7. B. S. Rowntree, *Poverty: A Study of Town Life* (London: Macmillan, 1901).
8. B. S. Rowntree, *Poverty and Progress* (London: Longman, 1941); B. S. Rowntree and G. R. Lavers, *Poverty and the Welfare State* (London: Longman, 1951).
9. Joanna Mack and Stewart Lansley, *Poor Britain* (London: Allen & Unwin, 1985); Joanna Mack and Stewart Lansley, *Breadline Britain: the findings of the television series* (London: London Weekend Television Community Education Office, 1991).
10. Mack and Lansley, *Poor Britain*, p. 9.
11. Mack and Lansley, *Breadline Britain*, p. 6.
12. Mack and Lansley, *Poor Britain*, p. 98.
13. Mack and Lansley, *Breadline Britain*, p. 9.
14. http://www.dss.gov.uk
15. Central Statistical Office, *Households Below Average Income*.
16. Oscar Lewis, *Five Families* (New York: Basic Books, 1959); Lewis, 'The Culture of Poverty', in D. P. Moynihan (ed.), *On Understanding Poverty* (New York: Basic Books, 1968).

17. Coates and Silburn, *Poverty: The Forgotten Englishman.*
18. Elaine Kempson, Alex Byrson and Katherine Rowlingson, *Hard Times? How Poor Families Make Ends Meet* (London: Policy Studies Institute, 1994).
19. *The Guardian* (2 August 1994), p. 4.
20. Office for National Statistics, *Social Trends, 1999*, no. 29 (London: The Stationery Office, 1999), p. 100.
21. *The Guardian* (3 August 1994), p. 3.
22. Alissa Goodman and Steven Webb, *For Richer, For Poorer* (London: Institute of Fiscal Studies, 1994).
23. Louie Burghes, *Living from Hand to Mouth*, 1980, quoted in Child Poverty Action Group Fact Sheet, *Poverty – What Poverty?* (London: Child Poverty Action Group), p. 2.
24. Ursula R. W. Henriques, *Before the Welfare State* (London: Longman, 1979), p. 12.
25. Report of the Royal Commission on the Poor Laws (1834).
26. Norman Longmate, *The Workhouse* (London: Temple Smith, 1974), p. 82.
27. Taken from Longmate, *The Workhouse*, pp. 96–7.
28. *Report on Social Insurance and Allied Service, Cmnd 6404* (London: HMSO, 1942).
29. The Child Poverty Action Group produces books on benefits, updated each year.
30. Lix Bisset and Jean Coussines, *Badge of Poverty, Poverty Pamphlet*, 55 (London: Child Poverty Action Group, 1982), p. 17.

4   Unemployment

1. *The Guardian* (4 March 1999).
2. *The Guardian* (15 January 1988).
3. *The Guardian* (15 January 1988).
4. Alan Walker, 'The Level and Distribution of Unemployment', in Louie Burghes and Ruth Lister (eds), *Unemployment: Who Pays the Price?, Poverty Pamphlet*, 53 (London: Child Poverty Action Group, 1981), p. 16.
5. *Labour Market Trends*, July 1999, pp. S51 and S59.
6. Peter Makeham, *Youth Unemployment*, Department of Employment, *Research Paper*, 10 (London: Department of Employment, 1980).
7. *Labour Market Trends*, July 1999, p. S40.
8. David J. Smith, *Racial Disadvantage in Britain, The PEP Report* (Harmondsworth: Penguin, 1977), p. 109.
9. Smith, *Racial Disadvantage*, p. 124.
10. Jeremy Seabrook, *Unemployment* (London: Granada, 1983), p. 113.
11. Central Statistical Office, *Social Trends 1994*, no. 24.
12. Seabrook, *Unemployment*, p. 144.
13. Seabrook, *Unemployment*, p. 197.
14. The Health Education Council, *The Health Divide*, quoted in *The Guardian* (3 April 1987), p. 3.

15. Dr Richard Smith, *Unemployment and Health*, quoted in *The Guardian* (17 September 1987), p. 2.
16. National Association of Citizens' Advice Bureaux, *The Cost of Living* (London: NACAB, 1992).
17. Jeremy Seabrook, 'Unemployment Now and In the 1930s', in Bernard Crick (ed.), *Unemployment* (London: Methuen, 1981), p. 14.
18. Seabrook, *Unemployment*, p. 128.
19. Seabrook, *Unemployment*, p. 199.
20. *Britain 1999* (London: Office for National Statistics, 1998), p. 175.
21. House of Commons, *Hansard*, 24 July 1987, quoted in *Poverty* (CPAG), Winter 1987–8, p. 5.
22. Balbir Chatrik, *Guide to Training and Benefits for Young People* (London: Unemployment Unit & Youthaid, 1999), p. xiii.
23. Reported in *Times Educational Supplement* (30 July 1999), p. 25.
24. *The Guardian* (13 August 1999), p. 20,
25. *The Guardian* (19 December 1998).

5 Housing and homelessness

1. Central Statistical Office, *Social Trends 1988*, no. 18 (London: HMSO, 1988), p. 133.
2. Office for National Statistics, *Social Trends, 1999*, no. 29 (London: The Stationery Office, 1999), pp. 42 and 167.
3. *Britain 1999* (London: Office for National Statistics, 1998), p. 346.
4. Central Statistical Office, *Social Trends 1988*, no. 18, p. 132; *Britain 1999* (London: Office for National Statistics, 1998), p. 348.
5. *The Guardian* (23 June 1999).
6. *Britain 1999* (London: Office for National Statistics, 1998), p. 350.
7. Henry Aughton, *Housing Finance* (London: Shelter, 1986), p. 64.
8. *Britain 1994* (London: HMSO, 1994).
9. Office for National Statistics, *Social Trends, 1999*, no. 29 (London, 1999) p. 168.
10. Shelter, *The Facts about Council House Sales* (London: Shelter, 1979), Appendix.
11. *Britain 1999* (London: Office for National Statistics, 1998), p. 349.
12. Central Statistical Office, *Social Trends 1988*, no. 18 (London: Office for National Statistics, 1988), p. 132; *Social Trends 1999*, no. 29 (London: Office For National Statistics, 1999), p. 169.
13. For example, *Housing Policy: A Consultative Document* (London: HMSO, 1977).
14. Central Statistical Office, *Social Trends 1994*, no. 24, p. 117.
15. *The Guardian* (10 March 1999), p. 17.
16. Short, *Housing in Britain*, p. 130.
17. www.shelter.org.uk
18. Joseph Rowntree Foundation, *A Competitive UK Economy*.

19. Commission for Racial Equality, *Factsheet 2: Housing* (London: CRE, 1978), p. 1.
20. Central Statistical Office, *Social Trends, 1994*, no. 24, p. 192.
21. Commission for Racial Equality, *Race through the 90s* (London: BBC and CRE, 1993).
22. Commission for Racial Equality, *Race through the 90s*.
23. Colin Brown, *Black and White Britain* (London: Heinemann, 1984), p. 79.
24. Commission for Racial Equality, *Race through the 90s*.
25. Brown, *Black and White Britain*, pp. 71–5.
26. www.shelter.org.uk
27. Office for National Statistics, *Social Trends, 1999*, no. 29 (London, 1999), p. 171.
28. *The Sunday Times* (8 February 1981), p. 17.
29. Central Statistical Office, *Social Trends 1994*, no. 24, p. 114.
30. Ron Bailey, *The Homeless and Empty Houses* (Harmondsworth: Penguin, 1977), p. 21.
31. *Roof* (July/August 1987), p. 13.
32. Shelter leaflet, *Homelessness in England: the facts* (London: Shelter, 1994).
33. *The Guardian* (23 January 1987), p. 3.
34. All figures from www.shelter.org.uk
35. Shelter, 1982, *Ordinary People* (London: Shelter, 1982), p. 23.
36. Shelter, *Homelessness in England*.
37. www.bigissue.com
38. University of York Centre for Housing Policy, *Foyers for Young People*: www.york.ac.uk/inst/chp
39. *The Guardian* (14 October 1998), p. 7.
40. *The Times Higher Education Supplement* (7 May 1999), p. 13.
41. Office for National Statistics, *Social Trends 1999*, no. 24 (London, 1999), p. 174.
42. Office for National Statistics, *Social Trends 1999*, no. 24 (London, 1999), p. 175.
43. Department of the Environment, *Better Homes: The Next Priority* (London: HMSO, 1973), p. 4.
44. J. Hillman, 'New houses for old – when?', *Observer*, 2 February 1969, reported in Paul N. Balchin, *Housing Policy and Housing Needs* (London: Macmillan, 1981), p. 177.
45. P. Walker, 1970, quoted in Balchin, *Housing Policy*, p. 182.
46. M. Young and P. Willmott, *Family and Kinship in East London* (London: Routledge & Kegan Paul, 1957).
47. Department of the Environment, *Old Houses into New Homes* (London: HMSO, 1968), p. 3.
48. *The Guardian* (6 June 1994), p. 3.

6 Living in cities

1. For example, L. Wirth, 'Urbanism as a Way of Life', *American Journal of Sociology*, 44 (1938), pp. 1–24.

2. www.regeneration.detr.gov.uk/utf/renais
3. Gill Burke, *Housing and Social Justice* (London: Longman, 1981), p. 113.
4. Lambeth Inner Area Study, quoted in Burke, *Housing and Social Justice*, p. 138.
5. Burke, *Housing and Social Justice*, p. 127.
6. www.regeneration.detr.gov.uk/98ild/indicate.htm
7. Lord Scarman, *The Brixton Disorders 10–12 April 1981* (London: HMSO, 1981).
8. Paul Harrison, *Inside the Inner City* (Harmondsworth: Penguin, 1983).
9. Harrison, *Inside the Inner City*, p. 32.
10. Harrison, *Inside the Inner City*, pp. 104–5.
11. Hackney Play Association, quoted in Harrison, *Inside the Inner City*, p. 310.
12. Harrison, *Inside the Inner City*, p. 345.
13. Community Development Project, *Gilding the Ghetto* (London: CDP Inter-Project Editorial Team, 1977), p. 4.
14. Benwell Community Project, *The Making of a Ruling Class* (Newcastle-upon-Tyne, 1978).
15. Reproduced by permission of the Controller of Her Majesty's Stationery Office with acknowledgement to ICD3 and the Cartographic Services of the Department of the Environment.
16. Department of the Environment, *The Urban Programme* (London: HMSO, 1981).
17. *Action for Cities*, The Cabinet Office (1988), p. 15.
18. *The Guardian* (9 December 1987), p. 27.
19. Quoted in *The Guardian* (10 November 1983), p. 20.
20. Information in this section taken from Central Statistical Office, *Britain 1994: an official guide* (London: HMSO, 1994).

7 Schooling in Britain

1. Office for National Statistics, *Social Trends 1999*, no. 29 (London: The Stationery Office, 1999), p. 68.
2. *Times Educational Supplement* (23 April 1999), p. 23.
3. *The Guardian* (7 December 1993), p. 4.
4. Quoted in *The Guardian* (18 March 1994), p. 3.
5. *The Guardian* (23 June 1999) p. 5.
6. *The Guardian* (17 March 1999).
7. Qualifications and Curriculum Authority (QCA), 148.
8. Office for National Statistics, *Social Trends 1999*, no. 29 (London: The Stationery Office, 1999), p. 148.
9. Dr Diane Reay, quoted in *The Guardian* (11 December 1998), pp. 2 and 3.
10. *The Guardian* (11 December 1998), p. 3.
11. *The Guardian* (1 November 1993).
12. Office for National Statistics, *Social Trends 1999*, no. 29 (London: The Stationery Office, 1999), p. 60.

13. www.dfee.gov.uk/eth/chapter3.htm
14. www.dfee.gov.uk/eth/chapter3.htm
15. Office for National Statistics, *Social Trends 1999*, no. 29 (London: The Stationery Office, 1999), p. 56.
16. *The Guardian* (3 May 1994), p. 7.
17. Julian Le Grand, 'Is privatisation always such a bad thing?', *New Society* (7 April 1983), pp. 7–9.
18. Office for National Statistics, *Social Trends 1999*, no. 29 (London: The Stationery Office, 1999), p. 56.
19. R. Klein, 'Using the Wrong Label', *Mind Out*, 33 (March/April 1979), pp. 16–18.
20. I. Reid, *Social Class Differences in Britain* (London: Open Books, 1977), p. 172.
21. R. Davie, M. Butler and H. Goldstein, *From Birth to Seven* (The National Child Development Study) (London: Longman, 1972).
22. Research by Ian McCallum reported in *Times Educational Supplement* (25 September 1998), p. 3.
23. Central Advisory Council for Education (England), *Early Leaving* (London: HMSO, 1954); Central Advisory Council for Education (England) *15–18* (The Crowther Report) (London: HMSO, 1959); J. B. W. Douglas, *The Home and the School* (London: MacGibbon & Kee, 1964).
24. A. H. Halsey, A. F. Heath and J. M. Ridge, *Origins and Destinations: Family Class and Education in Modern Britain* (Oxford: Clarendon Press, 1980); J. Gray, A. F. McPherson and D. Raffe, *Reconstructions of Secondary Education* (London: Routledge & Kegan Paul, 1983).
25. *1998 Youth Cohort Study*, Sheffield Hallam University.
26. Office for National Statistics, *Social Trends 1999*, no. 29 (London: The Stationery Office, 1999), p. 61.
27. *The Guardian* (12 January 1999), p. iii.
28. J. B. W. Douglas, *The Home and the School*.
29. M. Young and P. Willmott, *Family and Kinship in East London* (London: Routledge & Kegan Paul, 1957).
30. B. Bernstein, 'Social Class and Linguistic Development: A Theory of Social Learning', in A. H. Halsey, B. Floud and D. Anderson, *Education, Economy and Society* (London: Macmillan, 1961), ch. 24, pp. 288–314.
31. Department of Education and Science, *Education Survey*, 21 (London: HMSO, 1975).
32. N. Frazier and H. Sadker, *Sexism in School and Society* (New York: Harper & Row, 1973).
33. Commission for Racial Equality, *Race through the 90s* (London: BBC and CRE, 1993).
34. *Times Educational Supplement* (9 July 1999), p. 2.
35. Charles Husband (ed.), *Race in Britain*, quoted in *New Society* (17 February 1983), p. ii.
36. Commission for Racial Equality, *Race*, p. 15.
37. *The Guardian* (21 September 1993), p. 7.

38. *Education for All: the Report of the Committee of Enquiry into the Education of Children from Ethnic Minority Groups* (The Swann Report) (London: HMSO, 1985).
39. *Times Educational Supplement* (5 March 1999), p. 4.
40. From *The Times Educational Supplement* (15 March, 1985), p. 12.

8 Personal social services

1. *Local Authority and Allied Personal Social Services* (The Seebohm Report) (London: HMSO, 1968).
2. Tom Crabtree, 'The Double-bind of Social Work', in *New Society, Social Work* (London: New Society, 1981), p. 5.
3. Crabtree, 'The Double-bind', p. 4.
4. Reported in *The Guardian* (22 July 1999), p. 12.
5. Mary Langan, 'The Personal Social Services', in Nick Ellison and Chris Pierson (eds), *Developments in British Social Policy* (London: Macmillan, 1998).
6. Crabtree, 'The Double-bind', p. 5.
7. Reported in Mary Langan, 'The Personal Social Services', in Nick Ellison and Chris Pierson (eds), *Developments in British Social Policy* (London: Macmillan, 1998).
8. David Brockman, 'Trans-cultural social work: Time for attitudes to change', *Social Work Today* (24 November 1986), pp. 8–9.

9 Community care

1. Erving Goffman, *Asylums* (Harmondsworth: Penguin, 1968), p. 17.
2. Peter Townsend, *The Last Refuge* (London: Routledge & Kegan Paul, 1962).
3. Pauline Morris, *Put Away: A Sociological Study of institutions for the mentally retarded* (London: Routledge & Kegan Paul, 1969).
4. Leaflet on Elm Tree Close, Essex County Council.
5. Sir Roy Griffiths, *Community Care: An Agenda for Action* (London: HMSO, 1988).
6. Gillian Wagner, *Residential Care: A Positive Choice* (The Wagner Report) (London: HMSO, 1988), p. 60.
7. Barbara Meredith, *The Community Care Handbook* (London: Age Concern, 1993), p. 77.
8. Department of Health and Social Security, *Growing Older* (London: HMSO, 1981), p. 3.
9. N. J. Derricourt, 'Strategies of Community Care', in Martin Loney, David Boswell and John Clarke (eds), *Social Policy and Social Welfare* (Milton Keynes: Open University, 1983).
10. EOC, *Caring for the Elderly and Handicapped: Community Care Policies and Women's Lives* (Manchester: EOC, 1982), p. iii.
11. Janet Finch, *Family Obligations and Social Change* (Cambridge: Polity, 1989).

12. Finch, *Family Obligations.*
13. Carers National Association, *Community Care: Just a Fairy Tale?* (London: CNA, 1994).
14. Social Services Inspectorate, *Young Carers*, quoted in Eric Blyth and Allison Waddell, 'Young Carers – the Contradictions of Being a Child Carer', in The Violence Against Children Study Group, *Children, Child Abuse and Child Protection* (Chichester: John Wiley, 1999), p. 22.
15. Personal experience.

10   Children and young people in need

1. Government Statistical Service, *Health and Personal Social Services Statistics for England* (London: HMSO, 1993), p. 68.
2. *Times Educational Supplement* (5 March 1999), p 22.
3. *The Guardian* (11 May 1994), p. 12.
4. Participation Study, Rochdale ACPC, reported in *The Guardian* (11 May 1994), pp. 12–13.
5. Adrianne Jones and Keith Bilton, *Shape-up or Shake-up* (London: National Children's Bureau, 1994).
6. Reported in *The Guardian* (30 March 1994), p. 15.
7. Nigel Parton, *The Politics of Child Abuse* (London: Macmillan, 1985).
8. Noel Timms (ed.), *The Receiving End* (London: Routledge & Kegan Paul, 1973), p. 45.
9. Timms (ed.), *The Receiving End*, p. 47.
10. Quoted in *The Times* (28 August 1985), p. 9.
11. Commission for Racial Equality, *Fostering Black Children* (London: CRE, 1975), p. 34.
12. *The Guardian* (30 July 1987), p. 20.
13. R. Page and G. Clarke, *Who Cares?* (London: National Children's Bureau, 1977), p. 16.
14. Nicola Wyld, *Living Away From Home: Your Rights* (London: The Department of Health).
15. *The Guardian* (5 February 1999) p. 13.
16. Jenny Myers, Teresa O'Neill and Jocelyn Jones, 'Preventing Institutional Abuse: An Exploration of Children's Rights, Needs and Participation in Residential Care', in The Violence Against Children Study Group, *Children, Child Abuse and Child Protection* (Chichester: John Wiley, 1999).
17. Page and Clarke, *Who Cares?*, p. 42.
18. Page and Clarke, *Who Cares?*, p. 55.
19. Royal Philanthropic Society, *Leaving Care in the 1990s*, reported in *The Guardian* (21 April 1994), p. 8.
20. *The Guardian* (27 April 1994), p. 12.
21. Page and Clarke, *Who Cares?*
22. *Black and In Care*, Conference Report (London: Children's Legal Centre, 1984), pp. 34–5.
23. *The Guardian* (25 November 1994), p. 1.

24. www.homeoffice.gov.uk/cdact/csorddft.htm
25. Neale Pharoh, 'The long, blunt shock', in J. B. Mays (ed.), *The Social Treatment of Young Offenders* (Harlow: Longman, 1975), p. 57.
26. *The Guardian* (26 March 1999), p. 10.
27. *The Guardian* (19 April 1994), p. 19.
28. *The Guardian* (9 March 1988), p. 38.
29. Essex County Council, *A Community Based Provision for Juvenile Offenders Subject to Supervision Orders* (1988).

11   Mental health issues

1. Reported in *The Guardian* (25 August 1993), p. 14.
2. *Mental illness: what does it mean?* (London: Department of Health, 1993) and www.mind.org.uk
3. *The Guardian* (8 March 1994), p. 21.
4. *The Guardian* (3 February 1999), p. 9.
5. John Payne, *All in the Mind* (Oxford University Press, 1976), p. 18.
6. For a guide to the law on mental illness, see Larry Gostin, *A Practical Guide to Mental Health Law* (London: MIND, 1983).
7. Gostin, *A Practical Guide*, p. 6.
8. *The Guardian* (3 June 1994), p. 19.
9. *The Guardian* (10 May 1999), p. 17.
10. Dr Thomas Main, 'The Ailment', quoted in Joseph H. Berke, *I Haven't Had to go Mad Here* (Harmondsworth: Penguin, 1979), p. 49.

12   Learning disability

1. *Mencap Review* (London: Mencap, 1993), p. 2.
2. *Mencap Review*, p. 2.
3. From R. Edgerton, *The Cloak of Competence*, quoted in Joanna Ryan and Frank Thomas, *The Politics of Mental Handicap* (Harmondsworth: Penguin, 1980), p. 12.
4. Paul Williams, quoted in Ann Shearer, *Disability: Whose Handicap?* (Oxford: Blackwell, 1981), p. 54.
5. Mencap information, *Community Care: people and principles* (January 1993), p. 2.
6. *The Guardian* (26 July 1999), p. 8.
7. *The Guardian* (20 July 1983).
8. *The Guardian* (26 July 1999), p. 8.
9. From R. Kugel and A. Shearer (eds), in Ryan and Thomas, *The Politics of Mental Handicap*, p. 12.
10. P. Hunt, 'Comment: Single Rooms', *Cheshire Smile* (Winter 1968–69).
11. J. Mattinson, 'Marriage and Mental Handicap', quoted in Shearer, *Disability: Whose Handicap?*, p. 95.
12. Ryan and Thomas, *The Politics of Mental Handicap*, p. 58.

13. Ryan and Thomas, *The Politics of Mental Handicap*, p. 83.
14. Ryan and Thomas, *The Politics of Mental Handicap*, p. 42.
15. Mencap Resources Pack, *Community Care.*
16. *The Guardian* (26 July 1999), p. 8.
17. Mencap information, *Community Care: people and principles*, p. 2.
18. Paul Williams and Bonnie Shoultz, *We can speak for ourselves* (London: Souvenir Press, 1982).

13   Old age

1. Muriel Brown, *Introduction to Social Administration in Britain*, 5th edn (London: Hutchinson, 1982), p. 180.
2. *Older people in the United Kingdom*, factsheet from Age Concern (1994) and www.ace.org.uk/stat
3. *Older people in the United Kingdom* and www.ace.org.uk/stat
4. Family Policy Studies Centre, *An Ageing Population* (London: Family Policy Studies Centre, 1988), pp. 2 and 3.
5. For example, Peter Townsend, *Poverty in the United Kingdom* (London: Allen Lane, 1979).
6. www.ace.org.uk/stat
7. Child Poverty Action Group, *Poverty*, 52 (August 1982), p. 30.
8. Townsend, *Poverty in the United Kingdom.*
9. *Older People in the United Kingdom.*
10. www.ace.org.uk/stat
11. www.ace.org.uk/stat
12. www.ace.org.uk/stat
13. www.ace.org.uk/stat
14. www.ace.org.uk/stat
15. Rebecca Leathlean, 'Diary of a distressed daughter', in *The Guardian* (17 February 1999), p. 3; Central Statistical Office, *Social Trends 1982*, no. 12 (London: HMSO, 1981), p. 238.
16. www.ace.org.uk/stat
17. *Alzheimer's Disease – What is it?* Information sheet from Alzheimer's Disease Society (1994).
18. Printed in *Mind Out*, 33 (March/April 1979), p. 4.
19. Printed in Vida Carver and Penny Liddiard (eds), *An Ageing Population* (Kent: Hodder & Stoughton and The Open University, 1978), pp. ix–x.
20. Ellen Newton, *This Bed My Centre* (London: Virago, 1979), p. 38.

14   Disability

1. Michael Oliver and Colin Barnes, *Disabled People and Social Policy* (London: Longman, 1998), p. 14.
2. Ann Shearer, *Disability: Whose Handicap?* (Oxford: Blackwell, 1981), p. 10.
3. Reported in *The Guardian* (15 December 1998), p. 4.

4. Michael Oliver and Colin Barnes, *Disabled People and Social Policy*, (London: Longman, 1998), p. 18.
5. Reported in *The Guardian* (15 December 1998), p. 4.
6. Christopher Reeve, *Still Me* (London: Arrow Books, 1999).
7. Sue, in Jo Campling (ed.), *Images of Ourselves* (London: Routledge & Kegan Paul, 1981), pp. 47–8.
8. Angie, in Jo Campling (ed.), *Images of Ourselves*, pp. 11–12.
9. Quoted in *The Guardian* (9 June 1999), pp. 8–9.
10. Shearer, *Disability: Whose Handicap?*, p. 178.
11. *The Guardian* (4 August 1999), p. 3.
12. Daphne Saunders, 'Living on Benefit', in Alan Walker and Peter Townsend (eds), *Disability in Britain* (Oxford: Martin Robertson, 1981), p. 23.
13 Muriel, in Jo Campling (ed.), *Images of Ourselves*, p. 115.
14. Sarah, in Jo Campling (ed.), *Images of Ourselves*, p. 3.
15. Micheline, in Jo Campling (ed.), *Images of Ourselves*, p. 25.
16. Ros Franey, *Hard Times* (London: Disability Alliance, 1983).
17. *The Guardian* (9 April 1994), p. 8.
18. *The Guardian* (2 September 1998), p. 8.
19. *The Guardian* (4 November 1998), p. v.

15   Health and the health services

1. Office for National Statistics, *Social Trends 1999*, no. 29 (London: The Stationery Office, 1999), p. 119.
2. Colin Thunhurst, *It Makes You Sick: The Politics of the NHS* (London: Pluto Press, 1982), p. 3.
3. Thunhurst, *It Makes you Sick*, p. 4.
4. *The Guardian* (1 July 1988), p. 4.
5. *The Guardian* (1 July 1988), p. 4.
6. *Britain 1999* (London: Office for National Statistics, 1998), p. 193.
7. The Guardian (27 January 1999), p. 5.
8. Government Statistical Office, *Health and Personal Social Services Statistics for England*, 1988 Edition (London: The Stationery Office, 1998), p. 78.
9. National Association Health Authorities and Trusts, *NHS Handbook*, 13th edn (London: JMH Publishing, 1998), p. 7.
10. First Report of the Commons Social Services Committee on Resourcing the National Health Service (London: HMSO, 1988).
11. Summarised in *The Guardian* (2 March 1988), p. 2.
12. *The Guardian* (11 September 1987), p. 2.
13. *The Guardian* (4 June 1983), p. 17.
14. Central Statistical Office, *Social Trends 1994*, no. 24 (London: HMSO, 1994), p. 105.
15. Office for National Statistics, *Social Trends 1999*, no. 29 (London: The Stationery Office, 1999), p. 140.
16. Central Statistical Office, *Social Trends 1994*, no. 24, p. 105.

17. BUPA, *A Special BUPA Health Care Scheme* (London: BUPA, 1981).
18. *The Guardian* (4 June 1983), p. 17.
19. The Audit Commission, *A Prescription for Improvement* (London: Audit Commission, 1994).
20. The Haslemere Group, 'Who Needs the Drugs Companies?', quoted in Thunhurst, *It Makes You Sick*, p. 43.
21. The Audit Commission, *A Prescription*.
22. Thunhurst, *It Makes You Sick*, p. 39.
23. OPCS figures quoted in Ham, *Health Policy in Britain*, p. 191.
24. Ham, *Health Policy in Britain*, p. 193.
25. *Review of the Resource Allocation Working Party Formula: Final Report of the NHS Management Board 1988* (London: DHSS, 1988).
26. *The Guardian* (11 October 1998), p. 14.
27. For example, M. Stacey, 'People who are affected by the inverse law of care', *Health and Social Security Journal* (3 June 1977); A. Cartwright and M. O'Brien, 'Social Class Variations in Health Care', in M. Stacey (ed.), *The Sociology of the NHS*, Keele: *Sociological Review Monograph*, 82 (1976); M. R. Alderson, 'Social Class and the Health Service', *The Medical Officer* (17 July 1970).
28. TUC, *The Unequal Health of the Nation: A TUC Summary of the Black Report* (London: TUC, 1981).
29. Andrew Veitch and Nicky Hart, 'How the government buried its dead reckoning', *The Guardian* (30 July 1986), p. 21; The Acheson Report, 1998 www.offocial documents.co.uk/document/doh/ih
30. The Acheson Report, 1998 www.offocial documents.co.uk/document/doh/ih

16   The voluntary sector

1. *Britain 1999* (London: Office for National Statistics, 1998), p. 118.
2. *The Guardian* (22 June 1994), p. 10.
3. David Gerard, *Charities in Britain* (London: Bedford Square Press/NCVO, 1983), p. 17.
4. Quoted in *New Society* (7 April 1983), p. 3.
5. *Britain 1999* (London: Office for National Statistics, 1998), p. 120.
6. www.nspcc.org.uk
7. NSPCC, *Annual Review* (London: NSPCC, 1998).
8. NSPCC, *Annual Report* (London: NSPCC, 1993), pp. 3–4.
9. NACAB leaflet, *Seven million questions.*
10. Information leaflet from Alcoholics Anonymous.
11. David and Yvonne Robinson, *From Self-Help, to Health* (London: Concord Books, 1979), p. 21.
12. Robinson and Robinson, *From Self-Help*, p. 43.
13. *The Guardian* (27 January 1999), p. 6.
14. Information leaflet from Parentline.
15. Child Poverty Action Group publicity.

16. www.shelter.org.uk
17. WAFE, *What is Women's Aid Federation England?* (Leeds: WAFE).
18. The Terence Higgins Trust leaflet, *Service Users Guide to the Terence Higgins Trust* (London: The Terence Higgins Trust, 1994), p. 4.
19. Robinson and Robinson, *From Self-Help*, p. 57.
20. Robinson and Robinson, *From Self-Help*, p. 78.
21. David Robinson and Stuart Henry, *Self-Help in Health* (London: Martin Robertson, 1977), p. 118.
22. Robinson and Henry, *Self-Help*, p. 115.
23. Robinson and Henry, *Self-Help*, p. 115.
24. *The Guardian* (22 June 1994), p. 10.
25. *The Guardian* (22 June 1994), p. 10.
26. Reported in the *The Guardian* (18 May 1994), p. 12.
27. *The Guardian* (18 May 1994), p. 12.

17   Policy issues in welfare

1. Vic George and Paul Wilding, *Ideology and Social Welfare* (London: Routledge & Kegan Paul, 1976).
2. Report in *The Guardian* (2 October 1987).
3. Reported in *The Guardian* (6 September 1994), p. 1.
4. Yasmin Gunaratnam, 'Breaking the Silence: Asian Carers in Britain', in J. Bornat, C. Pereira, D. Pilgrim and F. Williams (eds), *Community Care: a reader* (London: Macmillan, 1993).
5. David Lipsey, *The Sunday Times* (14 February 1982).
6. J. N. Nicholson, 'Distribution and Redistribution of Income in the UK', in D. Wedderburn (ed.), *Poverty, Inequality and Class Structure* (Cambridge: Cambridge University Press, 1974), p. 81.
7. Commission for Racial Equality, *Race Relations Code of Practice in Primary Health Care Services* (London: CRE, 1992).
8. Commission for Racial Equality, *Race Relations Code.*

Glossary of terms

It should be noted that the explanations given here refer only to the way in which terms have been used in the context of this book and in the study of social policy. Some of the policies, provision and organisations referred to are no longer current, but remain of interest in studying the development of social policy.

absolute poverty: a lack of resources for survival

acronym: word made up only of initials, such as TEC

acute illness: an illness which comes sharply to a crisis and is of brief duration

adult training centre: see *social education centre*

advocacy: speaking up for someone's needs, *self-advocacy* can mean disabled people speaking up for themselves – perhaps with support and preparation in a self-advocacy group – but is also used when one disabled person represents another

agency: an organisation providing a service – could be a statutory, voluntary or privately run organisation

ante-natal clinic: a service for pregnant women, providing medical checks, relaxation classes and instruction

anti-collectivist: philosophy which believes in a minimum of state provision of welfare and believes individuals and families should help themselves and buy services if needed

anti-depressants: drugs given to people suffering from depression

anti-discrimination legislation: law prohibiting unfavourable treatment of particular groups

approved social worker: social worker with special training which allows her to be involved in cases needing compulsory admission to psychiatric hospital

arms' length (inspection): local inspection teams looking at services, for example residential homes, are supposed to be independent from the managers of the service, so they will report objectively

assessment: the process of deciding what a person needs

assessment centre: social services provision for children in care, aiming to provide an analysis of needs before placement

assisted places scheme: enables pupils to attend an independent school with fees partially or fully met by the government on the basis of a means-test, phased out from 1997

at risk register: a system of local reporting of children at risk from child abuse

attendance allowance: benefit for people aged over 65 requiring care or supervision *attendance centre*: provision for young offenders found guilty of an offence which, for an adult, would mean imprisonment, often run by the police on Saturdays with craft facilities, drills and sport

Audit Commission: government agency responsible for monitoring local authority and health services

binary system: a system containing two elements, as in the binary system which used to exist in higher education with polytechnics and universities; now polytechnics have become universities

bind over: an order of the court to a person found guilty of a crime that he or she will keep the peace and be of good behaviour or forfeit a sum of money

Borstal training: a court order now replaced by the youth custody order; it was a custodial sentence from the Crown Court for a person aged 15–21, with an emphasis on training and structured discipline

budget-holding GP: see *fund-holding GP*

bureaucratic: descriptive of administration based on rules and procedures

'cap': set a limit, for example the government can 'cap' local authority levels of council tax

capitalism: economic system which is dominant in this country and others in Europe and in the USA, based on private businesses employing workers to produce goods and services in order to make a profit

care manager: person responsible for someone receiving a community care package of services – involving the planning, monitoring and reviewing of services from various sources

care order: allows the local authority to take over legal custody of a minor

care package: services provided by various organisations which together allow a person needing support to remain at home

care plan: individual plan drawn up to provide care (perhaps from a variety for sources)

care proceedings: procedure in the family court for a child believed to be in need of care and control

carer: see *informal carers*

case conference: a multi-disciplinary meeting of professionals, for example from social services, education and the probation service, to discuss a case of child abuse

casework: a form of social work focusing on individuals and families in need of help and support

census: a study of the whole population; a census is carried out by the government every 10 years

central government: as distinct from local government, includes Parliament and Whitehall

centralisation: a process of concentration of decision-making in a central authority

cerebral palsy: a condition in which brain damage incurred before birth or at the time of birth and which results in symptoms that include an inability fully to control movement

charitable status: a legal category allowing a voluntary organisation to call itself a charity and entitling it to certain benefits such as reduced rates and taxation

charter: document written by the government or other organisation setting out standards of service which users can expect and often other information such as complaints procedures

chemotherapy: treatment with drugs

child health clinic: clinic providing for routine medical care of infants, screening of pre-school children and instruction for parents

Child Support Agency: government body which assesses the financial responsibilities of 'absent' parents for their children

chronic illness: a lingering, lasting illness with slow changes in symptoms

'Cinderella' service: part of provisions with less funds and less status than other services

City Technology Colleges (CTCs): secondary schools partly funded by industry and providing an emphasis on technical areas of education

class structure: an aspect of society whereby people sharing an economic position form groups with different access to wealth, power and prestige

client groups: different groups of people provided for by a service, for example, elderly people, children or people who are mentally ill

cohabitation: a couple living together without being married

collectivism: philosophy which believes in state provision of certain services for all

community care: exact definitions vary but basically the idea that people should be cared for at home or in small units in the community (rather than in institutions); services provided by outside institutions as an alternative to long-term residential care

community home: residential social services provision for people in the care of the local authority, replacing approved schools and remand homes

community psychiatric nurse: based in the community and working with people with mental illnesses living in the community

community service order: a court order requiring a person aged 16 or over to do unpaid work in the community under supervision

community school: secondary schools which did not become grant-maintained schools under the legislation which allowed schools to opt out of the control of the local education authority, previously known as county schools

community work: an ill-defined term which implies social work focusing on local groups rather than on families and individuals

comprehensive: descriptive of a service or facility provided for all

comprehensive school: a school attended by all children of secondary-school age in a particular area; some people suggest a school cannot be properly termed 'comprehensive' if there is an independent school in the area

congenital abnormality: a condition present at birth

consultative document: a report prepared for discussion and comment

contact order: this replaces the old idea of 'access' to children after a divorce, this is one of the 'Section 8' orders which the court can make under the 1989 Children Act – a contact order gives a person who the child does not live with the right to contact with the child

contempt of court: an offence, punishable by imprisonment, involving disobedience to a court, interference in court procedures or a show of disregard for the court

contract: an agreement between the provider and the purchaser of a service as to what will be provided

contributory benefit: a benefit paid only to those who have made sufficient national insurance contributions

cultural differences: differences in values and acceptable behaviour between groups or societies

culture of poverty: a concept associated with Oscar Lewis' explanation of the self-perpetuating way of life developed by the poor to cope with their situation

curriculum: the content of learning

custody: (1) the guardianship of minors

custody: (2) imprisonment

cycle of deprivation: a concept associated with Sir Keith Joseph, used as a means of explaining the way in which a poor background may lead to poor prospects

cycle of expectation: a process in which little is expected of a person's achievement and consequently little is achieved

cyclical unemployment: temporary unemployment caused by periodic slumps in the economy

day hospital: hospital care on a daily, non-residential basis – for example, for people who are mentally ill

dependency culture: a concept associated with right-wing politics; the idea of the dependency culture is that people on benefits become reliant on the state and as a result have no interest in trying to find work or living as economically as possible

depression: a mental illness, commonly described as a 'nervous breakdown' with symptoms of excessive sadness, feelings of hopelessness

deprivation: (1) individual – for example, emotional deprivation when people have been prevented from experiencing love or praise

deprivation: (2) collective – for example, urban deprivation as a result of multiple problems of poverty, poor housing, etc.

detention centre: residential provision for offenders aged 14–21 for periods of three weeks to four months

direct grant school: a form of private education which no longer exists whereby schools received finance from the Secretary of State for education and the local education authority could make use of up to 25 per cent of places

Disability Service Teams: provide specialist employment and training advisory services for disabled people

disabled person's tax credit: extra income for disabled people in low-paid work, included in wage packet, replaces disability working allowance

discretionary: if a service or benefit is discretionary, there is no automatic entitlement according to rules laid down by Parliament, the agency controlling the award can decide whether or not to give it

discrimination: treatment of a person differently on the basis of particular criteria

discriminatory practice: see discrimination

disruptive unit: provision within the education system for children labelled as 'difficult'

district general hospital: hospital providing all aspects of health care for a particular area

division of labour: separation of work into different tasks to be carried out by different people

divorce rate: the number of divorces expressed either as a proportion of marriages or as a ratio to population

domiciliary service: services provided in people's homes

dyslexia: a handicap involving difficulty in recognising or reproducing shapes or sounds of words and leading to impairment of reading, writing and language skills

earnings-related: benefits or contributions where the amount depends on the level of earnings

economic regeneration: financial revival of an area

ECT: electro-convulsive therapy, a method of treatment used in cases of depression and schizophrenia which involves the passing of an electric current through electrodes fitted over the temples whilst under anaesthetic

education action zones: groups of schools or single secondary schools in deprived areas receiving extra funding to improve provision

education welfare office: a person employed by the education authority concerned with school attendance and educational welfare

eligibility: entitlement

élite: a minority group which is believed to be superior and which has power and influence

enabler: people or organisations who do not provide a service themselves but allow clients access to services provided by other organisations

equality of opportunity: a situation in which everyone has an equal chance of success

ethnic group: see *ethnic minority*

ethnic minority: a term lacking a clear definition with the implication of membership of a group possessing a culture, often carries implication of discrimination and racial difference

extended family: a family group including other relatives in addition to parents and children

fair rent: a rent for privately rented accommodation set by a Rent Officer or Rent Assessment Committee, with regard to current prices and the condition of the property, but ignoring scarcity (now abolished)

family credit: a means-tested benefit for families in work, replaced by working families tax credit

field social worker: a social worker with families and individuals in the community

foster-parent: a person providing care for children under the supervision of a social worker; technically, fostering is called 'boarding-out'

foundation school: secondary school previously known as a grant-maintained school, created in 1999 when the system of schools opting out of the control of the local authority ended

frictional unemployment: unemployment caused by time-lags in people getting jobs

fund-holding GP: doctor or practice with a budget to pay for hospital and other services for his or her patients (abolished in 1999)

further education: education for people over 16, below degree-level

General Improvement Area: introduced in 1969, small areas of housing eligible for special grants and other provision for rehabilitation

General National Vocational Qualification (GNVQ): qualification related to an area of work, for example Health and Social Care, available at foundation, intermediate and advanced levels; advanced levels to be known as vocational 'A' levels

generic social work: social work which is not specialised but deals with all client groups

gentrification: process whereby professional people move into inner-city areas which become fashionable and expensive, displacing poorer people

geriatric: part of medicine dealing with illnesses associated with old age

'glass ceiling': a barrier to promotion to high levels of employment, usually used in connection with women

grant-maintained school: a school which 'opted-out' of the control of the local education authority and received a grant directly from central government, now returned to the local authority and known as a foundation school

group therapy: a form of treatment for mental illness involving group discussion of problems and possibly group living

guardian ad litem: a person appointed at the discretion of the juvenile court in care proceedings to safeguard the welfare of children by making independent inquiries, reports and recommendations to the court

half-way hostel: residential accommodation with some supervision for people moving from an institution to the community

health education: information to persuade people to adopt a life-style believed to be more healthy

health visitor: a person trained as a nurse with experience of midwifery and knowledge of preventative health, working in the community offering advice and support

hereditary: descriptive of a characteristic biologically transmitted from one generation to another

high-density: descriptive of areas with a high population relative to size

higher education: education at a level above 'A' level

home carers: staff working with people living at home and needing personal care (other terms may also be used)

Houses in Multiple Occupation (HMOs): shared houses or properties split up into bedsits, occupied by more than one household

Housing Action Area: introduced in 1974, a small area of housing where the local authority can improve housing, and housing associations are encouraged to buy and renovate properties

Housing Action Trust (HAT): an organisation set up by the central government to take over the running of council estates in poor condition, rehabilitate them, and sell them on to a new landlord

housing association: a part of the voluntary housing movement with the aim of buying and improving housing for rent at a non-profit-making price

Housing Corporation: a government organisation responsible for encouraging housing associations and distributing funds

housing tenure: the way in which properties are occupied, for example, rented or owned

hypothermia: accidental reduction of body temperature below normal range, particularly likely to happen to babies and old people

income support: a means-tested benefit for those not in work and not required to look for work whose income falls below a level set by Parliament

independent school: a school not maintained by the local education authority nor in receipt of a government grant

independent sector: non-government agencies providing services, and includes voluntary organisations and private organisations

indirect discrimination: a legal concept in the Sex Discrimination and Race Relations Act referring to discrimination by rules applied to all which effectively exclude certain groups

indirect tax: tax on goods and services, for example, Value Added Tax (VAT)

individualism: belief that individuals and families should take responsibility for meeting their own needs

industrial tribunal: an organisation, less formal than a court, which adjudicates on employment legislation, for example, unfair dismissal

infant mortality rate: number of deaths of children less than one year old as a ratio of live births

informal carers: people who care for someone who is elderly or disabled or otherwise needing care and for whom this is not a paid job, commonly just spoken of as 'carers'

informal patient: a patient in a psychiatric hospital without legal compulsion, retaining full rights

informal social control: control of itself by a community

injunction: court order stopping someone from doing something

institutionalisation: the process of becoming dependent on the routines of a protective environment

insurance qualification: a requirement attached to a benefit that the claimant has paid sufficient national insurance payments

interest rate: the price of borrowed money

intermediate treatment: a term with no clear definition describing a sentence for young offenders or provision for young people at risk of crime involving various activities and short residential courses

internal market: idea that services within one organisation, for example the NHS, compete with each other for contracts with purchasing sections of the organisation

invalid care allowance: a flat-rate benefit payable to people staying at home to care for a relative receiving an attendance allowance

inverse care law: idea which describes tendency for areas most in need of services to have least provision

IQ: Intelligence Quotient, the score from a test measuring a type of intelligence and compared with the mean for the age group

joint-funding: arrangement whereby two organisations, for example the health service and the local authority, share the cost of a project
joint roles: describes a marriage in which the husband and wife share tasks, social life and decision-making

laissez-faire: the philosophy that the government should not intervene in the economy
large-scale voluntary transfer: transfer of ownership of housing from local authorities to housing associations or other landlords
league tables: annually published lists showing schools' performance
learning difficulty: see *learning disability*
learning disability: someone is described as having a learning disability if they have considerably more difficulty in understanding and managing their everyday lives than others of the same age, as well as limited social skills
legal aid: means-tested financial help with the cost of legal advice and proceedings
legal system: the system of legislation and law enforcement
less eligibility: the principle, in the 1834 Poor Law, that a person receiving state help must live at a level lower than that of the poorest person living independently
life expectancy: a statistical concept giving the average number of years a person is expected to live from a given point in time
lobotomy: an operation on the brain intended to relieve a mental disorder
local authority: the local system of government run by councillors and officials

mainstream education: as distinct from special education; the education provided for most children
maintained school: a school where the running and staffing costs are met by the local education authority
maintenance payments: payments made by a divorced or separated spouse to the other for that person and/or the children of the marriage
maladjustment: a child is said to be maladjusted if he or she is unable to cope with normal situations
mandatory: compulsory
manic depression: a mental illness characterised by dramatic swings of mood from elation to depression
market forces: the idea that supply and demand for goods and services sets the price and availability of goods and services
Marxist: theories based on ideas of Karl Marx, basically seeing capitalism as a system of two classes, employers and workers, in which employers exploit workers to create profit for themselves
matrifocal family: a family type consisting of a woman and her dependent children

means-tested: benefits are means-tested when they are only available to persons whose income and savings fall below a certain level

modified extended family: separate nuclear families related to each other who share and provide significant services for each other

monogamy: the marriage of one man to one woman

mortality rate: the incidence of death in a population at a particular time

mortgage: a loan with property as security for the debt

mortgage default: failure to pay outstanding mortgage payments

multi-cultural education: education which relates to the cultures of ethnic minorities as well as dominant groups in a society, also known as multi-racial and multi-ethnic education

multi-disciplinary: involving staff from a number of different professions, for example social workers, doctors and community psychiatric nurses

multiple deprivation: a situation where many aspects of deprivation are combined in inner-city areas, for example poverty, poor housing and unemployment

multiple sclerosis: a chronic disease of the nervous system affecting young and middle-aged adults

national curriculum: content of education laid down by government to be taught in all state schools

national insurance contributions: payments made by employers, employees and self-employed people for national insurance benefits

National Vocational Qualification (NVQ): vocational qualifications for people in work, at various levels and covering most types of work

negative equity: the result of a fall in house prices, negative equity occurs when a house or flat has been bought with a mortgage which was higher than the current value of the property

neurosis: a less severe category of mental illness, typically involving an exaggeration of usual emotions, but retention of insight

New Right: people who believe in minimal state provision, families and individuals being responsible for themselves and the private provision of services

NHS Trust: with the split of the health authorities into units which purchase services and those which provide services, most hospitals and community health services are separately managed by Trusts; the Trusts remain part of the NHS but are managed by a Board of Trustees

non-accidental injury: injury inflicted on children in their homes, also known as child abuse

non-contributory benefit: entitlement to the benefit does not depend on having paid national insurance contributions

norm: social rule for behaviour in a particular group

nuclear family: a family consisting of parents and immature children only

obsession: a mental illness where activities are taken to extremes or repeated over and over again

obstetrician: a doctor specialising in the care of woman in pregnancy, childbirth and immediately after birth

occupational pension: a pension based on payments made whilst in work to a private fund

outreach: services are taken out to where clients are, for example in prison or hospital or even on the street

paranoia: a mental illness characterised by delusions and a false belief of persecution

parasitic disease: an illness caused by an organism living in the body, for example a virus

parity of esteem: descriptive of provision where different aspects are regarded as equal

Part III accommodation: accommodation provided for people needing care under Part III of the 1948 National Assistance Act

passport benefit: a social security benefit which provides automatic entitlement to other benefits

patch system: a system where small groups of social workers are based in neighbourhood offices instead of working from more centralised area offices

patent law: gives exclusive rights over a new invention or process for a period of time

paternalistic: limiting freedom by well-meant regulations and provision

patriarchy: feminist concept seeing society as controlled by men in their own interests

per capita: per head

personal social services: provision by local authority department employing social workers and others, such as home helps

phobia: mental illness involving an irrational fear

planning blight: environmental problems caused by indecision in planning

polyandry: marriage where there is one woman and several husbands

polygamy: marriage between more than one man or woman

polygyny: marriage involving one man and several wives

positive action: action to combat inequalities by giving extra resources or rights to disadvantaged groups or areas

poverty cycle: a concept describing changes in the standard of living of those near the poverty line in the course of their life, through, for example, the existence of dependent children or retirement from work

poverty line: a definition of poverty for research purposes, setting a level of income below which people are said to be in poverty

poverty trap: factors which prevent families from increasing net income through raising wages as a result of the interaction of increased income tax, national insurance payments and decreased benefits

pre-school education: education before the compulsory school age

pressure group: an organisation trying to bring about change by influencing those in power or changing public opinion

preventative medicine: medical services designed to prevent rather than cure problems

preventative services: as preventative medicine although more general in scope

primary care groups: responsible for commissioning and providing community-based health services for local areas of around 100,000 people

primary poverty: Rowntree's term for people living below the poverty line as a result of insufficient income

private sector: services provided outside state provision

probation officer: a person employed to advise, assist and befriend offenders and those leaving prison; also involved in preparing Social Inquiry Reports for the court

progressive tax: a tax which takes proportionately more from higher income groups

prohibited steps order: this is one of the 'Section 8' orders which the court can make under the 1989 Children Act in a divorce case; a prohibited steps order stops something from being done, for example stating that the child must not be taken abroad

provider: the organisation or person providing a service (health and social services are now split into 'provider' and 'purchaser' sections following the 1990 NHS and Community Care Act)

psychiatric social worker: a social worker attached to a mental hospital or child guidance clinic, specialising in mental illness

psychiatrist: a doctor who specialises in the study and treatment of mental disorders

psycho-geriatrician: a doctor specialising in the mental illnesses associated with old age

psychological: concerned with the human mind

psychologist: a person engaged in the study of the mind or working in the field of assessment and treatment of people with mental disorders

psychopath: a person suffering from a personality disorder with symptoms of anti-social behaviour, little feeling of guilt and an inability to form relationships

psychosis: a category of severe mental illnesses in which the sufferer loses touch with reality

psychosurgery: surgery on the brain believed to cure certain types of mental illness

psychotherapy: treatment of mental illness through talking with the aim of reaching an understanding of the illness

psychotropic drug: a drug affecting moods and emotions

public school: a term with no clear definition usually used for schools whose head belongs to the Headmasters' Conference

purchaser: the organisation or individual buying a service on behalf of clients (health and social services are split into 'provider' and 'purchaser' sections following the 1990 NHS and Community Care Act)

quango: stands for quasi-autonomous non-governmental organisation, an organisation set up by government but operating with some independence

quota system: scheme for proportional allocation to particular groups or individuals

racism: deliberate or unintentional practices, behaviour or attitudes which discriminate on the basis of race

reconstituted family: a family including step-parents and half- or step-children

redevelopment: the process of pulling down older buildings and replacing with new

red-lining: the policy of building societies of selecting areas where mortgages will not be given

redistribution of wealth: a means of achieving greater equality by transferring wealth from richer groups to poorer ones

registered social landlord: term introduced by the 1996 Housing Act, includes housing associations, local housing companies and housing societies which are registered with the Housing Corporation

regressive subsidy: allocation of government funds in such a way that people who are better off receive more

regressive tax: a tax which takes a decreasing proportion of income as income rises

rehabilitation: (1) programmes to help people to develop or relearn skills for independent living

rehabilitation: (2) renovation of old areas or housing, etc.

relative poverty: a lack of resources for the standard of living considered normal in a particular society

rent arrears: debts incurred as a result of not paying rent

residence order: this is one of the 'Section 8' orders which the court can make under the 1989 Children Act in a divorce case; a residence order decides where a child will live

respiratory disease: disease affecting breathing

respite care: temporary care provided to give carers and people being cared for a break; may be in a hospital, residential home or with another family

Restart: everyone who is unemployed for 6 months is invited for an interview with a claimant advisor; this may lead to placement on a course or workshop to help with finding a job

role: set of ways of behaving in a particular social position

role-conflict: there are several definitions for this term, it is used in this book to refer to a situation in which two or more of a person's roles interact in such a way as to cause stress

role-set: a collection of roles which fit together in a particular situation, for example, student and teacher

safety-net: idea of provision to support people who 'fall through' gaps in other forms of provision

schizophrenia: this is not a clearly defined term – it describes a severe mental illness characterised by loss of emotional responsiveness, loss of reality, often accompanied by delusions, hallucinations or bizarre imagery

secondary poverty: Rowntree's term for people in poverty because some of their income is spent on items not essential in terms of his definition of the poverty line

secure unit: accommodation in community homes or assessment centres for children who are violent or who continually run away

security of tenure: where tenants of rented property cannot be evicted without cause

segregated roles: descriptive of a marriage where the husband and wife carry out separate tasks and have their own friends and social life

segregation: setting some people apart from others

selective: descriptive of provision only available to particular categories of people

selective benefit: benefit allocated on the basis of set conditions, usually involving a means-test

selective education: a system of schooling which allocates children to different types of school

self-help group: an organisation in which members have common problems and help each other

senile dementia: a mental illness of old age, characterised by vagueness and disorientation

severe disablement allowance: a non-contributory benefit for people with disabilities

sheltered accommodation: independent housing with support from a warden or social worker if needed

sheltered employment: a protective work environment for people with disabilities

sheltered workshop: see *sheltered employment*

shorthold tenancy: tenancy of private rented property for a fixed period

shortlife property: property due for demolition or renovation, let cheaply or free for a short period

social deprivation factors: characteristics, for example, poor housing, which are used to measure need in an area

social education centre: (previously known as adult training centre) provides support in finding work, training or education for people with a learning disability; may include other facilities for people with severe disability

social exclusion: a wide term used to refer to a variety of ways in which people are denied full participation in society as a result of a combination of linked problems such as poverty, unemployment, poor housing, bad health and family breakdown

social housing: includes local authority (council) housing and housing provided by housing associations and other landlords registered with the Housing Corporation

social indicator: see *social deprivation factors*

social inquiry report: a report written by a social worker or probation officer (for a court) on the circumstances and home environment of a person

social policy: government action in the field of welfare

social security: the system of financial benefits for income maintenance, that is national insurance benefits and other means-tested benefits

social services: welfare provision, including education, health services and social security, sometimes incorrectly used to refer to the personal social services alone

socialisation: the process of learning the values and accepted behaviour of a society

special education: educational provision for children with learning difficulties

special school: a school for children with learning disabilities

specialist school: the specialists schools programme was launched in 1993; specialist schools are secondary schools which teach the full curriculum but also specialise in technology, modern languages, sport and the arts; such schools have the backing of private sponsors and extra grants from the government

specific issue order: this is one of the 'Section 8' orders which the court can make under the 1989 Children Act in a divorce case; a specific issue order takes away the parents' responsibility over particular issues and means decisions must be made by the court – an example of this could be decisions on education; it is quite rare for this order to be used

speech therapy clinic: provision to help people with speech problems

squatting: unauthorised occupation of empty properties

state sector: services and enterprises provided by the government rather than private individuals or organisations

'statementing': procedure under the 1981 Education Act whereby children with more complex learning disabilities are assessed by the local education authority

status: social position relative to others

statutory: by law

statutory duty: obligation by law

statutory organisation: organisation established by legislation

stereotype: type-cast mental impression

stigma: something which sets apart or results in unfavourable treatment

structural unemployment: unemployment caused by basic long-term changes in the economy

supervision order: a court order that a child being looked after by his or her family be allocated a social worker or probation officer to provide help

take-up: the proportion of those eligible for a benefit who receive it

targeting: the policy of focusing services on those thought to be in greatest need, usually meaning the poorest only

tax relief: freedom from taxation for specific reasons

tenure: see *housing tenure*

tertiary college: an education institution providing further education for all over 16, replacing sixth forms and colleges of further education

test case: a legal case brought to court in order to establish a ruling on an aspect of law

therapist: a person providing treatment, sometimes used to refer to psychotherapy, but also speech therapist, etc.

total institution: Goffman's term for an institution in which people live their whole lives, e.g. prison or army barracks

Training and Enterprise Councils (TECs): local organisations led by employers and responsible for training schemes and support for new businesses in their areas (LECs in Scotland)

tranquiliser: a drug which has a calming effect; major tranquilisers are used in the treatment of schizophrenia and other psychoses, minor tranquilisers are used for neuroses such as anxiety

tribunal: a decision-making body, for example in the fields of mental health, social security, rent and employment

tripartite system: organisation into three parts, for example, secondary education consisting of technical, grammar and secondary modern schools

universal: welfare provision is said to be universal when it is available for all
universal benefit: benefit available for all without a means-test

voluntary organisation: a non-profit-making organisation not established by legislation
voluntary school: a school established by a voluntary organisation but maintained by the local education authority
volunteer: an unpaid worker choosing to give services

welfare provision: a vague term for services provided to help people
welfare state: a term with no clear definition, originating in the 1940s after the introduction of the health service, national insurance, etc.; refers to all welfare provision or a state which provides welfare
White Paper: a document stating the government's policy prior to legislation
workhouse: institution in which poor people were provided for under the 1834 Poor Law
working families tax credit: extra income for families in low-paid employment, replaces family credit, and included in pay
work-sharing: a means of reducing unemployment by dividing work among the population, perhaps by shortening the working week

◼ ⍗ Index

absolute poverty 69, 399
access, for disabled people 315
Access Officers 315
Access to Work 309
Acheson Report 341
adult education 187
advocacy 281–2, 399
age (see also older people) 3–4, 8
Alcoholics Anonymous 350–1,
    356–7
anti-collectivism 361–4, 369, 399
anti-racism 368–9
approved social workers 268, 399
Area Health Authorities 322
Assisted Places Scheme 189, 399
assured tenancies 124
at risk registers 63, 239, 399
attendance allowance 91, 399
attendance centres 255, 400
Audit Commission 222, 336, 400
Aves Committee 347–8

Barclay Report 211
Barnardo's 235, 346
'bed and breakfast' accommodation
    135–6
Bevan, Aneurin 321, 331
Beveridge Report 88–90
Big Issue 139
Black Report 339–41
budgeting loans 95
Bulger, James 250
Butler–Sloss Report 63

CARE 356
care order 237–8, 400
Careers Officers 193
carers 228–31
Carers National Association (Carers)
    229
Carers (Recognition of Services) Act
    1995 230
case conferences 238
Catholic Rescue Society 346

Central Council for Education, Training
    and Social Work (CCETSW) 206,
    209–10
charities 345–6, 401
chemotherapy for mental illness 270,
    401
child abuse 62–4, 244–6
child assessment order 237
child benefit (see also family allowance)
    90, 91, 97–8
child curfew schemes 251
Child Guidance Clinics 193
child minders 174
Child Poverty Action Group (CPAG)
    351–2, 355, 356
child safety orders 251–2
child support 53–6
Child Support Agency (CSA) 54–6,
    401
child welfare clinics 322
children
    and divorce 50–1
    and social services 207–8, 236–49
    and voluntary organisations 346–7
Children Act 1989 207, 236–41, 246
Children and Young Persons Act 1933
    236
Children's Act 1948 236
Christmas bonus 91, 98–9
Chronically Sick and Disabled Persons
    Act 312, 315
'Cinderella' services 337, 401
Citizens' Advice Bureau 349–50, 401
City Action Teams 163, 164, 165
City Challenge 164, 165
City Technology College 182, 401
class see social class
collectivism 361–2, 364, 369, 401
communities 225–7
community care 211–12, 219–33
    and disabled people 312–14, 401
    and learning disability 279–80
    and mental health 268–70
    and older people 289–90

Community Care (Direct Payments) Act 1996   313
community care grants   95
Community Development Project (CDP)   159
Community Health Councils   322, 323
community health services   330
community psychiatric nurses   268, 401
community schools   169, 175, 401
community service orders   255
Compacts   185, 344
Comprehensive Community Programmes   159–60
comprehensive schools   181–2
constant attendance allowance   90, 91
council housing   see local authority housing
council tax benefit   94
counselling   268
Crime and Disorder Act, 1998   251–2, 256
Criminal Justice Act, 1982   253, 255
Criminal Justice Act 1988   253
Criminal Justice Act, 1991   251, 253
Criminal Justice and Public Order Act, 1993   254
crisis loans   95
Crowther Report   180, 181
culture of poverty   79–80, 402
Curtis Report   236
cycle of deprivation   79–80, 402
cyclical unemployment   101, 402

day centres   268
Dearing Report   176
dental treatment   93, 331–2
dentists   322, 325, 328
dependency culture   80–1, 363–4, 402
'deserving' poor   98–9
detention centres   252–3, 402
direct grant schools   189, 400
Disability Discrimination Act 1995   105, 310–11, 315
Disability Employment Advisors   309
disability living allowance   91
Disability Rights Commission   311
Disability Service Teams   112, 309, 402
disabled people   78, 90
   and education   190–3
   and social services   208, 301–16
   and voluntary organisations   347
Disabled Person's Act   313, 315
Disabled Person's (Employment) Act 1944   310

Disabled Person's (Employment) Act 1958   310
disabled person's tax credit   95, 309, 402
disablement benefit   90
distribution of wealth and income   81
District Health Authorities   323
District Management Teams   322
divorce   49–51
Divorce Law Reform Act 1969   50
doctors   see General Practitioners (GPs)
Domestic Proceedings and Magistrates' Court Act, 1978   60
domestic violence   see violence in the family
Domestic Violence and Matrimonial Proceedings Act, 1976   60

education   5, 64–5, 168–204
   and disability   311–12
Education Act 1944   168, 170, 180, 190, 194
Education Act 1980   170, 189, 194
Education Act 1981   191–2, 312
Education Act 1993   192
Education Action Zones   183–4, 403
Education Business Partnerships   185
Education Reform Act 1988   169
Educational Priority Areas (EPAs)   158, 178–9
electro-convulsive treatment (ECT)   271, 403
Elizabethan Poor Law 1601   83
emergency protection order   64, 237
employment   3, 107
   and disability   309–10
   lone parents and   52–3
   parents and   12, 47–8
   segregation in   17
empowerment   213, 305
Enterprise Zones   163, 164
environment   5
equal opportunities   38
Estate Action Programme   143
ethnicity   see race
European Regional Development Fund   165
European Social Fund   165
European Structural Fund   166
European Union (EU)   165–6
extended family   44, 403
eyesight tests   93

family allowance   89
Family Allowance Act 1945   89

family background 2–3
family credit 94, 97, 403
Family Fund 307
Family Health Service Authorities 323
Family Law Act, 2000 50
Family Practitioner Committees 322
Family Service Units 347
family structures 43–6
Family Welfare Associations 347
families 42–67
  and community care 227–8, 292–3
  and race 30–1
  and social services 209
feminism 368
foster-parents 241–3, 403
foundation schools 169, 175, 403
Foyers 139
free school meals 93, 97–8
frictional unemployment 101, 404
functions of the family 42–3
funeral payments 95
further education 169, 185–7

gender 4
  and education 197–9
gender roles 13–18, 48–9
General Improvement Areas 142, 404
General National Vocational
  Qualifications (GNVQs) 184, 186, 404
General Practitioners (GPs) 320, 322, 323, 325, 326–7, 332
'gentrification' 152–3, 404
Gingerbread 52
'glass ceiling' 17
grant-maintained schools 169, 404
Griffiths Report 211, 222–4, 344

health 318–19
  and older people 294–5
health care 65, 318–41
health education 322
Health Improvement Programmes 324–5
health visitors 322, 404
higher education 187, 404
home care services 216–17, 290, 312–14
homelessness 133–40
hospitals 328–30
  mental handicap 276–9
  and older people 295–8
hostels 268
Houses in Multiple Occupation (HMOs) 143, 404

housing 5, 118–47
  and older people 289
Housing Act, 1961 125
Housing Act, 1974 124, 125
Housing Act, 1980 127
Housing Act, 1988 143
Housing Act, 1996 126, 138
Housing Action Areas 142, 160, 404
Housing Action Trusts 128, 143, 404
housing associations 121, 124, 405
housing benefit 94, 122, 124
Housing Corporation 121, 125, 405
Housing (Homeless Persons) Act, 1977 126, 137
Housing (Homeless Persons) Act, 1985 137
housing legislation 144–5
housing tenure 121–33

immigration 27–9
incapacity benefit 92
income support 93, 94, 405
Independent Living (1993) Fund 313
independent schools 175, 188–90, 405
Individual Learning Accounts 187
Industrial Improvement Areas 160
inequalities in health 337–41
informal carers see carers
Inner Area Studies 160
inner-cities 148, 149–66
institutionalisation 266–8, 405
interim care order 238
internal markets 323–4, 405
invalid care allowance 91, 405

Job Interview Guarantee 112
Job Introduction Scheme 309
Jobclubs 112
Jobfinder's Grant 112
Jobfinder Plus 112
Jobplan Workshop 112
Jobseeker's Agreement 111
Jobseeker's Allowance 90, 92–4, 111
Jobseeker's Charter 111
joint roles 48–9, 406
Joseph, Keith 79
Juvenile Courts (Metropolis) Act, 1920 235

Kith and Kids 356

laissez-faire 86, 406
large-scale voluntary transfers 128, 406
Lawrence, Stephen 37

'league tables' 176, 193, 406
learning disability 9, 275–82
    and voluntary organisations 347,
    406
Liberal reforms 87
lifelong learning 187
local authority housing 121, 125–8
Local Authority Social Services Act 1970
    206
Local Government Act 1966 158
lone parents 2, 44, 51–6, 78
low pay 78

marriage 46–9
    arranged 31
Marxism 367–8, 369, 406
mature students 13
means-test 89, 90, 94–5, 97–8, 99,
    407
medical model, of disability 301–2
mental health 261–71
    and voluntary organisations 347
Mental Health Act, 1959 265
Mental Health Act, 1983 265, 266
Mental Health (Amendment) Act, 1982
    265
Mental Health Review Tribunals 266
mental illness
    and community care 232
    and social services 208–9
midwives 322
minimum wage 78
Modern Apprenticeships 115, 187
modified extended family 44, 407
Mortgage Interest Tax Relief (MIRAS)
    129–30
mortgages 130–1
    arrears 131
Motability 314
multi-cultural education 201, 407

National Assistance Act, 1948 89, 135,
    206
National Campaign for the Homeless
    see Shelter
National Children's Home 346
National Council for Voluntary
    Organisations (NCVO) 345
national curriculum 175–6, 178, 198,
    407
National Disability Council 310
National Health Service 319–33
National Health Service Act, 1946
    206, 321
National Health Service Act, 1973
    322

National Institute for Clinical Evidence
    (NICE) 319
national insurance 89, 91
National Insurance Act, 1946 89
National Insurance (Industrial Injuries
    Act), 1946 89
National Society for Prevention of
    Cruelty to Children (NSPCC)
    62–4, 238, 345, 348–9
National Statistics Socio-Economic
    Classification (NS-SEC) 22–4
National Traineeships 115
National Vocational Qualifications
    114, 186–7, 407
negative equity 131, 407
New Deal 112, 113–14, 116, 309, 366
New Deal for Communities 165
New Poor Law 84–7
New Towns Act, 1947 151
Newsom Report 180–1
NHS and Community Care Act, 1990
    206, 212, 219–20, 224, 268, 279–80,
    289, 313, 323, 326, 329, 344
NHS Direct 328
NHS Trusts 323–4, 325, 329, 407
nuclear family 44
nurseries 172–4
nursery schools 172

OFSTED (Office for Standards in
    Education) 173, 177
Old Poor Law, 1601 83
older people (see also age) 78
    and social services 208, 284–99
    and unemployment 105
    and voluntary organisations 347
opticians 322, 325, 328, 331–2
optometrists see opticians
owner-occupation 121, 128–31

parenting order 251
Parentline 351
passport benefits 93, 408
personal social services see social
    services departments
pharmacists 322, 325, 327–8
playgroups 173
Plowden Report 158, 170–1, 178–9
police
    and child abuse 63
    and violence in the family 59
'politically correct' language 6–9
poor law see New Poor Law and Old
    Poor Law
Poor Law Amendment Act, 1834 84,
    205

positive action   38–9, 376–7, 408
poverty   4, 68–82
  causes of   77–82
  definitions of   68–71
  effects of   82
  and older people   287–9
poverty   4, 68–82
  surveys   71–6
poverty cycle   76, 408
poverty line   72, 408
poverty trap   98, 408
pre-school education   170–5
Pre-School Learning Alliance   173
prescriptions   93, 327–8, 331–2
primary care groups   324, 409
primary health care   326–7
primary poverty   72, 409
primary schools   178–9
principle of less eligibility   84
private education   188
Private Finance Initiative (PFI)   330
private health care   329, 333–5
private medical insurance   333–5
privately rented housing   121, 122–4
privatisation   374–5
probation order   256
psychiatric hospitals   266–8
psychosurgery   271
psychotherapy   271
Public Health Act 1848   319
public schools   189

Qualifications and Curriculum
  Authority (QCA)   176, 184, 186

race   3, 24–39
  and children in care   248–9
  and education   199–201
  and fostering   242
  and housing   132–3
  and social work   214–16
  and special education   193
  and unemployment   105
Race Relations Act, 1976   38, 377
racial disadvantage   34–9, 132–3
racial violence   36–7
reconstituted family   44, 410
'red-lining'   130–1, 408
Regional Development Agencies
  165
Regional Health Authorities   322, 323
regional inequalities
  in employment   104
  in health   337–9
registered social landlords   121, 125,
  128, 410

Registrar-General's classification of
  occupations   21–2
relative poverty   69–70, 410
Relatives' Support Group   350
religious customs   31–3
Remploy   309
repossessions   131
residential care   9
  for children   243–9
  for disabled people   315–16
  for older people   290–2, 295–8
Resource Allocation Working Party
  (RAWP)   338
retirement   11–12
retirement pension   87, 91, 287–8
'Right to Buy'   127–8
Robbins Report   187, 196
role theory (see also gender roles)
  10–13
role-conflict   11, 410
  in social work   213–14
role-set   11, 410
Rough Sleepers Initiative   139
Rowntree, Joseph   72, 76–7
Royal Commission   84
Royal Commission on Mental Health
  and Deficiency, 1954–7   220,
  265

school meals (see also free school
  meals)   194
school milk   194
secondary poverty   72, 410
secondary schools   180–5
secure training orders   254–5
security of tenure   122–4, 411
Seebohm Report   206
segregated roles   48–9, 411
Sex Discrimination Act 1975   198
Shelter   352, 355
sheltered housing   290, 411
sheltered workshops   309, 409
shorthold tenancies   124, 411
single parents   see lone parents
Single Regeneration Budget   165
social class   4, 18–24
  and education   176, 195–7
  and health   339–41
social exclusion   70–1, 411
social fund   90, 95
social housing   121, 124–8, 411
social model, of disability   301–3
social policy   1–2
social security   65, 89–99
  and disability   305–8
Social Security Act, 1986   90, 95

social services departments 60–1, 205–17, 312–14, 345
social workers (*see also* social services departments) 205–16
and child abuse 63–4
socialisation 42, 411
special schools 190–3, 311–12, 412
Specialist Schools 183, 412
Speenhamland System 83–4
squatting 139–40, 412
standardised assessment tasks (SATs) 175, 178
'statementing' 191, 312, 412
statutory maternity pay 92
statutory sickness benefit 91
step-parents 13
stereotyping 14
structural unemployment 101
student loans 188
supervision order 238, 255
Swann Report 201

take-up 96–8, 412
Task Force 164, 165
Technical and Vocational Education Initiative (TVEI) 184
teenage mothers (*see also* lone parents) 53
Tenant's Charter 127
Tenant's Choice 128
Terence Higgins Trust 354–5
total institutions 220–1, 412
Training and Enterprise Councils (TECs) 111, 114, 115, 412
Travel to Interview scheme 112

underclass 81
'undeserving' poor 98–9
unemployment 3, 12, 78, 87, 101–17, 309–10
unemployment benefit 89
universities 187–8
University for Industry (UfI) 187

Urban Areas Act, 1978 160
Urban Development Corporations 162–3, 164, 165
Urban Programme 158–9, 160, 161–2, 164, 165, 171
Urban Task Force 149
Utting Report 245–6

violence in the family 56–64
vocational education 184–5
voluntary organisations 344–59, 413
voluntary schools 169, 175, 413
voluntary unemployment 101

Wagner Report 223
waiting-lists 329
Warnock Report 191, 311
welfare to work 112, 113
welfare state 88–9
and family 64–5
widow's payment 92
widowed mother's allowance 91, 92
Women's Aid 61, 353–4, 355, 356
work *see* employment
Work-Based Training for Young People 114
Work Trials 112
workhouses 84–6, 413
working families tax credit 94–5, 413

young offenders 235, 249–59
young offender institutions 253–4
young people 235–59
and caring 230–1
and unemployment 104
youth courts 251
youth custody 252–5
youth custody orders 253
youth justice centres 256–7
Youth Training 114–15
Youth Training Scheme 114–15
youth workers 193

Learning Resources
Centre